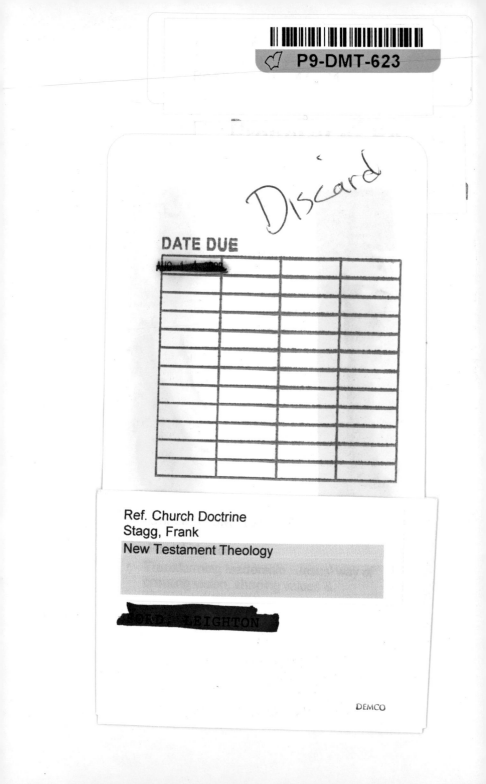

P9-DMT-623

Discard

DATE DUE

New Testament Theology

NEW
TESTAMENT
THEOLOGY

FRANK STAGG

Nashville, Tennessee   BROADMAN PRESS

© 1962 · BROADMAN PRESS
Nashville, Tennessee

All rights reserved
International copyright secured

ISBN–0–8054–1613–7

4216–13

Library of Congress catalog card number: 62–15328

Printed in the United States of America

Dedicated
to the memory
of my mother and my father,

DELLA and PAUL STAGG,

who between them
led me into biblical study
both devotional and critical

Preface

THIS BOOK has been in the making for many years. Since student days, the writer's major study has been the Greek New Testament, pursued in the pastorate and then in the classroom. Concentration upon New Testament theology was forced upon him by assignment of the Curriculum Committee of the New Orleans Baptist Theological Seminary. More than a decade ago he was asked to offer a course in New Testament theology. He "stalled" for three full years, seeking during that time to work out a satisfactory course. A sabbatical year, 1953–54, was devoted almost exclusively to the preparation of this course, and it has undergone constant revision in the years since.

The writer has sought to make this work distinctively New Testament theology as distinguished from historical, systematic, or philosophical theology. Of course the difference is in emphasis, there being inevitable overlapping in all of these theological disciplines; but the attempt here is to make the study basically an exegetical one. By some it has been called exegetical theology. Again, it is to be acknowledged that one brings to the task of exegesis much of his theological and philosophical conditioning. This writer is no exception. His plea is that he has purposed to give himself to the text, however miserable his failure at any given point. Once again, the writer was a preacher before becoming a professor, and it will be obvious that he does not always overcome the urge to preach his theology.

vii

A second guiding principle for this book is a practical one. The writer has sought to narrow the gap between the classroom and the pulpit and that between the technical scholar and the "layman." Too often the seminary student studies all week and then has to search for sermon material for Sunday. This writer is convinced that there should be a closer correlation between what is taught in the classroom and what is preached in the pulpit. He also believes that theology is as important for the "layman" as for the seminary professor. This conviction has governed the selection of subjects for study and also the treatment of the subjects. Purely speculative interests have been kept to a minimum. In truth this should not be difficult, for the New Testament is "down to earth" in its concern for life and death issues as they relate to all people.

This book is written in the hope that it may offer some challenge to the technical scholar and at the same time be intelligible to the serious layman. It is hoped that the layman will be patient when appeal is made to the technicalities of language. It is also hoped that the scholar will be patient when explanations are offered for the layman in particular. Employment of Hebrew and Greek is indispensable to biblical theology, but the attempt has been made in this book to make each paragraph understandable to one not familiar with these languages. Unless otherwise indicated, translations from the Greek New Testament will be the author's own. Translations from the Old Testament will be those of the American Standard Version, unless otherwise indicated.

The plan of the book has grown out of classroom procedure. The writer shares with many the conviction that the New Testament is concerned basically to proclaim *Heilsgeschichte,* the story of salvation. In truth, the whole Bible is the story of what God has done for man's salvation, his mighty acts in which he is self-revealed and in which he has sought to redeem man, reconciling man to himself and thus to his fellow man. The New Testament is concerned with the culminating event of all redemption history, the event in which the Word has come to us.

This book in New Testament theology attempts to trace out the meaning of this event. After an initial chapter on the nature and purpose of the Bible, it considers the plight of man or the doctrine of sin. From that point it turns to Christology, for the New Testament is Christocentric in its doctrine of God and of salvation. The doctrine of salvation is studied in its multiple aspects, a cluster of closely related terms offering focal points for its New Testament analysis. Because of the centrality of the death and resurrection of Jesus in salvation, a special chapter is devoted to this study. Chapter six is a study of the kingdom of God, a primary theme in both the Old and the New Testaments. This chapter could have appeared earlier in the book. The people of God, the ultimate goal of his purpose in redemption, are studied in terms of the church as the body of Christ, the fellowship of persons made one people under the kingdom or sovereign rule of God in Christ. Study follows of the ordinances, the ministry of the church, and the ministries within the church. The Christian is considered in his multiple relationships to the family, the state, and the world of people and things. The final chapter is devoted to eschatology, although this could have been treated at the outset; for the whole New Testament is eschatological, that is, concerned with the *goal* towards which God is moving man and history.

For some decades now biblical students have been concerned with the unity of the Bible underlying its diversities. Certain former generations gave major attention to the Bible's diversities; the present generation is more concerned with its unity. This is not merely the work of obscurantists; this interest is seen in the most critical and competent biblical scholars of today. This book has been written in the conviction that there is a New Testament theology, not merely varieties of Christian thought compiled in one collection of writings. This is not to disparage the critical analysis which sought to distinguish the varieties of thought in the New Testament, for that was and is a necessary work. This work, however, is profitable only as it leads finally to a better understanding of the theological sub-

structure giving unity to the whole New Testament. To understand a watch one must take it apart to see what makes it tick.
But if one wants to *hear* it tick, he must put it together again.
So in Bible study, one must see not only the parts but the
whole. The varieties of thought are to be observed in the New
Testament, but one does not read the New Testament with adequate discernment if he fails to see the basic concerns and
affirmations which set these writers apart and make them one in
their theology.

Basic presuppositions, tenets, and concerns which are common to the New Testament writers, giving to the New Testament its "unity in diversity" include the following: (1) The
reality of God is never argued but always assumed or affirmed;
he is sovereign Ruler, seeking Father, always holding the initiative in creation, revelation, and redemption. (2) Jesus Christ is
absolutely central; he is Lord and Saviour, the one in whom God
not only acted but in whom he came. (3) The Holy Spirit came
anew with Jesus Christ. (4) The Christian faith and life are
a calling, rooted in divine election. (5) The plight of man as
sinner means that he is completely dependent upon the mercy
and grace of God. (6) Salvation is both God's gift and his demand through Jesus Christ, to be received by faith. (7) The
death and resurrection of Jesus are the heart of the total event
of which he was the center. (8) God creates a people of his own;
they are designated and described by varied terminology and
analogies. (9) History must be understood eschatologically,
being brought along toward its ultimate goal when the kingdom
of God, already present in Christ, is brought to its complete
triumph. (10) In Christ all of God's work of creation, revelation, and redemption is brought to fulfilment.[1]

[1] Studies of the "unity in variety" to be found in the New Testament (and the
Bible as a whole) include: A. M. Hunter, *The Unity of the New Testament*
(Toronto: The Macmillan Co., 1943), *Interpreting the New Testament, 1900–
1950* (Philadelphia: The Westminster Press, 1952); Floyd V. Filson, *One Lord,
One Faith* (Philadelphia: Presbyterian Board, 1943); J. N. Sanders, *The Foun-
dations of the Christian Faith* (London: A. & C. Black, Ltd., 1951); H. H.
Rowley, *The Unity of the Bible* (London: Carey Kingsgate Press, Ltd., 1953);
C. H. Dodd, *According to the Scriptures* (New York: Charles Scribner's Sons,

The manuscript for this book is released with the awareness that it will reflect the limitations of its author, at best an "earthen vessel" unworthy of the "treasure" entrusted to us all and unequal to the demands of this stewardship. The book is offered simply as the best of which its author is capable at this point in his pilgrimage. His dependence upon the work of others will receive acknowledgment in the footnotes, but the debt goes far beyond these specific acknowledgments.

The writer's colleagues and students, especially those in the New Testament department, will find in the book many traces of his debt to them. Special thanks are due Professors William A. Mueller, William S. Garmon, Samuel J. Mikolaski, and Robert R. Soileau. These colleagues shared valuable insights and removed from the manuscript some of its errors and weaknesses. They are in no way to be held responsible for the errors or weaknesses which remain. For constant encouragement and for making the indices, I am indebted to my wife, Evelyn Owen Stagg. The editors of Broadman Press went beyond normal expectations in the many valuable services which they rendered.

1953); John Wick Bowman, *Prophetic Realism and the Gospel* (Philadelphia: The Westminster Press, 1955). Many books helped lay the foundation for this emphasis, and many others reflect the adoption of this approach to the Bible. These include: H. L. Strack and Paul Billerbeck, *Kommentar zum Neuen Testament aus Talmud und Midrasch* (München: Beck, 1922–1956); A. E. J. Rawlinson, *The New Testament Doctrine of the Christ* (New York: Longmans, Green & Co., 1949); Sir Edwyn Hoskyns and F. N. Davey, *The Riddle of the New Testament* (London: Faber & Faber, Ltd., 1931); Gerhard Kittel and Gerhard Friedrich (eds.), *Theologisches Wörterbuch zum Neuen Testament* (Stuttgart: W. Kohlhammer, 1933—); Dodd, *The Apostolic Preaching and Its Developments* (New York: Willett, Clark & Co., 1937), *The Present Task in New Testament Studies* (New York: The Macmillan Co., 1936); A. G. Hebert, *The Throne of David* (London: Faber & Faber, Ltd., 1941); Alan Richardson (ed.), *A Theological Word Book of the Bible* (New York: The Macmillan Co., 1950); and many others.

FRANK STAGG

Contents

The
Bible:
Its Nature
1 and Purpose

THE TEXTBOOK for New Testament theology is
the New Testament. Of course, the New Testament itself cannot
be studied apart from the Old Testament. This chapter will be
concerned with the nature and purpose of the Bible, with particular reference to the New Testament.

Terminology

Bible—The word "Bible" is derived from Byblos, a town in
Phoenicia also known as Gebal. This town gave its name to the
papyrus plant. Byblos is the correct Greek for the Egyptian
loanword "papyrus." The diminutive form of the Greek Byblos is
biblion. The Latins took the plural form, *biblia,* as singular, and
thus its usage has come into English. "Bible" is really the plural
of the diminutive form of Byblos, the Greek term for the Egyptian loanword "papyrus." Bible, then, strictly means little papyrus books.[1] Actually, for us it means the collection of Jewish and
Christian writings generally accepted by Christians as their
sacred Scriptures.

Canon.—Etymologically the term "canon" means cane or
reed, as is true of the Hebrew *qāneh* and the Greek *kanōn.*
In earliest Christian usage "canon" referred to a list of books
approved for public reading. These books were distinguished
from those not on the list—those called "apocryphal," books for

---

[1] Cf. Edgar J. Goodspeed, *How Came the Bible?* (New York: Abingdon
Press, 1940), pp. 11 f.

1

private reading only. Athanasius, for example, in his Easter letter of A.D. 367 employed the term canon in the sense of a list. He spoke of those books which were "canonized" as ones listed for public reading and those apocryphal as for private reading. His list is the oldest known to correspond exactly to the twenty-seven writings of our New Testament. Under Latin influence from the fourth century on, canon came to stand for a closed and authoritative list in the sense of rule or norm.[2]

Testament.—The Greek *diathēkē* is not adequately translated by either "testament" or "covenant." It is a covenant between God and man, but the covenant is unilateral. It is not an agreement worked out between God and man. God alone determines the nature, the grounds, the demands, and the provisions of the covenant. It is not coercive upon man, for man remains free to enter into the covenant or not; but the covenant is strictly God's covenant offered to man. In a real sense it is a "will" or "testament" in that it is God's "will" offered to man.[3] The term "New Testament" is a serviceable one, and no real gain would derive from the substitution of "New Covenant," as is frequently suggested. The "New Testament" is concerned with the "will" of God or the unilateral covenant, not a contract or agreement, which God has offered man in Jesus Christ.

The Old Testament

Canon.—The New Testament refers to the threefold division of the Hebrew Scriptures: the law, the prophets, and the writings. Luke 24:44 speaks of the law of Moses (the Pentateuch), the prophets (certain historical books in addition to most of the books now called "prophets"), and the psalms (the "writings" designated by its chief collection). Luke 11:51 and Matthew 23:35 reflect the arrangement of the Old Testament as begin-

[2] Cf. Alexander Souter, *The Text and Canon of the New Testament* (New York: Charles Scribner's Sons, 1913), pp. 154–156.

[3] Cf. W. F. Arndt and F. W. Gingrich, *A Greek-English Lexicon of the New Testament and Other Early Christian Literature* (trans. and ed. from W. Bauer's *Griechisch-Deutsches Wörterbuch zu den Schriften des Neuen Testaments und der übrigen urchristlichen Literatur,* 4th ed., [Chicago: University of Chicago Press, 1957]), p. 182.

ning with Genesis ("the blood of Abel," Gen. 4:8, 10) and concluding with 2 Chronicles 24:20–22. This is not the place for a study of the formation of the Old Testament canon, but probably it was "canonized" in these three stages: the law canonized before the Exile, the prophets by the time of the Syrian persecution of the Jews, and the writings shortly after A.D. 70.

This is not to suggest dates so late for the writing of these books; it is only to suggest that the formal listings were completed at these times. The fall of Jerusalem in A.D. 70 and the appearance of Christian writings accepted as "Scripture" by Christians, probably caused the Jews at Jamnia to formally close their "canon." [4] Thus they listed their own recognized Scriptures and at the same time excluded both the Christian writings and some Jewish writings known now as "apocryphal." In this canon, the thirty-nine books of our Old Testament were grouped together as twenty-two books, equaling the twenty-two letters of the Hebrew alphabet. This canon of Jewish Scriptures is attested to by Philo, Josephus, the New Testament (Luke 11:51; 24:44), and the Talmud.

Inspiration.—The New Testament writers assumed the inspiration of the Old Testament. Probably 2 Timothy 3:16 is nearest to a formal statement of inspiration. Because of the absence in the Greek text of a verb form (or copula), the translation may be rendered: "All Scripture is inspired of God" or "Every God-inspired Scripture is also profitable for teaching." In either translation the *fact* of inspiration is affirmed.

The writer was not concerned to discuss the nature or manner of inspiration. His concern, beyond affirming the fact of inspiration, is to stress the *purpose* of the God-inspired Scriptures. Their purpose is achieved in teaching, in reproof, in correction, in discipline in righteousness. The *fact* of inspiration he does

---

[4] Cf. George Foot Moore, *Judaism in the First Centuries of the Christian Era, the Age of the Tannaim* (Cambridge: Harvard University Press, 1927), I, 238 ff. For Talmudic references to Jamnia, see H. E. Dana and R. E. Glaze, Jr., *Interpreting the New Testament* (Nashville: Broadman Press, 1961), p. 20, note 20.

not argue, probably because this so clearly accords with the whole biblical emphasis upon God's initiative in self-revelation and redemption that it called for no argument. His concern rather is with the intention of the Scriptures. They are not an end in themselves; their purpose is served only when they bring one under the judgment and correction of God leading to righteousness.

Equally clear in the assumption of inspiration is 2 Peter 1:21: "For not by the will of man was prophecy borne at any time, but men being borne by the Holy Spirit spoke from God." The writer's concern here is with the interpretation of Scripture (v. 20); but in the development of this, he assumes inspiration to be essential both to the prophetic utterance (or Scripture) and to the interpretation. Again it may be said, this accords with a basic assumption of the whole Bible—the initiative is always with God and not with man. This is true in creation, in revelation, and in redemption. The Scriptures represent man's response to God, who has spoken to man.

Revelation

The New Testament, along with the Old, assumes the self-revelation of God. This is true in *Histoire* (so-called "secular" history) as well as in *Geschichte* (salvation history). The Bible knows God as God of nature, of all history, and of the "existential moment" when a man knows himself to be in the presence of God. God reveals himself to man through his mighty acts (cf. Rom. 1:19–20; Heb. 1:1–4). God is self-revealed in nature or in creation: "For the invisible things of him from the creation of the world are clearly seen, being known in the things made [or things done], even his eternal power and divinity" (Rom. 1:20). Paul was explicit in saying that God is seen in what God makes or does. It is important to observe that this is *revelation*, not discovery. It is God who thus makes himself knowable; it is not man who has discovered God in nature or in history (Rom. 1:19). In Acts 14:17 Paul is quoted as saying of God that "He has not left himself without witness in doing good, from heaven having given to you rains and fruitful seasons, filling your heart with food and gladness."

The writer of Hebrews was equally clear in seeing the self-revelation of God to have come in "various measures" and in "various manners" though supremely and ultimately in Jesus Christ (1:1–4). In some sense God is self-revealed in all that he does, yet he is supremely revealed in a person, Jesus Christ. Although God is not called a person, he is everywhere in the Bible thought of in personal terms. It is understandable, then, that his ultimate self-disclosure should be in one who is his Son (Heb. 1:2). This accords with Paul, who sees the divinity (*theiotēs*) of God revealed in the things made or done (Rom. 1:20) but the divine essence (*theotēs*) fully present in Christ alone (Col. 2:9).

The Old Testament is largely the prophetic witness of God-inspired men to the mighty acts of God in which God has revealed himself. The exodus from Egypt was not viewed as an escape but a *deliverance*. God was self-revealed in what he did to deliver his people from bondage and in his calling and creating of Israel.

The New Testament is the apostolic witness of God-inspired men to the mighty acts of God in the total event in which the Word became flesh and made his dwelling among us (John 1:14). The acts were God's acts and hence his revelation. This was not merely the giving of information *about* God (no man is saved by information); it was God's giving of himself. This was not a discovering (man's work) but an uncovering of God which he alone could accomplish. As John Baillie happily puts it, God offers himself to us in fellowship; he does not give us "information by communication; He gives us Himself in communion." Saving knowledge is not knowledge *that* God is, nor knowledge *about* God, but knowledge *of* God—personal acquaintance with him through direct encounter.[5]

In revelation, then, God is both subject and object; he is

[5] *The Idea of Revelation in Recent Thought* (New York: Columbia University Press, 1956), p. 47.

revealer and revealed. Revelation came to the biblical writers through events understood by faith as the mighty acts of God.[6] All the events of history (*Historie*) are in some sense revealing, but the Bible chiefly is concerned with special redeeming events of history (*Heilsgeschichte*). God who spoke creation into being, even he who was seen to have intervened in Egypt to deliver Israel, was the Word who became flesh and tabernacled among us. The written word is the prophetic (Old Testament) or apostolic (New Testament) witness to the mighty acts of God who is both above history and yet within it. God is behind the mighty acts, hence the written word is revelation. God is behind the receiving (the recalling, the attesting, the interpreting); hence, it also is inspiration.

Uniqueness of the New Testament

The uniqueness of the New Testament is to be seen in the nature of the witness it gives to the unique event of all salvation history. The New Testament is both history and interpretation of Jesus Christ, given by men who were eyewitnesses to that of which they wrote (1 John 1:1–4). It preserves and is built upon the witness of the community of believers who saw and heard Jesus.

Surely the New Testament writers were inspired; but their uniqueness is not in that. Behind all faith in God, behind every conversion, and behind all knowledge of God is the inspiration of God. It is God who speaks; man answers. Inspiration is as broad as is the response of man to God. The New Testament was written by men inspired of God; but inspiration, the impact of God's Spirit upon man, goes beyond the writing of the Scriptures. Otherwise, all our theology would be but philosophy, and prayer itself would be a monologue. Inspiration is a primary factor in every phase of Christian faith and life.

The New Testament writers were inspired, but there is much more to be said of them. It is these factors beyond inspiration

[6] *Ibid.*, p. 62.

that make their witness unique. The New Testament is complete; there will not be added to it books yet to be written. The New Testament is basically the "apostolic witness" to Jesus; it is the witness of the earliest community built around the apostles who were called by Jesus himself, trained by him, and commissioned to this very witnessing. The New Testament is the primary witness to a once-for-all event in salvation history.

When Christians through the early centuries struggled to arrive at a canon of scriptures, they were guided by the principle of apostolic authorship. For them a book was to be accepted as canonized if it came from an apostle or from an "apostolic man"—one like Mark or Luke, whose associations with the apostles were such as to assure him of the apostolic witness. The writings of others were valued, but the early Christians saw a uniqueness in the witness of those who stood in immediate relation to Jesus.

This accords with the requirement that the successor to Judas be "of the men therefore who have companied with us all the time that the Lord Jesus went in and went out among us, beginning from the baptism of John, unto the day he was received up from us" (Acts 1:21 f.). This one was to be a witness of the resurrection (Acts 1:22). Christianity is a historical religion, concerned with what God in Christ has actually done (Luke 1:1–4). The New Testament is the written word of men who saw and heard, and who gave witness to the great event in which God acted for man's salvation. God continues to speak, but what he accomplished in Christ Jesus is the center of all revelation and redemption. The New Testament as the witness to that central event must be normative in the understanding of what God has yet to say.

Authority

To affirm the uniqueness of the New Testament is to affirm its authority for Christians. It is important to see this authority in terms of its nature and purpose. It is basically the story of what God has done in Jesus Christ for man's salvation. It is *kērugma,* the proclamation of the gospel, the good news of what God has done. It is *didachē,* the teaching which is concerned for the *demand* embedded in the *gift* of God's grace.[7] The New Testament is our trustworthy authority in terms of its purpose.

It is a violation and rejection of this authority to claim either too little or too much for the New Testament. To reject what it has to say about God and man, about sin and salvation, about the gifts and demands of God, is to reject its authority. On the other hand, to go *outside* the New Testament to make claims for it which it does not make for itself is actually to find authority outside the New Testament and thus to reject its authority. That is to say, one may reject the authority of the New Testament by claiming too much for it as easily as by claiming too little for it.

Actual acknowledgment of the authority of the New Testament comes to realization alone in submission to its demands and acceptance of its gifts. Merely to say "Bible, Bible" is worth no more than to say "Lord, Lord" yet not do the will of the Father (Matt. 7:21).

No theory of inspiration itself, however strong, is actual acknowledgment of the authority of the New Testament. To support this, one needs only to remember that the Pharisees, who most stubbornly rejected Jesus, held to a high doctrine of the inspiration of the Scriptures. These made the Scriptures their life by day and night, yet were they blind to Jesus. One needs only to recall that the Council of Trent declared the Scriptures to be *Spiritu sancto dictante,* "dictated by the Holy Spirit." Despite this strict doctrine of verbal inspiration, the Roman Church has refused to grant to the Bible its true authority, subordinating it to its own tradition. One may loudly declare his claims for the Bible's inspiration and authority and yet use this as a smoke screen behind which to hide his own will to power.

---

[7] Timely caution against too rigid a separation between *didachē* and *kērugma* is made in A. J. B. Higgins (ed.), *New Testament Essays* (Manchester: Manchester University Press, 1959), pp. 306–314.

The Goal of the Scriptures

The purpose of the Bible is accomplished when men are brought into an actual knowledge of God through faith in Jesus Christ and submission to him as Lord. The writer of the Fourth Gospel is explicit as to his purpose: "Many other signs did Jesus in the presence of his disciples which are not written in this book; but these have been written in order that ye might trust that Jesus is the Christ, the Son of God, and that trusting ye might have life in his name" (John 20:30–31).

Again in 1 John 1:1–4 may be found a clear statement as to the purpose of Scripture: that the readers might enter into fellowship with God and with one another through Jesus Christ. In John 5:39 Jesus is quoted as saying: "Ye search the scriptures, because ye think in them to have eternal life, and these are they which bear witness concerning me." Thus the Scriptures are not an end in themselves but a witness to him in whom alone is life.

Luke's story of the encounter of the risen Jesus with the two men of Emmaus gives clear indication of the purpose or goal of the Scriptures. Luke says of Jesus that "beginning from Moses and from all the prophets, he interpreted to them in all the scriptures the things concerning himself" (24:27). The Bible is *Christuszeugnis*,[8] that is, witness to Christ. He is the ultimate Word of God. Luke reported the result of his witness in saying: "Their eyes were opened, and they recognized him; and he vanished from their sight. And they said to one another, Did not our hearts burn within us as he was speaking to us along the way, and he opened to us the scriptures?" (24:31–32). The Scriptures are trustworthy; and when trusted, they point one to Jesus. The goal not only of John but of all New Testament writers is that those who read fall at the feet of Jesus saying as did Thomas: "My Lord and my God!" (John 20:28).

[8] Cf. W. D. Davies and D. Daube (eds.), *The Background of the New Testament and Its Eschatology* (New York: Cambridge University Press, 1956), p. 22.

Basic Principles for Bible Study

The Bible is the rightful possession of all people. It should be in the hands of all as an open book. It is so written that its essential message is open to any humble person of faith. This is not to forget, however, that it is a difficult collection of writings, often baffling the most devoted and competent of scholars. The Bible thus should be entrusted to the humblest who would read it, and it should be entrusted to the most competent who spare themselves no toil or pain in seeking its meaning.

Luther, rebelling at the Roman Church's policy of denying the Bible to the layman, insisted that the Bible is *allgemein-verständlich*—understandable to all men. In a sense this is true. The common man, the untutored man, may read the Bible with understanding. Every person should be encouraged to read it. In another sense the Bible is not "understandable to all." Interpretation is the scholar's task. Peter was quite honest in affirming that Paul is hard to understand (2 Peter 3:15–16). Paul could have returned the compliment. The study of the Bible requires the discipline of a lifetime, and the Bible is never mastered by any scholar. The layman should be free to read the Bible, but he should also be encouraged to see the need for the scholar who gives himself devotedly to the special study of the Bible.

A speaker once drew applause by saying: "When a preacher shoots over the heads of his audience, all he proves is that he does not know how to shoot." That overstates the case. Jesus knew how "to shoot," but his most devoted followers do not understand all that he preached. Neither does any scholar understand all of the New Testament. To understand it, though, is the scholar's work. It is a disservice to a person to cause him to distrust scholarship simply because it is scholarship. The scholar must accept his task; he must acquire at any cost the competence for it. He must humbly share his findings—whether they are received or not.

A second basic principle for Bible study is that it should be done in faith and personal commitment. It should be existential in the sense of personal involvement. The study, if effective, cannot be merely a scientific, objective study. None can be a true student of the Bible unless it be subjective as well as objective. J. A. Bengel, in 1734, happily prefaced his edition of the Greek New Testament with a Latin couplet employed subsequently by Eberhard Nestle and his son in each edition of their Greek New Testament:

Te totum applica ad textum:
rem totam applica ad te.

That is: "Thy whole self apply to the text; the whole thing apply to thyself." Well does this sum it up! Bible study demands the whole self—a mind trained by every scholarly discipline, a heart of trust and devotion, and a willingness to come under the judgment and guidance of the Bible as it is studied.

A third principle, or a restatement of the above paragraph, is that study is to be both critical and devotional. In fact, true critical study must be devotional and true devotional study must be critical. By critical study is meant the effort to arrive at the true meaning of the writer, utilizing every grammatical and historical datum available. Critical study begins with the question, not with the answer. But one cannot be truly critical unless he comes humbly to the text, willing for it to speak its true message whatever its implication for, or impingement upon, the exegete. By the same token, true devotional study must be critical, otherwise it is but self-devotion, the attempt to impose upon the Bible one's own meditations.

A fourth principle is that the Bible is to be studied *ganzheitlich,*[9]—in its wholeness. The "proof text" method makes the Bible the victim of any irresponsible interpreter. A proof text is one which by itself misrepresents the writing as a whole; a "climactic text" is one which gathers up in one great sentence the theme or doctrine of the writer.[10] Sound exegesis requires that

---

[9] Wilhelm Vischer, quoted in Davies and Daube, *op. cit.,* p. 24.
[10] Cf. Frank Stagg, *The Book of Acts* (Nashville: Broadman Press, 1955), p. 62.

one always consider the total text of a given writing. One statement is not to be played against another; rather, each statement is to be interpreted in the light of the whole.

A fifth principle for Bible study is that of fellowship or *koinonia*. Paul prayed that the Ephesians "be made strong to apprehend *with all the saints*" the love of Christ and thus be filled with the fulness of God (Eph. 3:18 f.). The Bible is the story of what God has done and is doing in Jesus Christ to save man by creating a new fellowship of persons under the lordship of Christ. One cannot understand the Bible if he rejects the very fellowship it is concerned to affirm. One cannot in his estrangement understand the message of reconciliation (2 Cor. 5:20 f.). To study the Bible adequately, one must study *with his brethren.* One must humbly receive from the studies of previous generations of disciples and from the present one.

A final observation is that the Bible is *Christuszeugnis,* a witness to Christ, and eschatological. The whole Bible looks to Jesus Christ. As stated earlier, its goal is realized when the reader falls at the feet of Jesus as Lord. It is eschatological. That is, the whole Bible is written with a particular understanding of history. It sees God as before and above history and yet within it, moving it to its goal. The Bible's first affirmation is: "In the beginning God." History is not evolutionary; it does not move under its own power. It is not cyclic; it is not doomed to go in circles. It is eschatological; it has an *eschaton*—a goal. On the negative side the goal is judgment; on the positive side it is redemption in its fulness. The *eschaton* or goal is realized in Jesus Christ. He is the judgment and the redemption. Every man, as well as all history, stands under his judgment and is offered his redemption.

In New Testament theology, the textbook is the New Testament. It "opens its treasures to the man who comes in faith and prays for the inward witness of the Holy Spirit." [11]

---

[11] Davies and Daube, *op. cit.,* p. 25.

The
Plight
of Man
2   as Sinner

THAT MAN is in serious trouble from which he
needs deliverance is a fact assumed everywhere in the Bible.
This is made explicit at the outset of Genesis, and it is either explicit or implicit on every page of the New Testament. The
plight is one of *sin*, not merely one of finiteness, fate, involvement in material substance, or ignorance. The fact of sin is so
clear to biblical writers that it is scarcely argued. Its cause,
nature, results, and cure are matters of primary concern.

The Fact of the Plight

Biblical writers generally assumed the fact of sin as suffi-
ciently obvious. When occasion required, however, they clearly
affirmed it. Paul left little to the imagination in Romans 1:18 to
3:20 as he declared all men to be under sin—Jew and Gentile
alike. He insisted that every mouth be stopped among those
who would question either man's sin or God's righteousness. In
Romans 5:12 he affirmed the universality of sin: "Thus unto all
men did death spread because all did sin." John was equally
explicit: "If we say that we have no sin, we deceive ourselves
and the truth is not in us" (1 John 1:8). Again, he said: "Should
we say that we have not sinned, we make him a liar and his word
is not in us" (v. 10).[1]

The fact of sin as the human predicament is implied in the
mission of Jesus, and it is explicitly affirmed in that connection.

[1] For apparent teaching of "sinless perfection" in 1 John, see pp. 108 f.

13

John the Baptist, in a ministry foreshadowing that of Jesus, preached "a baptism of repentance unto [or, upon] the remission of sins" (Mark 1:4). Jesus defined his task as concerned with sinners in saying: "I came not to call righteous people but sinners" (Mark 2:17). His very name proclaimed his mission and assumed the fact of the human predicament: "And you shall call his name Jesus, for he himself shall save his people from their sins" (Matt. 1:21). Zacharias, speaking of the mission of John, prophesied that he would "go before the face of the Lord to make ready his ways, to give knowledge of salvation unto his people in the remission of their sins" (Luke 1:76–77). To Zacchaeus Jesus declared: "the Son of Man came to seek and to save the lost" (Luke 19:10). Jesus not only sought out sinners but justified this as the very point of his mission (Matt. 9:10 f.; 11:19). John the Baptist pointed up the nature of Jesus' mission in saying: "Behold the Lamb of God, the one bearing the sin of the world" (John 1:29).

The apostolic preaching everywhere assumed the plight of man and described it as sin. At the Feast of Pentecost even the worshiping pilgrims were told: "Repent ye, and get yourselves baptized, each of you upon the name of Jesus Christ unto [or, upon] the remission of your sins" (Acts 2:38.). Before the Sanhedrin in Jerusalem, Peter and the other apostles declared of Jesus: "This one did God exalt to his right hand, Prince and Saviour, to give repentance to Israel and the forgiveness of sins" (Acts 5:31). In the home of Cornelius, the God-fearing Roman, Peter declared the prophets to be witnesses to him through whose name every one who trusts shall receive remission of sins (Acts 10:43). In 1 Timothy 1:15 is found a clear statement as to man's plight and Jesus' mission as well as the rightful confession of every man: "Christ Jesus came into the world to save sinners; of whom I am number one."

Terminology

The Greek New Testament does not have one dominant term for what in English is normally called sin. A dozen or more

Greek words serve to describe sin in its various aspects. The following list will not be exhaustive, but it is hoped that it may be serviceable in defining the meaning of the terms most significant or most frequently used.[2]

The term *adikia* stands for unrighteousness, wrongdoing, wickedness, or injustice. Possibly the meaning is "misdeed" in 2 Corinthians 12:13, "Pardon me this misdeed," and in Hebrews 8:12, "For I shall be merciful toward their misdeeds." Probably "injustice" is the meaning in Romans 9:14, "There is not injustice with God, is there?" In Romans 1:18 it describes the unrighteousness or wickedness of men at enmity with the truth. First John 5:17 says that all *adikia* is *hamartia* (sin).

Hamartia is the term most used in the New Testament for the idea of sin, and it probably is best translated with the word "sin." The verb equivalent to the noun *hamartia* means to transgress, to do wrong, to sin against God. The older idea of "missing the mark" is not adequate to translate its New Testament meaning. It is failure, but it is more. In Mark 2:5 *hamartiai* (plural) require to be forgiven. In Hebrews 1:3 they require cleansing. In John 9:41 *hamartia* is more than failure; it is a responsible condition or characteristic involving guilt: "If ye were blind, ye would not have sin [*hamartian*]: but now ye say, We see: your sin [*hamartia*] remains." Paul speaks of *hamartia* almost in personal terms, as in Romans 5:12, "*hamartia* came into the world," and Romans 5:21, "*hamartia* reigned in death." In Hebrews 3:13 *hamartia* has deceptive power, as the warning implies: "Lest any of you be hardened by the deceitfulness of sin [*hamartias*]." Clearly, then, *hamartia* in the New Testament implies far more than just "missing the mark."

The term *anomia* denotes lawlessness, implying not ignorance of the law but the defiance of it. In Romans 6:19 it is contrasted with righteousness and holiness: "Just as ye did present your members slaves in uncleanness and lawlessness [*tē anomia*] unto lawlessness [*eis tēn anomian*], thus now present your members slaves in righteousness unto holiness."

[2] In the main the definitions will follow Arndt and Gingrich, *op. cit.*

The term *apistia* can indicate unfaithfulness, lack of belief, or even disbelief with the implication of obstinacy. In Romans 3:3 it seems to mean unfaithfulness or betrayal of trust: "Their unfaithfulness [*apistia*] did not nullify the faithfulness [*pistin*] of God, did it?" *Apistia* may denote lack of belief, usually with blame as in Hebrews 3:12, "Take heed, brethren, lest there be in any of you an evil heart of unbelief." Blame is not necessarily implied, however, in 1 Timothy 1:13, "But I received mercy, for unknowing I did it in unbelief [*apistia*]."

Impiety or want of reverence is the basic idea in *asebeia*. It may be translated "ungodliness," with the idea of irreverence, as in 2 Timothy 2:16, "But profane, empty voices shun; for they will advance in yet more ungodliness [*asebeias*]."

Appearing ten times in the New Testament, *aselgeia* carries the idea of licentiousness, debauchery, or sensuality. The meaning may be seen in Jude 4: "Ungodly ones [*asebeis*], changing the grace of our God into licentiousness [*aselgeian*]." The term seems to describe an unrestrained commitment to evil.

The essential idea in *epithumia* is desire. Only the context may indicate the moral character of the desire, whether good or bad. Matters of motive, intention, direction, and relationship to other concerns give to *epithumia* its moral character. Jesus, with emphasis, used the term for himself: "With desire I desired to eat this passover with you" (Luke 22:15). On the other hand, James 1:14 points to desire as the "base of operations" for temptation and sin: "For each is tempted by his own desire [*epithumias*], being dragged away and enticed [with bait]." Thus it becomes clear that desire is not of itself evil, but it becomes evil when egocentric, when it is improperly related to God, to other people, and to other concerns.

The term *echthra* describes hostile feelings or actions and may best be translated "enmity." This finds illustration in Romans 8:7: "Wherefore, the mind [mind set] of the flesh is enmity against God." Likewise, "The friendship of the world is enmity against God" (James 4:4). In Ephesians 2:14–16, Paul attributes to Christ the work of overcoming the *hostility* or *enmity* between Jew and Gentile and between each and God, reconciling "both in one body to God through the cross."

Kakia is one of the stronger terms in the New Testament for indicating wickedness or depravity as opposed to virtue. It describes character or disposition, not just outward acts. Peter (1 Peter 2:16) warned against the abuse of freedom as a cloak under which to hide wickedness (*kakia*). Once in the New Testament the term has only the connotation of trouble: "Sufficient to the day is its own trouble" (Matt. 6:34).

Used only about eight times in the New Testament (the manuscripts differ), *parabasis* makes a significant contribution to the understanding of the nature of sin. Among other things, it is transgression, an overstepping of the boundaries, a violation of the law. There is in the term a strong emphasis upon wilful, or at least conscious, violation of the law. This is explicit in Romans 4:15: "Where there is not law, neither is there transgression [*parabasis*]." This is likewise implied in Romans 5:14, "But death reigned from Adam to Moses, even upon those not having sinned [*hamartēsantas*] in the likeness of Adam's transgression [*parabaseōs*]." Paul was not exonerating those who sinned from Adam unto Moses. They, too, were guilty and suffered the consequences of their sin. He was saying that they did not have the Mosaic law, and his implication seems to be that their sin (*hamartia*) was not as flagrantly rebellious as was the transgression (*parabasis*) of those who had the advantage of the Mosaic law. In Hebrews 2:2 *parabasis* is linked with disobedience. In 1 Tim. 2:14 it is said that Eve fell into transgression (*parabasis*) by being deceived, but this was not to exonerate her of rebellion. The writer's purpose is not to reduce Eve's guilt, but to add the charge of gullibility to that of rebellion.

The term *ponēria* in the New Testament has the meaning of wickedness, baseness, or even maliciousness. It is similar to *kakia* in meaning, and the two terms appear together in 1 Corinthians 5:8, where the "old leaven" of baseness and wickedness (*kakia* and *ponēria*) is contrasted with the "unleavened bread of purity and truth."

The Cause of the Plight

In the Bible man's predicament from which he needs deliverance is traced back to a fatal choice. In both Testaments the plight is attributed to man's wilful abuse of his God-given freedom in choosing the basic course and character of his life. Genesis 3 sets this forth in a story so simple that a child may understand. Romans 1:18–32 sets forth the same truths in careful and forceful analysis. Both passages take one back as near the origin of sin as one may go. Both find the potential for sin in the very fountainhead in which is found the potential for good. It is the freedom for choice given to man.

Genesis 3:1 ff. is the story of a choice. Man was *thrust* into a freedom. He was free in his choosing, but he was not free to forego choice. He had no choice but to choose. As Jean-Paul Sartre has put it: "Freedom is freedom to choose but not freedom not to choose. Not to choose, in fact, is to *choose* not to choose." [3] Man was thrust into what someone has called his "dreadful freedom"; [4] he was "condemned to be free." This freedom was and is indispensable to moral values and personal life. The freedom itself is not evil, and the thrusting of man into the freedom was not evil. Man could not be given the potential for good without being given the potential for evil. These are twin potentials; they, to change the analogy, are the two sides of one coin.

This is not to say that there cannot be good without evil; it is to say that there cannot be the *potential* for the one without the potential for the other. This belongs to the essential nature of good and evil. Neither may be coerced; each must be free. There can be no trust unless one be free to distrust. A watch cannot trust or distrust. It cannot love or hate. It may be mechanically efficient or inefficient, but it cannot be morally good

---

[3] Quoted by Paul Foulquie, *Existentialism*, trans. Kathleen Raine (London: Dennis Dobson, 1950), p. 92.

[4] Cf. Marjorie Grene's book entitled *Dreadful Freedom: A Critique of Existentialism* (Chicago: The University of Chicago Press, 1948).

or bad. That God should make man free for the good involved, inescapably, that he should make men free for the evil. The God-given freedom into which man was thrust was the *occasion* but not the necessity for evil.

According to the biblical treatment, the essence of man's fateful choice was his choice to have his being in and of himself, apart from God. The Genesis story of the Fall is the story of man's revolt against his creature status and his attempt to be like God—to be complete in himself.[5] It is the story of man's self-love, self-trust, and self-assertion. First came the doubt of God: Is God's will really good for us? Are God's commands binding? Cannot one manage for himself? Doubt became distrust and then disobedience. The will to power came to expression in the denial of God and in the assertion of self. Man was unwilling to be a part; he wanted to be the whole. In a class lecture John Baillie aptly put it: "Man wanted to be the whole cheese." There followed an ugly train. Man's nakedness brought the sense of helplessness, uncertainty, shame, and exposure. In his flight, as John Olen Strange points out, the "godlike" hid like a naughty boy. Man sought to evade, rationalizing and blaming someone else. He knew condemnation, the realization of guilt. His estrangement from God brought inevitable estrangement from man.[6] Adam's estrangement from God was immediately reflected in his estrangement from Eve and next in Cain's killing of Abel. Man's fall, then, was his self-exclusion from the fellowship of God, a fellowship of love and trust. This self-exclusion man brought upon himself in his fatal choice of self-love, self-trust, and self-assertion. It was his choice *to be* apart from God.

Paul, in Romans 1:18–32, covers the same ground as does chapter three of Genesis. Verse 28 supplies the key to the plight

---

[5] Cf. Reinhold Niebuhr, *The Nature and Destiny of Man* (New York: Charles Scribner's Sons, 1949), pp. 178–207.

[6] For a cogent treatment of the Fall, cf. Gottfried Quell, "Sin in the Old Testament," *Bible Key Words,* trans. and ed. J. R. Coates (New York: Harper & Brothers, 1951), Vol. I, Sec. III, 23–32, from Gerhard Kittel's *Theologisches Wörterbuch zum Neuen Testament.*

of men: "They did not choose [*approve*] to have God in their knowledge." God made himself knowable to man (v. 19), but man preferred not to know him. The Greek verb *edokimasan* in verse 28 is very significant for Paul's meaning. The word describes a proof by testing; man considered the matter of knowing God and decided against it. Paul is not presenting man's plight merely as one of ignorance; that could be solved by information. He does not represent the plight as a fate coercive upon man; that would rob it of all moral value except for the author of the fate. Paul presents the plight as rooted in a wilful choice on man's part to seek the meaning of his existence apart from God; man chose not to know God.

The wrath of God is set forth as the outworking of this fateful choice made by man to his own ruin. Three times Paul states that God gave them over (*paredōken*) to their own choices (vv. 24, 26, 28). In verses 24–27 Paul traces out man's depravity in terms of sensual vices, the moral breakdown of man seen in the reduction of himself to the animal or subanimal level. In verses 28–32 Paul describes the same depravity in terms of antisocial vices, the breakdown of human society. All of this Paul attributes to the fatal choice of men "professing themselves to be wise" but actually become fools (v. 22), men who tried to give to the creature the place belonging alone to the Creator (v. 25).

Does the Bible present man as a sinner by nature? This is true, in the sense that man turns naturally (by nature) to evil. His natural tendency is to try to be independent, to live of and for himself. According to Genesis, this was true of Adam *from the beginning*. The self-trust, self-love, and self-assertion of Adam is not presented as the *result* of the Fall but as the *cause*. Man did not fall and then turn to sin. The man whom God created is presented in Genesis not only as capable of evil but as doing evil. This does not mean that God created man evil or that God created the evil. It means that God made man free, free for good and hence free for evil. Finding himself to be in the *likeness* of God, man wanted *to be* his own God.

The question is often asked, "Was man—is man—able not

to sin?" From the Bible, from logic, and from experience one is driven to answer, "yes and no." How high can a man jump—six feet, seven feet? Then why not eight or nine feet, or over the house? Theoretically there is no limit to the height he can jump; actually there is. In a real sense man is able not to sin, otherwise there would be neither good nor evil possible to man. The fact that the Bible throughout holds man *guilty* for sin is conclusive for its position that man does not have to sin.

In another sense the question must receive a negative answer: "No, man is not able not to sin." Actually man has found himself unable to give himself to the good instead of the bad. He finds a contradiction within himself; he does what he wills not to do and he fails to do what he wills to do, as Paul so painfully shows in Romans 7. Socrates taught that a man will do right if he knows right, but Paul, in keeping with the Bible generally, pointed out the fallacy of this. Man's problem is deeper than ignorance. There is a contradiction within man, and he destroys himself in the very act of seeking to save himself (Mark 8:35).

In a sense, then, man does not have to sin; he is not coerced from without. His sin he must confess as his own, himself as guilty before God. In another sense, man cannot escape sin: he has sinned; each man has sinned; and man, each man, will yet sin. Man requires redemption; he requires a Redeemer. Man, the sinner, needs a new way; but he must have a Way in terms of One who can work in him a deliverance which he cannot effect for himself.

Satan and Demons

That the cause of man's predicament has been discussed thus far without reference to Satan (or demons) is not untrue to the New Testament; for it, too, in major passages concerned with the cause of sin pursues the matter without reference to Satan. Outstanding examples would include Romans 1:18–32—or Romans in its entirety! The term "Satan" appears in Romans only at 16:20; the term "devil" does not appear at all. In the New Testament there is no more penetrating analysis of sin's cause than in James 1:13–16; and there the whole blame is placed upon man, with no reference to Satan.

On the other side, it is to be observed that reference to Satan and demons is far more prominent in the New Testament than in the Old. There are in the Old Testament only three explicit references to Satan as a particular personage, and in two of these (Zech. 3:1; Job 1–2) the term is yet a title: the Satan (i.e., the adversary). In 1 Chronicles 21:1 the term appears without the definite article: "And Satan stood up against Israel, and provoked David to number Israel."

In the Jewish apocalyptic literature Satan emerges as chief of the evil spirits or demons and as the enemy of God and man. He appears, however, along with Semjaza, Azazel, Mastema, Belial (or, Beliar), Sammael, and Satanail.[7] In the New Testament there are yet echoes of Beelzebul (Mark 3:22; Matt. 12:24; Luke 11:15) and Belial (2 Cor. 6:15), but Satan is dominant. He is known as Satan, the devil, the enemy, the evil one, Beelzebul, Belial, the dragon or the old serpent, and the prince of the world. His role is that of accuser, tempter, and destroyer.

Although the New Testament places the responsibility for sin directly upon man, it does give great prominence to Satan and demons in some way connected with man's plight. Ragnar Leivestad[8] has suggested that two patterns may be found in the New Testament: one pattern connecting Satan directly with the problem of sin, the other pattern connecting Satan indirectly, through the demons, with "possession," disease, and death. In the former pattern, Satan is the tempter and accuser; in the latter pattern, working through demons, he is the tormentor, contributing to mental and bodily ills. Approached from the other side, from the standpoint of man's plight, some causal connection is seen between sin and all of man's ills.

[7] Cf. Edward Langton, *Essentials of Demonology* (London: Epworth Press, 1949) pp. 107–144.

[8] *Christ the Conqueror* (New York: The Macmillan Co., 1954), p. 42 *et passim*.

Only where man himself is found guilty is reference made to Satan as tempter or cause. John 13:27 states that "Satan entered into Judas," but Judas is not in the least exonerated; he is responsible for this "entering of Satan." When the problem is that of disease or "possession," the reference is to demons as related to the plight, and the afflicted is viewed as a "victim" rather than as directly responsible for his plight. In the pattern where Satan is introduced, the victory is found by Christ through the cross. Satan is overcome by faith in God and submission to him. When the problem is that of "possession," mental ills, and disease, the term used is "demons," and the victory of Christ over demons is through the power of God.[9]

Thus, in the New Testament, Jesus overcame the same hostile power in overcoming temptation and sin as when healing the sick or casting out demons, but in so doing he followed different methods.[10] Temptation and sin (Satan) are overcome by *kenōsis* (self-emptying) and the cross; disease and "possession" (demons) Jesus overcame by power (*dunamis*) or miracle (cf. Luke 13:16; Acts 10:38).[11]

It may be suggested that the Satan-demon analysis found in the New Testament is deeper than the simple psychosomatic analysis of man's ills. Man's problem has a moral and spiritual base; and man needs God, not just a psychiatrist. Man needs salvation from sin, not just psychosomatic therapy. (This is no disparagement of psychiatry as such, surely not when practiced by men of Christian faith.) Behind all man's ills, the New Testament finds the problem of sin; but it does not always see mental and physical ills as standing in a direct causal relation to sin. The afflicted may be victims (of demons, not Satan); yet if there were no sin, there would be no ills. In the other pattern, man is the guilty sinner. Satan has tempted or entered him; yet is he guilty. He is responsible for this "entry of Satan" into himself.

[9] Cf. *ibid.*, pp. 52 f.
[10] *Ibid.*, pp. 42 f.
[11] *Ibid.*, p. 295.

The Seriousness of the Plight

The seriousness of man's plight may be understood only if the nature of man and of sin are understood. That is to say, the doctrine of sin is bound up with the doctrine of man. Man's plight is most serious because sin is concerned with the essential man and the whole man, not simply with an incidental or isolated aspect of his being. It is serious because it is at one and the same time a situation of bondage and of guilt.

The essential man.—Sin is not concerned merely with flesh or matter as in certain gnostic and rationalist systems. Were this true, salvation could be found through asceticism or some other overcoming of the flesh. Sin is not just a matter of the mind as with certain naturalists or romanticists. The former group would say that man is essentially reason and would relegate sin to flesh, considered at best a secondary aspect of one's being. The latter group would make "sin" only the figment of distorted thinking, urging man simply to be "natural," to follow his biological destiny, to obey the instincts natural to his body. Neither has a defensible doctrine of man. Neither has a serious view of sin, for each relegates sin to what is considered a secondary aspect of one's being. Each maintains that the essential nature of man is intact.

In the New Testament, as well as in the Old, sin is seen to belong to the essential man. Something is wrong with man where the damage is greatest. Wolf has stated it forcefully: "Sin is understood less as an outward act and more and more as a crippling disease at the center of selfhood." [12] It is not merely that there is skirmishing in some border province of the empire of the self; there is rebellion in the capital city itself. Sin does not simply concern some dispensable organ which may be amputated; it concerns the heart of the self which must be cleansed and renewed.

The whole man.—Despite varied terms which characterize

[12] William J. Wolf, *No Cross, No Crown* (New York: Doubleday & Co., Inc., 1957), p. 38.

man from different standpoints, the New Testament views man in his wholeness and sees sin as affecting man in his wholeness. The terms flesh (*sarx*), spirit (*pneuma*), body (*sōma*), and soul (*psuchē*) in the New Testament may seem to assume a dichotomous or trichotomous view of man, but actually this is not the case. Each term describes the whole man from its particular perspective. The whole man may be described as "flesh," or "spirit," or "body," or "soul." Each term is highly serviceable in the analysis of man or for emphasis of some aspect of his being, but this never becomes a thoroughgoing dichotomy or trichotomy.

This parallels current usage in psychology, where various terms are used in the analysis of the person, but where these distinctions never become absolute. Accordingly, a person may be analyzed in terms of reason, emotion, volition, or flesh; but these cannot in fact be separated one from the other. One's mind cannot be placed in one room, his emotions in another, his will in another, and his flesh in yet another. In the New Testament, man is a complexity of bodily, rational, emotional, volitional, moral, spiritual, and other factors, distinguishable in analysis but not separable in actuality. Sin affects all factors.

Flesh.—The term *sarx* appears about 140 times in the New Testament but not always with the same connotation. Sometimes it is to be taken in the most literal sense, as descriptive of "the material that covers the bones of a human or animal body" [13] as in 1 Corinthians 15:39: "Not all flesh is the same flesh: but there is one of men, another flesh of beasts, another flesh of birds, and another flesh of fish." Sometimes *sarx* is used for "the body itself, viewed as substance." [14] Repeatedly, however, *sarx* is employed, especially by Paul, to describe the whole man in his distance from God or in his weakness. Man may be "flesh" in his thinking, feeling, willing, even as in his sensual self.

That the whole person, with no necessary implication of

[13] Arndt and Gingrich, *op. cit.,* p. 750.
[14] *Ibid.*

estrangement or weakness, may be described as "flesh" is easy to demonstrate from the New Testament. When Paul wrote in Galatians 1:16, "I did not confer with flesh and blood," he simply meant that he talked with no person. In Galatians 2:16 (cf. Rom. 3:20) he said, "Out of the works of law shall no flesh be justified," obviously meaning no person. When Paul cited God's provision "that no flesh may boast in the presence of God" (1 Cor. 1:29), he clearly was referring to persons, not to literal flesh. In 2 Corinthians 7:5 Paul describes an arrival in Macedonia under circumstances which denied him rest for his "flesh," and the context clearly shows that the "rest" which eluded him was not primarily concerned with literal flesh; the whole self was in agony over unpredictable Corinthians to whom recently he had written a stern and painful letter (2 Cor. 7:8).

Similar use may be seen in Romans. In 6:19 Paul explained to his readers that the manner of his writing was because of the weakness of their "flesh." Obviously he did not thus imply that their problem was that of physical weakness. He spoke rather of a weakness both rational and moral. In Romans 7:18 Paul confessed that good does not dwell in his "flesh." The context makes it clear that the reference was to his person. In Romans 8:3 Paul attributed the impotence of the law for moral good to the weakness of the flesh. Surely the reference was to the total self and not simply to the literal flesh.

Paul was not alone among New Testament writers in employing the term flesh with the connotation of person. Genesis 2:24 was quoted by various ones, describing marriage as a union in which the two become "one flesh" (Mark 10:8; Matt. 19:5). At the Feast of Pentecost, Peter quoted Joel as prophesying of the time when God would pour out his Spirit "upon all flesh" (Acts 2:17). Surely the meaning is that the Spirit would come upon all people.

A comparison of John 6:51 with 6:56 and 6:57 is rewarding for this study. In 6:51 Jesus says: "I am the living bread, that having come down out of heaven; if anyone eat of this bread, he shall live forever; and the bread which I shall give is my flesh in behalf of the world." Here the living bread which one is to eat is his "flesh." In verse 56 Jesus gave this assurance: "The one eating *my flesh* and drinking *my blood* abides in me and I in him." Significantly, in the next verse Jesus declared: "The one devouring *me,* that one shall live through me" (57). So, in verse 51 the "bread" is equated with "flesh," and in verses 56 and 57 "flesh" is equated with "me." Here again "flesh" stands for the whole self.

Many times in the New Testament "flesh" is used for the whole man in his *distance* from God or for man in his natural state.[15] The phrase "according to flesh" occasionally denotes only one's natural state with no connotation of estrangement from God. This is true in Romans 1:3, where Jesus is said to be "of the seed of David according to flesh." Likewise this is true in Romans 9:3, where Paul refers to his "kinsmen according to flesh." Usually, however, the phrase "according to flesh" (*kata sarka*) describes one in his distance from God, thus contrasting with what is according to Spirit (*kata pneuma*). In Romans 8:4 the Christian is characterized as walking "according to Spirit" and not "according to flesh." This is not a dichotomous treatment of man. It is rather a contrast between the whole man trying to live apart from God (*kata sarka*) with the whole man living in relation to God (*kata pneuma*). The attempt to live independently of God is described variously as purposing according to flesh (2 Cor. 1:17), knowing according to flesh (2 Cor. 5:16), walking according to flesh (2 Cor. 10:2; Rom. 8:4), being according to flesh (Rom. 8:5), warring according to flesh (2 Cor. 10:3), living according to flesh (Rom. 8:13), and judging according to flesh (John 8:15). Obviously these functions belong to the total man, not simply to the literal flesh.

The phrase "in flesh" (*en sarki*) normally describes man in his necessary bodily existence, as in Galatians 2:20: "that

[15] This whole section is greatly indebted to John A. T. Robinson's monograph, *The Body: A Study in Pauline Theology* (Chicago: Henry Regnery Co., 1952).

which I now live in flesh." Second Corinthians 10:3 is instructive for different meanings of the word flesh: "For though we
walk *in flesh* we do not war *according to flesh.*" Here "in flesh"
describes one's natural and necessary state; while "according
to flesh" describes the renounced estrangement from God. But
"flesh" for Paul so characteristically stood for distance from
God that even the phrase "in flesh" sometimes carried this
connotation, as in Romans 7:5: "When we were in the flesh."
Surely Paul does not imply that he is now a ghost. In Romans 8:9
he wrote: "Ye are not in flesh but in Spirit." He is not saying
that they are "disembodied spirits"; they are people now living
in a relationship of trust in God rather than in estrangement
from him.

The "works of the flesh" are cataloged in Galatians 5:19–21,
and ten out of the fifteen are not basically sensual. These "works
of the flesh" include idolatry, sorcery, enmities, strife, jealousies,
anger, disputes (or, outbreaks of selfishness),[16] divisions, factions, and envyings. Thus ten nonsensual evils are grouped with
five sensual evils (fornication, uncleanness, licentiousness,
drunkenness, and carousing), and all of them are termed "works
of the flesh." In the list of fifteen the first three and last two sins
are basically sensual, the middle ten are nonsensual. In 1 Corinthians 3:3 Paul classifies jealousy and strife as "fleshly."

The New Testament does not view the literal flesh as evil;
this is a gnostic idea. In 1 Corinthians 3:1–3 Paul does not
chide the Corinthians for being "made of flesh" (*sarkinos*), for
they cannot help that. His censure is for their being "fleshly"
(*sarkikos*). They are necessarily of flesh (literally), but it is to
their shame that they are "fleshly," yet in too great distance
from God. That flesh in the literal sense is not viewed as evil
in the New Testament is once-and-for-all ruled out by its bold
statement, "The Word became flesh" (John 1:14).

Spirit.—That "spirit" in the New Testament may have the connotation of "self" or "person" is apparent in passages already
studied in connection with "flesh." Just as "flesh" may describe

[16] Arndt and Gingrich, *op. cit.,* p. 309, so translate *eritheiai.*

the whole man (the thinking, feeling, willing, moral, spiritual, bodily man) in his distance from God, so "spirit" may describe the total man in his relation to God. It was seen from Romans 8:4 that the Christian walks "according to Spirit" and not "according to flesh." In Romans 8:9 the readers were reminded that they were then not "in flesh" but "in Spirit." In Galatians 5:22 f. the fruit of the Spirit (love, joy, peace, patience, kindness, goodness, faith, gentleness, and self-control) is contrasted with the works of the flesh (fornication, uncleanness, licentiousness, idolatry, sorcery, enmities, strife, jealousies, anger, disputes, divisions, factions, envyings, drunkenness, and carousing). In each representation, as "flesh" or as "spirit," the total self is considered. In benedictions like that of Philemon 25, "The grace of our Lord Jesus Christ be with thy spirit," or 2 Timothy 4:22, "The Lord be with your spirit," one's spirit is one's self. When Stephen prayed: "Lord Jesus, receive my spirit" (Acts 7:59), he meant, "Lord Jesus, receive me."

This conclusion is reinforced by the fact that although terms are used which seem to imply a dichotomous or trichotomous view of man, the New Testament never envisions a "disembodied spirit." Whenever those who have died are pictured in the life beyond, it is in some kind of bodily form. When Moses and Elijah appeared with Jesus at the transfiguration, they were *seen* and *heard* as *men* (Luke 9:30 f.); and their appearance was such that Peter suggested the appropriateness of three tabernacles: one each for Jesus, Moses, and Elijah (Luke 9:33).

In Luke 16, the rich man, Lazarus, and Abraham are all envisioned as bodily men with all of the faculties belonging to full personality. They were not in a "disembodied state" as is often claimed. At least for the rich man it was not complete disembodiment, for he begged for water for his *tongue!* The idea of a "pure spirit" or "naked soul" belongs to Greek and other systems of philosophy and religion but not to the Bible. In biblical teaching (Gen. 2:7), God formed man from the dust of the earth and he became a living soul (*nephesh*). Genesis does not say that man *has* a soul, he is one.

Body.—It has just been observed that the Bible knows man only in somatic or bodily existence. The term "body" (*sōma*) sometimes interchanges with "flesh" (*sarx*), but generally the words differ in connotation. "Body" (*sōma*) has in common with "spirit" (*pneuma*) the fact that it can describe man in his relationship to God. "Flesh" is not used for this purpose. Frequently *sōma* is used with the meaning of self or person. This parallels English usage of "body," as in words like "somebody," "nobody," "anybody." In a familiar song, the line "If a body meet a body coming through the rye" does not stress the physical but rather the *personal* encounter. In the New Testament "body" is considered an essential aspect of personal being. Body *is* the person, viewed from one important aspect of his being.

The comparison of 1 Corinthians 6:15 with 12:27 is instructive for the meaning of *sōma:* "Do ye not know that *your bodies* are members of Christ?" (6:15) and "Ye are the body of Christ, and members individually" (12:27). There is virtual interchange between "your bodies" and "ye." Similar interchange may be seen in Romans 6:12–13 in the employment of "body," "members," "selves," where one reads: "Let not sin reign in your mortal *bodies* . . . , neither present your *members* . . . , but present *yourselves*." Probably Romans 12:1 is to be interpreted accordingly, where "present your bodies a living sacrifice" may mean "present yourselves a living sacrifice."

Soul.—In biblical usage, as indicated above, "soul" (*nephesh* in Hebrew, *psuchē* in Greek) describes the whole person from a particular standpoint and may be used for the person. Genesis 2:7 is clear in its statement that "man *became* a living soul." Many nonbiblical systems teach that "soul" has pre-existence over body and that "soul" survives apart from the body in the life beyond. In such systems the body is viewed as the tomb or the prison house of the soul, incarnation or embodiment is the soul's "fall," and physical death is the beautiful friend which liberates the soul from its prison.

Such ideas are foreign to biblical thought. In the Bible God is creator of the body, and it is essential to the self. "Soul" is not pre-existent and the idea of a "naked soul" in the Greek sense repels the biblical writer. Man is body, he is soul, he is spirit. He is all this at one and the same time. Body is not only the creation of God and essential to what man is, but body is included in redemption. A "soul" is a bodily, rational, emotional, volitional, moral, spiritual self.

That "soul" may have the meaning of self is clear in Luke 12:19–20, where the rich farmer dreams of his retirement: "I will say to my *soul, Soul,* you have many good things laid up for many years; take your rest, eat, drink, be merry!" What kind of "soul" is it that may eat, drink, and be merry? Even in verse 20 the meaning of soul is probably self: "And God said to him, Thou fool, in this night they [his material possessions?] are demanding from thee thy soul [thyself]."

Further evidences that in the New Testament "soul" may mean self or person may be seen in passages like the following. In Acts 2:41 the "three thousand souls" added to the church were certainly persons, not souls in the Greek sense. The same connotation is to be seen in Leviticus 23:29, quoted in Acts 3:23, "And it shall be, that every soul [person] who shall not hear that prophet, shall be destroyed out of the people." In Romans 13:1 Paul admonished every "soul" to be in subjection to the existing authorities. In Revelation 6:9–11 the "souls" under the altar are seen, they had voices, and they wore robes. These are not Greek souls but full persons.

This section on the biblical doctrine of man may seem to be unduly long and to have lost sight of the real subject: the plight of man. The plea to be made is that one must correctly understand the biblical doctrine of man in order to understand its doctrine of sin or salvation. Much of the inadequacy and even distortion of the doctrines of sin and salvation root in the confusion of nonbiblical ideas with the biblical doctrine of man. This writer believes that in the doctrine of man one stands at the crossroads for his theology. The road he chooses here determines the balance of his theology.

The conclusion to this point is that sin involves the total man;

it is not limited to separable or incidental aspects of one's being. The total man is in trouble beyond his own power to remedy. He is in trouble in his thinking, in his emotional responses, in his volitional choices, in his moral values, in his bodily expression, in his relationship to God, to other people, and to things. This means, then, that the salvation required must be more than information for the mind, the advantage of a good example, external application of a religious rite, a tranquilizer for the emotions, or ascetic discipline to curb bodily impulses. The salvation required must come from a source higher than man, and it must include the cleansing and renewal of the total person.

The Plight as Bondage

The irony of man's plight is that bondage is the result of his attempt to be free. Distrusting God, fearing his will, man turned to his own way in self-love, self-trust, and self-assertion. Wanting to be sovereign, he became slave to sin and to death. Jesus stated it unambiguously: "The one doing sin is the slave of sin" (John 8:34). Paul described the human predicament in saying: "Sin reigned in death" (Rom. 5:21). John A. T. Robinson neatly summarizes:

Consequently, men's state is equally one of slavery to sin (Rom. 6:6, 17, 20). In essence, indeed, sin is an act of human freedom, whose prime nature is disobedience (Rom. 5:19). But it is something which has long since got out of man's control. It is a symbol now not of freedom, but of determinism. Like death, it has become an alien power residing within the individual, denying him command of his own actions: "It is no more I that do it, but sin that dwelleth in me" (Rom. 7:17, 20). It has its own law under which the self is prisoner (Rom. 7:23). It exercises the functions of king (Rom. 5:14) and Lord (Rom. 6:14); it is a slave-owner to whom man has been sold as chattel (Rom. 7:14). In a phrase, all things have been shut up under sin [hupo hamartian, Gal. 3:22].[17]

Paul, in describing man's plight as one of bondage, employed three closely related phrases: "body of sin" (Rom. 6:6), "body

[17] Op. cit., p. 36.

of death" (Rom. 7:24), and "body of flesh" (Col. 2:11). He seems to imply not only the individual person's bondage but his solidarity with others in bondage. In some real sense the individual person is bound up with the human race and with history. To be *en sarki*, in flesh, is to be within the sphere, and, therefore, the jurisdiction, of the world and its forces. It is to be understood in the light of the contrasting phrases: "in Christ" and "in the Spirit." [18]

The Plight as Guilt

Man as sinner is caught in a solidarity with the human race and history, but the solidarity is never of such nature as to exonerate him. Man is guilty for his own sin. In a sense the individual is swept along in sin by the human race and by history, but this is never in such a way as to free him of guilt. The prophets cried out against any "passing of the buck" of responsibility for one's sin. In Deuteronomy 24:16 the judgment is given: "The fathers shall not be put to death for the children, neither shall the children be put to death for the fathers: every man shall be put to death for his own sin." Jeremiah made strong protest against any attempt to evade the fact of one's own guilt: "In those days they shall say no more, The fathers have eaten sour grapes, and the children's teeth are set on edge" (31:29). Ezekiel refuted the same proverb (18:2) and added the clear indictment: "The soul that sinneth, it shall die" (18:4).

The principles of solidarity with the group and individual guilt may be illustrated in terms of mob action. One may find himself swept along by a mob of which he is a part. Under its spell he may seem to be moved more by its will than his own. However, in looking back upon the scene, he must admit his personal guilt. However irresponsible one may be as he finds himself a part of a larger solidarity, he is yet responsible; he is responsible for becoming irresponsible. At some point he made a personal and responsible decision or commitment by which he

[18] *Ibid.*, p. 22, footnote 2.

gave way to, and became a part of, the solidarity of the group. At the time a drunken man may be irresponsible, yet he is responsible for becoming irresponsible. So it is with the individual in his bondage to sin, in his "body of flesh," "body of sin," "body of death." In the final analysis he must assume responsibility for his own sin.

One can hardly exaggerate the power exercised over an individual by his environment, by the force of history, by the human race. For all this, however, each man is guilty. As each faces the fact of his sin, it is with "total responsibility in total solitude" (Sartre). Alone, yes, and yet not alone. So soon as man is willing to acknowledge that the sin is his own and his alone, there is Another to bear it. But that is another story; that is the story of God's grace in Jesus Christ.

Man's difficult situation is bound up with his uniqueness, in which he is tempted from two sides. Man is created in the image of God. He is created in God's image, but he is not God. He is created but he is more than just another creature. On one side, man is tempted to reject his creature status and seek to be equal with God, or to be his own God. On the other side, man is tempted to forget that he is created in the image of God and to be a mere creature, to sink into creation as just another creature. Man's place is thus unique and difficult. He is created in the image of God, but he is not God. To try to be God is the sin of idolatry. He is created, but he is not just another creature. To try to be merely another creature is the sin of secularism or materialism. Man must find his true being in proper relationship with God, his creator, and with all else that God has created. It is the work of Christ to bring man to this true being.

The
Christology
of the
3 New Testament

THE NEW TESTAMENT is from first to last about Jesus Christ. He is the one alone indispensable to its concern. Every other person in the New Testament has importance only in relationship to Jesus: for or against him, friend or foe. He is the unmistakable center to the total event which the New Testament describes.[1] God has acted in self-revelation and in redemption, and this divine event is centered in One alone. God who "in many measures and in many manners of old" did speak to the fathers in the prophets has in these last days spoken in his Son (Heb. 1:1 f.).

The New Testament is about a person. It is about an event at the center of which is Jesus Christ. It is about the creation of a community of persons through an event at the center of which is a person, Jesus Christ.[2] In Jesus Christ, God has acted and spoken, but more is to be said. In Jesus Christ, God has *come*. He is the Word incarnate; he is Immanuel, God with us. The New Testament ascribes ultimate significance to Jesus of Nazareth, one "born of woman" (Gal. 4:4) yet one who was before Abraham (John 8:58). Christianity does not go back simply to an early community of disciples; it is rooted in Jesus of Nazareth. The redemptive activity of God came to its ultimate expression in Jesus, and the church is his creation.[3]

[1] Cf. John Knox, *On the Meaning of Christ* (New York: Charles Scribner's Sons, 1947), p. 49.
[2] *Ibid.*, p. 19 *et passim.*
[3] Cf. Rawlinson, *op. cit.*, pp. 8–11.

35

Characteristic Emphases

The historical Jesus.—Mark, the earliest of the Four Gospels, introduces itself as "The gospel of Jesus Christ" (1:1). This could well introduce the whole New Testament. It is the gospel of Jesus Christ. Luke's explicit concern was with "the things fulfilled among us" (1:1). The Gospel of Luke is from beginning to end about Jesus. In Acts 1:1 the author ties together this Gospel and Acts as being concerned with "all of the things which Jesus began to do and to teach." This two-volumed work, Luke-Acts, is concerned with Christ in the flesh and Christ present by the Holy Spirit and embodied in the church. Matthew is about "Jesus Christ, son of David, son of Abraham" (1:1). The Fourth Gospel (John) is about the Word made flesh (1:1, 14). Without Jesus the Christ, his person and teaching and works, the Four Gospels would shrink into nothing.

Outside the Gospels, the New Testament is likewise Christo-centric. That this should be true of Paul's letters would be expected from his boast, "I judged to know nothing among you except Jesus Christ and him crucified" (1 Cor. 2:2). The essence of his theology is to be found in the full meaning of "in Christ" and "Christ in you." Paul's concern with Christ as a living presence does not mean that he was unconcerned with "the historical Jesus." It is incredible that scholars ever so misread 2 Corinthians 5:16 as to understand Paul to mean that he was no longer interested in "the historical Jesus." His meaning is that he, Paul, no longer sees "according to flesh"—with the "eyes of flesh." He does not mean that he is indifferent to Jesus as over against Christ. He means that with the new "eyes of faith" he has come to see Christ in a new way.

For the writer of Hebrews, Jesus Christ is the Son in whom God has spoken his final word. Creation, revelation, and redemption are traced to Jesus. It is in him as mediator that God comes to man and that man is brought to God. For Peter, Jesus is the "living stone" (1 Peter 2:4), the one in whom alone we have a "living hope" (1:3). The book of Revelation is "the revelation of Jesus Christ" (1:1). It is the revelation which God has given *through* Christ, but from beginning to end Christ himself *is* the revelation. James alone of the New Testament writers fails to give prominence to the person and the event of Jesus Christ. He gives almost exclusive attention to the moral and ethical teachings of Jesus, probably because he was concerned with those who "accepted" the person and event but gave no evidence that their "faith" was real.

Emphasis on function.—The Christology of the New Testament is concerned with the person and nature of Jesus Christ, but its approach is through function, historical revelation, rather than through speculative questions of nature or essence.[4] The more speculative questions about the nature (or two natures) of Christ belong to the later Christological controversies.

Of course, the question of the identity of Jesus was raised in the lifetime of Jesus and became primary in the New Testament. He was recognized by all as truly human and by many as divine. Many who knew him as truly human also worshiped him as divine. He was to them the "Son of God." Paul declared that "God was in Christ" (2 Cor. 5:19). John affirmed that "the Word was God" (1:1) and that "the Word became flesh" (1:14). Thomas worshiped him as his Lord and God (John 20:28). But for all this, there was no real metaphysical speculation about his nature. The earliest believers began with an event which broke around them. In it they saw God acting and God present in self-disclosure and in redemption. God was acting eschatologically or ultimately, and he was acting in judgment and salvation. This divine act occurred in Jesus Christ, its center.

Titles of Jesus.—Jesus is set forth in terms of many titles or roles, adapted chiefly from the Old Testament but supplemented by terms belonging to the larger world in which Jesus and his early followers lived and with which they interacted. Jesus is

---

[4] Cf. Martin Dibelius, *Gospel Criticism and Christology* (London: Ivor Nicholson & Watson, Ltd., 1935), pp. 86 f.; William Manson, *Jesus the Messiah* (Philadelphia: The Westminster Press, 1946), p. 134; Oscar Cullmann, *The Christology of the New Testament,* trans. Shirley C. Guthrie and Charles A. M. Hall (Philadelphia: The Westminster Press, 1959), pp. 3 ff.

presented in the New Testament so as to be unintelligible apart from the Old Testament.

Some of the titles were self-designations on the part of Jesus. Some were employed by others in designating him. Jesus interpreted himself and his work in terms of basic Old Testament roles. In so doing he adapted, extended, and fulfilled them. These titles are more concerned with function than with speculative questions of nature. They describe what he came to do in bringing God to man and in bringing man to God. In some instances a role was described without the employment of an actual title. In the New Testament Jesus is known as Son of David, Son of God, Son of man, Messiah or Christ, Servant of God (the role but not title), Lord, Prophet, Saviour, High Priest, Lamb of God, Mediator, Logos, and even as God.

The Triune God

As W. O. Carver pointed out, the New Testament does not have a formal doctrine of the Trinity; it nowhere discusses the Trinity as such. It does speak repeatedly of the Father, the Son, and the Holy Spirit. It speaks of Father, Son, and Holy Spirit in such a way as to compel a trinitarian understanding of God. This never in the New Testament becomes a "tritheism"; the New Testament does not have three Gods, nor even two. The *Shema* of the Old Testament (Deut. 6:4) belongs to the New Testament also: "The Lord our God is one" (Mark 12:29). For several decades it was possible for Christians to worship at the Temple and in the synagogues and even to preach Christ in the synagogues of the Jews (Acts 17:1 ff.). Paul remained a monotheist who continued to worship in Temple and synagogue, yet he saw that "God was in Christ."

The New Testament recognized that in some real sense Christ and the Father were one (John 14:10 ff.). The Word who became flesh (John 1:14) was in the beginning with God and was God (1:1). One who has seen the Son has seen the Father (14:9). When the Son addresses the Father, the mystery is that belonging to the Incarnation, a mystery which faith accepts but does not explain. This does not imply two Gods. It does mean that the Word became incarnate in one who was human and who prayed to the Father. The "dialogue" in the prayer of Jesus is not one between two Gods; it is a mystery belonging to the God-man.

The New Testament likewise has much to say about the Holy Spirit. Especially was the Holy Spirit's presence felt following the ascension of Christ, although not to the exclusion of an earlier presence as attested by the Old Testament and all the New. The Holy Spirit was the Comforter (John 14:16) whose *coming* was to be realized through the *going* of the Son to the Father. The Holy Spirit is thought of in the New Testament in terms of a personal presence. Yet again it must be said that he was not another God. The Holy Spirit's continuing ministry was to be in relationship to the earthly ministry of Jesus. He was to convict the world with respect to sin, righteousness, and judgment (John 16:8 f.). This was to be done in relationship to the life and ministry of Jesus.

The Holy Spirit was to guide the disciples "into all truth," but this was to be accomplished upon the basis of what Jesus himself had taught (16:12 f.). The early Christians were to be empowered by the Holy Spirit, but this was at the command of the risen Christ, a command given to a community brought together around the risen Christ and commissioned to witness to the risen Christ (Acts 1:3, 6, 8, 21 f.). Thus the Spirit is the continuing presence of Jesus Christ (John 20:22). Paul could write of the risen Christ and the Holy Spirit in such a way as to make the terms almost interchangeable (Rom. 8:9 f.).

The New Testament knows God as Father, Son, and Holy Spirit, yet it knows God as one alone. One may suggest that in his transcendence he is known as Father, in his immanence as Holy Spirit, and in his ultimate presence and self-disclosure as Son. Yet to raise metaphysical questions and to offer rationales about the Trinity is to attempt to go beyond the New Testament. Its writers only knew that the "incredible" had happened: the God of the ages had visited earth in the person of Jesus of

Nazareth, and after the death of Jesus he continued his presence as the Holy Spirit. It is the uniqueness of the New Testament that the Father and the Spirit are understood in terms of Jesus Christ. To know the Father requires that one know the Son. It is through the Son that the Spirit comes.

New Testament theology, consequently, is concerned with the triune God, but this concern is basically Christological. Paul wrote in the name of the Father, the Son, and the Holy Spirit (cf. 1 Cor. 12:4–6; 2 Cor. 13:14), yet he "preached Christ" (1 Cor. 1:23; 2:2). New Testament theology to be concerned with the triune God must be concerned with Christology. Christ is God present, God acting in self-revelation, in judgment, and in salvation in the person of Jesus Christ.

Event, Person, and Community

Jesus Christ is "the same yesterday, today, and forever" (Heb. 13:8), yet he cannot be understood apart from the event which took place in Palestine almost two thousand years ago.[5] Christ is a living person who encounters us *here and now,* but he comes to us through the community whose preaching bears witness to that event in which the Word became flesh and accomplished the work of God on earth.

One cannot exaggerate the importance of the "existential encounter" with the living Christ here and now, but neither may he divorce the event of his coming now from the event of his coming long ago. In truth they are not two events, but one. The coming to us now is the extension of his coming then. The event which occurred then is yet occurring. The Word who became flesh must be embodied in us, the body of Christ (John 6:48–59; 1 Cor. 10:17; 12:12 f., 27). He who died at Golgotha must extend his death into us in so real a sense that we become "crucified with Christ" (Gal. 2:20). His resurrection from the dead must be extended into us in a sense so real that we be raised to newness of life. Christ's very sufferings are continued in those of his servants (Col. 1:24).

[5] This section draws heavily on Knox, *On the Meaning of Christ*

The "existential interpretation" of the New Testament associated with "demythologizing" of Rudolf Bultmann [6] stresses a primary truth, yet involves a fatal error. Although the idea is not new, Bultmann has given new focus and emphasis to the fact that Christ must be known as a presence here and now.[7] He must confront us now in the *kērugma* (preaching), forcing us into the agony of decision in which we must choose between remaining in our false existence, or giving ourselves to Christ and thus entering into our authentic existence in relationship to God and men. This is to say that we cannot be saved simply by an event two thousand years ago. Even as we recognize all that Christ did back there, we also have to recognize that millions are yet in their sins and unchanged as to life or destiny. To save us, it is necessary for Christ to accomplish a radical change in us.

Bultmann, however, is either wrong or inexcusably obscure in failing to do justice to the event that occurred in Palestine two thousand years ago. The Christ who comes to us now, comes through the community which preaches Christ in terms of that event. It is one continuing event which embraces both what Christ suffered under Pontius Pilate and his confronting us here and now. Correctly defined, "modernism" is any separation between "Jesus of history" and "Christianity." [8] This "modernism" must be avoided from whichever side it may come, either in the failure to do justice to Jesus of Nazareth or to Christ who is "the Presence of eternity" here and now. It is fatal to New Testament faith and theology to separate Jesus from the present,

[6] See Rudolf K. Bultmann, *The Presence of Eternity* (New York: Harper & Brothers, 1957); *Jesus Christ and Mythology* (New York: Charles Scribner's Sons, 1958); *Theology of the New Testament,* trans. Kendrick Grobel (New York: Charles Scribner's Sons, 1951), I, and other writings for his emphasis.

[7] It was in the earliest days of this writer's ministry that in the reading of Alexander Maclaren's *Expositions of Holy Scripture* Jesus ceased to be merely a person in the first century and became for him a living presence here and now.

[8] According to Rawlinson, *op. cit.,* pp. xii f., the term "modernism" was first used by Rousseau in 1769, next by Italian bishops in 1905 in denunciation of the views of Loisy and others, and then in 1907 in the Papal Encyclical *Pascendi dominici gregis.* The attempt to separate "Christianity" from Jesus was termed "modernism."

locking him up in the first century; and it is likewise fatal to
uproot the "contemporary Christ" from the event of the first
century.

Jesus' Understanding of Himself

The Christology of the New Testament is bound up with
how Jesus understood himself. The New Testament clearly
represents Jesus as struggling with the question of his own identity and mission. Much of the New Testament makes sense only
if one assumes that Jesus did struggle through to a strong conviction as to his person and work. Those about Jesus were at-
tracted or repelled by his claims for himself. They gave him their
devotion and allegiance or they sought to destroy him. Jesus
himself was the issue, even above what he said and did. He
deliberately made himself the decisive issue. He called men to
himself, not just to a teaching or an example.

The student of the New Testament cannot afford to be intimi-
dated by what has been written in disparagement of a "self-
interpretation of Jesus." [9] It is not naïve to understand Jesus as
concerned with his own identity and mission. The obscurantism
and naïveté rest with one who would seek to understand Christianity apart from Jesus as a person in history.

As the New Testament shows, Jesus consciously thrust himself into the center of history and made himself the object of
trust, obedience, and worship. Martyrs and "expendables" have
forsaken all—even father, mother, child, husband, or wife—
for him. We can understand them only as persons who have
come under the *claim* of Christ—the Christ who understands
himself as having the right to ultimate and absolute claim upon
each of us. To doubt that Jesus was concerned with understanding himself is to assume that he was *less* than an ordinary
person. It is not unusual for a person to ask, "Who am I?" [10] It is

---

[9] It is to the credit of W. O. Carver that in 1926 he published a book entitled *The Self-Interpretation of Jesus* (Nashville: Broadman Press) at a time
when many scholars rejected this as a valid investigation.

[10] Cf. Dietrich Bonhoeffer, *The Cost of Discipleship*, trans. R. H. Fuller (New
York: The Macmillan Co., 1949), pp. 15 f.

astonishing that serious scholarship should ever have doubted the fact of self-interpretation on the part of Jesus.

It is altogether proper to avoid extravagant statements about the "messianic consciousness" of Jesus, but one may be certain that "at some stage in his ministry Jesus stood self-disclosed as the Messiah or Son of Man to be." [11] It would be arrogant to boast that we can "read his mind" or look directly into his heart, seeing all that is there. We cannot do that with respect to those nearest and dearest to us. On the other hand, we are not without evidence of his self-interpretation.

That Jesus was somewhat reticent in speaking of his personal identity is reflected in the variety of answers given to the question, "Who do men say that I am?" (Mark 8:27). But whatever variety in the answers, the question *was* asked, and *Jesus* asked it. From the outset of his ministry, Jesus so spoke and acted as to indicate that he had some extraordinary sense of mission. William Manson neatly summarizes the evidences that Jesus saw his mission as creating a supreme crisis in the religious history of Israel, observing that his sayings ascribe to him:

1. The belief that a crisis is at hand for the nation, that the kingdom of God has suddenly appeared (*ephthasen*) or is forcing its way in (*biazetai*) or is present in the midst (*entos humōn*).

2. The conviction that prophecy is being fulfilled in his words and deeds, and that he is the bearer of a higher revelation than any given in the past: something greater than Jonah or than Solomon has appeared.

3. The claim not merely to supersede the tradition of the elders, but to set his own interpretations upon the commandments of the Torah (*egō de legō humin*) and to offer these not as matters of opinion but as authoritative declarations of the Will of God.

4. The consciousness of performing his mighty works by divine inspiration (*en pneumati Theou*), so that to indict him as a sorcerer is to blaspheme against the Holy Spirit.

5. The sense of authority not only to summon men to follow him, but to pronounce their salvation conditional upon their acceptance of what he reveals.[12]

[11] William Manson, *Jesus the Messiah,* p. 137.
[12] *Ibid.,* p. 139.

To attribute all of this to the community rather than to Jesus is to be unduly skeptical and to reduce research to ungoverned subjectivity. It takes more credulity to be asked to believe that Jesus is the creation of the community than to believe that he actually was such a person as the New Testament describes him. In the New Testament he is not a "stained glass window" type of Christ; he is a real person, stained with sweat, tears, dust, and blood. He is one who *agonized* over what he was to do and say. The portrayal of Jesus in the New Testament has the ring of truth. The magnitude of the event of which he is the center is not to be understood apart from Jesus himself or apart from his own realization that he was the center of the event.

Filial consciousness.—The core of the self-interpretation of Jesus was by every evidence his "filial consciousness." He knew himself to be God's Son in some unique sense. Luke's story of the lad of twelve years in his visit to the Temple is not to be unduly pressed for meaning, but at the least it points to Jesus' recognition of God as his Father and of himself as called to some special work (2:41–52). His work essentially proved to be that of enabling men to know God as their Father, this being the essence of eternal life (John 17:3). He himself so knew God and came to impart that knowledge (Matt. 11:25–27; Luke 10:21 f.).

The so-called "Johannine" passage in the Synoptics (Matt. 11:25–27; Luke 10:21 f.) represents Jesus as knowing God as his Father and as able to impart that knowledge to others. Because of the Johannine character of the passage, many see it as the nucleus from which the later Johannine understanding of the Fourth Gospel was developed. Others, however, see this as a genuine saying of Jesus, representing his own self-understanding.[13]

Apart from this controversial passage, there are clear evidences that Jesus understood himself to be God's Son. The par-

---

[13] See Rawlinson, *op. cit.*, pp. 251–264, for a critical analysis of the problem.

able of the wicked husbandmen (Mark 12:1–12) implies such understanding of himself. The avowal that knowledge of the future belonged to no one, "not even the Son," except to the Father alone is no doubt a statement which goes back to Jesus himself (Mark 13:32; Matt. 24:36). Scribes were troubled by this limitation upon the knowledge of Jesus and tried to delete the words, "not even the Son." This is best understood as a saying of Jesus which survived *because* it was genuine and in spite of the difficulty it caused early Christians.

The idea of "knowing God" is not to be written off as Hellenistic rather than Jewish, for the idea is found in the Old Testament (Deut. 34:10; Jer. 31:34; Hos. 4:1; 6:6; Amos 3:2) and in Paul (Gal. 4:9; 1 Cor. 13:12).[14] The idea is Jewish, and there is no sufficient reason for doubting that Jesus both knew God as his Father and that his conscious mission was to give us that knowledge.

The knowledge of God is deep-rooted in New Testament faith; the fact that we may know God is Jesus' gift to us.[15] Paul declared this to the Galatians: "God sent forth the Spirit of his Son into our hearts, crying, Abba, Father" (4:6). He likewise gave this reminder to the Romans: "Ye received not the spirit unto bondage again unto fear, but ye received the spirit of adoption, in which we cry, Abba, Father" (8:15).

What Paul thus ascribed to Jesus accords with the words which Mark attributed to him: "Abba, Father, all things are possible to thee; let this cup pass from me, nevertheless not what I will, but what thou wilt" (14:36). The agony of Gethsemane is not anything which the church would have attributed to Jesus unless it actually went back to him. From our earliest glimpse of Jesus until his death, this "filial consciousness" characterizes him. Likewise, the knowledge of God as Father is basically what he came to impart: "That ye may become sons

---

[14] *Ibid.*, p. 263.
[15] Cf. Manson, *op. cit.*, p. 151, who cites T. W. Manson, *The Teaching of Jesus* (New York: Cambridge University Press, 1935), pp. 89–115, to the same effect.

of your Father who is in heaven" (Matt. 5:45; Luke 6:35; cf. John 17:3).

Around this "core" of Jesus' awareness of his filial relationship to God as his Father grew his fuller understanding of himself and his mission. That Jesus "advanced in wisdom and stature and in favor of God and men" is explicit in Luke 2:52. To deny that he thus grew is to deny that he was truly human. Such denial is a new "gnosticism" which must be rejected. To deny that he struggled for self-understanding is to make him less than human. Although it is hazardous to try to trace out his growing self-interpretation, the assumption of such growth is required by the New Testament. This self-understanding seems to have developed as Jesus saw himself and his work reflected in many Old Testament figures and passages, especially the Suffering Servant of Isaiah (42:1–4; 49:1–7; 50:4–11; 52:13 to 53:12) and the Son of man in Daniel 7:13. These two "titles," plus a variety of others, will now form the basis for this study of the Christology of the New Testament.

Messiah or Christ

The word "Christology" would seem to imply that the Greek term "Christ" or the Hebrew "Messiah" is the basic one for the study. Actually this is not the case. Christology is not primarily concerned with the term "Christ." It is an irony that a term which Jesus accepted but did not encourage has become the major title for him. Already in the New Testament he is known as "Jesus the Christ" or as "Christ Jesus." The term had come almost to be used as a personal name, interchanging with "Jesus." But Jesus himself preferred other titles to this one, probably because it carried political overtones to most hearers. The study of the person and work of Jesus is called "Christology," but the study goes far beyond consideration of the term "Christ." On the other hand, Christ is an important term employed in the New Testament, and it must receive due attention.

Jewish usage.—The term "Christ" is of Greek origin and means "anointed." The Hebrew equivalent is "Messiah" and has the same etymology. In Jewish writings, Old Testament and noncanonical, there is no one uniform meaning or application.[16] The patriarchs were termed God's anointed (messiah or christ): "Touch not mine anointed ones, and do my prophets no harm" (Psalm 105:15). Prophets (1 Kings 19:16), priests (Ex. 28:41), and kings (1 Sam. 10:1; 16:13; 1 Kings 19:15 ff.) were anointed; and in a sense all of God's people were his "anointed," for all were intended to be prophets (Num. 11:29), priests (Ex. 19:6), and kings or at least a "royal priesthood" (1 Peter 2:9).[17] Anointing, probably by pouring oil over the head, was an act of consecrating one to office.

The term "Messiah" came to designate in later Judaism an eschatological figure, and as a title it always designated one who belongs to "the last time."[18] The word "anointed" appears in the Old Testament but not as a title "Messiah" or "the Anointed One."[19] Yet it is clear that late Judaism expected a Messiah, and the Jews and early Christians looked to the Old Testament for a description of this one.

Kings in Israel were known as God's anointed ones. Later an eschatological figure came to bear the title "Messiah," which was an abbreviation for "Yahweh's Anointed," his function being to "restore Israel as a people, free her from her enemies, rule over her as king, and bring other nations under her political and religious sway."[20] Thus the title was adapted from an earlier designation of Israel's kings, having a political meaning from its beginning. As a title, its new character was that of eschatology. The title also reflected the fact that what was looked for was not merely some king of Israel, but "the presence of God Himself in the midst of His people."[21]

Actually there were two messianic types expected by the Jews

---

[16] Cf. F. J. Foakes-Jackson and Kirsopp Lake (eds.), *The Beginnings of Christianity* (London: Macmillan & Co., Ltd., 1920), I, 347.

[17] Cf. Rawlinson, *op. cit.*, pp. 20 f.

[18] Cf. Sigmund Mowinckel, *He That Cometh*, trans. G. W. Anderson (New York: Abingdon Press, 1956), p. 3.

[19] *Ibid.*, pp. 4, 7, *et passim*.

[20] *Ibid.*, p. 7.

[21] *Ibid.*, p. 280.

when Jesus came.[22] The great majority of Jewish people, including the Pharisees and Zealots, expected a Messiah concerned with national, political, this-worldly interests. This view appears in much of the rabbinical literature and in the synagogue prayers and Targums (Aramaic translations of the Hebrew Old Testament for synagogue services). Some of the scribes anticipated a Messiah of a more other-worldly, transcendental, and universalistic type. This view is found especially in the Jewish apocalyptic literature. Each view somewhat influenced the other, neither being held in a pure form. In some form, Messiah was expected by most Jews at the beginning of the Christian era.

Conclusive evidence for the expectation of a this-worldly, nationalistic, political type of Messiah may be seen in the fact that various persons were actually acclaimed Messiah by the Jews.[23] Zerubbabel was so recognized by Haggai and Zechariah. Simon, the Maccabean, was not called Messiah, but his work was described in language almost messianic (cf. 1 Maccabees 14:4–15). A Hezekiah in the time of Herod was hailed as Messiah by Hillel (Babylonian *Sanhedrin* 98*b*, 99*a*). Hezekiah's two sons, Judas of Gamala and Menahem, Theudas in the time of Felix, and an unnamed Jew in the time of Festus were all acclaimed Messiahs (Josephus, *Ant.* xvii, 27; *Life,* ii, 266 ff.; *Ant.,* xx, 88). Rabbi Akiba acclaimed Simon Bar Cocheba as Messiah at the time of the second Jewish-Roman War about A.D. 132–135. The warnings of the New Testament against false Messiahs support this evidence (cf. Mark 13:22; Matt. 24:24).

Jesus' acceptance of the title.—Jesus accepted the title Messiah or Christ, but he did not encourage its use. This is understandable. The eschatological significance of the term accorded with his view of himself as being the center of the eschatological event.

The term "Messiah," however, carried political overtones for

---

[22] *Ibid.,* pp. 281–284.
[23] Cf. Foakes-Jackson and Lake, *op. cit.,* pp. 353–362 and Mowinckel, *op. cit.,* pp. 284 f.

first-century Jews that made its use difficult. Many understood Messiah's first task to be the overthrow of world powers. This meant specifically a deliverance of the Jews from Rome. Jesus rejected the role of mere national deliverer as that role was commonly understood. He was no "Judas," "Theudas," or "Barabbas" to lead Zealots into physical combat with the Romans. His kingdom would be established by the giving of life, not by the taking of it. It would be by a cross, not by the sword. Jesus accepted the title Messiah, but he interpreted his role as Messiah in terms of basic Old Testament figures, especially those of the Suffering Servant and the Son of man.

In the Gospel of Mark the term "Christ" appears only seven times, only three times in the mouth of Jesus (9:41, 12:35; 13:21). Only one reference is to himself as the Christ, and in it Jesus raised the difficult question about the relationship between the Christ and the Son of David (12:35). Mark entitled his book "The Gospel of Jesus Christ." Though he clearly saw Jesus as the Christ, he employed the term rarely. Jesus accepted the title, but he seemed more concerned to *correct* it than to claim it.

At Caesarea Philippi, in response to the questioning of Jesus, Peter confessed, "Thou art the Christ." What precisely Peter understood "the Christ" to mean is not clear. Probably he thought of the Christ more in terms of the scion of David than the Son of man.

Peter's behavior at the trial and death of Jesus would indicate that he had little understanding of Jesus. A nationalistic understanding of the Messiah's work seems to be reflected in the disciples' question: "Lord, do you at this time restore the kingdom to Israel?" (Acts 1:6). The reply of Jesus at Caesarea Philippi seems to indicate that Peter's confession required both acceptance and correction. Jesus insisted over the protest of Peter that "the Son of man must suffer many things, and be rejected by the elders, and chief priests, and scribes, and be killed, and after three days arise" (Mark 8:31). The narrative seems to be concerned more with the correction than with the confession.[24]

---

[24] Foakes-Jackson and Lake, *op. cit.*, p. 364.

The problem was not in getting the disciples, or Jews generally, to hail someone as the Christ but rather to get them to commit themselves to the kind of Christ that Jesus was.

Some interpreters hold that Jesus probably said "I" and that Mark or his source substituted "Son of man" for the personal pronoun. This is not likely. The striking statement that the Son of man must suffer, be rejected, and be killed was incredible to Peter, as it would have been to Jews generally.[25] It is best understood as going back to Jesus himself.

Even apart from the employment of "Son of man" in place of "Christ," the correction is clear. The Jews of the time did not conceive of a suffering or dying Messiah (cf. Mark 8:31; 9:31 f.; Matt. 16:21 ff.; Luke 24:20 f.; Acts 17:3; 1 Cor. 1:23; Gal. 5:11). The Targums on Isaiah identified the Servant of the Lord with the Messiah, but they so read Isaiah 53 as to make Messiah triumphant and exalted and the wicked defeated and humiliated.[26] Jesus alone is responsible for combining the understanding of Messiah with that of Son of man and the Suffering Servant of the Lord. He accepted the title Christ only when so interpreted.

In Mark 12:35 f. a question of far-reaching significance is attributed to Jesus: "How do the scribes say that the Christ is the son of David? David himself said by the Holy Spirit, 'The Lord said to my Lord, sit thou at my right hand until I place thine enemies under thy feet.'" Jesus presumably accepted the title Christ, but he either rejected the claim that the Christ was to be the Son of David or else he corrected the meaning of "Son of David."

Probably the latter is the truth. Jesus would accept either title, Christ or Son of David, but each must be properly defined. The genealogies in Matthew and Luke both stress the Davidic lineage of Jesus, and Acts says that he is to sit upon

---

[25] This is not to overlook the convincing evidence that the Old Testament did ascribe suffering to the Son of man as is shown by Dodd, *According to the Scriptures*, p. 117 n. It is to suggest that at the beginning of the Christian era suffering was not the role ascribed to the Son of man in Jewish thought.

[26] Mowinckel, *op. cit.*, pp. 329–333.

the throne of David (2:29 ff.). Paul made a distinction in writing that Jesus is out of the seed of David *according to the flesh,* but he is the Son of God (Rom. 1:3). So in Mark 12:35 f., Jesus probably was accepting both titles, Christ and Son of David, but not in the common understanding of either.

The Servant of the Lord

Jesus did not employ the title "Servant of the Lord" (Servant of Yahweh) as a self-designation, but he did see himself as fulfilling that role. He drew heavily upon the Servant passages of Isaiah (42:1–4; 49:1–6; 50:4–11; 52:13 to 53:12) for an understanding of his mission. He accepted the title "Christ," but he interpreted it in terms of the suffering and service of the Servant of the Lord. His favorite self-designation was "Son of man," but he described the role of the Son of man in terms of suffering and service.

With due respect for arguments to the contrary, it is best to trace back to Jesus himself the significant step of bringing together the concepts of Messiah and Son of man and of interpreting both in terms of the Suffering Servant of the Lord. Jesus not only fulfilled these roles, but it was he who first saw that he did so. Not only did these roles converge in him, but he was the first to recognize the fact. Bowman argues to this effect in saying, "Until and except for Jesus, no one ever thought of bringing together the three epithets that lay side by side in Hebrew prophecy and apocalyptic, 'Son of Man,' 'Messiah,' and 'Suffering Servant.' " [27]

It is true that, at least in the Targum on Isaiah, Jewish exegesis identified the "Servant of the Lord" in Isaiah with Messiah. Significantly, however, this identification was made only in those passages concerned with exaltation and glory, the passages con-

[27] John Wick Bowman, *The Intention of Jesus,* (Philadelphia: The Westminster Press, 1943) p. 144. See the cogent studies of the self-understanding of Jesus by E. A. McDowell, *Jesus and His Cross* (Nashville: Broadman Press, 1944), and William Manson, *op. cit.,* pp. 134–168. Manson finds that the mind of Jesus concentrated on three main concepts: Son of God, Servant of the Lord, and Son of man (p. 140).

cerned with humiliation and suffering being so interpreted as to refer to Israel.[28] Thus Hebrew exegesis could think of a glorious and exalted "Servant of the Lord" as Messiah, but it did not know Messiah in terms of a suffering "Servant of the Lord."

The contention of F. C. Burkitt that the term Servant of the Lord could have been applied to Jesus only by Greek-speaking Christians, and not by anyone knowing the Hebrew Bible, has been ably refuted by Rawlinson.[29] Burkitt's argument was that the Hebrew word *'ebhedh* in Isaiah means "slave" rather than "servant," and that Hebrew-speaking Christians would never have ascribed the role of a slave to Messiah. He contended that Greek-speaking Christians, using the Septuagint or Greek translation of the Old Testament, knew only the term *pais* which could mean "boy" or "servant," a term free of the offensiveness of "slave."

Rawlinson nullifies Burkitt's argument in pointing to the vast difference between the Hebrew understanding of "slave" and that of the Greeks. For the Greeks a slave was mere property, a *thing* with neither dignity nor rights. In Judaism a slave was always a *person* with basic dignity and rights. The "Slave of Yahweh" (*'Ebhedh Yahweh*) could be one devoted to the service and worship of God. There is no reason why the term could not have been applied to Jesus by Hebrew Christians or utilized by Jesus himself.

Although Rawlinson has discounted Burkitt's theory as invalid, it is really not necessary to thus remove the offense from the term *'Ebhedh Yahweh* to make it understandable as a title for Jesus. This follows certainly if it was Jesus himself who first utilized the Servant poems of Isaiah in self-portrayal. It is to remove the "scandal" from the cross and from the whole incarnation to belittle the offense of being the "Slave of Yahweh."

[28] Cf. Rawlinson, *op. cit.*, pp. 241 f., who follows W. O. E. Oesterley and G. H. Box, *The Religion and Worship of the Synagogue* (New York: Charles Scribner's Sons, 1907), p. 49.

[29] Rawlinson, *The Gospel According to St. Mark* (London: Methuen & Co., Ltd., 1925), pp. 255–256, and *The New Testament Doctrine of the Christ*, pp. 238–241.

It is precisely the message of the New Testament that the highest glory comes through the deepest humiliation, that true greatness is in the servant role, that life is through death, that triumph is through self-giving. It was by no quirk of Hebrew to Greek translation or by some softened Hebrew conception of "slave" that it became possible for Messiah to be described in terms of the "Suffering Servant" of Isaiah. Jesus fulfilled that role in its deepest humiliation and suffering and thus achieved true exaltation, glory, and triumph for himself and for all in whom he becomes embodied. Not only did he fulfil this role; from at least as early as his baptism he saw that it was his role to fulfil.

The baptism of Jesus.—Baptism for Jesus carried with it the idea of suffering and death (cf. Mark 10:38; Luke 12:50). Significant is what he heard when the "voice came out of heaven" at his baptism in the Jordan River: "Thou art my Son, the beloved, in thee I am well pleased" (Mark 1:11). This is most probably a reflection of Isaiah 42:1, "Behold, my servant, whom I uphold; my chosen, in whom my soul delighteth," and possibly of Psalm 2:7, "Thou art my son; This day have I begotten thee."

If both Isaiah 42 and Psalm 2 stand behind Mark 1:11, the idea of the messianic Son is combined with that of the Suffering Servant and the fusion of the two ideas is traced to the mind and experience of Jesus.[30] If Luke 2:49 may be understood as reflecting an early awareness on the part of Jesus that God was his Father in a unique sense, then at his baptism may be seen the extension of this "filial consciousness" to include his awareness of himself as God's anointed (Psalm 2:2) and as God's servant (Isa. 42:1). Consciousness of Sonship came first, and then came his awareness of his messianic function. In turn he saw that the messianic function was to be accomplished through suffering and not through physically overcoming Israel's foes.

It is impossible to exaggerate the significance of the servant

[30] Cf. Vincent Taylor, *The Gospel According to St. Mark* (London: The Macmillan Co., 1952), p. 162, for the substance of this statement.

passages of Isaiah (42:1–4; 49:1–6; 50:4–11; 52:13 to 53:12) which seem surely to stand behind Mark 1:11. Jesus rejected the Jewish messianic hope which was concerned with Israel's becoming a world power like that of the kingdom of David and Solomon. He interpreted the messianic function in terms of the Suffering Servant of Isaiah. T. W. Manson states the point succinctly in saying:

> The central violent contradiction between the Christian *kerygma* and the Jewish Messianic hope is that which sets the crucified Messiah of Christian experience over against the triumphant hero of Jewish fancy. . . . It is from this point of view of the fundamental contradiction between the Jewish Messianic hope and Jesus's convictions concerning his own Ministry that the Gospel story becomes, in the main lines, an intelligible piece of history.[31]

If Dodd [32] is correct in his thesis that quotations of the Old Testament in the New contemplated not isolated verses but blocks of material, then it is valid to assume that Jesus thought in terms of the Servant poems in their fulness and not merely of Isaiah 42:1. It is probably correct to assume that Jesus knew thoroughly the Servant poems and saw in them the basic description of his messianic function.

The Servant's mission.—The *work* of the Servant of the Lord is made prominent in the poems. He is to bring forth justice to the Gentiles (42:1, 4); he is to glorify God (49:3); he is to reclaim and gather Israel unto God (49:5, 6); he is to be a light to the Gentiles and be God's salvation unto the ends of the earth (49:6); he is to have an ear awakened unto the hearing of God (50:4 f.); he is to bear the griefs and sorrows of men (53:3 f.) and to suffer wounds, stripes, rejection, and death for sinners (53:5–9).

The *suffering* of the Servant is inseparable from his work. The Servant poems carry this refrain. He is to be despised and

[31] *The Servant-Messiah* (New York: Cambridge University Press, 1953), p. 36.
[32] Cf. Dodd, *According to the Scriptures,* pp. 59 f.

abhorred by men (49:7); he is to bare his back to the smiters, his cheeks to them who pluck out his beard, and his face to them who spit upon him (50:6). He appears among men as one by the world's standards altogether unsuited to any messianic role. He is like a root out of dry ground (53:2). He is one void of the appearance which attracts men. He is despised and rejected by men (53:3). He is beaten, cut off from men, and killed (53:5-9).

The Servant in Isaiah is identified with Israel (49:3), and yet the Servant's task is to bring Jacob again to God, and to gather Israel unto God (49:5). The picture of "Servant" thus seems to fluctuate between that of a nation and an individual, between the people of God and the One who gathers them together as God's people. Mowinckel argues strongly that the Servant is an individual prophet, though more than a prophet, and cannot mean Israel, for no Old Testament prophet would describe Israel as thus suffering innocently, silently, and patiently, or hold that Israel's sufferings were incomprehensible.[33] He does see the Servant in some sense to represent his people Israel.[34]

Cullmann makes more of "corporate personality" or the Semitic way of identifying collective and individual representatives; and he sees a triple reference, the three not mutually exclusive: the whole of Israel (Isa. 49:3), a part of the people (probably the remnant), and an individual person, representative of Israel. He holds that the Servant came to realization not in humanity as a whole, not in national Israel, not in the remnant, but in one individual person, who proved to be Jesus.[35] Jesus did see himself as the Servant and saw his function to be that of gathering unto God his people. He would redeem them through suffering and service with him. Only as the "true Israel," restored to God, could they fulfil the picture of the Suffering Servant in Isaiah.

[33] Op. cit., pp. 214–219.
[34] Ibid., p. 217.
[35] Op. cit., pp. 54 f.

Just as at his baptism Jesus saw himself in the role of Suffering Servant, so throughout his ministry he saw his role to be that of suffering and service. Of himself he said, "A baptism I have in which to be baptized, and how am I in anguish until it be accomplished" (Luke 12:50). Ambitious disciples were challenged with the question, "Are ye able to be baptized with the baptism with which I am baptized?" (Mark 10:38). In each case he was speaking of that utter self-renunciation which is "death to self" and which, in his case, led to his crucifixion at Golgotha.

To minister and to give his life.—As soon as Jesus was acclaimed by his disciples to be the Christ (Mark 8:29), he turned their attention to the true character of his mission. He began openly to speak the word, saying: "It is necessary for the Son of man to suffer many things, and to be rejected by the elders, and the chief priests, and the scribes, and to be killed, and after three days to be raised" (8:31). Thus he substituted for "Christ" the term "Son of man," and he described the Son of man in terms of the Suffering Servant. As Manson stated it, referring to the *'Ebhedh Yahweh* or Servant of the Lord in Isaiah, "Jesus turned his back on the desires and hopes of his time to revive the half-forgotten ideals of the great prophet of the Exile." [36]

But the role of suffering service was not to be that of Jesus alone; he called men to enter into that role with him. He said, "If anyone wishes to come after me, let him deny himself, and take up his cross, and follow me" (Mark 8:34). This demand belongs essentially to the Christian calling; it is not optional equipment for "de luxe model" Christians.

By "self-denial" Jesus did not mean mere denial of something to one's self. That is the easy attainment of misers, ascetics, tyrants, and egocentrics of all sorts. It is commonplace for selfish and ambitious persons to deny themselves leisure, pleasure, luxury, or certain bodily functions. What Jesus meant was not

[36] T. W. Manson, *The Servant-Messiah*, p. 58.

merely doing without something; he meant radical reversal of Adam's choice of asserting self in place of God. He meant radical commitment in affirming God and saying no to this pretentious self who wants to be God. It is to be crucified with Christ (Gal. 2:20). It is to be a grain of wheat which falls into the ground and dies in order to bear fruit (John 12:24).

Jesus described his role in saying, "The Son of man came not to be ministered unto, but to minister, and to give his life a ransom for many" (Mark 10:45). It is significant, however, that he thus spoke in rebuking and redirecting the ambitions of James and John (v. 35). This was to be their function, too. Of course, this was not a role which they could fulfil of themselves. Only he could do that. Yet he called them to that faith which is not only trust, but which is openness to him to receive the divine resources for such a life. Christ in the believer enables him, too, to give his life in suffering service. In some sense the "saved" become "saving." Paul dared write: "I fill up in my flesh the things lacking of the sufferings of Christ, in behalf of his body, which is the church, of which I became a minister according to the commission of God given me unto you, to fulfil the word of God" (Col. 1:24 f.).

Paul's suffering took place on at least three levels: (1) physical or outward sufferings in terms of hunger, thirst, coldness, destitution, toil, vigils, beatings with lashes and rods, stonings, imprisonments, shipwrecks, perils of robbers, rivers, sea, and wilderness; (2) those sufferings within caused by rejection, slander, humiliations, and indignities; and (3) vicarious sufferings of sorrow, anguish, and concern, inescapable to him because he so identified himself with other people that he could not help but weep with those who wept and rejoice with those who rejoiced (Rom. 9:3; 2 Cor. 6:4–10; 11:23–33; Col. 1:24; etc.). John saw himself to be "partner in tribulation, and sovereignty, and steadfastness in Jesus" (Rev. 1:9). Jesus is the Servant of the Lord, yet in some real sense, the church as his body becomes the Servant of the Lord. It is the suffering and ministering body of Christ.

The Son of Man

The characteristic self-designation of Jesus in the New Testament is the intriguing and significant though elusive title "the Son of man." This title is present in each major stratum of the Gospels: Mark, Q (non-Marcan material common to Matthew and Luke), M (material peculiar to Matthew), L (material peculiar to Luke), and John. It appears about seventy times in the Synoptics and about ten times in John. It is always a self-designation on the part of Jesus except in Acts 7:56, where Stephen declared, "Behold, I see the heavens opened, and the Son of man standing at the right hand of God." [37] Only an undue skepticism can deny that this is a self-designation which goes back to Jesus himself. Such skepticism is but a new obscurantism. Happily, many of the most able scholars of today recognize "the Son of man" to be a title employed by Jesus for himself.

Origin of the title.—The Greek term *ho huios tou anthrōpou* ("the Son of man") translates the Aramaic *bar "nāshā'* and it was a normal designation for a human being.[38] In Aramaic and Hebrew, an individual member of a species was commonly designated by prefixing "son (of)" to the name of the species.[39] Son of man would thus mean "a man" or some particular individual as "the man." Matthew Black holds that first-century Palestinian Aramaic fully attests *bar "nāshā'* as equivalent of the Greek for "son of man," or (the) "man." [40] At one time it was maintained that *bar "nāshā'* could only mean "a man" or "man" in general, but there is now general agreement that the term could mean "the man" and that it could thus designate the Messiah.[41]

---

[37] The phrase "one like a son of man," borrowed from Daniel 7:13, appears in Rev. 1:13 and 14:14, apparently designating the exalted Christ.

[38] T. W. Manson, *The Teaching of Jesus*, p. 212.

[39] Mowinckel, *op. cit.*, p. 346.

[40] *An Aramaic Approach to the Gospels and Acts* (Oxford: The Clarendon Press, 1954), p. 236.

[41] Cf. Taylor, *The Names of Jesus* (New York: St. Martin's Press, 1953), p. 25, for this position as against the older view of J. Wellhausen and H. Lietzmann.

In the Four Gospels the title "Son of man" clearly refers to Jesus, and the usage is chiefly derived from the seventh chapter of Daniel.[42] The full story of its antecedent usage and its full meaning to Jesus are difficult problems, allowing for no dogmatic conclusion. Many have held that Jesus (or the early church) was influenced by the Jewish apocalyptic book, the Similitudes of Enoch, in which "the Son of man" is a supernatural figure who comes in glory to execute judgment, but it is doubtful that Jesus drew from this source.[43] For Jesus, the foremost mark of the Son of man was that he was to give himself in suffering service and death, the figure of Son of man thus being combined with that of the Servant in Isaiah. It is now recognized that "nowhere in 1 Enoch is the main function of the Servant, his vicarious and redemptive suffering, ascribed to the Son of man." [44] In all likelihood, it was Jesus himself who blended the figures of Son of man with Servant of God, and it was from Daniel 7 and Deutero-Isaiah that he drew these figures. He applied these blended roles to himself and to the community which he came to create.

An eternal and universal kingdom.—The one "like unto a son of man" in Daniel 7:13 f. appeared before the "ancient of days" and there was given "dominion, and glory, and a kingdom, that all peoples, nations, and languages should serve him." It was further indicated that "his dominion is an everlasting dominion, which shall not pass away, and his kingdom that which shall not be destroyed." This is precisely the kind of kingdom which Jesus claimed to bring: universal and indestructible and in contrast to the earthly or political kingdoms belonging to the Jewish messianic hopes of the day (Luke 1:33; John 18:36).

This kingdom would not be confused with national Israel nor with any political structure. Jew and non-Jew were to be

[42] Cf. Black, "The 'Son of Man' in the Teaching of Jesus," *The Expository Times,* LX (1948), 2, 32.

[43] George S. Duncan, *Jesus, Son of Man* (New York: The Macmillan Co., 1949), p. 137.

[44] Black, "Servant of the Lord and Son of Man," *Scottish Journal of Theology,* VI (1953), 1, 10.

brought *under* its absolute and ultimate claim (Matt. 8:11 f.; Luke 13:29 f.). Jesus' preference of the title "Son of man" over "Christ" was due in part no doubt to the fact that the kingdom given to the Son of man was a dominion over "peoples, nations, and languages" and could not be confused with the glorification of a single nation. He had not come simply to "restore the kingdom to Israel" (Acts 1:6). His concern was with humanity—mankind—not just national Israel. T. W. Manson points out that instead of clearing the Gentiles out of Jerusalem, Jesus vindicated their rights to the Temple, for the part of the Temple which he cleansed was the court of the Gentiles.[45] His concern as Son of man is with *mankind*.

To create a community.—Further significance for the concern of Jesus was the fact that the "one like a son of man" (Dan. 7:13) was also identified with "the saints of the Most High" who were to "receive the kingdom" and who were "to possess the kingdom for ever" (Dan. 7:18). Thus in Daniel 7 the "one like a son of man" was described both as an individual person and as a community. Jesus saw his mission to be "to create the Son of man, the kingdom of the saints of the Most High."[46]

Jesus alone proved to be in truth the Son of man. Humanity had failed to be true mankind or "the saints of the Most High." The nation of Israel failed to be true mankind. The remnant itself proved to be elusive. Finally Jesus stood alone, "embodying in his own person the perfect human response to the regal claims of God."[47] He was *more* than man, but he was *man*. It was in him alone that the true destiny of man was achieved, and this was through suffering and death (Heb. 2:6–13).[48] The mystical

[45] *The Servant-Messiah,* p. 83.
[46] T. W. Manson, *The Teaching of Jesus,* p. 227.
[47] *Ibid.,* p. 228.
[48] Cf. Dodd, *The Interpretation of the Fourth Gospel* (New York: Cambridge University Press, 1953), p. 241, for the observation that Heb. 2:6–9 draws upon Psalm 8:5 rather than Dan. 7:13. He further writes: "Ps. 8:5 is applied to Christ as the representative Head of Humanity (of ideal, or redeemed humanity), and Dan. 7:13 is applied to Him as the 'Coming One' to whom everlasting dominion is given 'at the right hand of God.' As such He is also

yet real solidarity between Christ and his people is such that not only is he the Son of man, but his people become in him the "Son of man."

C. H. Dodd, with credit to T. W. Manson, forcefully demonstrates how the individual and corporate ideas are worked out, not only in Paul's analogy of the church as the body of Christ, but in the vivid language of the Fourth Gospel.[49] Commenting on John 12:32, Dodd observes: "In His death the Son of Man draws all men into union with Himself, and so affirms His character as inclusive representative of the human race." [50] The solidarity between the Son of man and his people is affirmed in the hard sayings of John 6, in which the disciple is to "eat the flesh of the Son of man and drink his blood" (v. 53). Elsewhere, Dodd argues convincingly that in Psalms 8 and 110, and Daniel 7, the Son of man is "a figure representative of a community, which may be Israel, as the people of God, or mankind, as 'visited' by God." In the New Testament "Son of man" as a title for Christ results from "the individuation of this corporate conception." [51]

The New Testament has much to say about the kingdom's being *given* to the people of Christ. The *demand* is that we yield to the kingdom of God—that we yield to the sovereign rule of God confronting us in his anointed, the Christ. The *gift* is that those thus yielding to the claims of God's kingdom as ultimate and absolute, also *enter into* his kingdom. Jesus said, "Fear not, little flock; it is the Father's good pleasure to give you the kingdom (Luke 12:32). That Christians reign through and in Christ, is a refrain in the New Testament (Matt. 5:3,10; Luke 12:32; 22:28–30; Rom. 5:17; 2 Tim. 2:11 f.; 1 Peter 2:9; Rev. 1:9; 5:9 f.; 20:4; 22:5). In Daniel 7 (vv. 13,18) the kingdom is given to the "one like a son of man"

---

called 'Messiah,' but Mark indicates (8:30–1; 14:61–2) that 'Son of Man' is the preferred title."
[49] *Ibid.*, pp. 241–49.
[50] *Ibid.*, p. 247.
[51] *According to the Scriptures*, pp. 117 f.

and to the "saints of the Most High." So in the New Testament, Jesus is the Son of man in whom is realized the universal and eternal kingdom; yet in a real sense his people become the "Son of man" and reign with him.

Role of suffering service.—The most significant modification of the "Son of man" idea was in Jesus' interpretation of that role in terms of that of the Servant of Isaiah.[52] Jesus taught that the Son of man was to suffer, to be betrayed, rejected, killed, and to rise again (Mark 8:31; 9:9,12,31,35; 10:45; 14:21,41; Luke 22:48,69; 24:7). The work of the Son of man was that of a servant. He would suffer, be rejected, and be killed. Precisely through this self-giving would he establish his kingdom and create his people. The role was his, but also he was to draw men into that role. The kingdom was to be given to them in the way it was given to him, through suffering and death (Luke 22:28–30).

T. W. Manson correctly observes that Jesus impressed upon his followers that "discipleship is synonymous with sacrifice and suffering and the cross itself." [53] So soon as Peter at Caesarea Philippi confessed, "Thou art the Christ" (Mark 8:29), Jesus began to teach that "the Son of man must suffer many things, and be rejected by the elders, and the chief priests, and the scribes, and be killed, and after three days arise" (v. 31). When Peter protested this teaching, Jesus branded Peter's protest as satanic. Jesus then extended the demand for self-denial to include all who would follow him: "If anyone wishes to come after me, let him deny himself, and take up his cross, and follow me" (v. 34).

Manson further observes that "there is not a hint that he would not have allowed them to go to the cross with him, had

[52] Cf. Black, *Scottish Journal of Theology*, 1, 11 who says: "The motif of redemptive suffering . . . is never associated with the figure in Enoch. It has been introduced into New Testament Christology, I submit, from quite a different source, the belief in the Prophet and his fulfilment of Isa. 53. With the recognition of this figure as Messianic, whether before Christ or after Christ (or by Christ), the gulf is bridged between the majestic Son of Man Messiah, and the great Servant."

[53] *The Teaching of Jesus*, p. 231.

their courage not failed." [54] That Jesus was crucified between two thieves rather than between James and John is traceable to the failure of James and John and not to any reduction of claims upon them on the part of Jesus (cf. Mark 10:32–40). Jesus, the Son of man, received the kingdom through utter self-denial which culminated in his death and resurrection (cf. Phil. 2:5–11). He came to create the "Son of man," the "saints of the Most High," the *ekklēsia* of God, his own body through which he continues his ministry in the world. The members of the body share the suffering of the Head.

The Son of man among men.—By every test, the combining of the roles of Son of man and Suffering Servant is most significant. It is not what was to be expected of first-century Jews or Jewish Christians, and the New Testament does not attribute this development to the community. It is the "Christology" of Jesus and not of the four evangelists or of the early church. This amazing combination is attributed to Jesus. The roles were fulfilled in him, and he was the one who saw that this was true.

Of the two terms, Son of man is the more inclusive, representing the present and the future.[55] The Servant role is concerned more with the earthly work of Christ, the lowly service which leads to the highest glory (Mark 8:31,38; 9:12,31,35; 14:21,41,62; Phil. 2:5–11). The Son of man is the glorious, eschatological figure who is to appear at the end of time to judge and to rule; yet he is in the person of Jesus a man among men. Although the Son of man had been thought of by the Jews as an eschatological figure belonging to the end time, Jesus was able to see himself as the Son of man because he saw the end time as having begun.[56] The *eschaton* had been inaugurated, yet it awaited its consummation. Judgment was given to the Son of man (John 5:27), but this judgment had already begun (John 3:19). Son of man was thus the glorious

[54] *Ibid.*, p. 233.
[55] Cullmann, *op. cit.*, pp. 160 f.
[56] *Ibid.*, p. 159.

heavenly man already present among men in the person of Jesus.

Lord

Ethelbert Stauffer writes that of all the Christological titles the richest is that of Lord.[57] Of course, no one title may be singled out as the richest. However, any list of primary titles should include this one. In the New Testament it is a "divine title," and it goes back to the earliest Christian worship.[58] It is found in all New Testament writings except Titus and the letters of John, although it has scant usage in Mark and Q.[59]

The evidence seems conclusive that Jesus was called "Lord" by the early Aramaic-speaking community. This is reflected in the Aramaic words surviving in the Greek New Testament: *Marana tha*, "Our Lord, come!" (1 Cor. 16:22). *Erchou Kurie*, the Greek equivalent of this, appears in Revelation 22:20: "Amen, come Lord Jesus!" Thus Jesus was the object of worship to his Jewish followers who spoke Aramaic. The transition from the Aramaic *Mārî* ("my Lord") or *Māran* ("our Lord") to the Greek *Kurios* ("Lord") "awaited only the conversion of the first Christian believer who spoke Greek as well as Aramaic—and that may have been only a matter of days." [60]

The position advanced by W. Bousset in *Kyrios Christos* (1913) that the title "Lord" was borrowed by the Gentile church at Syrian Antioch from the Hellenistic mystery religions has been rejected by most scholars.[61] It is generally agreed that the term was used in the church before it included large numbers of Gentiles and before the influence of the Greek mystery

[57] *New Testament Theology*, trans. John Marsh (London: SCM Press, 1955), p. 114.

[58] Frederick C. Grant, *An Introduction to New Testament Thought* (New York: Abingdon Press, 1950), p. 219.

[59] Cf. Taylor, *The Names of Jesus*, pp. 41–47; Jackson and Lake, *op. cit.*, 412–414.

[60] Grant, *op. cit.*, p. 220.

[61] Bultmann is an exception to this, holding that the term was derived from oriental Hellenism, which was widespread in Egypt, Asia Minor, and Syria. Cf. his *Theology of the New Testament*, I, 124 ff.

religions had been felt.[62] Rawlinson correctly observes that the
Aramaic expression *Marana tha* in 1 Corinthians 16:22 is "the
Achilles' heel of the theory of Bousset." [63] There is no evidence
that Jewish and Gentile Christians were divided over the worship of Jesus as Lord. Their tragic division came over another
issue: the inclusion of uncircumcised persons in a fellowship
requiring that they even eat together.

The recognition of Jesus as Lord may best be understood in
the light of multiple factors. Jesus himself had implied that he
was Lord in his comment on Psalm 110:1, "The Lord said
to my Lord, Sit at my right hand, until I place thy enemies
under thy feet" (Mark 12:36).[64] The fact of the resurrection
was most important in opening the way for the full recognition
of Jesus as Lord, for it was through the resurrection that all
could know assuredly that "God made him both Lord and
Christ" (Acts 2:36; see also Rom. 1:4; Phil. 2:9–11). The
employment of the Septuagint by Greek-speaking Christians
strengthened the usage of "Lord" as a title for Jesus. The Hebrew
YHWH ("Yahweh" or "Jehovah") was rendered *Kurios* in
the Septuagint, and thus "Lord" took on its highest possible
meaning. For Greek-speaking Christians, familiar with the
Greek Old Testament, the employment of "Lord" as a title for
Jesus carried with it the recognition of his divinity.

It is not suggested that the term *kurios* is always employed in
the full sense of "Lord" when referred to Jesus. Especially in its
vocative form it often means only "Master" or "Sir." Moreover,
the term probably did not take on its full meaning until after the
resurrection.

In Mark, Jesus is called "Teacher" with frequency and
"Rabbi" four times. He is called *Kurios* only in 7:28, where the
Syrophoenician woman probably means only to say "Sir," and
in 11:3 where "Master" is the likely meaning. In non-Marcan
material common to Matthew and Luke (Q) there are possibly

---

[62] Cf. Knox, *Christ the Lord* (New York: Willett Clark & Co., 1945), p. 77.
[63] Rawlinson, *New Testament Doctrine of the Christ*, p. 235.
[64] Cf. *ibid.* and Taylor, *The Names of Jesus*, p. 50.

six occurrences of "Lord" as a title for Jesus. In material peculiar to Matthew there are seven occurrences; and in material peculiar to Luke there are twenty-five.[65] It is clear that Luke, especially, had a fondness for the title. It would follow that Jesus was known first as Teacher, and that he came gradually to be known as far more. With the resurrection he came to be known as "Lord" in the highest sense of the term.

In the Fourth Gospel there are only five places through the nineteenth chapter where Jesus is called "Lord," and two of these readings (4:1; 6:23) vary in the extant manuscripts. Vincent Taylor points out that the last two chapters contain nine examples of *ho Kurios,* three in resurrection narratives (20:20, 21:7,12) and six in postresurrection sayings (20:2,13,18,25, 28; 21:7).[66] Paul's letters are saturated with the term. Occurrences in the general letters and the Revelation are frequent.

It has been said by many that the earliest Christian confession was probably, "Jesus is Lord." Thomas fell before the risen Christ and said, "My Lord and my God" (John 20:28). Paul declared that to Jesus was given "the name above every name," that at his name every knee should bow and every tongue confess, "Lord Jesus Christ" to the glory of God the Father (Phil. 2:9–11). In Revelation 19:16, his name is "King of kings and Lord of lords." In the New Testament Jesus is given the title employed in the Greek Old Testament for Yahweh, and in the New Testament he is worshiped as divine. This worship began among Aramaic-speaking Christians, and the title "Lord" was first given him in Aramaic, then in Greek.

The strongest New Testament evidence that Jesus considered himself to be Lord, however, is not in the term itself. It is rather in the fact that he moved among men with the air of one who had the right to *command* and to make absolute demands upon others. He demanded priority over the claims of father, mother, husband, or wife. He claimed to have authority over the

---

[65] Cf. Foakes-Jackson and Lake, *op. cit.,* 412–414, for tabulations and analysis of these usages.

[66] *The Names of Jesus,* p 43

Torah or Law. He claimed to have authority over the sabbath, so cherished by the Jews. He called men to himself, commanding them to forsake all else and all others to follow him. Apart from the question of the employment of the term "Lord" by himself or by his earliest disciples, his very manner was that of one who thought of himself as Lord in the highest sense.

Saviour

It may come as a surprise that "Saviour," a title very familiar to us today, does not have comparable prominence in the New Testament. Jesus did not use it as a title for himself. In the Gospels, he is called "Saviour" only in Luke 2:11 and John 4:42; in Acts, he is so designated only in 5:31 and 13:23; and in Paul's letters (excluding the pastoral epistles) only in Ephesians 5:23 and Philippians 3:20. In the pastoral and general epistles Jesus is called Saviour ten times. Thus the title became prominent only in the late epistles. It then grew in prominence and has become almost dominant today.

The above picture, although technically correct, somewhat obscures the situation in the New Testament, for the verb "save" occurs in some form more than one hundred times. Jesus did speak of his ministry as being "to seek and to save the lost" (Luke 19:10; John 12:47). His enemies knew him as one who sought to save others (Matt. 27:42; Mark 15:31; Luke 23:35). His name "Jesus" pointed to his mission "to save his people from their sins" (Matt. 1:21). The word "salvation" appears about fifty times in the New Testament. The function or mission of saving is thus emphatic, although the title "Saviour" is somewhat rare.

Vincent Taylor suggests that the New Testament writers hesitated to employ the title "Saviour" for Jesus because it was applied to the divinities of the mystery religions and to the Roman emperors in Caesar worship.[67] Cullmann observes that the same problem would have obtained with respect to "Lord," and he suggests the prominence of the title "Lord" prevented

[67] *Ibid.,* p. 109.

the wide usage of Saviour as a title.[68] He further suggests that "Saviour" could not have become a special title for Jesus in Palestine, since that would mean the simple repetition of the name, for Jesus means Saviour.[69] *Iēsous* (Jesus) is the Greek form of the Hebrew *Yēshû'a*.[70] To say "Saviour Jesus" in Hebrew would be but to repeat the word: *Yēshû'a Yēshû'a*. In Greek the redundancy would not be apparent except to those knowing both Hebrew and Greek. "Saviour Jesus" in Greek would be *Sōtēr Iēsous;* and although both mean "saviour," they are different in appearance and sound, *Sōtēr* being Greek but *Iēsous* being a Hebrew loan word. This could explain the late rise of the title for Jesus.

It is significant that God is called "Saviour" throughout the Old Testament. In the New Testament the title is given to Jesus chiefly in the very writings, especially the pastorals and 2 Peter, which bestow it upon God. Thus the divine function of saving is attributed to Jesus. This salvation is chiefly from sin and death (Matt. 1:21; Acts 5:31; Phil. 3:20 f.; Titus 2:13 f.; 3:4–7; 2 Tim. 1:10).[71] That the idea of saving is also related to a wide range of situations where threats to well-being come through disease or peril is as should be expected, for salvation is concerned with *persons,* not with Greek "souls." Thus one may be "saved" from disease or dangers, but essentially Jesus is the Saviour from sin and death.

Jesus as High Priest

The major theme of the epistle to the Hebrews is that Jesus is High Priest after the order of Melchizedek (5:10; 6:20). His high priesthood is thus outside the Levitical line (7:4–17); it is eternal and unchanging (7:1–3,22–25); and it is one of continuing intercession, providing a salvation "to the uttermost" for all who through him are drawn near unto God (7:25).

---

[68] Cullmann, *op. cit.,* p. 238.

[69] *Ibid.,* pp. 244 f.

[70] Gustaf H. Dalman, *Jesus-Jeshua,* trans. Paul P. Levertoff (London: SPCK, 1929), p. 6.

[71] Cf. Cullmann, *op. cit.,* pp. 242 f.

He is also called Son (1:2,5; 3:6; 5:8; 7:28), Son of God (4:14; 6:6; 7:3; 10:29), Mediator (8:6; 9:15; 12:24), and Shepherd and Lord (13:20) in this epistle, but High Priest is the dominant designation. As High Priest he offers up himself in sacrifice (7:27; 9:14). Also, he saves us by writing his laws upon our hearts and minds (10:16), opening up for us a fresh and living way into the presence of God because we are enabled in some sense to share in his death and life (10:19–20). He is High Priest, Sacrifice, and Temple all at once.

Function as High Priest.—It is the primary function of a high priest to represent man before God, and this function is ascribed to Jesus (Heb. 2:17). To the writer of Hebrews, Jesus is divine and human. He sees Jesus as God's Son, as the very "effulgence" of God's glory (reflecting the essential unity between light at its center and light diffused) and as the "impress" or image of God's essence or actual being ("impress" and God being distinguishable but not separable).[72] He is divine. Yet no New Testament writer describes his humanity so movingly.[73] Reference is made to his fidelity (3:2), trust in God (2:13), his prayer, tears and piety (5:7), his being made perfect or brought to his fulness through suffering (5:9; 7:27), and his death (9:12; 13:12). He is truly man.

It was Jesus' function to "bring many sons into glory" (2:10). This he could do only by expiating (overcoming) the sins of the people (2:17). He so identified himself with us as our brother (2:11), having fellowship (*koinōnia*) with "blood and flesh," that he could break the power of sin and death for us (2:14 f.). This identification was so real that he has been tempted in every way just as we, yet without sin (4:14 f.).

It is through suffering and death that Jesus as High Priest brings men unto salvation (5:9 f.). As High Priest after the order of Melchizedek he takes us into the very presence of God, "within the veil" (6:19 f.). As High Priest he is the forerunner

[72] Cf. H. R. Mackintosh, *The Doctrine of the Person of Jesus Christ* (New York: Charles Scribner's Sons, 1912), pp. 80 f.
[73] *Ibid.*, pp. 79, 83.

who goes before us into the holy of holies (6:19 f.). But he is more than example. He is the *cause* (source) of eternal salvation to all who obey him (5:9 f.), and he is the author and finisher of our faith (12:2). He is not just a High Priest alone with God in the holy of holies; he is a Person, joined together with those whom he takes into the presence of God.

As High Priest after the order of Melchizedek, Jesus is not a "Jew," for he transcends Israel. He does not belong to the priestly order of Levi or Aaron. He is "without beginning of days or end of life" (7:3), remaining "a priest forever" (7:3). He is a priest with the "power of an indissoluble life" (7:16, 21). In this capacity he is the "surety of a better covenant" (7:22), able to bring men to God and to save them utterly and forever (7:25).

Christ is at once High Priest, tabernacle, and sacrifice, his sacrifice being his own blood, i.e. himself; and it is thus that he gains for us redemption (release) and brings us into new covenant relationship with God (9:11–15, 26). What he offered is the only true sacrifice—one's self in obedience to the will of God (5:7–10). He takes us not into a "sanctuary made with hands," but into the very presence of God himself (9:24). He saves us through his own self-giving; and drawing us into a union with himself, he effects in us his will and his way (10:8–18). His work is *for* us; it is also *in* us, giving his laws into our minds and writing them upon our hearts (10:16).

As our great High Priest in the house of God, Christ has opened up for us a fresh and living way into the presence of God. We may enter through his blood or through his flesh (10:19–20). By being brought into a faith-union with him, by being made partakers in his life that is given and in his body, we enter into the true sanctuary. We are made "perfect" or "complete" only in him (2:10 ff.; 10:14). He participates fully in us (2:17) that we may participate in him. This accords with Paul's emphasis upon being "in Christ" and "Christ in you." It accords with Paul's portrayal of salvation as being "baptized into Christ" by being "baptized into his death" (Gal.

3:27 f.; Rom. 6:3–11) and thus being "baptized into his body"
(1 Cor. 12:13).[74] As High Priest he saves us by doing a creative
work in us: he so joins us to himself that we, too, give ourselves
to God in faith-obedience.

In the epistle to the Hebrews, Jesus is never called Servant of
the Lord, but his high priesthood is described in terms of the
Servant. Like the servant, "he offered up himself" (7:27), and
he was offered once "to bear the sins of many" (9:28; cf. Isa.
53:12).[75] Moreover, it is through self-sacrifice, like the servant,
that he is to come into his high-priestly glory (2:9 f.; 10:12 f.).

In Hebrews Jesus is "the Apostle and High Priest of our
confession" (3:1). He is sent from God, and thus he is able
to represent us before God. Precisely because he is "Apostle and
High Priest," true God and true man, he is also "mediator"
(8:6; 9:15; 12:24), a concept that will be developed in the section to follow.

In the Gospels.—A plausible case can be made to the effect
that Jesus saw himself as the true High Priest, even though he
did not actually employ the title.[76] Jesus twice referred to Psalm
110 in relationship to the Messiah (Mark 12:35 ff.; 14:62);
he thus may well have been claiming by implication the role of
High Priest after the order of Melchizedek. Psalm 110 begins
with the oft-quoted verse, "The Lord said unto my Lord, Sit
Thou at my right hand, until I make thine enemies thy foot-
stool." Verse 4 declares: "The Lord hath sworn, and will not
repent, Thou art a priest for ever after the order of Melchizedek."
Jesus was not necessarily disclaiming Davidic sonship or messiah-
ship, but at least he was correcting the scribal understanding of
"Son of David" and "Messiah." Possibly he also claimed here to
be the "High Priest after the order of Melchizedek," a High
Priest whom he thus related to the Christ (Mark 12:35).

Cullmann offers an intriguing and cogent argument that Jesus
at his trial before Caiaphas implied that he was High Priest,

---

[74] See chapter 8 for study of these passages.
[75] Cf. Cullmann, *op. cit.,* p. 91.
[76] *Ibid.,* p. 88.

but not an earthly one (Mark 14:62).[77] If so, a parallel may be seen to his claim before Pilate that he was King, but not an earthly one (John 18:36). As Cullmann puts it: "He tells the earthly ruler that his government is not earthly; he tells the earthly high priest that his priesthood is not earthly." [78] This follows if Daniel 7:14 and Psalm 110:1 are combined in Mark 14:62: "You will see the Son of man sitting at the right hand of power, and coming with the clouds of heaven." This blending is indicated by the fact that "sitting at the right hand" is closely associated with the idea of a High Priest after the order of Melchizedek. The argument is far from conclusive, but it points to the possibility that Jesus saw himself as High Priest after the order of Melchizedek.

Jewish expectation of a true High Priest.—That there was in the time of Jesus some expectation of a High Priest identified with Messiah is well attested. The Jewish high priests had been a disappointing lot, especially when the high priesthood became a political "plum" under the Syrian and Roman rulers, up for "grabs" to the highest bidder. Against this deplorable succession of political high priests, there was envisioned a nobler and ultimate high priesthood. This ideal priest would in the last days bring to fulfilment the true intention of the priestly office. Cullmann summarizes the evidence:

The Qumran texts (*Manual of Discipline* 9:11; *Serek ha'eda* 2:12 ff.), the *Damascus Document* (12:23; 14:19; 19:10; 20:1), and the *Testaments of the Twelve Patriarchs* (*Reub.* 6:7 ff.; *Sim.* 7:2, etc.) distinguish between a priestly and a political-royal Messiah, between a Messiah of Levi and one of Judah, between the "Messiah of Aaron" and the "Messiah of Israel." In each of these cases the priestly Messiah is superior to the royal one. The important thing is that the identification of the High Priest with the Messiah is accomplished in these texts.[79]

This expectation of a true priest and the fact of a corrupt high priesthood in Jerusalem form the background for a possible

[77] *Ibid.*, pp. 88 f.
[78] *Ibid.*, p. 89.
[79] *Ibid.*, p. 86.

self-interpretation of Jesus in terms of High Priest after the order of Melchizedek. The prayer of Jesus in John 17 has been known as his "high priestly prayer," since so designated by Chytraeus in the sixteenth century.[80] Also, the risen Lord seems to be described as High Priest in Revelation 1:13, although the term employed is "one like unto a Son of man." However, the real study of Jesus as High Priest is in the epistle to the Hebrews.

Jesus as Mediator

Jesus is called mediator four times in the New Testament (Heb. 8:6; 9:15; 12:24; 1 Tim. 2:5). In Hebrews he is mediator of a better covenant (8:6; 9:15) and of a new covenant (12:24). In 1 Timothy 2:5 alone is the title employed directly in reference to his saving work. Of course, the idea of mediation is more deeply embedded in the New Testament than the scant occurrence of this title would imply.

Jesus is mediator, but he is that in a richer sense than is indicated by the usual translation of 1 Timothy 2:5, or by appeal to a Greek lexicon for etymology, or by appeal to general usage in the first century. Applied to Jesus in the New Testament, the title means *more* than someone *between* God and man.[81] He is not just a third party between God and man. He is certainly not less than that; he is infinitely *more* than that.

It is most unfortunate that 1 Timothy 2:5 is commonly translated thus: "For there is one God, one mediator *between* God and man, himself man, Christ Jesus" (cf. A.V., A.S.V., R.S.V., New English Bible, etc.). The Greek text has no word for "between." That is supplied in translation, and it is misleading. Jesus came *to overcome the betweenness* between God and man. The Greek for mediator, *mesitēs,* is built upon a root used to designate "middle" or "midst"; and in first century usage it designated an arbitrator or guarantor. This, however, does not

[80] *Ibid.,* p. 105. Cullmann also cites Cyril of Alexandria in Migne, *Patrologia Graeca,* 74, 505, observing that in commenting on John 17:9 he saw Jesus as High Priest.

[81] My colleague, Professor Samuel J. Mikolaski, reminds me that words do not have meanings, only uses. Meaning is in the mind of the one using the word.

do justice to the meaning as applied to Jesus in the New Testament.

The translation of 1 Timothy 2:5 should be: "For one God, also one mediator of God and men, [the] man Christ Jesus." Jesus is God, and he is man. Only one who is God can bring God to man, and only one who is man can bring man to God. Christ Jesus is not a second god, for God is one. He is not just someone between God and man—that is a gnostic idea refuted in the New Testament (cf. John 1:1–18; Col. 2:9). In him God and men meet directly. In Christ, God comes to man personally and directly (John 14:8 f.; 20:28; 2 Cor. 5:19), for he is Emmanuel, "God with us" (Matt. 1:23). He is true man, not a docetic or gnostic Christ; and in him man is brought into the very presence of God (Heb. 10:19 f.).

In Hebrews, the only other New Testament writing to name him mediator, Christ Jesus is divine and human. No book is more explicit as to his deity or humanity. He is not a "middle man" or someone merely "between." As true God he brings God to man. As true man he brings man to God. He is God in God's ultimate self-disclosure and presence (1:1,8–13). In him alone man reaches his true existence or destiny, for in Christ alone man is brought into the very presence of God (see 2:8–10; 5:8–10; 6:19–20; 7:24 f.; 10:19 f.; 12:2). Jesus is mediator of a new and better covenant (8:6; 9:15; 12:24) precisely because in him God and man meet directly and personally.

The Lamb of God

Jesus is called "the Lamb of God" (*ho amnos tou theou*) twice in the Gospel of John (1:29,36). In Acts 8:32 he is likened to the lamb of Isaiah 53:7 f.: "As a lamb before his shearer is dumb, so he opens not his mouth." In 1 Peter 1:19 our redemption is declared to be "with precious blood as of a lamb without blemish and without spot, that of Christ." In the Revelation, one who unmistakably is Jesus is called "the Lamb" twenty-eight times (counting two in 17:14), the word being *arnion* rather than *amnos*.

In Revelation.—The usage in Revelation is clearer than that in John 1:29,36. In Revelation the Lamb has two basic functions: (1) to conquer (5:4–6; 6:16 f.; 14:1,4; 17:14), and (2) to give himself up in sacrifice (5:6, 9, 12; 12:11; 13:8). The two functions are in a sense one, for it is precisely through sacrificial self-giving that he conquers. R. H. Charles writes, "The Lamb who conquers is the Lamb who has given himself up as a willing sacrifice." [82] Older Jewish apocalyptic literature furnished the background for picturing the Messiah as the Lamb in the sense of leader (bellwether) of the flock.[83] In Revelation, Jesus is the Lamb who conquers the "scarlet-coloured beast" with "seven heads and ten horns," for he is "Lord of lords, and King of kings" (17:3–14). It is in this sense that "the Lamb" is "the Shepherd" of God's people (7:17). He is the bellwether or leader, the ram or lamb with "seven horns" (5:6) whose function it is to lead, defend, and conquer for the flock.

It is the major message of Revelation that "the Lamb" conquers through self-sacrifice. The "book and its seven seals" (5:5), i.e. the book of history or destiny, can be opened alone by the "Lion of the tribe of Judah, the Root of David" (5:5); and the Lion who "has overcome to open the book and its seven seals" is none other than the "Lamb standing as though it had been slain" (5:6). To him is sung the new song of triumph through sacrifice: "Worthy art thou to take the book, and to open its seals, because thou wast slain, and didst purchase to God with thy blood out of every tribe, and tongue, and people, and nation, and thou didst make them to our God a kingdom and priests and they shall reign upon the earth" (5:9 f.). Likewise, he is acclaimed by multiplied thousands: "Worthy is the Lamb that was slain to receive the power, and wealth, and

[82] *The Revelation of St. John* (New York: Charles Scribner's Sons, 1920), cxiv.

[83] Rawlinson, *The New Testament Doctrine of the Christ,* p. 192, cites *Ethiopic Enoch* 89:44, where Samuel is the "sheep whose eyes were opened," and Saul and David were indicated as "rams." He also cites *Ethiopic Enoch* 90:9,12, where the Maccabean leaders, especially Judas, are symbolized as "horned lambs."

wisdom, and strength, and honor, and glory, and blessing"
(5:12). To the honor that Christ has always had as God's Son is
now added honor won by his self-giving.

In Revelation then, through the picture of the Lamb who conquers through self-sacrifice, is once again set forth the basic
New Testament doctrine of the cross, Christ's way which must
become the way of "life through death" for those who trust him.
Charles observes that the aim of Christ's work is not to cancel
guilt but to destroy sin in the sinner: "The conquest of sin is
only to be achieved through self-sacrifice. Nothing but the self-
sacrifice of holy love can overcome the principle of selfishness
and sin that dominates the world." [84]

Self-sacrifice in redeeming love is not new, for Christ is "the
Lamb slain from the foundation of the world" (13:8). His way
of life and triumph through death is not coercive or externally
imposed, for it must be received in faith by his followers. Those
alone may sit with him on his throne who conquer as he conquers (3:21). This victory comes not from our efforts or resources but only as by faith we receive him into ourselves as a
transforming Presence (3:20).[85]

John 1:29.—John the Baptist hailed Jesus as "the Lamb of
God, the one taking away the sin of the world" (John 1:29).
Barrett probably is correct in finding no simple explanation for
the term "the Lamb of God" and in finding no single Old Testament allusion sufficient to account for it.[86] The question in Matthew 11:3 would indicate that John the Baptist did not think of
"the Coming One" in terms of suffering. The apocalyptic lamb
as conquering leader seems to have been closer to John's understanding of Messiah.

On the other hand, it is difficult to rule out some allusion to
the paschal lamb interpreted in terms of the Suffering Servant of
Isaiah, whatever other allusions there may be in the reference to

---

[84] *Op. cit.,* p. cxiv.
[85] See chapter 5 for doctrine of the cross.
[86] C. K. Barrett, "The Lamb of God," *New Testament Studies,* I, 3 (1955),
210.

"the one taking away the sin of the world." [87] Paul referred
to Christ as our passover who was slain (1 Cor. 5:7). The
readers of 1 Peter were reminded that they were redeemed
"with the precious blood of a lamb without blemish and without spot, that of Christ" (1:19). The Fourth Gospel presents
the suffering of Jesus in close relationship to the passover
(12:1; 13:1; 19:14). Early Christians interpreted the passover
in terms of Isaiah 53. The death of Jesus was so interpreted in
Acts 8:32: "He was led as a sheep to the slaughter; and as a
lamb before his shearer is dumb, so he opens not his mouth."

It is best to concede that the background to John 1:29 is not
clear. Many influences may have come together here. As in Revelation, however, so in the Fourth Gospel, Jesus is the Lamb of
God who overcomes sin through self-sacrifice. The grain of
wheat must die to bear fruit (12:24), and "the one loving his
life destroys it" while "the one hating his life in this world
shall preserve it unto life eternal" (12:25).

Logos

The Fourth Gospel begins abruptly with the term *ho Logos*,
best translated as "the Word." The author describes the Logos in
relation to God and the created order, then declares that he
"became flesh" (1:14), and finally identifies him with Jesus
Christ (1:17). That the writer could thus begin with an abrupt
reference to the Logos suggests that the readers were already
expected to have some acquaintance with the usage. Probably
the author is not so much describing Jesus Christ as the Logos
as he is identifying the Logos with Jesus Christ. His theme is
not the Logos, but the Logos become flesh (1:14).

The term Logos had already a long and varied usage: by
Heraclitus in the sixth century B.C., by the Stoics for the rational
principle behind the universe, and by the Alexandrian Jew,

[87] Dodd, *The Interpretation of the Fourth Gospel*, p. 233, lists four possible
interpretations: (1) the lamb of the sin-offering; (2) the paschal lamb; (3) the
Lamb or Suffering Servant of Isaiah 53; (4) the young ram, the Messiah as
King of Israel. He concludes that the fourth choice is the most likely one (p.
238).

Philo. It also had an Old Testament usage, being the Septuagint translation of the Hebrew *dābhār* (word). John [88] thus wrote against a background of Old Testament and pagan usage. Possibly other Christians of the time were experimenting with the term.

John probably had a twofold purpose: (1) to utilize the term Logos for whatever help it afforded in interpreting Jesus Christ to Jews and Greeks and (2) to give to the ancient term a new and Christian meaning. That is to say, he could begin with Christ and move to the term Logos in the interest of a more intelligible Christology. Or he could begin with the much-used term and give it a Christian meaning. Probably the latter most concerned him. It is as though he were saying: "You speak of the Logos? Let me identify him for you. He is Jesus Christ." From that point of departure, the author "presents the revelation of Jesus Christ as the fulfilment of the Biblical religion," and the language employed is "the language of the Greek Bible just as the main element in the background of the Gospel is the Biblical religion." [89]

The Fourth Gospel may give answer to three groups: Jews, Gnostics, and followers of John the Baptist. To the rabbis who spoke of the Torah (Law) as pre-existent, as God's instrument in creation, and as the source of light and life, John replied that these claims apply rather to the Logos. To the Gnostics who would deny a real incarnation, John's answer was most emphatic: "the Word became flesh" (1:14). To those who stopped with John the Baptist, he made it clear that John was not the Light but only witness to the Light (1:6 ff.). Although the term Logos is not retained as a title beyond the prologue, the whole book presses these basic claims.

As the Logos, Jesus Christ is God in self-revelation (Light) and redemption (Life). He is God to the extent that he can be present to man and knowable to man. [90] The Logos is God

---

[88] Authorship is not argued here.

[89] F. L. Cross (ed.), *Studies in the Fourth Gospel* (London: A. R. Mowbray & Co., Ltd., 1957), p. 43.

[90] Cf. Dodd, *Interpretation of the Fourth Gospel*, p. 277.

(John 1:1), and the risen Christ is worshiped by Thomas, who fell at his feet saying, "My Lord and my God" (20:28). Yet the Logos is in some sense distinguishable from God, for "the Logos was *with* God" (1:1). Cullmann observes: "God and the Logos are not two beings, and yet they are also not simply identical. In contrast to the Logos, God can be conceived (in principle at least) also apart from his revelatory action—although we must not forget that the Bible speaks of God *only* in his revelatory action." [91]

The paradox that the Logos is God and yet is in some sense distinguishable from God is maintained in the body of the Gospel. That God as he acts and as he is revealed does not "exhaust" God as he is, is reflected in sayings attributed to Jesus: "I and the Father are one" (10:30) and also, "the Father is greater than I" (14:28). The Logos is God active in creation, revelation, and redemption. Jesus Christ not only gives God's Word to men (17:14); he is the Word (1:14; 14:6). He is the true Word—ultimate reality revealed in a Person.[92] The Logos is God, distinguishable in thought yet not separable in fact.[93]

[91] *Op. cit.,* p. 266.
[92] Dodd, *Interpretation of the Fourth Gospel,* p. 267.
[93] *Ibid.,* p. 285.

The
Doctrine
4 of Salvation

SALVATION in its nature must answer to the plight of man as it actually is. Man's plight as sinner is the result of a fatal choice involving the whole man in bondage, guilt, estrangement, and death; salvation thus must be concerned with the total man. It must offer redemption from bondage, forgiveness for guilt, reconciliation for estrangement, renewal for the marred image of God. This chapter will be concerned with salvation in its initial meaning for the individual person, its divinely provided means, and its initial demands. Because of its primary significance for salvation, the study of the cross is reserved for the next chapter. Subsequent chapters will be concerned with this same salvation in its meaning for an individual person as a constituent member of the community of Christ, and in his relationship to his family, the state, the larger world, and to things.

The Grace of God

Salvation roots in the grace of God. For bankrupt sinners with no ground of their own upon which to stand, with nothing of their own to hold up to God for his reward, it is their only hope; but it is their sufficient hope. The encouragement to "come boldly to the throne of grace" (Heb. 4:16) is offered to sinners who are known so thoroughly to God that he discerns "the thoughts and intents" of their hearts and who stand "naked and exposed to the eyes of him with whom is our account" (Heb.

4:12–13). Man cannot conceal his sin nor remedy it of himself. His one hope, his sure hope, is in the sinless One who not only can feel for man in his weaknesses but who has conquered precisely where man has failed (Heb. 4:14–15). T. F. Torrance has cut to the heart of the matter in saying:

God has personally intervened in human history in such a way that the ground of man's approach to God, and of all his relations with God, is not to be found in man's fulfillment of the divine command, but in a final act of self-commitment on the part of God in which He has given himself to man through sheer love and in such fashion that it cuts clean across all questions of human merit and demerit.[1]

Moffatt described grace as "the love of God in power and beauty, shining against the dark background of human demerit." [2]

Etymology.—*Charis,* the New Testament word for "grace," seems to come from a root indicating what gives pleasure or joy. The Greek word for "joy," *chara,* comes from the same root as does the word for grace. Joy was to the ancients the emotion aroused by grace.[3] The basic ideas in *charis* are: (1) beauty, charm, or graciousness, (2) kindness, favor or good will, and (3) gratitude or thankfulness.[4] The first idea, beauty or graciousness, seems to appear in Luke 4:22 and Colossians 4:6; and the third idea, that of gratitude, appears in passages like 2 Corinthians 9:15, "Thanks [*charis*] be to God for his indescribable gift!" Of the one hundred fifty New Testament usages, however, the usual meaning is that of favor, good will, or benefit.

Grace in the Old Testament.—The word in the Old Testament most like *charis* in the New Testament is *chesedh,* even though in the Septuagint *chesedh* is rendered "mercy" (*eleos*) rather than "grace" (*charis*). The Hebrew *chesedh* is often ren-

---

[1] *The Doctrine of Grace in the Apostolic Fathers* (Edinburgh: Oliver and Boyd, Ltd., 1948), p. 21.
[2] James Moffatt, *Grace in the New Testament* (New York: Ray Long & Richard R. Smith, Inc., 1932), p. 5.
[3] *Ibid.,* p. 21.
[4] *Ibid.,* and Arndt and Gingrich, *op. cit.,* pp. 885 f.

dered "loving-kindness." This does not do justice to the richness of the term, for it omits the distinctive idea. In the Old Testament *chesedh* stands for God's self-giving to Israel *within a covenant relationship.*[5] The chief idea is that his active love is offered within a covenant relationship. The covenant is unilateral; God determines its demands and its provisions. It is not a bargain or an agreement reached between God and man. God offers the covenant, but it is not coercive. Man is free to receive or reject it, but he is not free to modify it. Bound up with this is the idea of God's choice of Israel apart from Israel's merit (cf. Deut. 7:6–11).

Chesedh is also bound up with the idea of God's righteousness. It is not cheap; it is not indulgence. God's love finds a righteous way to establish new ground upon which man may stand and be reclaimed for God's fellowship.[6] It is God's righteous love which prevails in *chesedh,* the Old Testament counterpart to the grace of the New.

To summarize, then, *chesedh* in the Old Testament stands for the righteous love of God. It is expressed in restoring the sinner to his personal fellowship within the framework of a covenant, the demands and provisions of which he alone determines. This is the Old Testament background to grace (*charis*) in the New Testament.

Grace in the Gospels.—In the Synoptic Gospels the term *charis* appears only once (Luke 2:40), and there it denotes the favor of God upon the baby Jesus. In the Fourth Gospel the word appears in three verses (1:14,16,17). Although the word for grace is absent from the teaching of Jesus, the idea is present everywhere. Jesus taught grace by what he did; and in effect he taught it by word, especially in parables like that of the good Samaritan (Luke 10:30–37) and in those of the fifteenth chapter of Luke. Brunner aptly writes that Jesus was "the grace of God in person" (*die Gnade Gottes in Person*).[7]

---

[5] Torrance, *op. cit.,* pp. 10–20.

[6] Cf. *ibid.,* p. 18.

[7] Emil Brunner, *Der Römerbrief* (Stuttgart: Oncken-Verlag, 1948), p. 122 (now in English as *The Epistle to the Romans*).

The Fourth Gospel, in its prologue, is emphatic in pointing to the Word made flesh as the One in whom grace (*charis*) reaches man: "Grace [*hē charis*] and truth [*hē alētheia*] came through Jesus Christ" (1:17). Here grace and truth correspond to the *chesedh* and *"meth* of the Hebrew Old Testament. The righteous love of God (*charis* or *chesedh*) and truth as ultimate reality (*alētheia* or *"meth*) reach us in Jesus Christ. "Out of his fulness we all receive: grace over against grace" (1:16). The elusive "grace for grace" probably means grace "received on the ground of sheer grace," not on the "ground of conformity to law." [8]

Grace in Paul's letters.—About one hundred of the occurrences of *charis* in the New Testament are found in the letters of Paul. With other writers, Paul saw grace as the giving and forgiving love of God in the person of Christ.[9] For him grace stood over against all ideas of merit or reward: "To the one working, the wage is not reckoned according to grace but according to debt" (Rom. 4:4). It was precisely "where sin abounded" that "grace superabounded" (Rom. 5:20). In a discussion of election, Paul clearly argued that grace is in no sense a reward for merit: "If by grace, no longer out of works, else grace no longer is grace" (Rom. 11:6).

In denying that grace is the reward of works, Paul did not neglect to affirm that grace produces works or a new life. He declared the purpose of grace to be: "That just as sin reigned in death, thus also grace might reign *through righteousness* unto life eternal through Jesus Christ our Lord" (Rom. 5:21). In Romans 6:1 ff. he argued that grace is not an invitation to continue in sin, for grace so operates as to bring about a new life. The grace of God which was embodied in Jesus (John 1:17) becomes embodied in any person who by faith receives Jesus Christ into himself as a living and transforming presence.

The grace of God is freely offered but is never coercive; it must be received in faith: "By grace are ye saved through faith"

[8] Torrance, *op. cit.*, p. 22.
[9] Cf. Moffatt, *op. cit.*, p. 291, and Torrance, *op. cit.*, p. 29.

(Eph. 2:8). In this striking passage at least three major truths of grace appear: (1) grace enters into a situation of sin and death, not of merit, (2) grace is not imposed but must be received in faith, (3) grace is a creative force yielding a harvest of good works. In 1 Corinthians 15:10, Paul attributed his new being to the grace of God, but at the same time he indicated that this grace may operate in a life only as it is received: "By the grace of God I am what I am, yet his grace unto me did not become void; but more abundantly than they all I labored, yet not I but the grace of God with me."

Cautions.—Grace in the New Testament never implies caprice as in some early pagan usage. Grace is never the expression of a passing mood in God; it is God's characteristic attitude towards man, and it is not awakened by anything good in man. That is, God's grace is not *eros,* the "love" that seeks to profit by something of beauty or value in its object; it is *agapē,* the love which is creative, the love which brings about beauty or value in its object. The grace of God seeks men; they do not seek it. The grace of God is not an abstraction; it may be known only in Jesus Christ. In grace God grants *favor* but not *favors.* God's favor does not imply favoritism. It knows no "double" predestination" (i.e., some predestined to salvation and some to damnation), nor does it know an arbitrary salvation imposed without moral change or imposed without faith. The New Testament knows no "irresistible grace"; it knows much of an almost incredible blindness of eyes and hardness of heart capable of despising God's grace even when it appears in Jesus Christ.

Calling and Election

The doctrine of election is deeply embedded in each stratum of the Bible. Election is here understood as God's purpose and initiative in man's salvation. It is not that God chooses some for salvation and some for damnation, thus determining the destiny of each. Were that true, even the so-called salvation would be damnation, for to coerce a person as though he were a thing would be his destruction. Election is God's choice of man as prior to man's choice of God. Salvation is a possibility opened up for man only because of God's calling and election. Did God not seek out man, man could not seek God. God does elect; he does call, but his calling is not coercive. Man is yet free in his answer to God.

The New Testament knows the Christian life as a calling (Eph. 1:18; 4:1; 2 Thess. 1:11; 2 Tim. 1:9; Heb. 3:1; 2 Peter 1:10). The basic call is the call to Christ. There are further callings to special ministries, but the basic calling is to Christ as Lord and Saviour. Christians are referred to as "called saints" (Rom. 1:7; 1 Cor. 1:2), just as an apostle is a "called apostle" (Rom. 1:1). "Called" is an adjective modifying apostle in Romans 1:1; Paul is an apostle by calling. Likewise, "called" is an adjective in Romans 1:7 and 1 Corinthians 1:2, where Paul addresses Christians as "called saints." This calling, to Christ, is the basic calling within which is to be found the calling to a special ministry as that of the apostle. Peter uses the adjective "elect" in the same sense in addressing "elect sojourners" (1 Peter 1:1).

The doctrine of calling and election accords with the fact that in the Bible God is one who *acts* and with whom is always the *initiative.* This is true in creation, revelation, and redemption. The Bible's first affirmation, "in the beginning God," is its basic affirmation. The Fourth Gospel accords with Genesis in saying, "In the beginning was the Word, and the Word was with God, and the Word was God" (John 1:1). All things came into being through the Word in whom are life and light (John 1:2–4). Just as God who acts and speaks in his Word stands behind all creation, so he has the initiative in all revelation and redemption.

Man does not discover God; God is self-revealed to man. Man does not initiate or achieve his own salvation; God alone can save. The doctrine of calling and election belongs to this larger doctrine of the priority of God over all that is. It concerns his initiative in creation, revelation, and redemption. Behind man's salvation stands the purpose and work of God.

God is known in the New Testament as a *seeking God*. He seeks worshipers (John 4:23); and "the Son of man came *to seek* and *to save* the lost" (Luke 19:10). Luke 15 portrays God as being like the shepherd who seeks the lost sheep, like the woman who seeks the lost coin, like the father whose love followed wayward sons, one a confused prodigal and the other a proud egocentric. John attributed our very power to love to the initiative of God: "We love, because he first loved us" (1 John 4:19). Paul implies as much about knowledge, that we may know God only because he first knows us: "Knowing God, rather having been known by God" (Gal. 4:9).

That it is impossible for man to initiate his movement toward God is made clear by Jesus: "No one is able to come to me except it be given to him from the Father" (John 6:65). Again, in John 15:16, it is made clear that the initiative in salvation is not on man's side: "Ye did not choose [*exelexasthe*] me, but I chose you." This choice, or election, is not coercive, for man is given the freedom to accept or reject it.

Salvation rooted in God's purpose.—In the Old Testament, God chose Israel; Israel did not first choose God. Salvation in both the Old and the New Testament is set forth as rooted in the purpose of God for man. In Ephesians 1:4 it is affirmed that God chose or elected (*elelexato*) us in Christ before the foundation of the world. There was never a time when God did not purpose our salvation. This choice was in no sense based on man's excellence as is implied in 1 Corinthians 1:27–29:

But the foolish things of the world God elected in order that he might put to shame the wise, the weak things of the world God elected in order that he might put to shame the strong, and the nameless of the world and the things despised God elected, the things not being in order that the things being he might put to naught, that no flesh should boast before God.

In Romans 8:28 Paul speaks of "the called according to purpose." The eighth chapter of Romans sets forth the assurance of salvation. Assurance is grounded in the purpose of God, who

from the beginning foresaw the goal to which he would bring
those that would respond to his love.

Not predestination.—Logic would have it that some are in-
evitably saved because God has chosen them for salvation. This
implies, of course, that others are lost because God has chosen
them for damnation, or at least has not included them in election
for salvation. But the New Testament does not draw this logical
deduction. It never says that some are elected to be lost. Never
does the New Testament say that God purposes or wills that any
man be lost. Logical efforts to defend either predestination or
double predestination are weak and unconvincing. They are
likewise unnecessary, for they defend what the New Testament
never affirms.

The issue is confused by saying that none deserves salvation,
so God cannot be blamed if he chooses to save only some. The
Bible nowhere justifies our accusing God of standing by, doing
nothing, simply resigning some to their fate. To say that if it is
right to save some only, it is right to *purpose* to save some only, is
poor logic and an inexcusable confusion of issues. This falsely
suggests that God offers salvation to some only, and obscures
the fact that the tragic failures are in the witnessing of Christians and in the response of the lost. Jesus himself said: "Thus
it is not a thing willed before your Father in heaven that one of
these little ones should perish" (Matt. 18:14). Men may perish,
but that is not a thing willed of God. Second Peter 3:9 says
that the Lord is "not willing that any should perish but that all
should come to repentance."

The New Testament insists that behind any man's salvation
is the initiative of God in calling and election. This rules out any
boasting on man's part. But behind any man's damnation is
man's sin and neglect. In the New Testament, the opposite of
election is not nonelection, but man's rejection of God's salvation. This suggests a limit on God's freedom and correctly so.
But God himself is the one who limited his own freedom. God
was free to make man free to accept or reject salvation. Man's
freedom is within the larger freedom of God. Man can say yes

or no to God only because God has given him this freedom.

The Greek word *proorizein*, usually translated to predestinate or foreordain, appears six times in the New Testament (Acts 4:28; Rom. 8:29, 30; 1 Cor. 2:7; Eph. 1:5, 11). Only the verses in Romans and Ephesians are concerned directly with salvation. If Paul meant by this a fixing of fate beforehand, his careful attention to man's guilt and his great concern that man repent and believe would be meaningless. Why should Paul pray to God for man's salvation (cf. Rom. 10:1) if he believed that this matter has already been fixed? One is strangely insensitive to the throb and pulse beat of the whole New Testament if he thinks that each man's fate is determined for him in advance. This is not a "rigged" television show. God is not playing with toys or manipulating gadgets; he is seeking men who stand in an awesome freedom where they may accept or reject the salvation which God alone can offer.

Romans 8 is not saying that God determines man's fate but that salvation is what God has *purposed;* it is no accident or afterthought. Salvation is certain for those "in Christ," for God who purposed it will carry it through to its consummation. Ephesians also attributes man's salvation to God, who alone can accomplish it. This he does by studied purpose.

In 2 Peter 1:10 the brethren are urged to make sure to themselves their calling and election. This does not assume that destiny is fixed for one apart from his own responsible choice. Jesus' cry over Jerusalem (Matt. 23:37 ff.) is enough to destroy any doctrine that fates are already fixed. In Romans 10:21 the real cause of man's damnation is isolated: "To Israel he says: All the day long did I stretch out my hands to a people disobedient and obstinate."

Redemption

Salvation in the New Testament includes redemption, *apolutrōsis*. The basic idea in redemption is release or liberation. The idea of cost is second only to that of liberation. The root of the Greek word is that on which the verb "to loose" is built.

Sin involves one in bondage, hence salvation includes a loosing from this bondage. The full cost of this redemption is known alone to God, who in Christ Jesus accomplished the redemption.

Liberation.—That the primary idea in redemption (*apolutrōsis*) is liberation may be seen not only from the root *lu–* but also from New Testament usage. This is clear in Hebrews 11:35, "Others were tortured, not accepting the redemption [release] in order that a better resurrection they might obtain." Likewise may this be seen in Luke 24:21, "For we were hoping that he himself was the one about to *redeem* [liberate] Israel." The two disciples of Emmaus were thinking about the liberation of Israel from Rome, not about the cost. In Colossians 1:13 f. the idea of deliverance or liberation is again the prominent one as thanks are given to the Father "Who delivered [*errusato*] us out of the power of the darkness, and transferred us to the kingdom of the Son of his love, In whom we have the redemption [*apolutrōsin*], the forgiveness of sins." Redemption here is a deliverance from the power of darkness that one may live under the sovereignty (kingdom) of God's love.

The doctrine of redemption is closely related to that of forgiveness, and this is understandable. Guilt enslaves, forgiveness frees.[10] In Colossians 1:14 redemption and forgiveness are almost equated: "In whom we have the redemption through his blood, the forgiveness of sins." Ephesians 1:7 closely parallels this: "In whom we have the redemption through his blood, the forgiveness of transgressions." Redemption here is liberation effected through life given and involving the forgiveness of sins. In thus bringing the ideas of redemption and forgiveness into close relationship, the New Testament does not actually equate them. Redemption is wider than forgiveness.[11] Redemption is deliverance from death and corruption (Rom. 8:21), from creaturely weakness and misery (Rom. 7:24 ff.), from the curse

---

[10] W. T. Conner, *The Faith of the New Testament* (Nashville: Broadman Press, 1940), p. 344.
[11] Rawlinson, *The New Testament Doctrine of the Christ*, p. 149.

of the law (Gal. 3:13), and from the present evil age (Gal. 1:4).
Guilt is one shackle from which man is to be redeemed (liberated) but not the only one.

Cost.—Almost as prominent as the idea of liberation in
redemption is that of cost. Liberation from guilt, from death,
from the present evil age, from the tyranny of self and of sin
comes at a cost beyond our power to measure. It is given through
Christ's blood (Eph. 1:7), that is, through his life. It is at the
cost to Jesus of himself, "Who gave himself for us, that he might
redeem us from all lawlessness and cleanse for himself a chosen
people" (Titus 2:14). Hebrews 9:12 emphasizes clearly the
cost of our liberation: "Neither through the blood of goats and
calves, but through his own blood he entered once for all into
the sanctuary, finding an eternal redemption." In 1 Peter 1:18 f.
is to be seen the same emphasis on cost: "Knowing that ye
were redeemed, not with corruptible things, silver or gold, from
your vain manner of life handed down from your fathers, but
with precious blood, as of a lamb without blemish and without
spot [even the blood], of Christ."

Present and future.—Redemption is presented in the New
Testament as both a present reality and that which is to be completed in the future. In Ephesians 1:7 and Colossians 1:14, redemption (release) is a present possession in Christ through the
forgiveness of sins. In Titus 2:14 the self-giving of Jesus was
for the purpose of liberating us from all lawlessness and the
cleansing for himself of a chosen people (*laon periousion*),[12]
zealous for good works.

In another sense, redemption is yet to be completed. It is
future, eschatological. In Ephesians 4:30, the day of redemption
is yet in the future: "Do not grieve the Holy Spirit of God, in
whom ye were sealed *until the day of redemption.*" Ephesians
1:14 is most difficult to translate, but Arndt and Gingrich [13]
may have the solution: "Who [the Holy Spirit] is the earnest
[or first instalment] of our inheritance, *unto a redemption*

[12] Cf. Arndt and Gingrich, *op. cit.,* p. 654.
[13] *Ibid.,* p. 95.

through which you become God's property [eis apolutrōsin tēs peripoiēseōs]." In verse 7 the redemption is present; in verse 14 it is in some sense future, surely in its fulness.

Redemption in the New Testament must be future as well as present because it includes the total man, and apparently even the creation. At least in Romans 8:18–25, Paul speaks of "the redemption of the body" (v. 23), apparently referring to the resurrection. He also sees the creation itself as awaiting a liberation from "the bondage of corruption unto the freedom of the glory of the children of God" (v. 21). The word redemption is not used for the creation (v. 21) as it is for the body (v. 23), but this seems to be the meaning. In its fulness, then, redemption seems to include at once the liberation from the tyranny of sin through forgiveness, and ultimately the redemption of the body through resurrection and of the creation through freeing it from corruption.

Forgiveness of Sin

Forgiveness is the overcoming of the barrier standing in the way of reconciliation [14] and of redemption (liberation). This is God's work first of all, and it necessarily becomes the work of all in whom he dwells, the work of all who receive it for themselves. Long ago Seneca said: *Errare humanum est.* Alexander Pope completed the statement: "To err is human; to forgive, divine." This divine work stands at the beginning of salvation; it continues in the saved as Jesus indicated when he taught us to pray: "Forgive us our debts, as we forgive our debtors" (Matt. 6:12).

The noun *aphesis* and the verb *aphiēmi* appear in the New Testament about fifty-six times, chiefly in the Gospels and Acts.[15] The verb may mean to send forth or discharge (Latin *emittere,* hence missile) or to send away, let go (Latin *dimittere,* hence dismiss).[16] There are other usages, but they are not con-

---

[14] Thesis argued strongly by Taylor, *Forgiveness and Reconciliation* (London: The Macmillan Co., 1941), *passim.*
[15] Richardson, *op. cit.,* p. 86.
[16] Cf. Bultmann in Kittel and Friedrich, *op. cit.,* I, 508.

cerned with the forgiveness of sin. The basic idea, when used in
connection with sin, is that of canceling debt—the removal of
the barrier to reconciliation, the banishing of the sin. In the
Greek construction, sin is the direct object of the verb and the
person is the indirect object. The typical New Testament pattern
is: "Forgive to us [dative case] our sins [accusative case]."
In forgiveness the sins are sent away or dismissed; the person is
drawn into a closer relationship. In justification the opposite follows; the sinner is justified but the sin is not justified.

Forgiveness removes the barrier to fellowship and releases
from bondage (see previous section on redemption), yet it does
not remove all the consequences of sin. Mackintosh had a true
insight in writing: "Sin would not be sin if it did not steal something which cannot quite be recaptured." [17] Fellowship between
two persons may be stronger after sin has been committed and
forgiven, but it is not stronger because of the sin; it is stronger
because of faith and love. There is always some damage which
cannot be repaired. A mother may forgive a wayward child,
and ties of love may be strengthened in the experience, but that
does not restore sleepless nights or undo hours of distress.

Forgiveness is *necessary*, it is *possible,* and it is *right*. It is
necessary where sin is real. It is indispensable to all concerned:
to the wrongdoer, to the wronged, and to the one in position to
help—one to offer and the other to accept forgiveness.

From the negative side, it is impossible to assess the damage
or loss to the one who remains unforgiving, to the one who
remains unforgiven, or to the one who fails in his opportunity
to bring others into the experience of forgiveness. To be unforgiving is to store up poison in the innermost self. To be
unforgiving requires that one be unforgiven (Matt. 6:14 f.).
This is not arbitrary; it is inescapable. To be unforgiving is to
remain unforgiven because one is thus unforgivable. To close the
door is to close it from both sides. To shut another out is to shut
one's self in. The barrier which one raises between himself and

[17] Mackintosh, *The Christian Experience of Forgiveness* (New York: Harper
& Brothers, 1927), p. 27.

another also separates himself from God. To be unforgiven is to have one's very foundations undermined and his whole personal structure threatened. To forego the opportunity to help bring about an atmosphere in which forgiveness is more easily offered and received is to rob one's self of one of his highest privileges, as indicated in the Beatitude: "Blessed are the peacemakers: for they shall be called the sons of God" (Matt. 5:9).

Positively, there are cleansing, healing, and release for both the sinner who forgives and the sinner who is forgiven. In the work of reconciliation the Christian proves to be ambassador for Christ (2 Cor. 5:20).

Forgiveness, the sending away of the sin in order that the sinner be reclaimed, is *possible*. God can so creatively deal with sins as to transmute their value.[18] A major reason for the triumph of Christianity is that God does receive sinners. Someone has called Christianity the sinner's religion. Jesus shocked his hearers in declaring: "I came not to call righteous ones but sinners" (Mark 2:17). God offers forgiveness, and he commands us to forgive.

Forgiveness is *right*. The very Christ who so stressed the all-importance of forgiveness gave the strongest doctrine of God's holiness and of God's judgment.[19] Forgiveness is not to be confused with indulgence. Forgiveness is positive and creative; indulgence is negative.[20] Forgiveness takes a serious view of sin and is concerned with overcoming it and banishing it. Forgetting has a place in forgiving. Before one may "forgive and forget" he must first remember, and the wronged and the wrongdoer must *remember together* in order that they may be able to *forget together*.[21] They must look at the wrong until they see it alike and condemn it together; only then may they forget together.

[18] *Ibid.*, pp. 11 f.
[19] *Ibid.*, p. 21.
[20] Fritz Kunkel, *Creation Continues* (New York: Charles Scribner's Sons, 1947), p. 237.
[21] Knox, *Chapters in a Life of Paul* (New York: Abingdon-Cokesbury Press, 1950), p. 147.

As R. E. Glaze has pointed out, in another sense the forgiving one cannot forget, for in forgiving one assumes the responsibility for the wrongdoer. He assumes responsibility for the rehabilitation of the wrongdoer and for repairing or absorbing the damage done.

Presuppositions to forgiveness.—Forgiveness is safeguarded from the character of indulgence by its basic presuppositions or conditions. It is connected with repentance, faith, confession, a forgiving spirit, and above all, the work of Christ. Forgiveness was never offered without conditions. In forgiveness there are *demands* as well as "giveness." John preached a "baptism of repentance unto [or upon] the remission [*aphesis*] of sins" (Mark 1:4). Peter voiced the same demand in saying, "Repent . . . unto the remission of your sins" (Acts 2:38).

Forgiveness calls for a new awareness of sin and a turning from it. The assurance is given that forgiveness and cleansing will certainly follow upon the confession of sins (1 John 1:9), but no promise is given where confession does not obtain. In the home of Cornelius, Peter related forgiveness to faith, declaring that to this one (Jesus) all the prophets bear witness: "that through his name everyone who trusts him shall receive forgiveness of sins" (Acts 10:43). In this trust, with its repentance and confession, one both "owns and disowns" his sin. This does not mean that repentance *wins* forgiveness; even repentance does not make one worthy of forgiveness.[22] As another has put it, the sinner must accept his rejection and accept his acceptance, although he knows himself to be unacceptable.[23] The sinner is not forgivable until he is willing to accept God's *no* in order to hear his *yes*.[24]

The forgiving spirit in its relation to forgiveness has already been discussed. The importance of this may be seen in the emphasis given in the Sermon on the Mount (Matt. 6:12,14–15)

[22] Taylor, *Forgiveness and Reconciliation*, p. 196.
[23] Cf. Paul Tillich, *The Courage to Be* (London: James Nisbet & Co. Ltd., 1952), pp. 155–156, *et passim.*
[24] Karl Barth, *The Epistle to the Romans*, trans. Edwyn C. Hoskins (London–New York: Oxford University Press, 1933), pp. 93, 163, *et passim.*

and the parable of the unmerciful servant (Matt. 18:21–35). It is not that God is unwilling to forgive the unforgiving but that the unforgiving is not able to *receive* forgiveness. Unforgiveness is a *condition* rendering one unforgivable.

Forgiveness is connected with the work of Jesus, or with Jesus himself (cf. Luke 1:77; Heb. 9:22; 10:18). It is a misconception, however, to say that Christ died in order that God might be able to forgive sins, for the New Testament never teaches that.[25] It would be nearer the truth to say that Christ died because he is one who does forgive sins. He does not indulge sins; he forgives. As one who out of free grace forgives, he also assumes responsibility for the sinner, as is evidenced in his life and death. This point will not be pursued here, for a special chapter is devoted to the meaning of the death of Jesus.

Justification

The term "justification," of Latin origin, does not adequately capture the meaning of the Greek which it seeks to translate. Usually it carries for Christian theology the meaning of "imputed righteousness," not actual righteousness but a "favorable standing." [26] Based on one Greek root, the words commonly translated "justification," "just," "justify," and "righteousness," must be studied together. In the New Testament these words describe God's work of free grace in which he brings man into the faith in which man receives a *new standing* and a *new way of life.* "Justification" is the creative work of God in which he is making man upright even as he gives man favorable standing.

Justification is concerned with God's *gift* and his *demand.* W. T. Conner is only partially correct in saying that justification is "a state of acceptance with God." [27] It is that, as is clear from Romans 8:33, "God is the one justifying; who is the one condemning?" But the idea of *standing* is only a part of what is here translated "justifying" (*dikaiōn*). Equally clear is the de-

---

[25] Cf. Taylor, *Forgiveness and Reconciliation,* p. 195.
[26] Bultmann, *Theology of the New Testament,* I, 272.
[27] Conner, *op. cit.,* p. 336.

mand which is embedded in the gift. This is explicit in Romans 2:13, "For not the hearers of the law are just ones (*dikaioi*) with God, but the doers of the law shall be justified (*dikaiō-thēsontai*).

A correct understanding of "justification" must do justice to the New Testament doctrine of the grace of God. The Reformation leaders reacted to the false doctrine of salvation by merit or works; but in so doing, they may have lost a part of the doctrine of justification. To see in justification God's provision for both new standing and new life is to heighten the doctrine of grace. In "justification" the sinner is brought into the faith by which—to adapt Paul Tillich's striking expression—he "accepts God's acceptance of the sinner although the sinner is unacceptable." But the grace which offers acceptance also offers a new direction and a new life. To see justification as a "making upright" as well as the giving of a new standing is not to adopt a merit religion of human works, but it is more adequately to see what God accomplishes in salvation rooted in his grace.

One gets even nearer the New Testament idea of uprightness or justification when he sees it as one's being brought into right relation to the will of God. One is "just" or "righteous" when he is brought under the will of God.[28] This illumines the meaning of Matthew 6:33, "Seek ye first his kingdom [God's sovereign rule] and his righteousness [right relation to God's will]." Romans 1:17, usually translated, "The just shall live by faith," may be paraphrased: "The one who by faith is brought into conformity to the will of God shall live." The idea is not to be confused with the Greek idea of "virtue" which man achieves; it is rather an uprightness derived from God when one is brought into covenant relationship with God.

Cognates and etymology.—The word for "justification" (*dikaiōsis*) appears only twice in the Greek New Testament (Rom. 4:25; 5:18). There are many cognate forms, including adjective, substantive, and verb forms: *dikazō*, judge or con-

[28] Gottfried Quell and Gottlob Schrenk, "Righteousness" in Coates, *op. cit.*, Vol. I, Sec. IV, 23–25, 35, *et passim*.

demn; *dikaiokrisia,* righteous judgment; *dikaios,* upright, just, righteous; *dikaiosunē,* uprightness, righteousness; *dikaioō,* to justify, vindicate, treat as just, make free or pure; *dikaiōma,* regulation, requirement, righteous deed; *dikaiōs,* justly, uprightly; *dikastēs,* judge; and *dikē,* justice personified as a goddess.[29]

The root upon which all of the above words are built is *dik–.* The basic idea is to show or point out. This is true in Greek, Sanskrit, Latin (*in-dic-co,* indicate), and the Germanic. The idea of "way" belonged to ancient usage, and in certain combinations it could mean "to put into the right way."[30] It is precarious to assume that New Testament usage abandons the idea of "putting into the right" for that of "treating as right."

The Greek *dikaiōsis,* as stated above, appears in the New Testament only in Romans 4:25 and 5:18. Usually, it is translated "justification." In these two passages the idea may be that of making righteous. At least in 4:25 *dikaiōsin* is set over against *paraptōmata* (transgressions). The meaning may be that Jesus was "delivered because of our transgressions and raised with a view to our being made righteous." In 5:18 *dikaiōsin* is set over against *katakrima* (condemnation) and in its context may mean "acquittal that brings life."[31] The term may denote "a putting into the right way" rather than simply an acquittal. In any event, two occurrences of *dikaiōsis* in the Greek New Testament scarcely *justify* any dogmatism in limiting the translation to "justification." It is not certain that this term preserves the New Testament meaning, for the meaning may be that of a setting right.[32]

The verb *dikaioun,* depending on context, may mean to justify, vindicate, treat as righteous; or it may mean to make

---

[29] Cf. Arndt and Gingrich, *op. cit.,* pp. 194–197.

[30] Cf. George Curtius, *Principles of Greek Etymology,* trans. Augustus S. Wilkins and Edwin B. England (London: John Murray, 1875), I, 165, and Schrenk, "Righteousness," *op. cit.,* p. 56.

[31] Arndt and Gingrich, *op. cit.,* p. 197.

[32] See Goodspeed, "Some Greek Notes," *Journal of Biblical Literature,* June, 1954, pp. 86–91, who argues convincingly for the meaning "made upright" as against the Reformation idea of "counting right."

free or pure. In Luke 7:29 the meaning is to vindicate as right: "And all the people and the publicans, having heard, justified [counted righteous] God." In Luke 10:29 the lawyer wanted to justify himself, not actually make himself upright. But in Luke 16:15 the Pharisees are accused of wanting to appear upright, not just to be treated as though righteous. In Acts 13:38 f. the meaning probably is more than acquittal or justification, for uprightness seems better suited to the text: "Through this one forgiveness of sins is proclaimed to you, and from all of which ye were not able to be freed [dikaiōthēnai] by the law of Moses; in this one everyone trusting has been made upright [dikaioutai]."

In Romans 6:7 the meaning is that of uprightness or freedom: "The one having died has been made free [or, made upright] from sin." The Reformation idea of justification as mere accounting right but not actual uprightness makes no sense in 1 Corinthians 6:11, where former pagans, encouraged to live a new quality of life, are told: "Ye were washed, ye were sanctified, ye were made upright [edikaiōthēte]." They were not simply treated as though righteous. Arndt and Gingrich give evidence which would support the translation, "Ye were made pure." [33] The claim in 1 Timothy 3:16 is not that Christ was only credited with a righteousness not actually possessed. The emphasis in the verse may well be on the idea of vindication, but surely it was a vindication because of his uprightness. Paul in Romans 3:4 was concerned that God be proved righteous (dikaiōthēs), not just counted righteous.

The adjective dikaios may describe men as upright, righteous, or just. It is not merely a forensic term, describing one as counted righteous, even though actually unrighteous. The richer meaning is inescapable in 1 John 3:7, "The one doing righteousness [dikaiosunēn] is upright [dikaios]." The strong contrast to the one doing sin (v. 8) makes it clear that the idea is not forensic justification (counting right even though not right) but that of actual uprightness. Equally clear is Revelation

[33] Op. cit., p. 197.

22:11, "The one doing unrighteousness let him do unrighteousness still, the filthy let be filthy still, the upright one [*dikaios*] let do righteousness [*dikaiosunēn*] still."

The sharp contrast in 1 Timothy 1:9 f. forbids the idea that the Christian is merely counted righteous without actually being made righteous: "Knowing this, that law is not made for an upright [*dikaios*] man, but for the lawless and disorderly, the ungodly and sinners, the unholy and profane, murderers of fathers and mothers, manslayers, fornicators, homosexuals, kidnapers, liars, perjurers, and any other resisting healthy teaching." In Matthew 13:42 f. the upright are contrasted with those doing lawlessness; in 1 Peter 3:12, with the wicked; in 1 Peter 4:18, with the ungodly and sinners. The same meaning for *dikaios* (upright, not merely counted upright) may be seen in Matthew 10:41; 23:28; 25:37; Mark 6:20; Romans 5:19; and Hebrews 12:23.

Habakkuk 2:4 is quoted three times in the New Testament (Rom. 1:17; Gal. 3:11; Heb. 10:38), usually translated: "The just [*dikaios*] shall live by faith." A truer translation may be: "The upright out of faith shall live." This translation does not suggest the untenable idea that man achieves his own uprightness, nor does it follow the Reformation idea of the sinner's being counted righteous though actually unrighteous. The idea would be that God brings about uprightness in the one who receives it by faith, and this is the one who lives. This does not reduce the idea of salvation by grace. It does see the grace of God as creative, not only granting to the sinner an undeserved status (treated as righteous) but also made upright.

The substantive *dikaiosunē* is usually translated righteousness, as is proper. In the New Testament this word, built upon the same root as words often translated "justification" or "to justify," describes actual uprightness, not what is merely counted righteous. This is clear in passages like Romans 14:17. "For the kingdom of God is not eating and drinking, but uprightness [*dikaiosunē*] and peace and joy in the Holy Spirit." Paul is explicit in contrasting *dikaiosunē* (righteousness, uprightness) with *anomia* (lawlessness) in 2 Corinthians 6:14, "What have righteousness and lawlessness in common?" There is no idea here of "imputed righteousness" but of actual righteousness.

There is no reason for taking *dikaiosunē* to mean actual righteousness but the verb *dikaioō* to mean only to count as righteous. There is one basic idea in the two cognates: that of actual uprightness. This may be seen in Romans 1:17, "For God's uprightness is being revealed in it [the gospel], uprightness grounded in faith and leading to faith, just as it is written: The upright out of faith shall live." In Galatians 2:16–21 Paul interchanged these two terms, giving to each the same basic idea of uprightness. He contended that a man is not made upright (*ou dikaioutai*) out of the works of law but through trust in Christ (v. 16). Next he argued that one thus made upright will not continue in the same old life of sin, for a creative work has been accomplished, resulting in a new life in Christ (vv. 17–20). Having thus traced uprightness to Christ, he concluded that it (*dikaiosunē*) is not of the law.

The same interchange between *dikaiosunē* and *dikaioō* may be seen in Romans 3:21–26. Uprightness (*dikaiosunē*) is again what God effects in one who trusts Christ (vv. 21–22). All sinners are made upright (*dikaiosunē*) by God's grace (vv. 23 f.). In this creative work of God's grace is shown his uprightness (*dikaiosunē*). God is shown to be both upright (*dikaion*) and the one making upright (*dikaiounta*) those who are of faith in Christ (v. 26). Paul's point is twofold: salvation is not man's work but God's work; it is not indulgence of sin but the overcoming of sin. Were this only forensic "justification," then it would not be just or right. God gives both new standing and new life in his "making upright" of those who by faith in Christ receive of his grace. God is the one making upright the ungodly (*ton dikaiounta ton asebē*), not just giving the sinner a new standing (Rom. 4:5).

Paul stated that faith is accounted or reckoned unto righteousness, but the context points to two ideas: (1) new standing which may only be received by grace and (2) new life which God effects in those of faith. This is the uprightness based on faith and coming from God (Heb. 11:7; Phil. 3:9). The New Testament doctrine of "making upright," inadequately translated as "justification," thus represents both God's *gift* and *demand*.

Edgar J. Goodspeed, in his convincing argument that *dikaioun* means more than "to justify," that it means to make upright, points out that this accords with the New Testament emphasis upon the Christian as a new creation, saying: "This tremendous idea that through faith, the believer becomes a totally new being, united with Christ, and with the prospect of participating in the righteousness of God himself, far surpasses in daring my translation of *dikaioō* to make upright!" [34] The Latinized idea of "justification" as imputed righteousness, counting as righteous those who are not, correctly stresses that salvation is by God's grace and not by man's works, but it does not do justice to salvation as a creative work accomplished by that same grace.

Justification and forgiveness.—It is sometimes said that whereas Jesus taught forgiveness, Paul spoke of justification and that these ideas cannot be reconciled. This is not a correct statement of the case. Paul did use Greek words usually translated "to justify," "just," or "justification," but his meaning, as shown above, is far richer than such translation implies. Paul's doctrine of "justification" is really that of God's "making upright" or "rightwising" [35] those who trust Christ.

By the same token Jesus' doctrine of forgiveness is creative; he did not indulge sin. Too, Jesus brought "justification" or "rightwising" into close relationship with forgiveness. This may be seen in Luke 18:14, where the sinner who cried out for mercy went down to his house "justified" or "made upright" (*dedikaiōmenos*). One may expect to hear Jesus say that the

---

[34] "Some Greek Notes," p. 88.
[35] Cf. Bultmann, *Theology of the New Testament*, I, 253, 270, *et passim*, for term "rightwise," though used in forensic sense.

sinner went home "forgiven," but Jesus said that he went home "justified." Surely this included forgiveness, and it implies a creative work of making upright, not merely a crediting of righteousness to one who is not righteous.

Alan Richardson, in discussing "justification," aptly says, "Salvation is the result, not of our own meritorious works, but of the outgoing righteousness of God, which brings salvation to sinners who could not have attained it for themselves." [36]

Reconciliation

The doctrine of reconciliation belongs to the very heart of the New Testament doctrine of salvation, and it may be stated more simply than is true of "justification." The *idea* of reconciliation is found throughout the New Testament, but the term itself belongs chiefly to four great passages in Paul's letters: 2 Corinthians 5:18–20, Romans 5:10 f., Ephesians 2:16, Colossians 1:20 f. Reconciliation is God's work of overcoming the estrangements bound up with man's sin. Just as sin involves man in a dual estrangement, from God and from his fellow man, so reconciliation is God's work in bringing man into proper relationship with himself and with his fellow man.

Etymology.—The Greek *katallagē* in its literal sense has to do with a change or an exchange, to render someone "otherwise." The English "reconciliation" is derived from the Latin *conciliare,* to bring together or unite, in turn based upon the Latin *concilium* from *con-calare,* to call. Obviously, the Greek and Latin words are distinct in origin and in the pictures drawn. Despite this, reconciliation, a bringing together, correctly represents the New Testament idea. Once only in the New Testament does the King James Version of 1611 employ the word "atonement," so rendering *katallagē* in Romans 5:11, "through whom we now have the atonement." This forceful term has yet another origin and draws another picture, yet it within limits correctly interprets *katallagē* as at-one-ment (*mens* is Latin for mind).

[36] *An Introduction to the Theology of the New Testament* (New York: Harper & Brothers, 1959), p. 233.

The difficulty is in the fact that atonement thus means "at one mind," which is only a part of the meaning of *katallagē*. Reconciliation as restoration of a personal relationship comes nearer expressing the idea, for persons are more than minds.[37]

Reconciliation to God.—Sin is more than estrangement from God, but it is that. Reconciliation is first of all God's work in so overcoming man's sin as to restore man to his fellowship. This God does through Jesus Christ, and the place of reconciliation is the "cross." Paul forcefully stated this in Romans 5:10, "For if being enemies we were reconciled to God through the death of his son, by much more, having been reconciled, shall we be saved in his life."

Man's sin and estrangement are to be traced to his self-love, self-trust, and self-assertion; man's reconciliation to God can begin only at the "cross" where the "self" is crucified and where God is trusted. One enters into the life of Christ at that point where he is "crucified with Christ." Man does not "crucify" himself, but he is brought into the death that means life. Verse 11 is explicit in saying that in Christ we *receive* the reconciliation (at-one-ment in the ASV). Man does not overcome his own problem of estrangement, but by faith he receives this reconciliation to God.

God as agent.—In reconciliation God is the active agent; he is the subject, not the object. God is not appeased; it is he who takes the initiative to overcome man's estrangements. The problem underlying estrangement is in man's sin, not in God himself. The classic statement of this is in 2 Corinthians 5:19, "God was in Christ reconciling the world to himself."

This is not to say that God is not affected by his own work of reconciling man to himself. Man's sin and estrangement certainly affect God, and so does God's own work in reconciliation. The parables of Luke 15 eloquently describe God's joy over one sinner reclaimed—like the joy of a shepherd in finding a lost sheep, a woman recovering a lost coin, a father regaining a son. Estrangement is personal and affects all persons involved.

[37] Of course the Latin *mens* means more than intellect.

Likewise, reconciliation is personal and affects all persons involved.[38] It is contended here, however, that reconciliation is not the appeasement of God; it is God's own work in restoring man to proper relationship with himself and with other persons.

Reconciliation to other persons.—The Bible never allows a divorce between one's relation to God and that to man. Just as one's estrangement from God is reflected in his estrangements from his fellow man, so reconciliation to God also means reconciliation to others. Christ's purpose to unite Jew and Gentile is declared in Ephesians 2:16, "that he might reconcile both in one body to God through the cross." The same emphasis is found in Colossians 1:20 ff. The church itself is the great accomplishment of God in thus making of these formerly hostile people "one new man" (Eph. 2:15).

Man is not only to be the recipient of a dual reconciliation, to God and to others; he is given the "ministry of reconciliation" (2 Cor. 5:18). The Christian's primary ministry is this: "In behalf of Christ we are ambassadors, as though God were entreating through us; we beg in behalf of Christ, be reconciled to God" (v. 20). All basic elements come to expression here: God's initiative, man's estrangement, God's work accomplished in Christ, the responsibility of the reconciled to be an instrument in reconciliation.

Sanctification

In the New Testament, followers of Jesus are frequently called saints; and the reader repeatedly encounters the terms "sanctify," "sanctification," "sacred," "holy," and "holiness." Sanctification belongs to salvation from its inception and concerns it until its consummation.

Terminology.—In the Greek New Testament is a family of words built upon the root *hag–*. The verb *hagiazein* means to

---

[38] It is argued by some that God is not a person, but at least the Bible describes him in personal terms. Also, part of the theologians who protest use of the term appear to think of God as having personal qualities.

make holy, consecrate, sanctify. The substantives *hagiasmos,* *hagiōsunē,* and *hagiotēs* mean holiness, consecration, sanctification. The adjective *hagios* means holy, consecrated, sanctified, and in the plural it describes Christians as saints. Thus several English words translate the same basic idea in Greek. Sanctification, holiness, and consecration all mean the same thing in the New Testament.

In ancient Greek *hagios* (holy) signified the object of *awe* in the sense of either reverence or a curse.[39] The adjective *hagēs* approximated the sense of *katharos,* meaning "pure." [40] This agrees with Curtius, who suggests that *hagios* means holy and *hagnos* means pure.[41] In the Septuagint *hagios* translates the Hebrew *qādhôsh,* the root of which may mean to separate, contrasting with to profane.[42] In its original usage *hagios* was cultic, with no necessary moral connotation. Things could be "holy," and even heathen temple prostitutes were "holy" women, separated from life otherwise and devoted to one purpose.

In biblical usage, moral and ethical meaning is included because one is separated unto God. In a covenant relationship with God one is made holy or whole. The holiness or wholeness is derived from God, not from man. J. Wash Watts sees the further meaning of peace (*shālôm*) to result from the covenant relationship and the "holiness" or "wholeness" which comes to the person who is brought into covenant relationship with God, the person being subject to the corrective judgments of his grace or zealous love (*chesedh*).

The words "sacred," "sanctify," "sanctification," "consecration," "holy," "holiness," and so forth are serviceable in translating the Greek New Testament; but it must be remembered that they are derived from different word roots. Sanctify and saint (Latin *sanctus*), and sacred (Latin *sacer*) are based on the

---

[39] Otto Procksch in Kittel and Friedrich, *op. cit.,* I, 87.
[40] *Ibid.*
[41] *Op. cit.,* I, 209.
[42] Procksch, *op. cit.,* I, 88. Cf. also Francis Brown, S. R. Driver, and C. A. Briggs (eds.), *A Hebrew and English Lexicon of the Old Testament* (Fair Lawn, N. J.: Oxford University Press, 1952), p. 871.

Latin root *sa–*, which is akin to the Greek *saos* with the meaning of wholeness or soundness.[43] The English word holy is derived from the Anglo-Saxon *hālig* (root *hal*) meaning whole or well (hence, *hallowed*). Thus "holy" and "sacred" are distinct in origin from one another as well as from *hagios,* yet both are serviceable in representing the New Testament idea of *hagios* (and the Old Testament idea of *qādhôsh*).

The basic New Testament idea is that of separateness, but it is separation to God from whom is derived "holiness" or wholeness. Words which in their earliest usage were void of moral or ethical connotation take on strong moral and ethical meaning in biblical usage precisely because they describe persons who become God's people, sanctified by him and unto him.

An accomplished fact.—Sanctification is from one standpoint a completed work of Christ through the Holy Spirit. It stands at the beginning of the Christian life; it is not an optional or extra feature added to salvation. The Christian grows in, but not into, sanctification.[44] It points to, and is the ground for, moral and ethical growth. In other words, it stands for something to be accomplished as well as something already accomplished. Paul looked upon the problem-laden Corinthians even as having been sanctified: "But ye were washed, but ye were sanctified, but ye were justified [rightwised] in the name of our Lord Jesus Christ and in the Spirit of our God" (1 Cor. 6:11). In writing the Thessalonians he indicated that sanctification belongs to God's purpose in salvation: "God chose you a firstfruit unto salvation in sanctification of Spirit and true faith" (2 Thess. 2:13). In Ephesians 5:25 f. Christ is said to have given himself in behalf of the church in order that he might sanctify it.

Christians characteristically are addressed in the New Testament as saints (*hagioi*). These are not people canonized after death nor sinless or even exceptional followers of Jesus. The term is applied indiscriminately to the followers of Jesus. All Christians are saints. Fifteen of the twenty-seven New Testa-

---

[43] Curtius, *op. cit.,* I. 474; cf. also I, 210.
[44] Richardson, *Theological Word Book,* p. 218.

ment writings refer to the saved as saints. The term, based upon the same Greek root as are the words translated "sanctify," "sanctification," "holy," and "holiness," describes one as separated unto God and thus brought into a covenant relationship providing for a new quality of life. The Corinthians who so vexed Paul, people who were neither sinless nor dead, were addressed as "saints by calling" (1 Cor. 1:2).

It has been said with keen discernment that at Pentecost, Christians were endowed with power, not with sinlessness! [45] Conner has pointed out that even non-Catholics show confusion about the meaning of "saint" when they speak of the "sainted dead" and those of "sainted memory." [46]

Goal and task.—Sanctification in the New Testament is a goal or task, as well as a fact accomplished. Paradoxically, it is both gift and demand. The very writers who wrote of sanctification as a provision of God in salvation also made much of the moral and ethical demands upon the Christian. This is clear and emphatic in 1 Thessalonians 4:3–7: "This is the will of God, your sanctification, that you abstain from fornication: that each of you know how to possess his vessel in sanctification and honor, . . . for God called you not for uncleanness but in sanctification." In this passage the Greek *hagiasmos* may be translated "sanctification" or "holiness," the words meaning the same thing. In 2 Corinthians 7:1 Paul exhorted: "Let us cleanse ourselves from all defilement of flesh and spirit, completing sanctification [holiness] in the fear of God." The Romans were urged to present their members in righteousness unto sanctification (6:19,22). Sanctification is thus not completed in a single act but is a continuing discipline throughout the Christian life.

God as active agent.—Sanctification is always a divine work, in Christ through the Holy Spirit. In 1 Thessalonians 5:23 Paul prayed, "May he, the God of peace, sanctify you wholly!" In Ephesians 5:26 it is Christ who sanctifies the church. New Testament writers are never embarrassed by such an apparent

---

[45] Taylor, *Forgiveness and Reconciliation*, p. 154.
[46] *Op. cit.*, pp. 340 f.

discrepancy, for to them, as to Jesus, the Father and the Christ
are one and their work one (John 1:1; 14:9 ff.; 17:22).

The believer's sanctification is bound up with that of Jesus:
"For them I sanctify myself, in order that they might be
the ones sanctified in truth" (John 17:19). Jesus as the only true
man gives himself fully to the Father, completely "separated"
unto the Father; and only as one by faith becomes "a man in
Christ" does he become sanctified in truth. This in effect is declared in Hebrews 2:11, "The one sanctifying and the ones being
sanctified are all out of one." Thus sanctification is God's work
(cf. John 17:17), and it is accomplished as *in Christ* men are
brought into the presence of God.

How one is sanctified in Jesus Christ is set forth in Hebrews
10:10, "In whose blood we have been sanctified through the
offering of the body of Jesus Christ once for all." It is shown in
verses 5–7 that there is no substitute for self-giving in obedience to God. The self-giving of Jesus (9:14; 10:10) stands over
against the self-love, self-trust, and self-assertion of man. His
blood (9:14; 13:12) is his life given, the life being in the
blood. In 10:19 f. the writer explains that "the entrance of
the saints" into the presence of God is "in the blood of Jesus"
—by participating in his self-giving. Thus one is "separated unto
God" or brought into his presence as Christ effects in him his
will and his way (10:16).

No sinless perfection.—The New Testament knows no short
cut to sinless perfection by some special blessing or endowment
of the Spirit. This idea is a false "holiness" doctrine which
evades the hard demands of salvation. One "being sanctified"
is a person brought into a covenant relation with God and thus
brought under the corrective discipline of his zealous love. At
Pentecost, as already stated, the disciples were endowed with
power, not with perfection.

The First Epistle of John is appealed to by those who seek
support for the claim to sinless perfection. Ironically, this epistle
was a refutation of just such claims made by self-styled
spirituals. There were those who claimed to be "in the light" and

to be above sin. Claiming that they were above sin, they ignored the contrary evidence of their own practices.

First John rejects outright the theory of sinless perfection, saying: "If we say that we have not sin, we deceive ourselves and the truth is not in us" (1:8); and again, "If we say that we have not sinned, we make him a liar and his word is not in us" (1:10). In 2:1 and 5:16 the writer recognized the sin problem as still being real in the lives of God's children. In 3:6,9 and 5:18 the writer *seems* to teach sinless perfection. Surely he was not guilty of hopeless confusion and contradiction. Instead, he probably here was condemning the lives of those who boasted that they were "in the light" and above sin. In 3:6, John protested: "Everyone abiding in him does not go on sinning; everyone who goes on sinning has not seen him neither has he known him." In 5:18 he declared, "We know that one having been begotten of God does not go on sinning." Evil lives refuted the false claims of those who boasted that they were above sin. No epistle more forcefully refutes proud claims to sinless perfection than 1 John does.

Not to be evaded or explained away is Matthew 5:48, with its demand: "Ye shall be perfect as your Father in heaven is perfect." There are escapes through exegesis, but probably this verse is to be taken at face value, in its most obvious meaning. This is our Lord's command or demand. What else should one expect? Does one expect him to say, "Be nine-tenths pure"? God never compromises his standard; it is perfection. Jesus demanded absolute trust, obedience, love, loyalty. He gave his all, and he demands our all.

The other side of this is that salvation is absolutely free, the gift of God's grace. The Christian lives in the tension of *gift* and *demand.* His salvation is never earned, yet it places him under absolute demand, under the sovereignty of redeeming love, under the kingdom or rule of God. One does not become a child of God by deserving it, and he does not cease to be a child of God by failing to be perfect. Neither does God relax his demand in saving sinners by grace. The parent ideally holds over the child the highest standard he knows, but the parent-child relationship is not based on the fulfilment of the standard. When the child falls short of the demand, two amazing things follow: the child is retained and so is the standard; the child is not disowned nor is the standard thrown out. Jesus offers us salvation as a pure gift, yet the demand remains: "Ye shall be perfect as your Father in heaven is perfect."

Adoption

Adoption (*huiothesia*) is one of many analogies employed in the New Testament to portray salvation. Analogies may be correlated, but in their nature they do not require logical harmony. They are analogical, not logical. Illustration may be seen in Revelation 7:17, where the *Lamb* is the *Shepherd!* This poses a problem for the prosaic logician but not for the poet. Adoption is an analogy employed in the New Testament by Paul alone. It somewhat parallels the analogy of "regeneration," so prominent in the Johannine writings, and Paul's own analogies of a "new creation" and a making alive in resurrection. It does not follow, however, that the analogies may be interchanged without loss. Conner was correct in holding that adoption and regeneration are "two terms for the same thing," [47] but this must not obscure the fact that the two analogies say *different* things about the same thing.

Adoption stresses the family relationship in salvation, the free grace by which one is adopted into God's family, and the fact that one is not a child of God by nature. Another set of analogies, including "regeneration," "creation," and "resurrection," describes the same salvation in terms of its divine origin and its new quality of life. All of these analogies describe salvation but without redundancy. The description would be less adequate were any one analogy lost.

Paul employed the term adoption (*huiothesia*) to point up the fact that sonship is "not the common property of all men by creation," but something conferred through God's free choice,

---

[47] *Op. cit.,* p. 339.

determined not by man's merit but as an act of pure grace.[48]
Israel was God's son by adoption (Rom. 9:4), chosen not upon
the basis of Israel's merit, but God's free grace (Rom. 9:11 f.).
Sonship is not universal, for "not the children of flesh are the
children of God, but the children of promise are reckoned as
seed" (Rom. 9:8).

Adoption also suggests the privileges which belong to salvation, privileges growing out of the Father's grace, not the children's merits (Rom. 9:4). The saints are not slaves living in fear,
but adopted children living in security, knowing that they were
deliberately chosen: "For ye received not the spirit of slavery
again unto fear, but ye received the Spirit of adoption, in which
we cry Abba, Father!" (Rom. 8:15). As adopted children, we
are "heirs of God, and joint-heirs of Christ," the inheritance including both suffering and glory (Rom. 8:17 and Gal. 4:6 f.).

Fuller [49] neatly summarizes the "three moments" of adoption
as (1) determined by God before the creation, the choice resting
on his grace alone (Rom. 8:29; Eph. 1:4 f.), (2) made possible
by the sending of the Son (Gal. 4:5), and (3) actually received
when by faith one is brought into vital union with Christ (Gal.
3:26–29). Indeed, a fourth moment awaits the children of God
when at the *parousia* (future manifestation of Christ) the
"adoption" is completed in the "redemption of our body" (Rom.
8:23). Because of their present suffering, the children of God do
not appear to be his children, but what is now hidden will at the
parousia be revealed.[50]

Newness of Life

Eternal life.—Life, or eternal life, is a primary concern in the
New Testament. Jesus said, "I came that they might have life
and that they might have it abundantly." The life, or eternal
life, which he brings is the life of God himself, the life of the

[48] Richardson, *Theological Word Book,* p. 16. Cf. Dodd, *The Johannine
Epistles* (New York: Harper & Brothers, 1946), pp. 67 f.
[49] Richardson, *Theological Word Book,* p. 16.
[50] *Ibid.*

"coming age" already present in Jesus, life under the kingdom or sovereignty of God. As U. E. Simon puts it, eternal life is "the absolute, ontologically real Life-of-the-World-to-come which is the Life of God Himself." [51] Eternal life is the opposite of "destruction" or "perdition"; it is participation in the "theocracy" or kingdom of God.[52] Eternal life is the life of God given to those who by faith know him as King and who thus live under the absolute and ultimate claim of his rule.

The meaning of "life" or "eternal life" is to be seen in contrast to "destruction." This is seen in Matthew 7:13–14, where one way leads to destruction (*apōleia*) and the other to life (*hē zōē*). Destruction here represents the pseudo being of one who tries to live to, and of, himself. Life is the possession and status of one yielding to the sovereignty of God. That "life" (always with definite article, *hē zōē*) is the short form for "eternal life" (*zōē aiōnion*) is clear from Matthew 19:16–17, where the question, "What good thing shall I do in order that I might get life eternal?" receives the answer: "If you wish to enter into life. . . ."

Eternal life is life under the kingdom of God. In Matthew 19:16–24 may be seen the interchange of eternal life (v. 16), life (v. 17), the kingdom of heaven (v. 23), and the kingdom of God (v. 24). This is not to say that "life" and "kingdom" are equated in the New Testament. The kingdom of God (Hebrew, *Malkhûth Yahweh*) always stands for the *sovereignty* or *rule* of God (see chap. 6). Eternal life is life given to man under that theocracy.[53] The close relationship between life and the kingdom of God may be seen in Mark 9:43–47 in the change from "to enter into life" (vv. 43,45) to the phrase "to enter into the kingdom of God" (v. 47). The same ease in changing from one expression to the other may be seen in Mark 10:17–25, where "life eternal" (v. 17) becomes "the kingdom of God" (vv. 23,25).

[51] Cross, *op. cit.*, p. 109.
[52] Dalman, *The Words of Jesus* (Edinburgh: T. & T. Clark, 1902), p. 161.
[53] *Ibid.*, pp. 91–162.

Eternal life is a present possession for those under the kingdom of God. It is "the life of the age to come," but paradoxically this age has come. As Dalman stated it: "The idea of the 'sovereignty of God' filled the place of that of the 'future age.'" The opposite of "this world" or "this age" in the New Testament is not "that other world" or "that age," but "the sovereignty of God" and the "eternal life." [54] This is explicit in John 3:36, "The one trusting the son has eternal life; but the one distrusting the son will not see life, but the wrath of God remains upon him." Here eternal life is present; yet its contrast is not something future, but the wrath of God. So in John 5:24, "The one hearing my word and trusting the one sending me has eternal life; and he goes not into judgment but he has passed out of death into life" (see also 6:47,54).

It is not enough to say that eternal life is endless life, even though that be true. If it be thought of in terms of time, then it is everlasting, "a life not measured by months and years, a life which has properly speaking neither past nor future, but is lived in God's eternal Today." [55] But eternal life is best understood as qualitative, not quantitative, as the contrast to the "death" or "destruction" which is separation from God. Since eternal life is God's own life, it is known only in knowing him.

Probably the most significant statement about eternal life is that in John 17:3, "This is eternal life, that they should know thee, the only true God, and whom thou didst send, Jesus Christ." Knowledge here is personal acquaintance, not the possession of factual data. In biblical usage knowledge of God is not by pure contemplation, as with the Greeks; it is intercourse or fellowship with God, the acknowledgement of him and his works in a response of obedient faith to his claims (his kingdom) as ultimate.[56] One encounters God directly and personally in Christ (his anointed King) and is thus brought into the life of God. John Baillie correctly states it: "He [God]

[54] Ibid., p. 148.
[55] Dodd, Interpretation of the Fourth Gospel, p. 150.
[56] Ibid., p. 152.

is not an inference but a Presence." [57] Again, "Ultimate reality meets us, not in the form of an object that invites our speculation, but in the form of a demand that is made upon our obedience." [58]

The conclusion that eternal life is life received and lived under the kingdom (rule) of God accords with the word of Jesus that eternal life is to know God—to yield in obedient faith to his ultimate claim as he confronts us in a personal encounter.

The beginning of life.—Newness of life, or the new being, which belongs to salvation has a beginning; and this beginning is set forth under several analogies, chief of which are "creation," "resurrection," and "birth." The birth analogy is variously set forth as regeneration, as birth from above, and as being begotten of God. All of these analogies have it as their common purpose to emphasize and describe the inception of the new life, as well as to characterize the life itself.

A new creation.—Paul saw the Christians as a new creation: "So, if any one be in Christ, there is a new creation" (2 Cor. 5:17). The Greek substantive *ktisis* may describe a result, but normally it describes an act. It is well to remember that salvation in every respect is God's work and that it is a *creative* work. It is not indulgence of sin or the juggling of account books. God has acted creatively, and man is made new.

Nothing short of a creative work of God may effect salvation or newness of life, as affirmed in Galatians 6:15, "For neither circumcision is anything nor uncircumcision, but a new creation." Paul bluntly declared that one has not understood Christ if he fails to see salvation as the putting off of the "old man," corrupted and destroyed by the deceitfulness of desire, and the putting on of the "new man," *created* of God in uprightness, holiness, and truth (Eph. 4:20–24). The "new man," "new being," or newness of life is not a human possibility; it comes only by a new creative act of God.

[57] *Our Knowledge of God* (New York: Charles Scribner's Sons, 1939), p. 126.
[58] *Ibid.*, p. 157.

Resurrection.—Newness of life is set forth under the analogy of resurrection in Colossians 2:12 f., "Having been buried with him in baptism, in which also ye were raised together through faith in the energizing of God who raised him out of the dead, and you being dead . . . he made you alive with him." The same picture of being "dead" and of being "raised up" is given in Ephesians 2:1,5,6. With yet fuller implications, Jesus represented life as resurrection, claiming himself to be the embodiment of each: "I am the resurrection and the life" (John 11:25). Revelation 20:5 f. refers to a "first resurrection," which probably describes one's entrance into the new life. In Romans 5:10, Paul speaks of being "saved in his life," referring to the risen life of Jesus.

Begotten from above.—Newness of life is described through the "birth" analogy, but probably the stronger New Testament emphasis is seen in its tracing the new life to a divine begetting. John 3:3 may best be translated: "Except one be begotten from above, he is not able to see the kingdom of God." The familiar "born again" misses the meaning at two points. The Greek *anōthen* means "from above," not merely again. It is not just another beginning but a new kind of beginning that is required. Bultmann rightly affirms that one must have a new *Ursprung* (fountain spring or source); he must have a new *whence* (*Woher*) if he is to have a new *whither* (*Wohin*).[59] Man needs more than improvement; a new destiny requires a new origin, and the new origin must be from God.

But even "born from above" leaves something to be desired in translation. Probably "begotten from above" is the meaning. The Greek verb *gennaō* may describe the mother function of bearing a child (cf. Luke 1:13,57; 23:29; Matt. 2:1,4; 19:12; John 16:21), but normally it describes the father function of begetting. In effect John 3:3 may declare: "Except one be begotten of God, he is not able to see the kingdom of God." This underscores the fact that one enters the new life through an act

[59] Bultmann, *Das Evangelium des Johannes* (Göttingen: Vandenhoeck & Ruprecht, 1953), pp. 97, 98.

of God. The act is not coercive, but it is essential and indispensable.

The doctrine of new life through God's begetting occurs in the Gospel of John as early as 1:12–13, where it is said: "To as many as received him, he gave authority to become children [tekna] of God, to those believing on his name, those not out of bloods, nor out of the will of flesh, nor out of the will of man, but those begotten of God." Here it is affirmed that man is unable to produce his own sonship to God, but that it must be a gift received. In this context "flesh" may be taken in either a literal or an ethical sense. Taken in a literal sense, it asserts the inadequacy of the natural or physical birth to make one a child of God. If ethical, it describes the total man in his estrangement from God, just as spirit describes the total man in relation to God. To say that salvation is not of "flesh" is to say that it is not possible to human striving. "Flesh" in this sense would describe all religious striving, including that of Nicodemus.

If the above be correct, John 3:6 becomes clear: "That begotten of flesh is flesh, and that begotten of Spirit is spirit." Although some reference to flesh in the literal sense is not to be ruled out, the force of the verse is seen best when "flesh" is understood metaphorically or ethically. Here "flesh" may stand for the whole religious system known to Nicodemus. All of his effort at salvation through ritual and works may be summed up as "flesh." Nicodemus represented a religious system at its best, but he also reflected its limitations. The life he wanted could come only from above, from Spirit and not flesh. One must be begotten of God to see (3:3) or enter (3:5) the kingdom of God; he must trust to receive eternal life (3:15–16).

John 3:5 is the most enigmatic verse of the chapter: "Except one be born [or, begotten] of water and Spirit, he is not able to enter the kingdom of God." Although not without difficulties, probably the best solution is in seeing the contrast between John's baptism in water (1:26) and that of Jesus in the Spirit. John's repentance baptism was valid and the conversion it called for essential, but John himself pointed to Jesus, who would bring the Spirit. That John did not attribute to baptism a saving function is conclusive from the fact of his refusal to baptize many who sought it, first demanding evidences of repentance. Had he viewed water baptism as effective for salvation, he would have been unjust in withholding it. Whatever may be meant by "water," it is clear that the new being must be from God. Nicodemus must *receive* from above, he cannot produce eternal life.

The Johannine emphasis upon entrance into life through being begotten of God is not singular in the New Testament. First Peter 1:3 speaks of "the One according to his great mercy having begotten us unto a living hope through the resurrection of Jesus Christ from the dead." Again in 1:23, 1 Peter speaks of those "having been begotten through the living and abiding word of God." James, using another Greek word, *apekuēsen*, attributes the new life to God, saying: "Having purposed it, he brought us forth by the word of truth" (1:18).

Regeneration and renewal.—It may come as a surprise to some to realize that the familiar word "regeneration" appears only twice in the New Testament. In Matthew 19:28 Jesus promised his followers that they would reign with him "in the regeneration [*palingenesia*]." The parallel to this in Mark 10:30 and Luke 18:30 has "in the coming age" instead of "in the regeneration." Luke 22:29, in a similar statement, has "in my kingdom." *Palingenesia* is eschatological in Matthew, describing a new order under the sovereignty of Christ.

In Titus 3:5 appear two closely related words: regeneration (*palingenesia*) and renewal (*anakainōsis*):

When the generosity and the love for humanity of our Saviour God appeared, not out of works in righteousness which we did, but according to his mercy, he saved us through the washing of *regeneration* and the *renewing* of the Holy Spirit, whom he poured out upon us richly through Jesus Christ our Saviour, that being made upright out of his grace we might become heirs according to the hope of eternal life" (3:4–7).

Whatever may be meant by "washing," whether "baptism" as many argue or not, the passage could not more clearly and em phatically attribute the "regeneration" and "renewal" to God alone. In no sense did the writer credit man's works with this newness of life. All is credited to the generosity, love, and grace of the triune God as Saviour. If there be an allusion to baptism in verse 5, it certainly does not suggest anything which man can manage (see chap. 8 for baptism). Regeneration and renewal belong to God alone.

Anakainōsis, the word for "renewal," is an action noun, and it is employed in the New Testament, along with verb forms, to describe a continuing renewal, as in Romans 12:2, "Be ye transformed according to the renewing of your mind" and 2 Corinthians 4:16, "Our inward man is being renewed day by day." Colossians 3:10 describes the "new man" as "the one being renewed unto thorough knowledge according to the image of the one having created him." Thus the "new man," the newness of life, the "regeneration," or "renewal," however designated, is traced to an initial act and a continuing act of God as the giver and sustainer of eternal life.

Repentance and Conversion

The prophetic call to repentance was revived in the ministry of John the Baptist, who came "preaching a baptism of repentance unto [or, upon] the remission of sins" (Mark 1:4). Jesus announced the "hour of decision," the *kairos,* in view of the kingdom of God, calling men to repentance and faith (Mark 1:14–15). In Jesus Christ, God had come as King, confronting men with his claim to their obedient trust. This claim was absolute and ultimate; the summons was to man's unconditional surrender to God as King. In the early church the call was to repent (Acts 2:38) or to repent and be converted (Acts 3:19).

The repentance (*metanoia*) to which men are called is more than sorrow, though it includes that. It is more than a change of mind, though it includes that. The Greek *metanoein* literally means "to change the mind," but in New Testament usage it includes more, as it calls for a basic change of way. The force of *metanoein* is probably like that of the Hebrew *shûbh,* to turn.[60] The idea of conversion, which involves the whole man, more adequately represents the Greek noun *metanoia* than does repentance. New Testament salvation is concerned with persons, not merely with minds, and certainly not with "souls" in the Greek sense. The whole self is addressed in the call to God: the thinking, feeling, willing, moral, spiritual, bodily self. "Soul-winning" is person-winning, a fact too often forgotten in much of the dubious "soul-winning" of today.

The call to "repentance," then, was a call to *persons* for a radical turn from one way of life to another. In effect it was a call to *conversion* from self-love, self-trust, and self-assertion to the way of obedient trust and self-commitment to God in Christ as sovereign. The New Testament offers no salvation which leaves as optional the Lordship of Christ. He is the Lord Jesus. He is Lord (*Kurios*) or he is not Saviour (Jesus). One thus enters the Christian life at the point of a decision made as he stands in the presence of God. One must be thrust into the agony of decision and by God's Spirit be led to accept his true existence in a new relationship to God and as the gift of God.

The repentance in a real sense is God's gift, not man's achievement (cf. Acts 5:31; 11:18; Rom. 2:4; 2 Tim. 2:25), yet it is not imposed. Men cannot achieve but only receive repentance, yet they must receive it. By faith a man receives Christ into his innermost person; and Christ, as a transforming presence reverses the course of that life from self-trust to trust in God, from self-assertion to self-denial. This conversion is the reversal of the Fall, in which man sought to find the whole meaning of his existence within himself.

Faith

Closely linked with repentance is faith. It is more than belief, though it includes that. Faith is trust. It is openness of mind, heart, and life to God to receive what he has to give

[60] Cf. R. N. Flew, *Jesus and His Church* (London: The Epworth Press, 1938), p. 37, and Taylor, *Forgiveness and Reconciliation*, p. 7.

and to yield what he demands. Chief difficulty comes in translating the verb *pisteuein*, for English does not have a verb "to
faith." Much is lost as we are compelled to translate *pisteuein* as
"to believe." The biblical idea is that of confidence, reliance,
trust. This is clear in John 2:24, which says that Jesus was not
trusting (*episteuen*) himself to certain ones, for he knew what
was in them. The ideas of persuasion and obedience may be
expressed by words built on the Greek root *pith–* from which
comes *pistis* (faith).[61]

Brunner is correct in observing that faith is a "relationship
of trust between persons," directed to persons, not things.[62] Hence
there is no surprise in the close connection between faith and
obedience, as in the "faith-obedience" of Romans 1:5. In one
sense, faith is God's gift, yet it must be a gift received. In
Ephesians 2:8 the "gift of God" probably refers to salvation
rather than to faith; but in Philippians 1:29 "to trust"
(*pisteuein*) is clearly the gift of grace (*echaristhē*). Man
could not trust if God did not offer himself to man; but
trust is never coercive. Faith is the response of trust to
God's gracious self-giving. It is openness of heart, mind, and
life to God. It is an openness to God to receive what he has
to give and to yield what he demands.

In the Fourth Gospel the noun form for faith does not appear,
but the verb form is prominent. There is a close relationship
between faith and vision in this Gospel. G. L. Phillips [63] clearly
demonstrates this relationship, showing that faith is "the consummation of an act of illumination, which derives its quality
from what it sees, rather than a decision which we make with
reference to some external object." [64] On the other hand, the interpreter must not overlook John 11:40, where faith is given
priority over sight. Jesus said to Martha, "Did not I say to you that
if you should believe [*pisteusēs*] you would see [*opsē*] the
glory of God?" In one sense "to see is to believe," but here the

---

[61] Curtius, *op. cit.*, I, 325.
[62] Brunner, *op. cit.*, p. 119.
[63] Cf. Cross, *op. cit.*, pp. 83–96.
[64] *Ibid.*, p. 83.

truth is that "to trust is to see." Possibly this is near the meaning of Hebrews 11:1, "Faith is the assurance [*hupostasis*] of the things hoped for, the inner conviction of things unseen."

For Paul, faith is not sharply distinguished from knowledge. It is not just the rational acceptance of factual data; it is the "knowledge of Christ" in the sense of personal acceptance of Christ and acquaintance with him.[65] To have faith in Christ is to know him as an actual presence. It is that trust in him that means openness of life to Christ. It is to be "in Christ" and to have "Christ in you." It is important to believe in facts, but facts cannot save a person. One is saved by Jesus Christ, our Lord and Saviour. One is saved by Christ when faith is quickened within him, a faith which is also the knowledge of him as a living and transforming presence.

[65] Cf. Knox, *Chapters in a Life of Paul*, pp. 131 f.

The
Death and
Resurrection
5 of Jesus

THE GOSPEL which Paul both received and delivered, the gospel which to him was rudimentary, began by declaring that "Christ died for our sins according to the scriptures, that he was buried, and that he was raised on the third day according to the scriptures" (1 Cor. 15:3 f.). Thus the death and resurrection were proclaimed as belonging together at the very heart of the gospel. Paul's reluctance to speak of one without the other is reflected in Romans 8:34: "Christ Jesus, the one having died, rather having been raised." The death and resurrection are not pitted against one another, and they are not to be compared as to their significance. Both are ultimate in revelation and in salvation.

Primacy

Within the limits of a single letter, 1 Corinthians, Paul placed the full weight of faith on both the death and the resurrection of Jesus Christ. Of the death he wrote: "We preach Christ crucified" (1:23) and "I judged not to know anything among you except Jesus Christ and him crucified" (2:2). Of the resurrection he wrote: "If Christ has not been raised, indeed our preaching (kērugma) is empty" (15:14) and "If Christ has not been raised, then is your faith futile and ye are yet in your sins" (15:17).

The death of Jesus is ultimate in confronting us with God's *way of life* for us. Paradoxically, the cross is death, yet it is the

122

way to life. It is the way of *life through death.* It is the deepest paradox of the New Testament that life is found by losing it; that the grain of wheat must die in order to yield its fruit (John 12:24 f.). It was at the cross that this *way* came to its ultimate expression. It was there that the "mind" of Christ expressed itself in utter self-giving, the very mind which ought to be in us (Phil. 2:5 ff.). The mystery of the cross is so deep that to the world's wisdom it is "weakness," "foolishness," and an "offense" (1 Cor. 1:23 f.). Only to the "called" is it true wisdom and power (1:24).

The death of Jesus is ultimate in revealing the true way of God for man; the resurrection is ultimate in revealing the *victory* of that way. Life is stronger than death; good is stronger than evil; self-giving is stronger than self-assertion. As will be seen presently, both cross and resurrection are far more than revelation.

The cross alone would *show* us how to die in order to live, but the resurrection *enables* us to die the death that leads to life. The cross without the resurrection would be the ultimate *example,* but the cross with the resurrection becomes the *dynamic* making possible for us the way of the cross. Without the resurrection we would be left alone in the frustration of trying in vain to follow the example of his death. With the resurrection we are confronted with the living Christ, a living and transforming presence, able to bring us through death into life. Because of the resurrection, the One who announced to John, "I was dead and behold I am living unto the ages of the ages" (Rev. 1:18), can come to us to crucify "the old man," "joining us together in the likeness of his death and also of his resurrection," enabling us to die with Christ that we might live with him (Rom. 6:3–11).

Christ died for us. He died for our sins. Except for our sins there would have been no need nor occasion for his death. But the New Testament says more. Not only did he die for us; he died in order to enable us to die the death that issues into life.

The New Testament "rings the changes" on this fact. Jesus declared his commitment to death, a yielding up of life, a death into which he would draw all men: "And I, if I be lifted up from the earth, will draw all men to myself" (John 12:32). This he said signifying the manner of death he was to die. In some sense man would be drawn into that death with him. Paul is clear at this point: "For all he died, that those living no longer to themselves should live, but to the One having died and having been raised for them" (2 Cor. 5:15). When Jesus warned that none could follow him except he take up his cross, he was speaking of a requirement, not an elective, and he was speaking of that which belongs to the Christian life or salvation from its inception, not as some optional accessory to be subsequently added.

God's work received.—Salvation is completely God's work, not ours. At Golgotha and in our personal salvation Christ does for us what we are unable to do. That is beyond dispute in the New Testament. Equally clear is the fact that this salvation is never imposed; it must be received. Christ does not save us against our wills or apart from our personal response to him. There is no external compulsion in the cross, no automatic change of status or condition for us. Millions are as lost to God and to life as though Christ had not come. The cross is not some kind of automatic sacrament, and it is not a mere example. The cross is saving for us when it comes not as an abstraction but in the person of the living Lord Jesus Christ. Through him we are "joined together in the likeness of his death" that we might be joined together with him in his life.

The death which issues into life is the accomplishment of Christ alone. Paul, for example, never boasted that he crucified himself. The "old man" was slain but not by Paul. Man's one part is faith, the faith which is trust, the faith which is openness to Christ to receive: "With Christ I have been crucified; I live yet not I, but Christ lives in me; that which I now live in the flesh, I live in faith in the Son of God, the One having loved me and having delivered himself for me" (Gal. 2:20). This was not something externally imposed upon Paul, nor was it Paul's achievement in following an example. John Knox aptly says of the cross as the way: "In Christ—that is, in the entire event—the love of God was not simply made known, as a fact is made known to our understanding; it was actually 'poured into our hearts' (Rom. 5:5)."[1]

The prominence of the cross in the New Testament.—It would be difficult to exaggerate the importance of the cross to the New Testament. About one-fourth of the material in the four Gospels is concerned with the cross.[2] These Gospels are concerned to show historically how the death of Jesus came about and theologically what it means. The earliest preaching, as reflected in Acts, shows the same concern with the death of Jesus. Paul wrote the Galatians that he renounced all glorying except in "the cross of our Lord Jesus Christ" (6:14). To the Corinthians he wrote: "I judged not to know anything among you except Jesus Christ, and this one crucified" (1 Cor. 2:2). This emphasis may easily be traced throughout the New Testament as well as subsequent Christian history.

The cross is given major attention because to New Testament faith it is that important. The fact that it is given more space than is given to the resurrection is what requires explanation. It is not that one is more important than the other. It is that the cross is more difficult to explain and more difficult to accept. It is supremely the cross which comes to grips with the sin of man; it is there that man must enter into the life that saves.

Difficult to explain.—The cross was not more important than the resurrection, but it was more difficult to explain. The resurrection required only to be announced by those who saw the risen Lord. No elaborate resurrection narrative or defense was required. The New Testament alludes to about ten separate appearances of the risen Christ, but no one New Testament writer lists all ten. On the other hand, the death of Jesus called for an elaborate narrative which would serve both as a defense and a positive declaration of its meaning.

---

[1] Knox, *The Death of Christ* (New York: Abingdon Press, 1958), p. 159.
[2] Filson, *Jesus Christ the Risen Lord* (New York: Abingdon Press, 1956), p. 111.

The death of Jesus came as a shock to his closest followers. It was a major problem to faith in Jesus as the Messiah. Paul spoke of the "scandal" of the cross (1 Cor. 1:23). Jewish Messianic expectations of the day did not provide for a suffering and dying Messiah. Peter reflected the feeling of all when he protested the idea that the Christ would suffer and be killed (Matt. 16:21 f.). Not only would the unbelievers scoff at a crucified Saviour who could not even save himself (Matt. 27:40–42), but those most sympathetic were required to rethink the messianic function in order to see how Messiah could suffer and die. The first task of apostolic preaching was to deal with the "scandal of the cross." Only in the light of the resurrection were the earliest Christians able to restudy the Old Testament, as well as the life and death of Jesus, and see new meaning in the death.

In order to set forth the death in its true light, the disciples were compelled to tell the whole story of how, historically, Jesus came to be crucified and what, theologically, this meant. Consequently, the early *kērugma,* embodied finally in the four Gospels, told how Jesus came, what he did and said, how he was misunderstood, how the opposition formed and on what grounds, how both Jews and Romans finally brought him to his death. The apology and the interpretation of the death of Jesus could not be reduced to a few summary statements. It called for an extended narrative, which came to be repeated by the various individuals and in the various communities in a somewhat standardized form.

Difficult to accept.—Another reason why more attention has been given to the cross than to the resurrection in the New Testament and in subsequent theology is that the cross is more difficult *to accept.* Some do not believe in the resurrection, but probably most people would like to. (Exceptions would include those who desire escape from bodily existence, not its perpetuation, as is true of those holding that the body is the prison or tomb of the soul.) To most people the idea of resurrection is attractive. But the cross is always "foolishness" or a "scandal" to the world's wisdom. It offends reason to suggest that God's anointed should so suffer as did Jesus. Also, it is a hard saying (John 6:60) which repels when one is told that he must "eat the flesh" and "drink the blood" of the Son of man (John 6:53 ff.).

Life is attractive to us, but life through death is not attractive. We must be won to the cross, and this is never easy. The cross is such in character that even Jesus prayed in Gethsemane for the removal of the cup if there were any other way (Mark 14:36). It is not surprising that we cry out for an alternative to the cross.

Life through death.—Writing of Jesus, Paul declared: "We shall be saved in his life" (Rom. 5:10). In the context he stressed the importance of the death of Christ, closely relating death and resurrection. Actually we are saved by Christ himself as Paul affirms (v. 9), not by anything in the abstract, either death or resurrection. We are saved by the Saviour. We are saved by being brought into the life of the risen Lord.

Of utmost importance to observe is that the point at which he brings us into his life is the cross. It is at the point where we die with him that we live in him. In Pauline language we can be "baptized into Christ" only by being "baptized into his death" (Rom. 6:3). Only as we are crucified with Christ, as he lives in us (Gal. 2:20), are we saved in his life (Rom. 5:10). Along with the fact of its primary importance, the difficulty of bringing us to the acceptance of the cross goes far to explain what may seem to be a disproportionate attention that has been and must continue to be given to the cross. The remainder of this chapter will be devoted to the death of Jesus; further attention will be given to the doctrine of the resurrection in the final chapter of the book.

Basic Facts in the Passion Narrative

The theology of the New Testament is rooted in an event, in something which occurred in history. Any valid attempt to understand the meaning of the death of Jesus Christ must begin with the narrative of his death as set forth in the New Testament. Probably certain excesses in various atonement theories could have been avoided had the four Gospels received more careful attention. Any rationale must be subject to this rigid discipline at every point.

On Man's Side, a Life Taken

On man's side the death of Jesus was *rejection, betrayal,* and *murder.* The Gospels are clear and emphatic at this point. Redemption is to be found at the cross, but the redemption is in what Christ did, not in what man did. In man's part is depravity, not redemption. There is no redemption in fear, blindness, selfishness, malice, envy, jealousy, deceit, cowardice, betrayal, hate, and murder.

Rejection.—On man's part the death of Jesus was *rejection:* "He came unto his own, and his own received him not" (John 1:11). He was the stone which the builders rejected, said the New Testament writers repeatedly (cf. Mark 12:10; Acts 4:11; Rom. 9:32; 1 Peter 2:7). This rejection was real. That it was *rejection* has meaning only on the assumption that man did what he did not have to do. There was a choice.

Betrayal.—On man's part the death of Jesus was *betrayal.* Mark records that Jesus thrice warned that the Son of man would be rejected and betrayed into the hands of men who would kill him (8:31; 9:31; 10:33). Again it records that Jesus said: "The hour is come; behold, the Son of man is betrayed into the hands of sinners" (14:41). Paul, in our earliest account of the Last Supper, introduced the narrative with these words: "The Lord Jesus in the night in which he was betrayed." Nowhere in the New Testament is man's crime relieved by any doctrine of a determinism which made man an unwilling instrument in the death of Jesus. The choice was free and responsible; it was a shameful betrayal on the part of trusted religious leaders.

Murder.—On man's part the death of Jesus was *murder.* In what is possibly Paul's earliest extant letter, he is blunt in his reference to "the Jews, who both killed the Lord Jesus and the prophets" (1 Thess. 2:14 f.). On the day of Pentecost, Peter said: "Him ye by the hand of lawless men did crucify" (Acts 2:23), and again: "This Jesus ye crucified" (Acts 2:36). Stephen employed yet stronger language, saying: "They killed them that showed before of the coming of the Righteous One; of whom ye have become *betrayers* and *murderers*" (Acts 7:52). Paul, likewise, is quoted in Acts as charging his countrymen with betrayal of the innocent, saying: "Though they found no cause of death in him, yet asked they of Pilate that he should be slain" (13:28).

Thus the New Testament traces these acts of rejection, betrayal, and murder not to God's will but to man's perverted will. What is traced to God's will belongs to another world.

On Jesus' Part, a Life Given

Jesus did not speak of dying so much as of giving his life, thus stressing the positive nature of his death. This emphasis appears in Mark, our earliest Gospel: "The Son of man also came not to be ministered unto, but to minister, and to give his life a ransom for many" (10:45). The same emphasis appears in the latest Gospel, in John 10:11: "I am the good shepherd: the good shepherd layeth down his life for the sheep"; in verse 15, "I lay down my life for the sheep"; and in verses 17 f., "Therefore doth the Father love me, because I lay down my life, that I may take it again. No one taketh it away from me, but I have power to lay it down, and I have power to take it again. This commandment received I from my Father."

Not a helpless martyrdom.—The death of Jesus was not that of a victim, caught in circumstances from which he could not escape. Jesus maintained that he could have escaped those who sought to destroy him. In Matthew 26:53 he is quoted as asking: "Or do you think that I cannot beseech my Father, and he shall even now send me more than twelve legions of angels?" In John 19:11 he is quoted as saying: "You would have no authority at all against me, except it be given you from above."

Not a fate fixed by the Father.—The death of Jesus was not a

fate fixed for him by the Father. No individual was required to
reject, betray, or murder Jesus. His own could have received
him had they been willing. Judas did not have to betray him.
Caiaphas was self-willed and arrogant in his decision to put his
selfish interests and what he called "expedient" above truth and
right. Pilate's cowardice in surrendering to the accusers one
whom he recognized as innocent is exposed as a guilty and
shameful act. There was no external coercion that determined
the action of any who conspired to put Jesus to death.

This was no drama staged by the Father and the Son with a
carefully chosen cast of actors or "play villains," manipulated
like puppets. These were true villains, not unlike us, sinners all.
This was no television show reproduced by transcription; it
was live! Choices and decisions were real on both sides. Jesus
died at a place of execution at the hands of brutal men, not on
a stage nor on an altar in the Temple. The *Passion Play* is
given each tenth year at Oberammergau in Germany, a grip-
ping, dramatic enactment of the trial and crucifixion of Jesus;
but it is played by actors, however beautiful or reverent the performance. But Golgotha was not Oberammergau. It was not
a stage production.

Were the crucifixion of Jesus due to some divine coercion or
determination, then Judas, Caiaphas, Pilate, and all the others
would be exonerated and Jesus would be robbed of glory. Millions go to an unwilling or inescapable death, but that is not
the way the death of Jesus Christ is represented in the Gospels.

It is true that some New Testament passages seem to teach a
determinism behind the death of Jesus. Acts 2:23 may seem to
be of such teaching: "Him, being delivered up by the determinate counsel and foreknowledge of God, ye by the hand of
lawless men did crucify and slay." It is to be observed, however, that it is *the giving up,* and that alone, that is traced to
God's "determinate counsel." On God's side, the Son was given
up freely. On man's side, it was also a free act, an act of
murder. This verse very clearly portrays God's part and man's
part. Peter did not say that God determined that his Son be

rejected or killed, only that God gave him up as a free act.

Probably Acts 4:27 f. comes nearest to affirming a determinism behind the death of Jesus: "For of a truth in this city against the holy servant Jesus, whom thou didst anoint, both Herod and Pontius Pilate, with the Gentiles and the peoples of Israel, were gathered together *to do whatsoever thy hand and thy counsel foreordained to come to pass.*" But in this very context Peter charged the Gentiles and Israel with rage, vain imaginations, and *rebellion.* The passage is nowhere concerned to relieve the guilt of those who thus acted. Guilt would be excluded were their actions determined from above. Peter's concern seems rather to affirm the sovereignty of God over even the rebellions of men. Theirs was real rebellion, but not even at Golgotha was God overtaken by the unexpected or overthrown by men's rebellions. God was able to turn man's evil act to a good result.

The cry of Jesus on the cross, "My God, my God, why hast thou forsaken me?" is by some taken as an actual abandonment of the Son by the Father, or a giving over of the Son to his fate. Such interpretation suggests the impossible idea of two Gods at Golgotha. It would represent the Son friendly to man and the Father hostile. Such division between Father and Son is forbidden by the New Testament and especially protested in the Fourth Gospel. However insoluble the cry may be to us, it must not be so interpreted as to contradict the New Testament's insistence upon the oneness of Father and Son and the fact of the Father's love as being behind all redemption. God does not love because Jesus died for us; Jesus died for us because the Father loved us.

It seems best to understand the cry as that of one who was truly human and who felt forsaken. The Docetic view which refused to take the humanity seriously was clearly rejected in the New Testament. John A. Broadus, commenting on Matthew 27:46, cautioned us that: "We must remember that a human soul as well as a human body was here suffering, a human soul thinking and feeling within human limitations (Mark 13:32), not psychologically unlike the action of other devout souls when in some great and overwhelming sorrow." [3] W. T. Conner took the same position: "Put to death by his foes, very largely deserted by his friends, he feels as if he were deserted by God also." [4] God did not forsake Jesus; all others did. Jesus did not die *in* sin, but *to* sin.[5] He died *for* sinners but he was no sinner.

Even in this dark hour which wrung from his lips such a cry, his trust in God came to firm expression; the cry was addressed *to God,* whom he did feel to be near and to whose will he gave himself. The truth that he who died at Golgotha is one with the Father, that God was in Christ, and that at the same time he cried out to the Father belongs to the mystery of the incarnation and is far beyond our power to fathom. We can only accept what the New Testament affirms: Jesus Christ is the beloved Son in whom the Father is altogether pleased (Mark 1:11); he is in the Father and the Father in him (John 14:9 ff.; 17:22); yet the Son thus cried out to the Father.

Jesus gave his life, and he did so in accord with the Father. Paul is explicit about this in Galatians 1:3 f.: "Grace to you and peace from God the Father, and our Lord Jesus Christ, Who *gave himself for our sins,* that he might deliver us out of this present evil world, *according to the will of our God and Father."* Jesus gave his life; it was not given away for him by the Father. This giving was in accord with the Father's will. The giving of himself was not to deliver men from an angry Father but from sin, from this present evil world! There is no New Testament basis for rejecting this, as there is none for rejecting Paul's classic statement: "God was in Christ, reconciling the world to himself" (2 Cor. 5:19).

A bitter cup, not sought but accepted.—For Jesus, death was no beautiful friend but a bitter cup. Plato represents Socrates as

---

[3] *Commentary on the Gospel of Matthew (An American Commentary on the New Testament,* ed. Alan Hovey, Vol. I [Philadelphia: The American Baptist Publication Society, 1886]), p. 574.

[4] *Op. cit.,* p. 177.

[5] Conner, *The Cross in the New Testament* (Nashville: Broadman Press, 1954), p. 34.

remaining calm and composed as his hour of death drew on.[6] In part this is traceable to the fact that for him death was the friend which freed the soul as the true self from its prison, the body.[7]

To Jesus, death was an enemy to be overcome. In the Bible the body is seen as an essential part of man, calling for redemption, not destruction. In Gethsemane Jesus prayed: "Abba, Father, all things are possible to thee; remove this cup from me; howbeit not what I will, but what thou wilt" (Mark 14:36). There was more than physical death in the "cup," but it is not to be overlooked that death itself was to him a bitter cup. To this was added the suffering and shame of this particular death: rejected and despised, publicly condemned as a blasphemer and a traitor. To this was added the bitterness of seeing his own people exposed in their depravity and driven to new depths of depravity by the very love which sought to save them. From this cup he shrank, yet did he accept it.

In the Fourth Gospel, although there is no Gethsemane story, there is strong emphasis upon his hour and his cup. The hour he foresaw and accepted (2:4; 7:6,8,30; 12:23); the cup he accepted and drank (18:11). His death was self-denial in its ultimate expression, trusting obedience to the will of God. At the cross the Fall was reversed: whereas Adam had in distrust denied God and asserted himself, Jesus denied himself and in submissive faith affirmed God.

The death foreseen and not evaded.—The Gospels represent Jesus as foreseeing his death from the outset of his public ministry. At his baptism he was conscious of his role as the Suffering Servant (Isa. 42:1 ff.) and possibly also as God's anointed King (Psalm 2:2), the first role (Servant) certainly and the second (anointed King) possibly reflected in the words: "Thou art my beloved Son, in thee I am well pleased" (Mark 1:11).

[6] Cf. *The Dialogues of Plato,* trans. B. Jowett (5 vols.; Oxford: The Clarendon Press, 1953), II, 371–384, 407–477. See especially *Crito* and *Phaedo* 115e, 117c, 118.

[7] Cf. Cullmann, *Immortality of the Soul or Resurrection of the Dead* (New York: The Macmillan Co., 1958), pp. 19 f.

In the wilderness temptations which followed, Jesus refused any selfish road or short cut to personal comfort or glory. He gave himself in trusting obedience to the will of God, accepting the servant role and the self-denial which led to his death. When the messengers of John the Baptist came inquiring if he were the "Coming One," he pointed to the role of service which was his (Matt. 11:2 ff.). At Caesarea Philippi where he was acclaimed the Christ, he pointed to death for himself and for his followers (Mark 8:31,34). Peter's suggestion that Christ would not die was termed satanic.

The transfiguration pointed to Jesus' death, for it was of his decease (exodus) which he was to accomplish at Jerusalem that Moses and Elijah spoke with him (Luke 9:31). The coming of certain Greeks to see him apparently posed for him an alternative to suffering, but this became the occasion for a new commitment of himself to the will of God and to the cross (John 12:20 ff.). He would not take the easy road out, but would offer himself to his own people, even though he foresaw rejection and death.

Finally he set his face toward Jerusalem with such force of commitment that even the nearest disciples were awed by his action (Mark 10:32 ff.). His challenge to ambitious disciples was in terms of a death clearly foreseen: "Are ye able to drink the cup that I drink; or to be baptized with the baptism that I am baptized with?" (v. 38). He observed the Last Supper with his disciples, conscious of the death which awaited him. In Gethsemane he faced the whole basic choice again, and he gave himself finally and fully to the will of God, accepting the cup, however bitter. Death was neither sought nor desired but it was freely accepted.

The death a moral inevitability.—Two ways met at Golgotha as redeeming love sought to reclaim its own. In Jesus the love of God came to full expression in the relentless exposure of sin and in the complete offering of self. There, too, did man's false way come to its ultimate expression in self-will, self-trust, self-love, self-assertion. That Jesus should go all the way in the offering of himself to man is in keeping with what love is: "Having loved his own that were in the world, he loved them to the uttermost" (John 13:1). Jesus was not driven by fate or outward circumstances, but he was impelled by the love which prompts one to lay down his life for his friends (John 3:16; 15:13) and even for sinners (Rom. 5:8).

Man the sinner in rejecting Jesus, acted consistently with the false principle of self-love, self-trust, and self-assertion which he had taken into his bosom and by which in vain he had sought to live. That God in love should give himself was inevitable to love. That man in his self-centeredness should blindly strike back was also inevitable to his depravity.

No Rationale Adequate

The death of Jesus is bigger than any definition, deeper and more profound than any rationale. Although man must seek to make it intelligible to himself and to others to whom he would proclaim it, all of its mystery will not yield to rational analysis. Rational man has a mania for explaining and frets when all does not yield to his analysis. But religion is not to be emptied of all its mystery, and that holds for the cross of Christ. In the New Testament the cross is a constant theme, but nowhere is it reduced to one comprehensive and final rationale. By a rich variety of terms and analogies it is set forth, but it is never completely captured in any verbal net.

Probably in all the historic theories of atonement there is truth, but also in each is limitation. This will continue to be true. It is not simply that man is not profound enough; he is not good enough to understand the cross.[8] The divine love behind the self-giving of Jesus at the cross is so far beyond our egocentric way that we cannot adequately understand the cross. To man's wisdom, the self-denial of the cross is always foolishness (1 Cor. 1:23).

Fortunately for us, the power of the cross to save is not bound by our inability to comprehend it. Man is not saved by his own

[8] Cf. Wolf, *op. cit.,* p. 209.

works, not even by his own work in theology. Salvation is not
the award for passing an examination in the doctrine of atonement. Salvation is the work of divine grace, the newness of life
effected by the Saviour who becomes in the believer a personal
and transforming presence, somehow releasing in man the very
creative power which brought Jesus to the cross and to the
resurrection.

Although its full meaning is not to be fathomed by man, the
cross yet stands before us and bids us open our hearts and minds
to its reality and its meaning.

The Meaning of the Death of Jesus

Even though no final rationale of the cross is to be achieved,
we must seek its meaning again and again. Much, though not
all of its meaning, does come to us through the New Testament
and through life in Christ.

Christ's death as judgment.—In counseling today much is
said about accepting the client without raising the barrier of
moral judgment. Whatever the defense for this in psychiatry, in
the Bible major place is given to judgment in the therapy that
is salvation. Sin is real, and sin is judged as sin.

The death of Jesus stands over man as the most devastating
judgment conceivable. John 3:19 refers to the whole impact of
Christ upon our world, but it has special reference to the cross:
"This is the judgment, that light is come into the world, and men
loved darkness rather than the light." At the cross, man's way is
exposed in its ultimate expression and it is rejected. What man
the sinner did at the cross is the final fruit of the self-centered
way upon which he had embarked long ago. The first word of
the cross is *no* to all man's sin expressed in his self-worship-
ing way. Man is branded as guilty of betrayal, rejection, and
murder. To the Romans, Paul wrote: "For what the law could
not do, in that it was weak through the flesh, God, sending his
own Son in the likeness of sinful flesh and for sin, condemned
sin in the flesh" (8:3). As he approached his death, Jesus said:
"Now is the judgment of this world" (John 12:31). At the

cross the "prince of this world" has been judged (John 16:11).

No defense can be made for man's part in the rejection, betrayal, and murder of Jesus. No defense can be made for man's cherished way which led him to so shameful a deed. From one side the cross is man's deed, standing for his fear, his blindness, his will to power, all rooted in his self-love, self-trust, and self-assertion. In condemning Jesus, who alone was true and right, man condemned himself. The cross is judgment over every man. To those who do not accept it as judgment, it remains *only* judgment.

The New Testament does not relate the term "wrath" to the cross, but in a real sense the wrath of God is to be seen there— in and upon man. Nowhere does the New Testament declare that God's wrath was poured out upon Jesus.[9] The wrath was at work in and upon man. Of course, Christ suffered because of the wrath of God which overtook man at Golgotha, but God was not punishing Jesus. It is precisely at Golgotha that God's wrath is most fully revealed against man's sin. Precisely there is man's sin seen in its full force: the blindness, the senseless heart, the will to power, the ungodliness, and the inhumanity of man. What sin does in and to man is seen at the cross as nowhere else. Sin can so blind and corrupt man that he thus crucifies the Son of God.

The New Testament has much to say about the wrath of God (e.g., John 3:36; Rom. 1:18; Rev. 19:15) and even about the wrath of the Lamb (Rev. 6:16). God's wrath is revealed against the ungodliness and iniquity of men (Rom. 1:18); it comes upon the sons of disobedience (John 3:36; Eph. 5:6). Revelation paints vivid pictures of the wrath of God Almighty and that of the Lamb poured out upon the rebellions of men (6:16 f.; 11:18; 15:1, 7; 16:1, 19; 18:8; 19:15).

Paul devoted a long paragraph to an analysis of "the wrath of

[9] Conner, *Faith of the New Testament*, p. 319, warns against "literalizing" certain passages and against the perils of "lexicon and logic" applied to words like debt, ransom, and redemption, concluding: "I doubt, therefore, if a man is interpreting Paul (or any other part of the New Testament) when he talks about God as punishing Christ, or Christ as suffering the pangs of Hell, etc."

God revealed from heaven against all ungodliness and iniquity of men" (Rom. 1:18–32). He described its nature, traced out its cause, and showed its results. To Paul the wrath of God is his delivering of man over to man's own choice of the way of disobedience and self-worship. Three times he said that God "gave them over": (1) to "the desires of their hearts unto uncleanness to dishonor their bodies in themselves" (vv. 24 f.); (2) unto passions of dishonor, expressed in homosexuality and other sex perversions (vv. 26 f.); and (3) to a reprobate mind resulting in every sort of personal and antisocial vice (vv. 28 ff.).

This depravity, self-ruin, moral and social breakdown, blindness, senselessness, and false existence was to Paul the "revelation from heaven of the wrath of God." This he traced to man's fatal choice "not to have God in his knowledge" (v. 28); to man's rejection of the truth (v. 19); to man's substitution of the creature for the Creator (v. 23). In trying to be wise, man became foolish; rejecting God's truth, man's "senseless heart was darkened" (v. 21).

Paul's analysis of the wrath of God follows that given by Jesus as he declared the inescapable penalty of rejecting God's light: "Unto judgment I came into this world, that those not seeing might see; and those seeing (those satisfied with their sight) should become blind" (John 9:39). When one rejects the light, he does not put out the light; he puts out his own eyes. This is the wrath of God against ungodliness and iniquity. It is the outworking of sin in the life separated from God. Nowhere is this more clearly seen than in the outworking of sin in man at Golgotha. God did not pour out his wrath against Christ; God's wrath was at work within and upon man.

Christ's death as triumph.—The work of Christ was not merely that of restoration; it was a creative work beyond restoration.[10] Jesus met head on all that had brought man to ruin and made it serve a different end. He brought to naught the power of the devil, him who had the power of death, freeing man from the fear of death (Heb. 2:14). Jesus absorbed the evil and made

---

[10] Cf. Wolf, *op. cit.*, p. 97.

it become the raw material for good.[11] As Jesus faced his "hour" he said, "Now is the prince of this world cast out" (John 12:31). Again he said, "Be of good courage, I have overcome the world" (John 16:33). On the cross, not as a cry of defeat or despair but in triumph, he shouted, "It is finished!" (John 19:30).

Where man failed, Christ triumphed. Where man had abused a God-given freedom by self-worship rather than self-giving, Jesus gave himself in trust to the Father and in love to the very men who sought to destroy him. Not alone in words but supremely at the cross, he brought to triumphant reality the truth that he who would lose his life shall find it. The death of Jesus was the victory for faith in God, for submission to God's will, for the principle of the denial of self over the principle of self-assertion. Jesus as the Word made flesh, validated and brought to triumph in the sphere of the flesh—precisely where man had failed—the very way of life for which man was made.

Liberation at immeasurable cost.—Redemption is a major word in the New Testament, and it is vitally linked to the cross. Jesus gave his life a ransom for many (Mark 10:45); he redeemed those under the law (Gal. 4:5); redemption is through his blood or life as given (Eph. 1:7); we are redeemed through the precious blood of the Lamb (1 Peter 1:19); Jesus is the one who has loosed us from our sins by his blood (Rev. 1:5); he did purchase to God in his blood of every tribe of men (Rev. 5:9).

The basic idea in the Greek word for "redemption" is release or liberation (see chap. 4). Jesus broke the bondage of sin, the bondage of self-will, self-love, self-trust, self-worship. He freed man for God and for life as a person in the fellowship of God and man. Of course this was not automatic. Only as man by faith admits Christ into his own person and life does he become in man a personal and transforming presence. As man is brought to drink the cup which he drank and to be baptized

[11] Cf. Leonard Hodgson, *The Doctrine of the Atonement* (London: James Nisbet & Co., 1951), *passim*.

with his baptism (Luke 12:50; Mark 10:38; Rom. 6:3), so is man freed from the tyranny of sin and freed for the creative life in the fellowship of God.

Although the basic idea in redemption is liberation, also stressed is its *cost*. This redemption was by Christ's blood, his life given. He redeemed us by becoming a curse for us (Gal. 3:13). This of course does not mean that Jesus became a sinner. Never does the New Testament say that he died *in* sin. Redemption is related to forgiveness of sin (Col. 1:13 f.). He absorbed our sin. In forgiving he took the responsibility for us as sinners. Always in forgiveness, the one forgiving must in some sense assume responsibility for the other's sin, lest it be not forgiveness but indulgence. To be more precise, in forgiveness one takes responsibility for the *person* forgiven, not for the sin committed, as when one takes responsibility for a parolee—responsibility for his restoration. Precisely because Christ was righteous love and because he was without sin, he could so identify himself with man that man's sin became his very own.

Jesus *paid* to liberate us from our sin. Of course he paid no one, neither the Father nor the devil. He simply paid. He saved us at the cost of his own life. He paid in the humiliation of the Incarnation, in life and in death, in submitting to rejection, betrayal, and murder. The taunt at Golgotha, "He saved others, himself he cannot save" (Matt. 27:42), had far more meaning than his tormentors knew.

Christ's death as expiation.—Propitiation and expiation are alternate translations for the same Greek word, *hilasmos*. Neither is satisfactory. Because propitiation is so linked to pagan ideas of the appeasement of God, it is not suitable for translating New Testament ideas. Expiation is not satisfactory, but it is not so definitely linked to pagan usage. It is not sound exegesis to obscure by the pagan idea of propitiation or appeasement the biblical emphasis upon the initiative of God in man's salvation. God reconciles man to himself; God does not await appeasement. In the New Testament, God is the subject behind redemption, not the object. The problem of estrangement is in man, not in God. This does not mean that God remains unaffected by his own work of expiating man's sin and reconciling man to himself (see chap. 4).

Calvin taught that God was our enemy until he was reconciled to us by Christ, writing that Christ satisfied and propitiated the Father—"by this intercessor his wrath has been appeased." [12] But this is Calvin, not Holy Writ! This is Calvin, and he spoke with no infallible word.

Paul clearly referred to Jesus "Whom God set forth an expiation through faith in his blood" (Rom. 3:25), and John said of Jesus that "he himself is the expiation for our sins" (1 John 2:2). But that is not to say that the Son by taking man's punishment satisfied or appeased the Father. The New Testament never thus drives a wedge between the Son and the Father. "God so loved the world, that he gave his only Son" (John 3:16). Conclusive should be 1 John 4:10: "In this is love, not that we have loved God, but that he himself loved us and sent his Son an expiation for our sins." The meaning of expiation is seen in Luke 18:13, where the publican prays: "O God, have mercy on [expiate] me the sinner." Expiation is God's work, not man's. It is concerned with man's sin, not with God's wounded feelings.

God is free to forgive. The Father does not need to punish the Son in order to win the right to forgive. Were the Father paid off, then there would be no forgiveness. God himself forgives, and in so doing he assumes the responsibility for the sinner.

As Abelard asked, if Christ's death were a "satisfaction" for Adam's sin, what would give satisfaction for the sin of those who crucified Jesus? This, of course, is not at all representative of the thought of the New Testament and may well be left to the side. Sin in the New Testament is not viewed as an entity which can be offset by a good act; it is a broken relationship which must be restored, a sickness which must be cured.[13]

---

[12] John Calvin, *Institutes of the Christian Religion,* trans. John Allen (2 vols., Grand Rapids: Wm. B. Eerdmans Publishing Co., 1949), I, 552–553 (Bk. 2, Chap. 16, Sec. 2).

[13] Cf. Wolf, *op. cit.,* p. 107.

Christ's death as reconciliation.—Reconciliation through the death of Jesus is God's answer to man's estrangement from God (cf. Rom. 5:18–20; Col. 1:21 f.; Eph. 2:16). The dual estrangement, man from God and man from man, is overcome through the cross. Paul was eloquent at this point: "But all things are of God, who reconciled us to himself through Christ and gave us the ministry of reconciliation; to wit, that God was in Christ, reconciling the world unto himself, not reckoning to them their trespasses" (2 Cor. 5:18 f.). Just before this statement, Paul had indicated how this reconciliation is effected through the cross: "He died for all, that they that live should no longer live unto themselves, but unto him who for their sakes died and rose again" (v. 15). That is, the believer is brought into the very death to self or self-denial seen in Jesus at the cross. Adam was estranged from God by seeking to live unto himself; man is reconciled to God when in Christ this fall is reversed.

In this reconciliation, God is always the active agent, never the passive object. There is no picture of appeasement of the Father. This, of course, is not to overlook the obvious fact that in the estrangement of persons both are affected, however innocent one may be. Although it is man who is estranged from God, the love of God is thus frustrated, and he is denied the relationship with man for which he made man. As God overcomes the estrangement, surely new meaning is brought into the relationship for God himself. But this is not to be confused with the nonbiblical idea that the Father is appeased by the Son. Such a theory would seem to assume that John 3:16 reads, "God was so peeved with the world" rather than that "God so loved the world."

Christ's death as revelation.—The death of Jesus is far more than revelation, but it is certainly that. Not only does it expose man's depravity as it is nowhere else so clearly seen, but it lays bare the heart of God as nothing else does. The cross reveals the love of God as is made clear in Romans 5:8, "But God commendeth his own love toward us, in that while we were yet

sinners, Christ died for us." Only as we take seriously the insistence of Jesus of his oneness with the Father (cf. John 17)
may we see how God's love is set forth in Jesus' death. That
God is for us (Rom. 8:31) is the gospel's most glorious and almost incredible declaration, and this is most conclusively seen in
the death of Jesus, even in "the Son of God, who loved me, and
gave himself up for me" (Gal. 2:20).

But not only is the death of Jesus revelation of God's love;
it reveals his power and wisdom. It is revelation *in fact* as it is
received in faith, and only as received. It was not revelation to
the disciples when they picked up their belongings and returned
to Galilee, nor was it revelation to those who stood at the cross
and scoffed. To the Greek it is foolishness and to the Jew an
offense; but to the man who knows it through personal faith, it
is God's power and God's wisdom (1 Cor. 1:23). To the pagan
who believes that one must further his own interests by assertion
of self and one's "rights," the cross seems to reflect weakness
and foolishness. To the Jew, clamoring for vindication and glory,
the role of suffering and death seemed contradictory to that of
Messiah and his people. In the cross is seen true power and true
wisdom. Power is seen in self-denial, not in self-assertion. Wisdom, too, is there, for only the grain that falls into the ground
and dies bears the fruit.

Christ's death as sacrifice.—It is in Hebrews mainly that the
death of Jesus is set forth as sacrifice (5:9; 7:27; 9:12,26–28;
10:11–12; 13:20). To best understand this approach, one
needs to observe the problem with which the writer was concerned. Some of those to whom the letter was addressed were
tempted either to revert to Judaism or to linger too close to their
Jewish background.[14] The writer is calling them onward from a
religion of shadows and types to a freer following of Jesus in the
religion of fulfilment and reality. He shows the provisional and
symbolic value of the old and the finality of Christ. Hence, he
sets forth Jesus as the true sacrifice, making obsolete the ritual

---

[14] Cf. thesis of William Manson, *The Epistle to the Hebrews* (London:
Hodder & Stoughton, Ltd., 1951), pp. 15 f.

sacrifices. This presentation of the death of Jesus met the peculiar needs of his readers, meeting them on their ground and with their terminology. It is not in conflict with other New Testament portrayals of the death of Jesus.

It goes far beyond the writer of Hebrews to add the idea that this death was an appeasement or satisfaction offered to the Father. What he affirmed is that Jesus is the true High Priest and true sacrifice; Jesus offered himself! In Hebrews as well as elsewhere, the Father and the Son are one. The writer began with the assertion that God had spoken to us in his Son. What then Jesus did in his death represents the mind of the Father and not just that of the Son. Christ's sacrifice, his self-giving, is the self-giving of the Father in the Son, not an offering of the Son to the Father.

If one takes seriously John's assertion that the Word who became flesh is the Word who was from the beginning, the Word who was with God, and the Word who was God, then must he recognize God in the Incarnate One. He must recognize that at Golgotha the Father is present. If one takes seriously the assertion of the author of Hebrews that the very God who had previously spoken in the prophets, had now spoken in his Son, then at the cross the Father is to be heard and not only the Son. This is to say, if in Jesus is the supreme manifestation of God, then at the cross we are to see God—the Father and the Son—in suffering, redeeming love. We are not to see an angry Father being appeased or satisfied by the sacrifice of a loving Son. Rather at the cross we see the Father in the Son.

Christ's death as substitution.—The substitutionary aspect of the death of Jesus is set forth in various passages. Galatians 3:13 is clear in this respect: "Christ redeemed us from the curse of the law, having become a curse for us: for it is written, Cursed is every one that hangeth on a tree." Surely he suffered because of our sins and not his own. But this suffering is not to be excluded from the Father and ascribed only to the Son. The parable of the father and two sons in Luke 15 will not allow for any picture of the Father free of suffering. Jesus became a curse for us, yet surely not in the sense that he himself became a sinner. The picture of the Father's turning from the Son because the Son had become sin does not come from the New Testament. William J. Wolf has well observed:

God did not punish Christ. It is monstrous to picture the Father deliberately inflicting punishment on his beloved and obedient Son as a scapegoat. The truth of these affirmations is that God's love in Christ leads Christ to identify himself with the full consequences of human sin.[15]

The death Jesus died is for us; he did for us what we cannot do ourselves. But the further truth is that by this death which he died, he would enable us to die with him. His cup we are to drink, and his baptism we, too, are to be baptized with (Mark 10:38). In 2 Corinthians 5:14 f. Paul's very point is that the death he died we also are to die, in order that we no longer live to ourselves but unto him. The cross has saving value as Christ enables us to die to self that we might live to God.

Substitution is a serviceable term for the death of Jesus if properly employed. To transfer to it all that belongs to the word in current usage is to obscure the New Testament doctrine. In modern sports, a player may be taken from the game and be replaced by a "substitute." But Jesus never becomes our substitute in that sense. We are never taken out of the game. Rather Jesus quickens in us the faith by which we admit him into ourselves and our struggle. He in us brings about the victory over death unto life as he effects the death of the old man and the birth of the new. Jesus alone can save, but he does not send us to the bench while he plays the game for us. In us he achieves what we could never achieve of ourselves.

Existential: a way of life shared.—Salvation is not only a rescue; it is a cure. In Acts the disciples were followers of the way. In conversion one is brought into the way of God, which is the way of the cross. Man is delivered from the Adamic way of self-love, self-trust, self-assertion, self-worship to the way of the

[15] *Op. cit.,* p. 87.

cross, the way of self-denial and self-giving rooted in faith in God.

It is this writer's conviction that the chief weakness of each "rationale" of the cross, including this one, is in the failure to represent adequately the *demand* of the cross. The *gift* cannot be exaggerated, nor can the *demand* be exaggerated. What Jesus did *for* us and what he does *in* us must be kept in proper balance.

The New Testament knows of no salvation except one. That is accomplished in the human self as God in Christ Jesus gains such entrance into man as to transform him from within. The cross must become a living reality within the heart of man, else it is for him only judgment and not redemption. So soon as he had set forth the fact of his own death, Jesus called men to that same death, set forth as his "cup" or his "baptism" (Luke 12:50; Mark 10:38). He proclaimed that the grain of wheat must die to bear fruit and that to seek to save life is to lose it, while to surrender it is to gain it (John 12:24 ff.).

Paul followed the teaching of Jesus in making central in his message the death in which the disciple is to follow the Master. Galatians 2:20 tells us that he was crucified with Christ; 2 Corinthians tells us that he always bore in his body the dying of Christ. In Romans 6:1–11 the believer is baptized into Christ's death; in Romans 7:4 believers are made dead to the law through the body of Christ. In Philippians 2:5–11 the readers are summoned to the mind of Christ, which mind is set forth as his utter self-renunciation. In Philippians 3:10 f. Paul told how he yearned to know Christ in the fellowship of his sufferings, conformed to his death. In Colossians 2:20 the readers are described as having died with Christ. These are not isolated proof texts but are the heart of the New Testament. The cross is *God's gift and God's demand.* Christ died for us; and again, in Christ we are crucified that we may be delivered from the false way of Adam to the true way of Christ.

This is *not* to be seen as in the final analysis a work of man by which he effects his own salvation. It is first and last the work of Christ effected in man. Although the New Testament speaks of the death of Jesus as an example which we are to follow (1 Peter 2:21), it says far more than that. It holds out no hope that any man can simply through his own power follow that example. Rather it calls man to man's one part, that of faith. Faith is trust, and faith is receiving.[16] It is openness of heart and life to him that he might come in to live and save.

By faith man receives into his person and life Jesus, who alone can bring about the death of the old egocentric man and in his stead create the new man in whom the cross becomes a way of life. Paul wrote of being crucified with Christ, and it is significant that he used the passive voice. Paul never boasted that he slew the old self or crucified himself; rather, this crucifixion of the old self he attributed to Christ Jesus. There is salvation only in the cross, but the cross is encountered only in the person of Jesus, who in the man of faith is a personal and transforming presence.

We are saved by a Saviour, redeemed by a Redeemer. From first to last, salvation is *personal*. Salvation cannot be reduced to a set of abstract propositions. Christ saves us. First Peter cites Christ's suffering for us as "an example" that we "should follow in his steps" (2:21). But the epistle says more than this. Jesus bore our sins for us "that we, having died unto sins, might live unto righteousness" (v. 24). He is the Healer, the Shepherd, and the Overseer of us whom he saves. The writer of Hebrews pictured Christ as the one who makes a "fresh and living way" for us into the presence of God through his life that is given (10:19 f.). Thus he is our example, but he is more. He personally rescues, heals, and delivers us. He comes to get us and to take us home by the "way of the cross."

A child is lost in a heavy snow; he is unable to make his way home. His father goes to him to bring him home. Several plans could be considered. The father could set an example, asking the child to make his way home by imitating the father, each making his path through the snow. But example is not enough; the

---

[16] Cf. Brunner, *Der Römerbrief*, p. 10.

snow is too deep for the child. A second plan could be considered. The child could remain where he is, and the father could go home for him. This would leave the child in the snow. A third way would be for the father to take the hand of the child and *lead* him home, breaking through the snow for the child. Thus the child returns home, but as one *rescued*. He walks in the strength of another.

Christ saves us in his work of deliverance. He does something for us; but more than that, he does something in us.

The
Kingdom
6 of God

THE KINGDOM of God means the kingship or kingly rule of God. The kingdom of heaven, the kingdom of the Father, and the kingdom are variant expressions for the same New Testament claim, namely, that God is King. His kingship is to be acknowledged over all.

God's Rule Through Christ

Yahweh as King.—A basic idea in the Old Testament is that Yahweh is King (Num. 23:21; Deut. 33:5; 1 Kings 22:19; Isa. 6:5; Zech. 14:9). At an early time Israel thought of God as Lord, demanding obedience and offering his protection and help.[1] In Isaiah 43:14 f. Yahweh is Creator, Redeemer, and King; in Micah 5:2,4 he is King and Shepherd. The great coronation psalms (cf. 47; 93; 95; 97; 99) present Yahweh as King. Von Rad points out that "the pre-exilic passages mostly describe Yahweh as Israel's King and promise help, deliverance, justice, and joy for the chosen people, whereas in the exilic and post-exilic there are also pointers to Yahweh's kingship over the world."[2]

Malkhûth or kingship.—The Greek *basileia* in the New Testament corresponds to the Hebrew *malkhûth* of the Old Testament. The Jewish expression corresponding to *hē basileia tōn ouranōn*

---

[1] Gerhard von Rad, *"Melek* and *Malkûth* in the Old Testament," in Coates, *op. cit.,* Vol. II, Sec. VII, 9.

[2] *Ibid.,* p. 11.

149

is the Hebrew *malkhûth shāmayim* and the Aramaic *malkhûthā' dishmayyā'*.[3] The word *malkhûth* means kingship; *malkhûth shāmayim* designates the kingship of heaven (i.e., of God). In the New Testament, accordingly, "the kingdom of heaven," "the kingdom of God," and "the kingdom" are expressions for the kingship or rule of God.

Malkhûth is employed in the Old Testament usually in a secular sense for political kingship (cf. 1 Sam. 20:31; 1 Kings 2:12); but it is used also for the sphere of the sovereignty of Yahweh, who is *Melek* (king), as in Psalms 103:19; 145:11, 13; and Daniel 4:17,25.[4] In Daniel 7:14,18,22,27 the Aramaic word *malkhû* is employed to designate the rule given to the righteous in Israel over all the nations. Flew says of this passage in Daniel, "It does not mean that the saints of the Most High constitute a community among themselves; they exercise a sovereignty delegated to them by God Himself." [5] "Kingdom" in this usage means rule, sovereignty, kingship. Dalman is emphatic as to the meaning of *malkhûth:*

> No doubt can be entertained that both in the Old Testament and in Jewish literature *malkhûth,* when applied to God, means always the "kingly rule," never the "kingdom," as if it were meant to suggest the territory governed by Him. . . . Today as in antiquity an Oriental "kingdom" is not a body politic in our sense, a people or land under some form of constitution, but merely a "sovereignty" which embraces a particular territory.[6]

The Jewish use of *malkhûth shāmayim,* kingdom of heaven, reflects the tendency of late Judaism to avoid verbal references to God, replacing them with abstract formulations, presumably out of reverence for God. Kuhn, writing to this effect, says that the term

. . . is, therefore, closely connected with the term *shekînah.* Just as the latter is simply a substitute for the Old Testament sentence

---

[3] Dalman, *The Words of Jesus,* p. 91.
[4] Von Rad, *op. cit.,* pp. 12 f.
[5] Flew, *op. cit.,* p. 21.
[6] *The Words of Jesus,* p. 94.

shâkhan Yahweh "God dwells" . . . "God is present," so the expression *malkûth shâmayim* appears in late Judaism in place of the Old Testament *"malak Yahweh,"* "God is King." [7]

The Targums, Aramaic translations of the Hebrew Old Testament, made the substitution of "kingdom of God" for "God is King." The statement "Yahweh reigns" in Exodus 15:18 is given in the Onkelos Targum as "God's kingdom stands firm"; and the Targum to Isaiah 24:23 has "God's kingdom is revealed" for the Old Testament "The Lord is King." [8] Clearly, then, "kingdom" meant "kingship" or "rule."

Kingdom of God and kingdom of heaven.—There is no difference in the meaning of "the kingdom of heaven," peculiar to the Gospel of Matthew, and "the kingdom of God," used consistently by Mark and Luke and occasionally by Matthew. This interchange roots in the Jewish avoidance of the name of God by replacing it with "heaven." The Hebrew *malkhûth shâmayim* is given a literal translation in Matthew as *hē basileia tōn ouranōn* (the kingdom of heaven); but Mark and Luke preserve the actual meaning in the rendering *hē basileia tou theou* (the kingdom of God). From this Jewish origin of "kingdom of heaven" or "kingdom of God" it is clear that the meaning cannot be kingdom in the sense of territory but in the sense that God is King. [9]

Comparative study of the Gospels will show conclusively that there is no difference in meaning between their use of "kingdom of God" and "kingdom of heaven." According to Mark 1:15, Jesus preached, "the kingdom of God has drawn near." The parallel in Matthew 4:17 reads: "the kingdom of heaven has drawn near." "Kingdom of God" appears fourteen times in Mark, thirty-two times in Luke, and four times in Matthew. "Kingdom of heaven" appears thirty-three times in Matthew and nowhere else in the New Testament. Mark 1:15 has "kingdom of

[7] Karl Georg Kuhn, *"Malkûth Shâmayim in Rabbinic Literature,"* in Coates, *op. cit.,* Vol. II., Sec. VII, 9.

[8] *Ibid.*

[9] *Ibid.,* p. 16.

God" where Matthew 4:17 has "kingdom of heaven." Matthew
5:3 has "Blessed are the poor in spirit: for theirs is the kingdom
of heaven" whereas Luke 6:20 has "Blessed are ye poor: for
yours is the kingdom of God." Of John the Baptist it was said in
Matthew 11:11 that "he that is but little in the kingdom of
heaven is greater than he"; in Luke 7:28 one reads: "Yet he
that is but little in the kingdom of God is greater than he." The
same equivalence may be seen by comparing Mark 4:11 and
Luke 8:10 with Matthew 13:11.

The Gospel of John has "kingdom of God" twice (3:3,5).
The term "eternal life" is used by John in relationship to the
kingdom of God, but the terms are not equated. Eternal life is
life received and lived under the kingdom or rule of God. The
term "kingdom of God" appears occasionally in Acts, Romans,
1 Corinthians, 2 Thessalonians, and Revelation. The same reality is set forth variously as "the kingdom," "his kingdom," "thy
kingdom," and "the kingdom of the Father."

Fallacy of building the kingdom.—Popular ideas have equated
the kingdom of God with Utopia, some establishment of peace
on earth by man's efforts. To Albrecht Ritschl it meant "the
organization of humanity through action inspired by love," and
to Wilhelm Herrmann it meant "the universal moral community, the aspect under which humanity is included in God's
purpose for Himself." [10] This view held sway at the height of
"liberalism's" nineteenth-century optimism about man. It yet
survives in principle among those who speak of "building the
kingdom of God." The kingdom or rule of God, however, does
not come by human decision or work. The kingdom of God
comes to us; God is King apart from our decision or work. In
the Model Prayer the petitions "Thy kingdom come" and "Thy
will be done in earth as it is in heaven" are not synonymous,
for the second depends upon the first.[11] It is God's coming to us
in his kingship which enables us to do his will.

[10] Quoted by Flew, *op. cit.*, p. 20.
[11] Cf. Rudolf Otto, *The Kingdom of God and the Son of Man*, trans. Floyd
V. Filson and Bertram Lee-Wolf (London: Lutterworth Press, 1951), pp.
38 f.

THE KINGDOM OF GOD

Much well-meaning effort today seems to be unwittingly based on the "liberal" idea that man is the master of things. Evangelism, the proclaiming of the good news of what God has done and is doing, is easily exchanged for a "soul-winning" which relies upon salesmanship gimmicks, the manipulation of people through the power of practical skills, the winning of arguments by having all the answers. The inescapable duty of witnessing to God's salvation becomes the Christian's high privilege; but it is not to be confused with man's conceit in trying through his own smartness and energies (sometimes quite nervous ones) to bring in the kingdom of God. The kingdom of God *comes to us* (Mark 1:15; Matt. 3:2); we do not bring it to earth.

At least fourteen different verb forms are employed in the New Testament in reference to the kingdom, but not once does it speak of man as *building* the kingdom. It is God's alone to give or to establish; it is man's to await, to receive, to enter, and to proclaim. If the piling up of references may be pardoned, the following paragraph will demonstrate this significant fact.

The New Testament speaks of God's *giving* (*dounai*) the kingdom (Luke 12:32), his *appointing* (*diatithenai*) the kingdom (Luke 22:29), Christ's *restoring* (*apokathistanein*) the kingdom (Acts 1:6), his *delivering* (*paradidonai*) the kingdom (1 Cor. 15:24), God's *translating* us (*metatithenai*) into the kingdom, of *preaching* (*kērussein*) the kingdom (Mark 1:14; Matt. 4:23; 9:35; Luke 4:43; 9:2; 16:16; Acts 8:12; 20:25; 28:31), *proclaiming* (*diangellein*) the kingdom (Luke 9:60), *speaking* (*lalein* and *legein*) the kingdom (Luke 9:11; Acts 1:3), *witnessing to* (*diamarturesthai*) the kingdom (Acts 28:23), *awaiting* (*prosdechesthai*) the kingdom (Mark 15:43; Luke 23:51), *inheriting* (*klēronomein*) the kingdom (Matt. 25:34; 1 Cor. 6:9; 15:50; Gal. 5:21; Eph. 5:5); *seeing* (*idein*) the kingdom (Mark 9:1; Luke 9:27; John 3:3); *receiving* (*dechesthai*) the kingdom (Mark 10:15; Luke 18:17); and *entering* (*eiselthein*) the kingdom (Mark 9:47; 10:25; Matt. 5:20; 7:21; Luke 18:25; John 3:5; Acts 14:22).

Nowhere does the New Testament speak of our *building* the

kingdom. The kingdom is God's rule, and we do not establish it. It is our part to receive it and to proclaim it.

Kingdom and church.—A common error is that of equating the kingdom of God with the church. There is a close relationship between the kingdom of God and the church, but they are not identical. Whereas the kingdom is the sovereignty of God, the church is the fellowship of persons made one people under that sovereignty. God's kingdom in one sense is absolute, over all that is. There are rebels who reject his rule, but God is not thereby dethroned and he has not abdicated his throne. He remains God and he remains King, whatever man's decision. On the other hand, the New Testament is chiefly concerned with the kingdom of God as his rule over willing subjects who yield to his sovereign claims as ultimate. The church, the body of Christ, is God's own community of people: called, redeemed, made new, and made one people under one King.

Kingdom and decision.—It has just been said that God's kingdom does not await man's decision. God's being King does not depend upon man's consent. That is not to say, however, that the kingdom of God has not approached us with the call to repentance, a turning to God, in view of the fact that the kingdom of God has drawn near (Mark 1:15; Matt. 3:2). Man's decision does not determine the fact of God's being King, but it does determine the nature of man's relation to the kingdom. Man decides for himself to be either rebel—who nonetheless must answer to God—or willing subject now made participant in God's rule.

The fact that the kingdom calls for decision is emphasized in the New Testament by the employment of the term *kairos,* which here is an eschatological term designating "the time of crisis" or "the last times." [12] When Jesus came preaching the gospel (good news) of God, he declared that "the *kairos* has been fulfilled, and the kingdom of God has drawn near" (Mark 1:15). This was not just a matter of chronology (*chronos*) but of the season of fulfilment.

[12] Arndt and Gingrich, *op. cit.,* p. 396.

This season of fulfilment was also crisis (*krisis* means judgment). In the presence of the kingdom, man is compelled to make a decision. He may, to his own destruction, cling to the false way of self-worship or he may yield tc the absolute claim of God, confronting him as the kingdom or rule of God in Jesus Christ. The idea of *opportunity* belongs to that of *kairos*—opportunity which God has provided. This *kairos, season of opportunity, is also one of demand, calling for man's response to the opportunity.*[13] So, in announcing that the "*kairos* had drawn near," Jesus proclaimed the God-given season of judgment (*krisis*), of opportunity, and of demand. This *kairos* came in terms of the kingdom of God, God's active ruling in Christ, calling men to repentance and faith.

The Kingdom as Present

That in the New Testament the kingdom of God is seen to have come—in some sense to have newly come—seems to be an unmistakable fact. The *kairos* has been fulfilled and the kingdom has drawn near! (Mark 1:15). God has already, in the person of Jesus Christ, inaugurated his rule. A. M. Hunter wisely asks, "To begin with, what is the sense in saying that 'the appointed time has fully come' if in fact the Kingdom is still around the corner?"[14]

Near or present?—Much debate has centered around the meaning of *ēngiken* in Mark 1:15, whether the meaning is "drawn near" or "has arrived." C. H. Dodd[15] has argued that the translation should be: "The Kingdom of God has arrived." Others insist that the meaning is only that the kingdom is "at hand" or "near." In this context, the difference between the two meanings is slight, though important. The Greek verb is based on the adjective *engus* meaning "near." The verb may be used to describe that which is *very* near, so near as to be pres-

[13] Cf. Richardson, *Theological Word Book,* p. 258.
[14] *Introducing New Testament Theology* (Philadelphia: The Westminster Press, 1957), p. 27.
[15] *The Parables of the Kingdom* (London: James Nisbet & Co., 1946), pp. 44 f.

ent,[16] as may be seen in Matthew 26:46 f., "Behold, the one betraying me has drawn near (*ēngiken*). And while he was yet speaking, behold Judas came." Probably the question of whether or not the kingdom has arrived is not to be settled from this verb. Other evidences are more conclusive for the view that the kingdom has already arrived. Passages with *engazein* probably stress its imminence.

Arrived.—The verb *ephthasen* seems more definitely to describe the kingdom of God as already inaugurated (cf. Matt. 12:28: Luke 11:20). The idea of actual arrival, possibly sometimes the further idea of anticipation, is clearly present in Romans 9:31; 2 Corinthians 10:14; Philippians 3:16; 1 Thessalonians 2:16; 4:15, though these references are not to the kingdom. Actual arrival of the kingdom is unmistakable in Matthew 12:28, "If I by the Spirit of God cast out demons, indeed the kingdom of God has come [*ephthasen*] upon you." Here two kingdoms have already met; the kingship of God is overcoming that of Satan.

The parallel in Luke 11:20 reads: "If by the finger of God I am casting out demons, indeed the kingdom of God has come [*ephthasen*] upon you." In the Old Testament the "finger of God" describes his power in creation (Psalm 8:3), in redemption from bondage (Ex. 8:19), and in revelation (Ex. 31:18). The very power of God which came to expression in these mighty acts of creation, redemption, and revelation is now at work in Jesus. This is the kingdom of God overcoming the kingdom of Satan. The miracles are signs of the kingdom, already having been inaugurated. The analogy that the strong man must be bound before he can be robbed, maintains that Satan is already being overcome as evidenced by the casting out of demons (Mark 3:27).

Among or within?—An ambiguity is encountered in the announcement in Luke 17:21: "Behold, the kingdom of God is *entos humōn* [within or among you]." The adverb *entos* may

---

[16] The English "present" is from the Latin *prae* (before) and *esse* (to be), hence *to be before*, with no fixed distance specified.

mean "within" or "in the midst of." The meaning may be that the kingdom of God is not to be identified with a rebellion led by Zealots, but it is the rule of God within those who respond in obedient faith. Perhaps the meaning is that the kingdom is not that which awaits some "messianic" war; it is already present in their midst. Otto was probably correct in attributing to Jesus the unique idea "that the kingdom—supermundane, future, and belonging to a new era—penetrated from the future into the present . . . and was operative redemptively as a divine *dunamis* as an inbreaking realm of salvation." [17] With either meaning, "within you" or "in your midst," the claim is clear that the kingdom is already present.

Messianic works reflecting kingdom's presence.—In Matthew 11:2–19 (Luke 7:18–35) the question of the identity of Jesus is answered in terms of his works. John the Baptist sent his messengers to Jesus asking: "Are you the Coming One, or shall we await another?" In reply, Jesus pointed to his works of giving sight to the blind, strength to the lame, cleansing to the lepers, hearing to the deaf, life to the dead, and the gospel to the poor (11:5 f.). The allusion apparently is to the promises in Isaiah (29:18 ff.; 35:5 ff.; 61:1), promises to be realized under the gracious reign of Yahweh: "For Yahweh is our judge, Yahweh is our lawgiver, Yahweh is our king; he will save us" (Isa. 33:22).

Although John's question was about "the Coming One," the idea is bound up with that of God's kingdom. The works to which Jesus was giving himself did not conform to the ones expected by those wanting the overthrow of foreign rule, reestablishment of Israel as a glorious nation, with open judgments and vindications for the "wicked" and the "good." Jesus said in effect, that these very works which he was doing, however unmessianic they may have appeared to be, were true signs that he was "the Coming One." That he also meant that these were signs of the inbreaking of the kingdom would seem to follow from Matthew 11:11–15.

[17] *Op. cit.*, p. 72.

The translation of Matthew 11:12 is debated, but the weight of evidence favors this: "From the days of John the Baptist until now, the kingdom of heaven is being violently assaulted and violent men seize it by force." Possibly Jesus referred to those like the Zealots who wanted to *use* the kingdom for their own political purposes. Whatever the precise meaning, at least it is clear, as Kümmel well says, "that Jesus considers his presence to be a time in which the Kingdom of God can already be attacked as being present." [18] In Luke's parallel account, it is clear that the kingdom is viewed as being present: "The law and the prophets were until John: from then the kingdom of God is being proclaimed and everyone violently assaults it" (16:16).

Parables of the kingdom.—Many of the parables of Jesus are concerned with the kingdom of God. Whether or not they teach the presence of the kingdom is endlessly debated. It seems to this writer that at least they do not exclude the idea of the presence of the kingdom even though that may not affirm it. Much depends upon subjective conclusions in difficult exegesis.

The parable of the sower (Mark 4:3–25; Matt. 13:3–23; Luke 8:5–18) is concerned with the "mystery" of the kingdom of God (Mark 4:11; Matt. 13:11; Luke 8:10). Two facts are emphasized: (1) The knowledge of the kingdom is *given*, not discovered or achieved, and (2) the responsibility for receiving rests upon the hearers; it is not imposed. Hearers differ, as do the soils (impenetrable, shallow, mixed, fallow). Seeing and hearing are possibilities which God alone can open up to man, but man is responsible for receiving. The crowds are sifted not by arbitrary fate but responsible hearing. They were being confronted then and there with the "mystery of the kingdom," but this leaves open the question of whether or not the kingdom itself was present.

It is widely held today that the real point of the parable as in-

---

[18] W. G. Kümmel, *Promise and Fulfilment: The Eschatological Message of Jesus*, trans. by Dorothea M. Barton, (Naperville, Ill.: Alec R. Allenson, Inc., 1957), p. 123.

tended by Jesus is to be found in the certainty of the harvest, not in the variety of soils. Despite hard ground, birds, and thorns, the harvest is assured. Thus understood, the parable is eschatological, proclaiming the inbreaking of God's kingdom and the certainty of its triumph.

In the parable of the seed growing of itself (Mark 4:26–29) the point is that the kingdom of God is in truth *of God* and not of man. Bultmann is of this judgment:

From this *parable of the seed growing of itself,* in which "of itself" is the point, one must not draw the conclusion that God's Reign (or Kingdom) is an entity growing in history; rather it assumes that its coming is a miracle independent of every human act—as miraculous as the growth and ripening of seed, which proceeds without human help or comprehension.[19]

Probably Kümmel, to be more precise, is correct in seeing the point of the parable to be the certainty of the arrival of the "harvest," that is the eschatological judgment, which man cannot influence.[20] This parable supports the evidence elsewhere that the kingdom of God is his reign or kingship and that its reality does not depend upon man's decision. The parable is not conclusive as to whether the kingdom is viewed as already present or future.

The parable of the tares (Matt. 13:24–30) and that of the dragnet (Matt. 13:47–50) both seem to present the kingdom as judgment. In a sense it is delayed judgment. Those looking for the kingdom of God expected judgment to come at its inauguration. Kingdom ideas of the day did not expect Herod Antipas to remain on the throne, Judas to continue in the inner circle, or John and Jesus to be put to death. They expected something catastrophic, the open overthrow of the evil and the vindication of the good.

The simplest interpretation of these parables seems to be found against that background of confused kingdom hopes.

[19] *Theology of the New Testament,* I, 8.
[20] *Op. cit.,* p. 128.

Jesus was teaching that the kingdom includes judgment, but this in its open expression marks the consummation, not the inauguration of the kingdom. The separation of the good from the bad is God's business, and it will be done at the last judgment. The *present* already had an eschatological character, for the ultimate judgment is bound up with the inbreaking of the kingdom in the person of Jesus. These parables do not affirm that the kingdom is already present, but they are congenial to that idea.

The parables of the mustard seed (Mark 4:30–32) and the leaven (Matt. 13:33) alike seem to contrast the small beginning and the great ending of the kingdom. From the tiny seed comes the large plant; from the inconspicuous leaven comes the unexpected result. Kümmel holds that these parables stress only the fact that "the glorious finish is completely certain in spite of the humble start," that the "Kingdom of God will come, even if the all too small beginnings appear to gainsay it." [21] But apparently the kingdom is in some sense viewed as already present. The kingdom was present in Jesus, in what he did and said. The quiet beginnings of the ministry of Jesus did not accord with the expected "ax at the root of the trees" or with the expected expulsion of the Romans by force of arms. Jesus is saying that the kingdom *will come* in its magnitude, but is he not also saying that it *has come* already in what seems to be an insignificant beginning?

The parables of the hidden treasure (Matt. 13:44) and the pearl of great price (Matt. 13:45–46) form another pair, setting forth not only the supreme worth of the kingdom, but especially underscoring the demand for decision. The kingdom of God confronts man with the urgency of decision, at whatever cost. The demand is ultimate and absolute. One must, like the men in the parables, "sell all." This is not to suggest that the kingdom may be bought or earned. It is to say that God's absolutely free *gift* is also absolute *demand*. These parables do not say whether the kingdom is present or not; but the very

[21] *Op. cit.,* pp. 131, 132.

urgency for decision arises out of the fact that the kingdom is in the person of Jesus confronting man here and now. These parables, in their implication, parallel the earlier preaching of Jesus: "The *kairos* [season] has been fulfilled, and the kingdom of God has drawn near; repent and trust in the gospel" (Mark 1:15).

The Kingdom as Future

The kingdom of God is in some sense both present and future in the New Testament. In the Model Prayer we are taught to pray, "Thy Kingdom come" (Matt. 6:10); and also in the Sermon on the Mount we are taught to "seek first the kingdom of God" (Matt. 6:33). But in the Beatitudes of the same Sermon is the repeated assurance that the kingdom belongs to the poor in spirit (Matt. 5:3) and to those persecuted for righteousness' sake (v. 10). There is no hint that this is a promise to be fulfilled only in the future. Present and future are bound together in the Sermon on the Mount, as elsewhere in the New Testament.

A coming in power.—Mark 9:1 seems to point to some future coming of the kingdom, with no necessary denial that it has already come, and with the possible implication that it has come. Jesus gave assurance that there were some who would not die until "they see the kingdom of God having come [*elēluthuian*] in power." C. H. Dodd [22] understands that by this Jesus meant that some of his generation would live to see that the kingdom had already come, the emphasis being on the seeing, not the coming of the kingdom. Others find the emphasis upon its coming at that time "in power," as contrasted with its earlier coming. The point is inconclusive, but probably the verse is best seen as a reference to a future coming, with no necessary denial that already the kingdom has come in some sense.

At the Last Supper, Jesus indicated a future coming of the kingdom: "Not at all shall I drink of the fruit of the vine from

[22] *Parables of the Kingdom*, pp. 42, 53 f.

now until the kingdom of God come" (Luke 22:18). The parallel in Mark 14:25 (Matt. 26:29) reads: "until that day when I drink it new with you in the kingdom of God." The Lukan reading clearly anticipates a future coming, but this does not necessarily deny a past coming of the kingdom.

There is strong evidence throughout the New Testament that Christ was expected to come in a future sense, and this is bound up with the kingdom as future, or the consummation of the kingdom. The expectation made explicit in Acts 1:11 is in effect found throughout the New Testament: "This same Jesus, the one received up from you into heaven, thus shall come in which manner ye saw him going into heaven."

The *parousia* passages are difficult, and it is not always clear whether the meaning is "presence" or "coming," but the early Christians did expect a coming of Christ beyond history.[23] In 1 Thessalonians 3:13 the reference to "the *parousia* of our Lord Jesus with all his saints" most plausibly refers to a coming beyond history rather than only a coming within history. Paul's assurance in 1 Thessalonians 4:15 that those alive at the *parousia* will have no advantage over the Christian dead unmistakably refers to a coming of Christ at the end of this stream of history as we now know it. The Aramaic expression *Marana tha* ("Lord, come!") of the New Testament clearly reflects the expectation of the earliest Christians of a coming of the Lord. That this may preserve their prayer that the Lord come to them in the observance of the Lord's Supper is probable, but that does not exclude their expectation of his coming beyond history, bringing to consummation the kingdom of God.

To see the kingdom of God as culminating at the "end of history" in judgment and a fulfilled redemption accords with the eschatological orientation of Hebrew and Christian faith. The conviction that history is being "guided to a destination by

---

[23] George R. Beasley-Murray in *Jesus and the Future: The Eschatological Discourse, Mark 13 with Special Reference to the Little Apocalypse Theory* (London: The Macmillan Co., 1954), seems to this writer to have a sounder argument than does Robinson in *Jesus and His Coming* (New York: Abingdon Press, 1957).

God" [24] is basic to the faith of Old and New Testaments. History is not cyclic, doomed to retrace its steps as though on a treadmill. Neither is it evolutionary, improving under its own power. Eschatology stands for the faith that God who is before and above all history is also within it, carrying it forward to a goal, an *eschaton*.

On the negative side this goal will mean judgment, the complete rejection and overthrow of the powers of evil. On the positive side this will be vindication of the right and the completion of redemption in the "redemption of the body" (and the cosmos?). Judgment and redemption are already real, but they will be completed. The kingdom of God (his sovereign rule), already at work in judgment and salvation, will at the end of history triumph fully. Eschatology, the biblical doctrine of a goal to which God is bringing history, requires the conclusion that the God who will stand at the end of history as King is already present as King. In Christ the kingdom has come and in him it will come.

Conclusion: present and coming.—The view that the kingdom of God is present already and the view that the kingdom is yet to come are both securely based in New Testament faith. The harmony of these views is to be found in Jesus Christ himself. The kingdom has already come in Christ, and it will come at "the end of the world" in the same Christ. The inauguration and the consummation of the kingdom alike are in him. The powers already at work in Jesus, overcoming the forces of evil, are the powers of the age to come. In Jesus the coming age has broken into this age. Otto correctly sees as included when the kingdom of God is preached:

Divine dignity and glory; sovereign claim and the requirement that the will of the Lord be effective; realm of sovereignty and heavenly realm; heavenly world coming into this world; miraculous power and coercion of the devil; healing and performance of miracle; charismatic preaching and seeking of the lost; consciousness of mission

[24] John Bright, *The Kingdom of God* (Nashville: Abingdon-Cokesbury Press, 1953), p. 29.

as the secret Son of Man; divine judgment and sternest call to repentance; new righteousness with strongest tension of will, and yet praise of childlike attitude which no will can create and no man confer on himself; transcendental domain of salvation, which does not harass the will by threatening but draws it by attraction; purely *a coming and future reality,* and precisely as such on the point of breaking in, indeed, *already in the process of breaking in;* mysterious, imperceptible, but visible to "blessed" eyes; an operative and penetrating power.[25]

In Christ we are called *now* to decision which determines one's relationship to the coming kingdom (Mark 8:38; Matt. 19:28; Luke 12:32). Kümmel neatly shows the relationship between "promise and fulfilment" as they are brought together in Jesus:

Jesus linked the present in a quite peculiar way to the future by speaking of his return as judge and by making the attitude of men to the earthly Jesus the criterion for the verdict of Jesus, the eschatological judge. This in itself turns Jesus' presence into a *real* eschatological present, instead of its being merely a period for awaiting the eschatological consummation.[26]

This is to say that the kingdom of God confronts us as a person; it has come, it comes, and it will come in Jesus Christ. The kingdom of God is "realized" or inaugurated already; it will be brought to consummation in Christ: "The kingdom [*basileia*] of the world became [*egeneto*] that of our Lord and his Christ [Anointed], and he shall be King forever!" (Rev. 11:15).

The Kingdom of Christ and Kingdom of God

Does the New Testament distinguish between the kingdom of Christ and the kingdom of God? According to one view, this distinction is real.[27] There are passages which seem to teach this. The kingdom of Christ is referred to often (cf. Matt. 13:41; 16:28; Luke 22:30; 23:42; John 18:36; 2 Tim. 4:1,18). The passage which seems most explicitly to make the kingdom of

[25] *Op. cit.,* p. 57; italics not in original.
[26] *Op. cit.,* p. 153.
[27] Cf. Cullmann, *Königsherrschaft Christi und Kirche im Neuen Testament* (Zollikon-Zürich: Evangelischer Verlag, 1950).

Christ of limited duration, ultimately giving way to the kingdom of God is 1 Corinthians 15:23–28:

Each in his own order: Christ the firstfruits; afterwards those of Christ
at his coming [*parousia*], then the end, when he shall deliver the
kingdom to God, even the Father; when he shall abolish every rule and
authority and power. For he must reign until he puts all enemies
under his feet. . . . When he shall subject to him all things, then
he himself, the Son, shall be subjected to the one having subjected
to him all things, in order that God may be all in all.

This seems clearly to anticipate an end to the kingdom of Christ,
finally yielded to the Father.

Christ's kingdom permanent.—There are passages in the New
Testament which reflect the view that the kingdom of Christ is
without end. Luke 1:33 says of Jesus: "He shall reign over the
house of Jacob forever, and of his kingdom there shall be no
end." Jesus said to Pilate, "My kingdom is not of this world"
(John 18:36). In 2 Timothy 4:1 Christ's appearing (*epi-
phaneia*) and his kingdom are so related that possibly Christ's
kingdom is thought to survive beyond his coming. In 2 Timothy
4:18, the writer expresses the faith that his Lord will save him
"into his heavenly kingdom." Probably "the Lord" here designates Jesus. A passage as explicit as Luke 1:33 in affirming the
permanency of Christ's kingdom is 2 Peter 1:11: "Thus richly
he shall supply to you the entrance into the eternal kingdom of
our Lord and Saviour, Jesus Christ."

One continuing kingdom.—The above quoted passages declare that the kingdom of Christ is eternal and that it will be
given over to the Father. Unless all be lost in hopeless conflict,
the kingdom of Christ and the kingdom of God must be seen
as one kingdom. This is explicit in various passages. Approach
to this may be seen in the Synoptics where Mark 10:29 "for my
sake, and the gospel's" becomes in Matthew 19:29 "for my
name's sake" and in Luke 18:29 "for the sake of the kingdom of
God." In Ephesians 5:5 *one* kingdom is attributed to the Father
and Son, where it is said of some that "they have not inheritance
in the kingdom of Christ and God."

The book of Revelation reaches a climax when it says, "The kingdom [rule] of the world became that of our Lord and his Christ, and he shall reign forever" (11:15). One kingdom forever is thus attributed to our Lord and his Anointed. In chapter 19 of Revelation is the shout, "The Lord, our God, the Almighty reigns!" (v. 6). In verse 16 of the same chapter is given the name of "the Word of God," i.e., the Christ, it being "King of kings and Lord of lords!"

The kingdom of Christ is the kingdom of God in the sense that the Father and the Son are one (cf. John 14:9–11; 17:11, 21–22). This is not to explain away the plain statements in 1 Corinthians 15:23–28 about delivering the kingdom to the Father, who is thus to be all in all. It is simply to recognize that the New Testament never abandons its monotheism, even in its doctrine of Incarnation. The kingdom of God comes in Jesus Christ, and in Christ it is yet the kingdom *of God*. That it is *one* kingdom will become clear at the consummation when the kingdom of God has triumphed completely over all.

Reigning with Christ

To enter the kingdom of God is not only to become a willing subject under the sovereignty of God; it is to participate in his reign! The amazing paradox is that man reigns with Christ precisely when he gives up all notions of reigning. Adam sought to rule and thus became a slave. Man always has sought to be sovereign. In Christ alone may man actually reign, and this is a reign which comes when least sought.

At a time when he was beleaguered by many foes determined to destroy him, and when his following was small and insignificant as measured by the world's standard of greatness, Jesus gave an amazing promise to his followers: he promised them that they should reign, saying: "Fear not, little flock; for it is your Father's good pleasure to give to you the kingdom!" (Luke 12:32). Paul built upon this promise in Romans 5:17, "For if by the transgression of one, death reigned through the one, by much more shall those receiving the abundance of the grace of the free gift of righteousness reign through the one, Jesus Christ."

Participation in the kingdom of God is recognized as an accomplished fact. Even when the Christian seems least to reign, as in times of persecution, he is assured of his present and continuing reign in Christ. Peter wrote at a time when sudden persecution had struck, and he assured those threatened disciples that they were "an elect race, a royal priesthood [*basileion hierateuma*], a holy nation, a people of God's own possession" (1 Peter 2:9).

The book of Revelation was written during a major crisis for the Christian world, at a time when the Roman emperor demanded that he be worshiped as God. In those dark days of persecution, when it seemed that every true Christian was already marked for martyrdom, when it seemed that the church was an insignificant community about to be destroyed by brute force, then it was that the seer proclaimed them to be a kingdom, already reigning with Christ. In Revelation 20:4 it is said of the martyrs, who had died for their witness to Christ, that "they became alive [*ezēsan*] and reigned [*ebasileusan*] with Christ a thousand years." This is taken by some to refer to a literal thousand years, yet future; but every principle of apocalyptic method and of the Revelation itself points to something far greater. The writer is not speaking of a future and limited reign; numbers in Revelation are symbolic. He is declaring a present and endless reign of *all* persons in Christ.

Every Christian is a person who has "died" in order to live. The first chapter of Revelation declares that the saints already reign in Christ, and the last chapter declares that they shall reign forever. In 1:9, John introduces himself as "your brother, and fellow participant in tribulation, and kingdom [*basileia*] and constancy in Jesus." In 5:9–10, Jesus is declared to be worthy of breaking the seals of the little book (of history and destiny?), because he was slain, and did purchase to God in his blood of every tribe, and tongue, and people, and nation; and it is said of him: "Thou didst make them to our God a kingdom and priests, and they reign [*basileuousin*] upon the earth." The manuscripts are about equally divided between the present and future tense for the verb "reign." Verse ten declares that they have been made a kingdom (*basileian*), so the present tense best suits the sentence. In 22:5 is the assurance given the saints that "they shall reign forever."

The "secret" to the participation of the saints in the kingdom of God is disclosed. In the Beatitudes the kingdom is said to belong to the poor in spirit (Matt. 5:3) and to those persecuted because of righteousness (Matt. 5:10). The "poor in spirit" are the "people of the land" ('*ammê hā'ārets*),[28] rich and poor, who know that they do not meet the demands of the law; they are sinners who know themselves to be undeserving. Precisely those who renounce all claims upon God, including the right to rule, are the ones who do reign. Those persecuted for the sake of righteousness, upbraided and slandered, seem by the world's standards to be discredited and defeated. Precisely they are the ones who reign.

Jesus gave a clear answer to the question of sitting with him in his kingdom. James and John (Mark 10:35), or their mother (Matt. 20:20), requested that they be permitted to occupy the places next to him in his "glory" (Mark 10:37) or in his kingdom (Matt. 20:21). He pointed them to the "cup" which he was to drink, to the "baptism" with which he was to be baptized (Mark 10:39; Matt. 20:22), referring to his death. He thus indicated that to reign was not a favor passed out, but a privilege which comes with the renunciation of all privilege and even of life itself.

Luke's parallel to this is found in 22:24–30, where the disciples were rebuked for seeking "greatness" by the world's false standards. He indicated the road to participation in his kingdom, saying, "But ye are they who have continued with me in my trials; and I appoint unto you a kingdom, even as [*kathōs*] my Father appointed to me; . . . and ye shall sit on thrones judging the twelve tribes of Israel" (22:28–30). His kingdom was

[28] Cf. Strack and Billerbeck, *op. cit., in loco.*

by sacrifice, not by seeking greatness. His throne was first of all a cross! A true understanding of Jesus prompted his interpreters to declare: "No cross, no crown!"

A most beautiful affirmation of faith in the true reign of the saints in Christ appears in 2 Timothy 2:11–12, all the more beautiful if, indeed, from the pen of one battle-scarred through years of missionary campaigning and now awaiting trial for his life. Said he, "If we died together, we also shall live together; if we endure together, we also shall reign together [sumbasileusomen]." The kingdom is God's reign and his alone. Yet a part of its mystery is that it is given to those who yield themselves to his claim as absolute and ultimate. Wanting to be king, man is slave. Willing to be slave, he becomes king, but king only as in Christ, God's Anointed, he is made to reign.

The
People
7 # of God

THIS CHAPTER could be entitled "The Church," but "The People of God" was selected as more flexible for the purpose. As employed here, "The People of God" will designate that fellowship of persons in Christ variously described in the New Testament as the *ekklēsia* (church), the body of Christ, the *koinōnia* of the Spirit, flock, Israel of God, elect race, royal priesthood, holy nation, God's own people, temple of God, seed of Abraham, and otherwise. Special attention will be given to the meaning of *ekklēsia, body of Christ, and *koinōnia*.

The term "church" has dominated Christian usage in describing the people of God. In the New Testament, the equivalent term is *ekklēsia;* and it is a major designation, especially in Acts, many epistles, and the Revelation. However, it is by no means the only major New Testament designation for the people of God.

The Bible is from first to last concerned with God's purpose to create a people for himself. Although there is understandable hesitation to speak of God as a person—certainly he is not just another person among persons—the Bible itself speaks of him in personal terms. God is never spoken of impersonally as "the First Cause," or "the Unmoved Mover." He is referred to as one who is, who speaks, who sees, who hears, who acts, who loves. It is no wonder, then, that he is represented as primarily concerned with people. When Jesus put man above the sabbath,

170

he did in principle exactly what God always is represented as doing. Man is God's first concern, according to the Bible. But man is a true person only in relationship, hence the creation of a community of persons is God's purpose or plan of the ages (Eph. 3:11).

The Old Testament is largely the story of the calling and creation of "Israel." Strictly speaking, God did not call Israel; he called individual persons to become Israel. A nation has no ears and cannot be called. God speaks to individuals; his calls are "person to person" and not "station to station." He calls individuals to become persons related to other persons in community.

When Adam missed his true destiny, giving himself to the fallacy of self-sufficiency, God turned to the creating of a true people for himself. The call of Abraham, Isaac, and Jacob was with a view to the creation of a people for his own possession. When national Israel proved to be "flesh," seeking as did Adam to be sufficient within herself, God turned to the creation of a remnant. The remnant itself proved elusive, and it finally came into realization in one person, the true Son of man, the true servant of God, even Christ Jesus. But he came, paradoxically, to be both an individual person and a "community." In him was created "one new man" (Eph. 2:15); the true Israel of God (Gal. 6:16; Rom. 9:6); the seed of Abraham (Gal. 3:29); an elect race, a royal priesthood, a holy nation, a people of God's possession (1 Peter 2:9).

The purpose of God to create in Israel his people, traced through the Old Testament, is a continued story in the New Testament. In Christ, God has come to call and create his people. The community of persons in Christ is Israel "purged and reconstituted." [1] The *ekklēsia* in the New Testament is a new creation, yet in a sense it is reconstituted Israel. Abraham, Issac, and Jacob will sit together with Peter, James, and John, as well as with people "from the east and the west" (Matt. 8:11). This true "Israel" is the church, the *ekklēsia* of God.

---

[1] Flew, *op. cit.*, p. 88.

The Intention of Jesus

Jesus came to create a fellowship of persons under the kingship of God. It has been pointed out by many that the word "church" appears in the Gospels only in Matthew 16:18 and 18:17; and because of this it has been argued that Jesus did not intend to establish a church. The virtual absence of the word "church" from the Gospels is a problem demanding attention, but only an inexcusable neglect of basic evidence can obscure the fact that Jesus did intend to create his church.

The absence of the term "church" from the Gospels, except in Matthew 16:18 and 18:17, is to some extent explained in the occurrence of many alternate terms used to describe the people of God. The contemplation of a divinely called and created people is reflected in the ideas of his "flock," the Son of man, the true vine, and the new family. The idea of a new Israel, explicit in the Epistles, is implicit in the Gospels. In their very nature the preaching and teaching of Jesus contemplate a special people. What we know almost exclusively as the "church," the New Testament knows by many terms.

Flock.—The "shepherd" and "flock" picture is a prominent one in both Old and New Testaments. Well known are the beautiful pastoral descriptions of the Old Testament, like the familiar twenty-third Psalm and Isaiah 40:11, "He will feed his flock like a shepherd, he will gather the lambs in his arm, and carry them in his bosom, and will gently lead those who have their young." These passages have their counterpart in the New Testament in a passage like Luke 12:32, "Fear not, little flock, for your Father was pleased to give you the kingdom." Chapter 10 of the Fourth Gospel gives great prominence to the analogy of shepherd and flock. Verse 16 preserves the concern of Jesus for a people who with himself may be "one flock, one shepherd."

The risen Lord's commission to Peter was given through the pastoral analogy: "Feed my lambs" (John 21:15), "Shepherd my sheep" (v. 16), and "Feed my sheep" (v. 17). On the night of his betrayal, Jesus described his followers as a flock as he said, "All of you shall be offended in me this night; for it is written, I will smite the shepherd, and the sheep of the flock shall be scattered" (Matt. 26:31). It is not surprising to find that Peter exhorted his fellow elders, "Shepherd the flock of God which is among you" (1 Peter 5:2).

Although "flock" and *ekklēsia* are quite distinct in history and usage, they do describe the same people of God. Actual interchange occurs in Paul's exhortation to the Ephesian elders, as found in Acts 20:28, "Take heed to yourselves, and to all the *flock,* in which the Holy Spirit placed you as bishops, *to shepherd* [*poimainein*] the *ekklēsia* of God, which he acquired through his own blood." What is explicit here may be implied in the Gospels. The "flock of God" is the *"ekklēsia* of God" under another designation. This is not to say that either term may be dropped without loss. To the contrary, each term is rich and meaningful in Jewish and Christian usage. The presence of the "flock" analogy in the Gospels does supply a part of the answer to the problem of the few occurrences of *"ekklēsia"* in the Gospels.

The true vine.—The term *ekklēsia* does not appear in the Fourth Gospel, but the idea is present. When Jesus said, "I am the true [real] vine" (John 15:1), he was claiming to be the true Israel of God. The vine was the familiar emblem for the nation of Israel, as it appeared on the coins of the Maccabees with this significance.[2] National Israel had failed to become the true people of God. At best the nation typified God's people. Jesus was the true (*alēthinē*) vine, the actual or true Israel.

The analogy of vine and branches describes the vital union between Christ and his followers, the fruit bearing natural to this union, and the cleansing or discipline proper to this relationship (John 15:1–8). But first of all, this passage indicates that God's purpose in Israel is realized in Jesus Christ; God's true people are those who by faith are made one with him. The word

[2] J. H. Bernard, *St. John* (*The International Critical Commentary* [Edinburgh: T. & T. Clark, 1928]), II, 478.

ekklēsia is not employed, but the idea of the people of God is there. Paul's analogy of the body and its members somewhat parallels that of vine and branches. Paul explicitly equates the "body" with the *ekklēsia* (cf. Col. 1:24; Eph. 1:22 f.). In the Fourth Gospel the "vine" is not explicitly equated with the *ekklēsia,* but the idea is there.

Son of man.—The favorite self-designation of Jesus was Son of man. This term, already established in the Old Testament and other Jewish literature, seems to have had a dual role in designating a person and a community.[3] Since this has received detailed examination in chapter 3, demonstration will not be undertaken here. Here it needs only to be said that in Daniel 7, "Son of man" is identified with "the saints of the Most High." This community becomes actual in Jesus Christ, the Son of man. The point is difficult and elusive, the nearest approach in the New Testament to the explicit employment of "Son of man" for mankind being in Mark 2:27 f., "The sabbath was made for man, and not man for the sabbath; so then the Son of man is Lord even of the sabbath," and in Hebrews 2:6–13, where man and Son of man are equated and where the destiny of man is seen to be realized in Jesus Christ, true man or Son of man.

If this view of the Son of man be correct, a view having the support of a host of distinguished and credible scholars, then it supplies strong evidence that Jesus did come to create "the saints of the Most High." The term is deeply embedded in the Synoptics and the Fourth Gospel. Of its presence in the Fourth Gospel, Dodd writes, "Thus the term 'Son of Man' throughout this gospel retains the sense of one who incorporates in Himself the people of God, or humanity in its ideal aspect."[4] Unless scholars for a generation have missed completely the meaning of Son of man, it remains a solid evidence that Jesus saw

[3] Cf. Flew, *op. cit.,* p. 54, who credits Ferdinand Kattenbusch, *Der Quellort der Kirchenidee,* 143–72, with the pioneer work in this study. Cf. also T. W. Manson, *The Teaching of Jesus,* p. 227, and also "The Son of Man in Daniel, Enoch, and the Gospels," *Bulletin of the John Rylands Library,* XXXII (1950), 171–193.

[4] Dodd, *The Interpretation of the Fourth Gospel,* p. 242.

himself as having come to create the people of God. The near absence of *ekklēsia* from the Four Gospels does not cancel this evidence.

The new family.—Jesus called persons to himself; he did not simply offer a new teaching. "Follow me" was his bold summons to all who would receive life from him (cf. Mark 2:14; 8:34; 10:21; Matt. 4:19; 8:22; 9:9; 16:24; 19:21; Luke 5:27; 9:23,59; 18:22; John 1:43; 10:27; 12:26; 21:22). His gracious invitation to all who were wearied and burdened was, "Come unto me" (Matt. 11:28). The Gospels are saturated with references to invitations to follow him.

Jesus not only called people to himself, but he called them into a relationship closer than that of the natural family. He demanded a loyalty to himself beyond anything known within the natural family, saying, "The one loving father or mother more than me is not worthy of me" (Matt. 10:37). Jesus himself affirmed that his true family was not determined by flesh but by those doing the will of God. His striking reply to those who reported that his family were calling for him yet rings out: "Who is my mother, and who are my brothers? And looking about at those seated around him, he said, Behold my mother and my brothers. Whoever does the will of God, this one is my brother, and sister, and mother" (Mark 3:33–35). The term *ekklēsia* is not employed in this connection, but the idea of the people of God as a new family is inescapable.

The twelve.—Why Jesus chose as apostles twelve men, no more and no less, is somewhat speculative. One can hardly resist the suggestion that the number had a symbolic value. The twelve apostles were probably the nucleus to the new Israel. This is not mere speculation, for the idea of new Israel is itself secure in the New Testament, and the coupling of the twelve with new Israel is suggested. When the "twelve tribes of the dispersion" are addressed in James 1:1, the thought may be of the church as the true "twelve-tribed Israel." In Revelation 21:12–14 the twelve tribes of Israel and the twelve apostles are brought into close relationship in the description of "the holy city Jerusalem." In Matthew 19:28 is the word to the disciples, "Ye also shall sit on twelve thrones, judging the twelve tribes of Israel." Too much must not be read into these somewhat obscure passages, but at least there is some evidence for seeing in the number twelve a deliberate suggestion within the Gospels of a new Israel.

It is significant that when Jesus called the twelve, whatever the significance of the number, that the first purpose in the calling was that they be with him, "He constituted twelve *in order that they be with him,* and that he might send them out to preach, And that they might have authority to heal sickness and to cast out demons" (Mark 3:14 f.). In calling the twelve, Jesus was concerned with the formation of a fellowship, probably of a new Israel.

The prayer for oneness.—John 17 consists of a prayer attributed to Jesus on the night of his betrayal. Its burden from first to last is for his people, those with him then and those yet to believe (v. 20). He prayed for the preservation of his people in separateness [5] from the world (vv. 12–19) and for their unity (vv. 11,21–23). Jesus called men into the very relationship with the Father that he himself enjoyed: "That they all may be one, just as thou, Father, art in me and I in thee, in order that they also may be in us, that the world may believe that thou didst send me" (v. 21).

Not only did he pray for this two-dimensional relationship of man to God and man to man, but he made this *the conclusive evidence* for the validity of his own work. This heart of his concern was repeated as he prayed, "And I have given them the glory which thou didst give me, in order that they may be one just as we are one: I in them, and thou in me, in order that they may be perfected into one, in order that the world may know that thou didst send me and thou didst love them just as thou didst love me" (John 17:22–23).

[5] Proper relationship rather than separation may better describe the concern of the prayer. Jesus prayed that as to responsibility we be in the world but that as to character we be not of the world.

This prayer for the purity and the unity of his people in union with himself closely parallels what Paul says of the *ekklēsia* as the body of Christ. In Romans 12:4 f. Paul stressed the unity and diversity which belong to the solidarity of the body. In 1 Corinthians 12:12–31 Paul pleaded for the unity of the church, employing the analogy of the body. In Ephesians the church (*ekklēsia*) is termed his body (1:22 f.), and the bold claim is made for the church that precisely through it is the purpose of God through the ages brought to realization, and through it is the wisdom of God manifested (3:9–12). True unity is thus inherent in the nature of the church.

In John 17 there is no occurrence of the term *ekklēsia,* but the purity and unity of Christ's people, then and in the future, represented the *object* of his prayer and the *evidence* that his mission was of God and that God's love had come to expression through him. In Ephesians where *ekklēsia* is employed, this same unity of the people in Christ is presented as the realization of God's eternal purpose and the evidence of his wisdom. Surely John 17 gives evidence within the Gospels that Jesus did intend to create the "church." The designations vary, and with the varied terms are the varied descriptive emphases, but the basic fact remains: in Christ, God has purposed and actually created his own people.

Persons in community.—That Jesus came to save is itself evidence that he came to create a community of people. He came to save persons, not just "souls" in the Greek sense (see chap. 2 for the meaning of *psuchē*). Persons are individuals but they are more than that. When one is described as an individual, he is described in terms of his limits; when one is described as a person, he is described in relationship. Personality is not closed and exclusive, as once thought; rather, it is open and inclusive. Personal relationships are of such nature, and persons are so conditioned and made by one another, that it is impossible to isolate one person from other persons.

In truth, one may become a true person only in relationship with God and other persons. Nicholas Berdyaev is to the point:

"Where there is no God, there is no man." [6] It is true that man is only a sham self apart from God. Man is made for God and cannot be saved as a person except in the presence of God. So Jesus taught in saying, "This is eternal life, that they should know thee, the only true God, and Jesus Christ whom thou didst send" (John 17:3). God makes man a true person only in relationship with other persons. Friedrich Gogarten wisely said, *"Ich bin durch dich—"* "I am through you." [7] When God said, "It is not good that man should be alone" (Gen. 2:18), it was with a view to giving him a marriage partner. But the truth extends beyond the need for a spouse, as is witnessed to by God's concern to create a community of people made one under his lordship.

Salvation then implies community. A person is saved by being made a true person. Man, broken by sin, estranged from God and man and even divided within himself, to be saved must be restored to new relationship to God and to man. Precisely that is the salvation offered in Jesus Christ. He never offered a salvation of one dimension or direction. To be restored to God involves a new relation to man. The New Testament knows no salvation in isolation. One is lost as an *individual,* vainly seeking to find the meaning of existence in and of himself. When saved, one is a *person* in the truest sense, brought into new relation to God and man.

Cyprian said, *"Salus extra ecclesia non est"*—"There is no salvation outside the church." Precisely what he meant, this writer does not profess to know. If he meant by "church" some institutional or organizational structure, he obviously was mistaken. If he meant by "church" the people of God—the body of Christ, that community of persons created by the Spirit of God—he was profoundly right. There is no salvation which leaves the individual separated from the people of God.

This in no way is meant to obscure the fact that one may

---

[6] *The End of Our Time,* trans. Donald Attwater (London: Sheed & Ward, 1933), p. 80.

[7] Quoted by Baillie, *Our Knowledge of God,* p. 208.

enter into eternal life only through the narrow gate which admits us only singly (see chap. 12, p. 44), that individually we must be brought in repentance and faith to Jesus Christ. It does mean that to be "in Christ" is to be related to his own people in being related to him. One enters the Christian life by being "begotten from above," and one thus begotten is begotten into God's family. It belongs to the essence of salvation to belong— to belong to God and to his people.

There are many analogies in the New Testament employed to describe the people of God. *Ekklēsia,* or "church," has dominated the terms in Christian usage, but it by no means has a monopoly in the New Testament. In addition to terms discussed already, three will command major attention for the balance of this chapter. They are: *ekklēsia,* the body of Christ, and *koinōnia.* These three almost fall into a trinitarian formulation in the New Testament, but the patterns do not always hold. Although other patterns are observed in the New Testament, the following are familiar: (1) the *ekklēsia* of God, (2) the body of Christ, and (3) the *koinōnia* of the Spirit.[8]

The Ekklēsia of God

The English word "church" is not derived from *ekklēsia,* the New Testament term usually translated "church." The word "church" is of uncertain origin, but probably it comes from *kuriakos,* an adjective meaning "of the Lord" or "belonging to the Lord." This adjective appears in 1 Corinthians 11:20, in the expression "the Lord's supper" (*kuriakon deipnon*). It also appears in Revelation 1:10 in the phrase, "on the Lord's day" (*en tē kuriakē hēmera*). It never occurs in the New Testament as descriptive of the Lord's people. Apparently the term was applied at an early date to Christians as "the Lord's people" or to the house in which they met as the Lord's house. The larger phrase presumably was shortened to the simple word "church" (*kuriakos*).

[8] Cf. Duke K. McCall (ed.), *What Is the Church?* (Nashville: Broadman Press, 1958), pp. 18–27; 115 f.

Although a precise equivalent to our English word "church" is not employed in the New Testament as a description of the people of God, the English word is serviceable, correctly understanding the nature of the "church" as the Lord's people. By a happy development the postbiblical usage "church," if, indeed, from *kuriakos,* preserves the essential meaning of the biblical *ekklēsia,* for the *ekklēsia* is *of God;* it belongs to the Lord (*kuriakos*). "Ye are not your own" (1 Cor. 6:19) was a reminder to individual Christians that their individual lives were not their own, to be lived as they pleased; but this truth also holds for the "church." It, too, is the Lord's. The church cannot do as it pleases and remain the "church." It is truly the church when it is a fellowship of persons brought together under the kingdom or lordship of God. If "church" is actually from *kuriakos* then it is a happy designation, stressing *whose* we are. This is the *first* fact belonging to the idea of the church.[9]

Ekklēsia.—The New Testament word usually translated as "church" is *ekklēsia.* The full expression is "the *ekklēsia* of God" (Acts 20:28; 1 Cor. 1:2; 10:32; 11:16,22; 15:9; 2 Cor. 1:1; Gal. 1:13; 1 Thess. 2:14; 2 Thess. 1:4; 1 Tim. 3:5,15). This puts the study of the "church" in proper focus. There is one occurrence of "the churches [*ekkēsiai*] of Christ" (Rom. 16:16). First Thessalonians is addressed to "the church [*tē ekklēsia*] of the Thessalonians in God the Father and Lord Jesus Christ." There is one occurrence of "the churches of the saints" (1 Cor. 14:33). In Romans 16:4 reference is made to "the churches of the Gentiles." Presumably, the idea in the last three references is respectively: "the Thessalonian Church in God the Father and Lord Jesus Christ," "the churches made up of saints," and "the Gentile churches." In no case is the idea necessarily other than that the *ekklēsia* belongs to God, or to God and Christ Jesus (1 Thess. 1:1).

The term *ekklēsia* was widely used in the Greek-speaking world of the first century, but it is a mistake to seek the New Testament meaning in pagan Greek usage. The term is based

[9] Richardson, *Theological Word Book,* p. 47.

upon a root meaning "to call," and *ekklēsia* was used in Greek cities to designate town assemblies. The primary background to New Testament usage, however, is the Old Testament. The doctrine of calling and election is basic in the Bible, and the *ekklēsia* is made up of "called saints," but this is not what is stressed in the term "the *ekklēsia* of God."

Likewise, the emphasis is not upon local assembly. To argue for this is to be true to etymology and to pagan Greek usage, but it is not to approach the study through biblical usage. The idea of local assembly is not ruled out, and sometimes it is affirmed; but local assembly does not belong to the essence of the New Testament idea. The *ekklēsia* of God refers to *God's own people*. Ownership, not local assembly, is the emphasis. *Whose people*, not *where* or *whether* assembled, is the New Testament idea. This can be demonstrated only by showing how the pertinent Hebrew words were translated into Greek.

The Old Testament Background

The New Testament expression "the *ekklēsia* of God" appears first in the Old Testament. The Septuagint (Greek translation of the Old Testament) contains the very term found often in the New Testament: *hē ekklēsia tou Theou* (the church of God). In the Old Testament this expression is used to describe God's people when assembled locally and also with no reference to assembly.

In the Septuagint *ekklēsia* almost always stands for the Hebrew *qāhāl,* but *qāhāl* is not always translated by *ekklēsia*. In its earliest Old Testament usage, *qāhāl* was employed to describe the people of God *assembled*. The Hebrew word *'ēdhāh* was employed to describe God's people whether assembled or not. Later in the Old Testament, especially after the Exile, the term *qāhāl* came to be used much as *'ēdhāh,* that is, to describe the people of God whether assembled or not.[10] Consequently, when Jewish people in the first century heard the expression in

---

[10] Cf. F. J. A. Hort, *The Christian Ecclesia* (London: Macmillan & Co., Ltd., 1897), pp. 3–7, and Coates, *op. cit.,* Vol. I, Sec. II, 51–56.

Greek "the *ekklēsia* of God," they would think of the people of
God with no necessary reference to localization and certainly not
to organization.

To see that *'ēdhāh* in the Old Testament may describe the
people of God assembled or not requires only the reading of
passages like Numbers 31:16, "Behold, these caused the children of Israel . . . to commit trespass against Jehovah . . .
and so the plague was among the congregation of Jehovah
[*ba'"dhath Yahweh;* LXX, *en tē sunagōgē kuriou*]." Here the
Hebrew *'ēdhāh* stands for all Israel and is translated in the Septuagint as *sunagōgē* (synagogue). In the early part of the Old
Testament *qāhāl* was used to describe the assembly of the
'ēdhāh, as in Exodus 12:6, "and the whole assembly [*kōl
q'hal*] of the congregation of Israel [*'"dhāth–Yisrā'ēl*] shall kill
it in the evening." Here *qāhāl* clearly describes the assembly
of the people of Israel (*'ēdhāh*).

Later, *qāhāl* was employed as was *'ēdhāh* to describe Israel
assembled or not, as may be seen by comparing Numbers 27:21
with 1 Chronicles 28:8. Numbers 27:21 reads: "At his word
they shall go out, and at his word they shall come in, both he,
and all the children of Israel with him, even all the *congregation*
[*'ēdhāh*]." Here Israel is designated *'ēdhāh,* which is regular
in the oldest literature of the Old Testament. In 1 Chronicles
28:8 reference is made to "all Israel, the assembly of Yahweh
[*q'hal*]." The Septuagint uses *ekklēsia* here. In Deuteronomy
31:30 and Micah 2:5 the *qāhāl* of Yahweh is in the Septuagint
the *ekklēsia* of the Lord, apparently all Israel. In Numbers 20:4
the *qāhāl* of Yahweh is in the Septuagint the *sunagōgē* of the
Lord, apparently all Israel. In Nehemiah 13:1 the *qāhāl* of
'"lōhîm is in the Septuagint the *ekklēsia* of God, apparently
equated with Israel in verse 3. In Ezra 2:64 and Nehemiah
7:66 all the *qāhāl* (*ekklēsia*) numbered 42,360 persons, be-
sides 7,337 servants and 200 (or, 245) singers. All those return-
ing from Babylon were considered one *qāhāl* or *ekklēsia.*

So *qāhāl* and *'ēdhāh* came to be employed alike, as did the
Greek *sunagōgē* and *ekklēsia* (cf. Num. 20:4 with Deut. 31:30;

Micah 2:5). The *qāhāl* of Yahweh came to be described in Greek as *hē ekklēsia tou Theou*. This is the necessary background to understanding the New Testament term, the *ekklēsia* (church) of God.

Summary.—To summarize, *'ēdhāh* in the Hebrew Bible describes the Israel of God. Before the Exile, *qāhāl* was employed to describe Israel assembled, but after the Exile it could describe Israel either assembled or not. In the Septuagint, *sunagōgē* usually translated *'ēdhāh*, but it also translated *qāhāl* in the Pentateuch. The usual translation for *qāhāl* was *ekklēsia*. *Ekklēsia* takes on fuller meaning in Septuagint books referring to the postexilic period. It still translates *qāhāl*, which itself now included the fuller meaning of *'ēdhāh*. Thus, in the Septuagint, the Bible of the earliest Christians, the *ekklēsia* of God meant the people of God. It had no necessary reference to localization and certainly none to organization.

Strange developments may be traced in the usage of *sunagōgē* and *ekklēsia*. In the earliest Old Testament usage, *sunagōgē* represented *all* Israel, whereas *ekklēsia* described the assembly. Next, the two terms were used almost interchangeably as became true for *'ēdhāh* and *qāhāl*. Finally, *sunagōgē* became fixed as the term for the local Jewish assembly, while *ekklēsia* came to describe the body of Christ as a whole, the people of God.

Universal and Local

Ekklēsia in the New Testament designates the people of God in their totality and any local congregation of his people. The basic New Testament idea is that of the one *ekklēsia*. Repeatedly in the New Testament the reference is to the one *ekklēsia* as the body of Christ. The term "invisible" is never employed; [11] it is simply "the *ekklēsia*" or "the *ekklēsia* of God" or "the *ekklēsia*, the body of Christ." To belittle the idea of the one *ekklēsia* of God is to belittle precisely what the New Testament

[11] Emil Brunner, *The Misunderstanding of the Church*, trans. Harold Knight (Philadelphia: The Westminster Press, 1953), p. 9.

submits as the highest expression of the wisdom of God, the realization of his "purpose of the ages" (Eph. 3:10 f.).

The local usage is equally clear in the New Testament. Actually there are more "local" than "universal" occurrences in the New Testament, but the statistics are misread should they prompt one to conclude that the New Testament has only an incidental interest in the universal church. The local references predominate simply because people are found in localities.

The "local" church is the embodiment of "the church" in a given locality. It is the one church as that church is expressed at Corinth, at Thessalonica, at Philippi, and so forth. It may contradict logic but not fact to say that there is but one church, yet it is found at many places at one time. The same seeming contradiction in logic *but not in fact* obtains in the recognition that there is but one Christ, yet he is present wherever two or three are gathered together in his name (Matt. 18:20). The employment of *ekklēsia* to designate a local church is uncontested and requires no demonstration. Even the plural, "churches," is employed many times. The nonlocal usage is challenged in some quarters.

Nonlocal use of ekklēsia.—There are undeniable occurrences of *ekklēsia* in a nonlocal usage. The correct reading in Acts 9:31, according to overwhelming manuscript evidence, is "the *ekklēsia* throughout the whole of Judea, Galilee, and Samaria was having peace." Later manuscripts changed the reading to the plural. In two letters Paul confessed that he had persecuted "the *ekklēsia* of God" (Gal. 1:13; 1 Cor. 15:9). In Philippians 3:6 he pointed to his former zeal in "persecuting the *ekklēsia*," clearly not restricting the reference to a local situation.

Allusion is made in 1 Corinthians 10:32 to the "three races," as early Christians called them: Jews, Greeks (i.e. Gentiles), and the *ekklēsia*. To the old twofold division of humanity into Jews and non-Jews (Greeks), Paul now saw the addition of a third, the *ekklēsia*. This accords with his understanding of the work of Christ to be that of overcoming these divisions by "making both one," overcoming the enmity that "he might create the two in himself into one new man, thus making peace" (Eph. 2:14–16). First Corinthians 12:28 submits a list of those whom God placed in the *ekklēsia:* apostles, prophets, teachers, powers (miracles?), gifts of healing, and so forth. Not all of these are found in all the local churches; hence this describes *the ekklēsia of God.*

Hebrews 12:22–23 assures the readers that they have come to "Mount Zion, the city of the living God, the heavenly Jerusalem, to myriads of angels, to the festal gathering [*panēgurei*], and [or, even] the *ekklēsia* of the firstborn who are enrolled in heaven." Local limits are forever foreign to this glorious picture.

There are nonlocal occurrences of *ekklēsia* in Colossians and Ephesians. Because of their primary importance, and because of their employment with another term, "the body of Christ," study of these passages will be reserved for a separate section on "The Body of Christ." At this point, attention must be given to the three occurrences of *ekklēsia* in the Gospel of Matthew, in 16:18 and 18:17 (twice).

Ekklēsia in Matthew

The most difficult passage on the *ekklēsia* is Matthew 16:18, "And I say to you that thou art Peter, and upon this rock I will build *my ekklēsia,* and the gates of Hades shall not prevail against it." The genuineness of the verse itself as a saying of Jesus has long been contested. Many critical scholars today, however, are convinced of its genuineness.[12] It has already been shown that the idea of the *ekklēsia* is present in the Four Gospels, set forth under various terms. The absence of Synoptic parallels is not in itself sufficient reason for the rejection of a passage. Schmidt very plausibly argues that the presence of Johannine and Pauline circles in the early church makes it difficult to see how this passage, with its special reference to Peter, could have been introduced unless it actually represents

[12] Cf. Coates, *op. cit.,* Vol. I, Sec. II, 35–50.

something that Jesus said.[13] The passage is in Matthew and must be reckoned with as it stands.

His ekklēsia.—The personal pronoun is prominent in the Greek text and may give a clue to the meaning when Jesus said, "On this rock I will build *my ekklēsia.*" This could be paraphrased thus: "On this rock I will build my people," or "On this rock I will build my *qāhāl.*" The *qāhāl* of Yahweh comes to realization in the people of Christ, divinely created and indestructible for all time.

The *ekklēsia* of which Jesus spoke is in Matthew 16:18 considered in its universal sense. The promise of its indestructibility could not describe an organization of any kind; it could not describe any "church" limited by time and place. Men are able to organize and dissolve organizations. The *ekklēsia* of which Jesus spoke is not of human making; and death, or Hades, is unable to destroy it. Bitter controversies over what church is meant are based on ideas altogether foreign to anything meant in the passage.

To contend that *ekklēsia* can refer only to a local church is to dig a fatal pit for one's self. By that interpretation *only one* local church could qualify, and that one cannot be found. There is no local church now in Palestine which was there in the first century. Those who find the passage to refer to a particular "denomination" have no New Testament ground on which to stand, for *ekklēsia* is never used in that sense in the New Testament. In the New Testament, *ekklēsia* means either the church in its totality, or the church in some particular local embodiment. In Matthew 16:18 the reference is to the church or *ekklēsia* in its totality, that which God alone in Jesus Christ can create and which death, or Hades, cannot destroy.

Schmidt argues for the Aramaic word *k*ʿ*nishta*' as the original behind the Greek *ekklēsia,* holding that it was used both for *ekklēsia* and *sunagōgē,* designating here the whole *ekklēsia* or the whole as represented in the local congregation.[14] It seems,

[13] *Ibid.,* pp. 43 f.
[14] Cf. *ibid.,* pp. 46–50, 60–69.

however, quite precarious to attempt any conclusion as to the language employed by Jesus. Especially with the new light from the Qumran Scrolls, it is difficult to rule out Hebrew as a spoken language in the first century. Whether Hebrew or Aramaic (whether *qāhāl*, *'ēdhāh*, or *kᵉnishta'*) stands behind *ekklēsia*, the reference is most plausibly understood to be to the people of God, or the people of Christ. In Matthew 16:18 these are contemplated as a whole. In Matthew 18:17, on the other hand, they are thought of as a local congregation embodying the church as a whole.

It is quite obvious that in Matthew 18:17 a local assembly is contemplated, for only before such could an erring brother be brought. This thoroughly accords with the character of the *ekklēsia* of God as the reconstituted *qāhāl* of Yahweh. It was seen earlier in this chapter that *'ēdhāh* described Israel or the people of God whether assembled or not and that *qāhāl* came to have this same usage. It belongs to the very essence of the "local church" that it is *the church* in a local embodiment. The New Testament never represents a local *ekklēsia* as a *part;* it always has the character of wholeness.

This is true because Christ himself is present in his people; and he is present in his wholeness in each local church. The church at Antioch is *the church*—the *whole* church as it is manifest at Antioch. The church at Corinth is *the church*—at Corinth. This is true in the sense that the Christ who is present where any group is gathered together in his name is *the Christ,* the only Christ. It may contradict logic, but it does not contradict fact to affirm that the one Christ may be fully present both here and there. Likewise, it may contradict logic but not fact to affirm that the one *ekklēsia* may be both here and there.

The "autonomy of the local church" is to be seen in this connection; the local church is not a part but a whole. Hence it has authority to preach, teach, evangelize, and transact business without appeal to ecclesiastical headquarters. Because Christ is present, not as a torso but in his fulness, the local church is in a real sense a whole. Thus in Matthew 16:18 the universal *ekklēsia* is contemplated, the people of Christ, indestructible for all time; and in 18:17 this same *ekklēsia,* embodied locally, is contemplated.

The gates of Hades.—Jesus gave assurance regarding his *ekklēsia* that "the gates of Hades will not win the victory over it" (Matt. 16:18). The Greek word *hadēs* designates the place of the dead, literally the "unseen," which was thought of as being entered through gates, sometimes the plural being used when only one gate was meant. The meaning seems to be that death itself, the gate to Hades, will not win the victory (*katischuein*) [15] over the *ekklēsia.* This assurance was most important in the light of Jesus' own death. He spoke of that immediately, insisting that he must be put to death (16:21) and that his followers, too, must follow in the way of the cross (16:24 f.). Death would come to him and to them, but death could not destroy his *ekklēsia.*

A further reason for Christ's stressing the indestructibility of his *ekklēsia* was to contrast it with what his many would-be followers urged him to build—a national order after the pattern of David's kingdom. Jesus refused to build their "dream world," for it would be simply another destructible nation among perishing nations. He came to build not with a sword but a cross, not by taking life, but by giving it. He came to create his *ekklēsia,* the church which death itself could not destroy.

On this rock.—Unfortunately, the claims which the Roman Church arrogates to itself make it exceedingly difficult for anyone to study objectively the statement of Jesus: "Thou art Peter, and upon this rock I will build my *ekklēsia*" (Matt. 16:18). The Roman claims are so flagrantly abusive of the New Testament teaching and of early Christian history that it is almost incredible that anyone should find them credible. To begin with, whatever Jesus meant, it was said to Peter at Caesarea Philippi, not to anyone in Rome. Whether or not Peter ever saw Rome is not known, although the tradition that he was martyred

[15] Arndt and Gingrich, *op. cit.,* pp. 16, 425.

there must be respected as possibly true.[16] Leaving out Rome and all the extravagant claims which substitute men for Christ, the interpretation of the verse yet so baffles that it forbids dogmatic conclusions to even the most competent exegetes. Over against the unfortunate claims of the Roman Church have been the prejudiced "answers" to Roman claims. This writer obviously does not escape the pressures of controversy; he at least acknowledges that they are there.

It seems best to this writer to follow the simplest interpretation that would do justice both to the immediate context and to the whole New Testament. In some sense Peter himself is probably the rock.[17] He is not the rock in the sense claimed by the Roman Church. The whole weight of the New Testament cannot be offset by a single verse, and the New Testament will allow no rival to Jesus as the founder and the foundation of the church, "for other foundation can no man lay than that which is laid, which is Jesus Christ" (1 Cor. 3:11). In that sense, Jesus alone is the Rock. The very word *petra* is used of him by Paul, "the Rock was Christ" (1 Cor. 10:4).

Peter never claimed for himself what a misguided church later ascribed to him. When Cornelius fell at his feet to offer him worship, Peter refused it, saying, "I myself also am a man" (Acts 10:26). Never did he claim to be the rock; but, employing a similar analogy, he did acclaim Jesus as the living, elect, and precious chief cornerstone (1 Peter 2:4–7). The church could be a reality without Peter as without any one of us, but there could be no church without Jesus Christ. He is its founder and foundation, its head and body, its being and life.

Although Peter is not the rock in the sense claimed by the Roman Church, he was called the rock in some sense. The New Testament gives evidence that in some way he had primacy among the apostles. In some sense the church was built upon him, yet not in an exclusive sense; for what is said of Peter is said

---

[16] For this study see Cullmann, *Peter: Disciple, Apostle, Martyr*, trans. Floyd V. Filson. (Philadelphia: The Westminster Press, 1953).

[17] Cf. Broadus, *op. cit., in loco.*

of all the apostles. In Ephesians the household of God is said to be "built upon the foundation of the apostles and prophets, Christ Jesus himself being the chief cornerstone" (2:20). At least by some, James, Cephas, and John were thought to be "pillars" of the church (Gal. 2:9). In Revelation 21:14 the heavenly Jerusalem is said to have "twelve foundations, and upon them the twelve names of the twelve apostles of the Lamb." [18]

Jesus built his church, and yet builds it, upon just such frail and fallible men as Peter. What is stressed is probably not his rocklike qualities—which are difficult to find. Although called *Cephas* (from the Aramaic for rock) or *Petros* (Greek for stone), he was not rocklike, but often fearful, impulsive, and unpredictable. But this is the very point; Christ builds his *ekklēsia* of just such men.[19] He declared early in his ministry that he "came not to call righteous persons but sinners" (Mark 2:17). He did not come to pin blue ribbons on prize human stock at the county fair; he came to seek and to save the lost.

No scholar knows in what language Jesus first spoke these words: Hebrew, Aramaic, or Greek. Either to affirm or deny subtle word play (as between *petros* and *petra* in Greek) is more than validly may be claimed. Possibly the meaning is this: "You are Peter, called rock yet not rocklike, yet upon just such a 'rock' I will build my church." Jesus had just asked his disciples, "Who say ye that I am?" Peter had correctly answered, "Thou art the Christ, the Son of the living God." Possibly Jesus then replied in effect, "And I know who you are and what you are, yet upon just such a 'rock' I will build my *ekklēsia*." Should this be a correct interpretation, it would point up the meaning of the assurance which followed: "and [*kai* may mean "yet"] the gates of Hades [death] will not win the victory over it." Jesus, marching to the cross and summoning weak men to the cross, would build his *ekklēsia* out of just such unrocklike people as Peter; yet it will be indestructible through all eternity.

[18] For the study of the apostles, see chapter 10.
[19] Cf. Coates, *op. cit.*, Vol. I, Sec. II, p. 44.

The keys of the kingdom.—Neither too much nor too little should be read into the difficult statement: "I will give you the keys of the kingdom of heaven, and that which you may bind upon earth shall be [or, shall have been] bound in heaven, and that which you may loose on earth shall be [or, shall have been] loosed in heaven" (Matt. 16:19). The "keys" do not represent exclusive authority of which to boast, but a common trust to acknowledge. The power to bind and loose is in Matthew 18:18 extended to the church. This power of the "keys" is not even limited to the church, for "the scribes and Pharisees, hypocrites" are said "to shut [literally, to lock, *kleiete*] the kingdom of heaven in the faces of men," neither entering themselves nor allowing others to enter (Matt. 23:13–14).

In some sense, then, both disciples and hypocrites affect the opening or closing of the doors of the kingdom. In each case it is a matter of stewardship responsibility. In Luke 11:52 the "keys" are more clearly identified: "Woe to you lawyers, for ye took away the key of knowledge; ye yourselves did not enter, and those in the process of entering ye hindered." Salvation is God's free gift to man, yet men themselves may be "instruments of righteousness," those in whom Christ continues his own ministry, or they may be barriers blocking the way. It is too much to claim that the "keys" represent some arbitrary and exclusive power given to any man; but it is too little to fail to see that the "keys" point on the one hand to the solidarity between Christ and the church, and on the other hand to the inescapable obligation of the church to the world. Christ confronts the world in the church, his body.

Conclusion.—*Ekklēsia* in the New Testament designates first of all the people of God in Christ, one fellowship of persons, made one people under the kingship of God. *Ekklēsia* may also designate any local community of the saints, the whole being represented in the part. The *ekklēsia* is not arrived at by adding separate churches into a total; neither are the local churches mere fragments of the whole. There is the reality of wholeness in the local church precisely because Christ is embodied in it, and

he is never a fragment. The New Testament thought is first for
the whole *ekklēsia*, then for the same whole *ekklēsia* as it is
manifest in a given place.

The "autonomy of the local church" is rooted in the fact that
a local church is *the church*. Christ is in it, and it is his body.
Paradoxically, the whole is present in the part. Autonomy is not
a New Testament word, and it is not a choice one. Autonomy
means self-rule. The New Testament idea is that of *theocracy*,
the rule of God, or the lordship of Christ. Local churches are
"autonomous" in the sense that each, being a whole, may function as the whole. But actually a true church is a theocracy; it is
the church only when it is a fellowship of persons brought together under the kingship of God in Christ.

The church is a *democracy* in the sense that all members are
equally precious and equally members of the one body and are
to participate in its deliberations, life, and work. But, again,
democracy means the rule of the people. In the church the rule
does not belong to the majority; it belongs alone to the Lord
Christ. Neither a majority nor unanimity necessarily reflects the
will of God. A group of individuals is not the church simply because a majority has its way; it is the church when brought together as one fellowship of persons under the sovereign rule of
God present in Christ, his anointed King, our Lord and Saviour.

Organization and institutional developments do not belong
to the essential idea of the *ekklēsia*. The New Testament nowhere says that Jesus "organized" a church. However, organization and institutional developments were practical and necessary
developments for the life and work of the *ekklēsia* in the world.
These developments began in the New Testament period and
continue unto the present, as the church seeks to meet the
demands of its day. Organizational structures are valid to the
extent that they serve the church in its life and work.

The Body of Christ

A major Pauline analogy for the *ekklēsia* is the body of Christ.
This analogy may be taken too literally but it cannot be taken

too seriously. Paul never speaks of a "body of Christians"; it is always the body of Christ of which he speaks. The idea of the oneness of Christ and his people did not originate with Paul, for Jesus himself gave major stress to this throughout his ministry. What is new is this particular analogy of the body.

Paul gained his understanding of the solidarity of Christ and his *ekklēsia* from Christ himself, and it was at his conversion that he was introduced to it. Robinson is correct and profound in his insight into Paul's conversion as he writes, "The appearance on which Paul's whole faith and apostleship was founded was the revelation of the resurrection body of Christ, not as an individual, but as the Christian Community." [20] In persecuting Christians, Paul was made to see that he was persecuting Christ. The probing question of Jesus was, "Saul, Saul, why are you persecuting me?" (Acts 9:4 f.; 22:7 f.; 26:14 f.). This accords with what Jesus had taught: "In that ye did it to one of these my brothers, ye did it to me" (Matt. 25:40). Paul appealed to this same truth in warning the Corinthians that to divide the church was like dividing Christ (1 Cor. 1:13) and that in sinning against their brethren they sinned against Christ (1 Cor. 8:12).

The ekklēsia as the body of Christ.—The most explicit equation of the *ekklēsia* with the body of Christ is in Colossians and Ephesians. In Romans and 1 Corinthians, Paul is explicit that Christians are the body of Christ. In his letters generally, Paul's emphasis upon being "in Christ," or "Christ in you," is concerned with the concept of the body of Christ even where this latter expression is not used.

Colossians is strongly Christological, contending that in Christ "dwells all the fulness of the Godhood bodily" (2:9). But the Christology of this letter includes the view that Christ is embodied in the church. The equation of this body with the *ekklēsia* is explicit in 1:18, "He is the head of the body, that is of the *ekklēsia*." Again in 1:24 this identification is made as Paul boldly claimed that the sufferings of Christ are continued

[20] *Op. cit.,* p. 58.

in his own sufferings "in behalf of his body, which is the *ekklēsia*." This is not to confuse the church with Christ, for they do stand over against one another in an "I-Thou" relationship. But it is to recognize that the personal relationship of Christian to Christ and of Christian to Christian is such that the suffering of one is the suffering of the other. Less conspicuous, yet present, is the idea of the body of Christ in Colossians 2:16–19, where the body is seen to be dependent upon its head for its life and growth. Again, the idea is implicit in Colossians 3:15, where the readers are exhorted to the peace unto which they were called "in one body."

Ephesians makes even more of the analogy of the *ekklēsia* as the body of Christ. This letter is Paul's climactic treatment of the great theme that in Christ is brought to realization the eternal purpose of God to create "one new man" out of estranged peoples. This accomplishment is the *ekklēsia*, the body of Christ. In 1:22–23 is the statement that God "gave him [Jesus] head over all things to the *ekklēsia*, which is his body." The balance of the verse may be translated "the fulness of the one being made full as to all things in all ways" or "the fulness of him who makes full all things in all ways." In either case, the *ekklēsia* is itself, as the body of Christ, that which gives him his fulness. This is a daring thought, but Paul dared to express it here and elsewhere. In this daring thought he did not go beyond the teaching of Jesus.

In Ephesians 2:14–16 neither the term *ekklēsia* nor "body of Christ" is present, but the idea is apparent:

For he is our peace, the one having made both [i.e., Jew and Gentile] one and the middle wall of partition having broken down the enmity, in his flesh having annuled the law of commandments expressed in dogmas, in order that the two he might create in himself unto one new kind of man, thus making peace, and might reconcile both *in one body* to God through the cross, having killed the enmity in the same.

In his incarnate state (v. 14) Christ has, through the cross, made the breakthrough for the overcoming of the enmity separating man from man and man from God. His accomplished work is realized in the "new kind of man" created out of those formerly estranged.

In Ephesians 3:3–13, Paul expounded the mystery, or open secret, concerning God's eternal purpose to unite mankind in Christ. He described the Christians variously, and he apparently coined a word to stress the solidarity of Gentiles with Jews in Christ. In verse 6 he called them "fellow members of the body," or literally "synsomatic" (*sussōma*). He represented the heavenly being as seeing at last the manifold wisdom of God as it comes to light *through the ekklēsia* (v. 10). That is, what God's eternal purpose has been (v. 11) in his dealing with Jew and Gentile, and what his wisdom is, they see at last when they look upon the *ekklēsia*. In it those once estranged are made *synsomatic*, "bodied together" (v. 6). This is the *ekklēsia*, the body of Christ.

Ephesians 4:1–16 is a prayerful exhortation to the readers that they measure up to their high calling in Christ. Measuring up is set forth in terms of the unity and maturity of the one body which they are (vv. 4,12,16). Verses 4 through 6 set forth their sevenfold unity: "one body, one Spirit, . . . one hope . . . one Lord, one faith, one baptism, one God and Father of all, the one over all and through all, and in all."

The very Christ who ascended is then described as the one who descended and who gave the apostles, the prophets, the evangelists, the pastors, and teachers to the church. Their function is to equip the saints for the ministry: devoted to the building up of the body of Christ that all together become "a perfect man," conformed to the fulness of Christ (vv. 9–13). The church is thus both the ministering church and itself the fulness of Christ as the body of Christ. Never losing sight of the fact that for all the reality of the body of Christ, the *ekklēsia* itself is not Christ, Paul pointed to Christ, the head, from whom the body draws its life, by whom it is co-ordinated and nourished (v. 16). Again, however, in this long paragraph, the goal of redemption is the building up of the one body of Christ.

196 NEW TESTAMENT THEOLOGY

The *ekklēsia* is never explicitly called the bride of Christ, but that is approached in Ephesians 5:22–33, as in Revelation 21:9. But again the great analogy is that of the body. Husband and wife are to be "one flesh" (v. 31) and this for the writer describes the relationship of Christ and *ekklēsia* (v. 32). Husbands were exhorted to love their wives "just as Christ loved the *ekklēsia* and gave himself for it" (v. 25). The appeal to the husband to love his wife is furthered by the reminder that in loving his wife the husband loves himself, *for she is his body* (v. 28). The analogy is then drawn to show that the Christ-*ekklēsia* relationship is like the husband-wife relationship. When Christ nourishes and cherishes the *ekklēsia,* he nourishes and cherishes his own flesh. As the *ekklēsia,* "we are members of his body" (vv. 29–30). Clinching his argument, Paul then quoted Genesis 2:24: "For this cause a man shall leave father and mother and be joined to his wife, and the two shall become one flesh." This great "mystery" he applied to Christ and the *ekklēsia* as well as to husband and wife.

It is understandable that many fear this analogy, remembering the absorption theories of the mystery religions, as well as the extravagant claims of the Roman Church, virtually equating itself with Christ. Those dangers are real, and they are to be shunned. But the alternative to those errors is not to be the minimizing of the New Testament emphasis upon the *ekklēsia* as the body of Christ. Christ and the Christian remain distinct, and yet paradoxically become one, just as husband and wife remain two persons yet become one. *The analogy may be taken too literally but it cannot be taken too seriously.*

Unity and diversity in the body.—In a moving appeal in the Roman letter, Paul employed the analogy of the body to stress the importance of unity in diversity, as well as the interrelationships of Christ and believers: "Just as in one body we have many members, but all the members have not the same function, thus the many of us are one body in Christ, and individually members of one another" (12:4–5). Since we are one body in Christ, his body, there is no room for competition and jealousy. Both diversity and unity belong to the nature of the body. The kinship is inclusive of all.

It was upon the Corinthians, probably because they most needed it, that Paul pressed hardest the claims of the body of Christ for unity in diversity. All charismatic gifts he traced to one Spirit, one Lord, one God (1 Cor. 12:4–6,11), and then he stressed the unity and diversity necessary to the body.

The body is one body, but it cannot be one member. It must be many members, yet one body. A foot is not a body, however big. Were all eye, it would be a monstrous eye but no body. Paul's point was that the Corinthians were the body of Christ, and as his body they necessarily must be a unity in diversity. Verse 12 reads: "Just as the body is one and has many members, and all the members of the body being many are one body, thus also Christ." Thus also Christ—what? Thus Christ is one body of many members! Jews, Greeks, slaves, freedmen, "all of us were baptized into one body" (v. 13). In verse 27 is the positive pronouncement, "Ye are Christ's body and members individually." In the next verse he dropped the term "body" for *ekklēsia,* designating the one universal church to which God gave the apostles, prophets, teachers, and others.

The Koinōnia of the Spirit

In the benediction to 2 Corinthians, *koinōnia* is placed alongside grace and love: "The grace of the Lord Jesus Christ, the love of God, and the *koinōnia* of the Holy Spirit be with you" (13:13).[21] This alone would suggest its importance. The term appears in many significant passages and represents one of the key ideas in the New Testament. It is not out of place alongside grace and love.

Koinōnia, along with its cognate forms, is difficult to reproduce in English, the usual translations being "communion," "fellowship," "sharing," and "participation." The Greek word designates that which two or more have in common. No English

[21] 2 Cor. 13:13 in the Greek text, Nestle editions, is 13:14 in various English translations.

word is fully adequate, so the transliterated form is followed here.

In New Testament usage, *koinōnia* may describe the life shared in Christ, the life embodied in the *ekklēsia*. It may describe the common life which has its source in God.[22] Sharing may be of two kinds: one may have a specific and limited part out of a whole, like a share of stock or a piece of pie; or he may participate in the whole of something, like "belonging" to a family. The *koinōnia* of the Spirit is more like the latter; it is not to monopolize a separable part but to participate with others in the whole of a common life. It is our joint participation in the life of God through Jesus Christ, as constituent members of the body of Christ, as one people under the kingship of God. The people of God are not called the *koinōnia* of the Spirit, but *koinōnia* goes far in describing the inner life of the *ekklēsia*.

Vertical and horizontal.—First John, noted for its great emphasis upon love, indicates at the outset that its concern is with *koinōnia:* "That which we have seen and heard we proclaim also to you, in order that ye might have *koinōnia* with us. And our *koinōnia* is with the Father and with his Son Jesus Christ" (1:3). *Koinōnia* has for the Christian two basic dimensions: with God and with man. These may not be divorced. To be brought into *koinōnia* with the Father through the Son is also to be brought into *koinōnia* with others so related to him. The New Testament never gives the option of salvation with vertical dimension alone. This is a constant reminder, as in Matthew 10:40, "The one receiving you receives me, and the one receiving me receives the one having sent me."

Jesus taught that at the last judgment one's true attitude and relation to himself would be found reflected in one's relationship to his own people: "I hungered and ye gave me to eat, I was thirsty and ye gave me to drink, I was a stranger and ye took me in, naked and ye clothed me, sick and ye visited me, in prison and ye came to me. . . . Inasmuch as ye did it to one

---

[22] Cf. L. S. Thornton, *The Common Life in the Body of Christ* (London: The Dacre Press, 1950), pp. 4, 6.

of the least of these my brethren, ye did it to me" (Matt. 25:35–36,40). Saul of Tarsus, persecuting Christians, was stopped by the appearance of Christ with the question, "Saul, Saul, why are you persecuting me?" (Acts 9:4). Corinthians were charged with sinning against Christ in sinning against their brethren (1 Cor. 8:12).

In 1 John 1:3 the vertical and horizontal dimensions of *koinōnia* are made emphatic. The very *koinōnia* which obtains between the Father and the Son is that offered to the one who in faith will receive it. But the *koinōnia* offered not only binds one to God but to his brother. *Koinōnia* is participation with one's brethren in the very life of God, made available by faith in Christ. The purpose in declaring the great event of the Word made flesh is that "ye may have *koinōnia* with us" (v. 3).

Koinōnia is God's gift, never man's achievement. It is gift and demand: "God is faithful, through whom ye were called into *koinōnia*, that of his Son Jesus Christ our Lord" (1 Cor. 1:9). This is not mere co-operation, which is an easy achievement, even for pagans. Co-operation is in itself neutral as to moral value; bank robbers can achieve it as well as the "saints." *Koinōnia* is not mere accord, being of "one heart." The book of Acts describes beautiful acts of prayer and devoted service as being done by those "of one accord" (cf. 1:14; 2:1,46; 4:24; 5:12; 8:6; 15:25), but Acts also describes the arrogance and rage of madmen as being done "of one accord" (cf. 7:57; 12:20; 18:12; 19:29).[23]

Koinōnia of the Spirit is more than accord; it is that accord which is possible only in the creative calling of God. The *koinōnia* of the Spirit is not just a society of men, a congenial fellowship of "buddies." John Macmurray points out that a *society* mày be made up of strangers who have a common interest (cf. a burial society), but a *community* is made up of persons related through a common life.[24] Further, the *koinōnia* of the

---

[23] Cf. Stagg, *op. cit.,* p. 69.
[24] John Macmurray, *Conditions of Freedom* (London: Faber & Faber, 1950), p. 54.

Spirit is not just any community; it is that fellowship of persons created by the Holy Spirit in Christ Jesus, that fellowship of persons made real as together they are brought under one ultimate claim, the sovereignty or kingdom of God.

Demands of koinōnia.—Jesus protested and made obsolete all priestly and legalistic religions which sanctify separation on artificial and superficial grounds. He brushed aside all claims to "purity" or "godliness" achieved by food laws and ceremonial cleansings. But Jesus did not repudiate the idea of *separation.* Good and evil, right and wrong, light and darkness are to be distinguished. Israel had majored on separation: Jew from non-Jew, the priests from the people, the high priests from the lower priests, the "clean" from the "unclean." Jesus rejected these superficial walls of separation. At his death "the veil of the temple was rent in two from top to bottom" (Matt. 27:51), and Christ there "broke down the middle wall of partition" (Eph. 2:14).[25] But Jesus did not reject the fact that one may be unclean or defiled (Mark 7:15); he put it on a true basis.

The *koinōnia* of the Spirit overrides old distinctions which men have blindly cherished, but it has its own distinctions and demands. It is a fellowship in *light,* not in darkness. John placed light and purity among the tests of *koinōnia:* "If we say that we have *koinōnia* with him, yet walk in darkness, we lie, and do not the truth. But if we walk in the light as he is in the light, we have *koinōnia* with one another, and the blood of Jesus his Son cleanses us from all sin" (1 John 1:6–7).

Paul was as emphatic as John in contending that there can be no *koinōnia* between light and darkness (2 Cor. 6:14). In a remarkable paragraph (2 Cor. 6:14–7:1), Paul blended several analogies, seeing believers as God's temple in which he dwells (6:16), as his people with whom he dwells (6:16), his sons and daughters to whom he is Father (6:18), and yet subjects under his command as the Lord Almighty (6:17–18).

The one major concern of the paragraph is with the demand

[25] Cf. Marcus Barth, *The Broken Wall* (Philadelphia: The Judson Press, 1959), an exposition of Ephesians.

for separateness on a new basis: the "temple" must be clean, his people must be separate, there must be no confusion between righteousness and lawlessness, light and darkness, Christ and Belial, the trusting and the distrusting one, the temple of God and idols. God offers to live with us but not with our sin. Thornton sums it up in saying, "A contrast is drawn between the two communities, the Church and the pagan world, the *koinōnia* of light and an opposite *koinōnia* of darkness." [26]

The *koinōnia* of the Spirit demands *unity* as well as purity, light, and separateness. When the Philippian church was threatened with a rupture of fellowship, Paul made a strong appeal for unity, basing it in part on the claims of *koinōnia:* "If there be any summons [*paraklēsis*] in Christ, if any solace afforded by love,[27] if any *koinōnia* of the Spirit, if any affection and compassion, make full my joy that ye have the same mind, having the same love, minding the one thing" (2:1–2).

Koinōnia makes the demand of *acceptance.* Where there is *koinōnia* one must accept the other, even if by the world's standards one be slave and one a free man. There is not a more touching appeal in the New Testament than that of Paul for the run-away slave Onesimus. Paul began with the prayer that "the *koinōnia* of faith" become energetic in the knowledge of all good, that in Christ (Philemon 6). Finally, Paul made the direct appeal, "If you hold me partner [*koinōnon*], receive him as me" (v. 17). "Partner" is not an adequate translation for this cognate form of *koinōnia.* Paul made the test of *koinōnia* here the accepting of Onesimus as Paul; not just *as though* he were Paul, but *as* Paul. In the *koinōnia* of faith, Onesimus is Paul, just as in a real sense Christ is the hungry, the thirsty, the lonely, the persecuted.

Thus, in a situation which is not speculative but one belonging to life itself, demonstration is found for the New Testament principle that persons in *koinōnia* are distinguishable but not separable from one another.

[26] *Op. cit.,* p. 13.
[27] Arndt and Gingrich, *op. cit.,* p. 626.

Outward expressions of koinōnia.—The early chapters of Acts describe "the multitude of those believing" (4:32) as a *koinōnia* of persons. They were one in heart and life, manifesting their oneness normally and naturally in many ways, including the sharing of their material substance (2:42,45; 4:32,36–37). Following the outpouring of the Spirit on the day of Pentecost, over three thousand who had responded to the gospel "were continuing together in the teaching of the apostles, in the *koinōnia,* in the breaking of bread, and in the prayers" (2:41–42). Those trusting drew together, "holding all things in *koinōnia* [*koina*]," selling and distributing their property and belongings as any had need (2:44–45).

Later (Acts 4:32) it was said of the multitude of believers, now over five thousand, that "Not even one was saying anything of his belongings to be his own, but all things were to them common [*koina*]." They still held legal title to private property and they did not demand of the other that he surrender his property. It was made clear to Ananias that he was not required to give up his property (5:4). The *demand* did not come from without; it came from within. That is the point. There was something about the *koinōnia* of the Spirit which prompted them to disclaim ownership in favor of stewardship. However wisely or not they may have administered their property, their disposition to have all things common gave expression to something essential to the *ekklēsia* of God.

At a critical time when the *ekklēsia* was threatened with a major cleavage between the Jewish and Gentile Christians, Paul gambled with his own life, seeking to draw together these two groups. His whole effort found outward expression in the form of a collection of money which he called a *koinōnia.* Appealing to the Corinthians to contribute generously, he cited the Macedonians. In spite of deep poverty they had begged for "the favor [*charin*] and the *koinōnia* of the ministry unto the saints" (2 Cor. 8:4).

A short time later he wrote the Romans from Corinth, happily reporting that "Macedonia and Achaia were pleased to make a certain *koinōnia* unto the poor of the saints in Jerusalem" (Rom. 15:26). This he declared to be the rightful response to those who had "fellowshiped" the Gentiles, or who had *koinōnia* [*ekoinōnēsan*] with the Gentiles, in things spiritual. Thus *koinōnia* was expressed both in the preaching of the gospel and in sharing with the poor in material things.

Calling the giving of money a *koinōnia* was characteristic of Paul, as may be seen in various writings. In describing the behavior of love, he included its "having *koinōnia* with the needs of the saints" (Rom. 12:13). He exhorted the Galatians, "Let the one being taught the word have *koinōnia* [*koinōneitō*] with the one teaching in all good things" (Gal. 6:6). He gave thanks to the Philippians for their *koinōnia* in the gospel "from the first day until just now" (1:5). In its very nature, *koinōnia* is a "giving and receiving," and this Paul made explicit in commending the Philippians for their generosity in a difficult time, as he wrote, "When I went out from Macedonia, no *ekklēsia* had *koinōnia* [*ekoinōnēsen*] with me in the matter of giving and receiving except you alone" (4:15).

Suffering was another expression of *koinōnia*. Paul testified that he counted all things loss for the knowledge of Christ Jesus his Lord, his one concern being "to know him in the power of his resurrection and the *koinōnia* of his sufferings, being conformed to his death," thus to attain unto the resurrection of the dead (Phil. 3:8–10). He paid high tribute to the Philippians, saying, "Ye did beautifully [*kalōs*], having *koinōnia* with my distress" (4:14). Peter comforted and encouraged persecuted Christians as he wrote, "But just as ye have *koinōnia* with the sufferings of Christ, rejoice" (1 Peter 4:13).

A major meaning of the Lord's Supper is in the *koinōnia* which it is, both expressing and extending itself in the shared Supper (cf. 1 Cor. 10:16 f.). This study, however, is reserved for chapter 9.

Baptism: Origin
8 and Meaning

THERE IS no formal treatment of baptism in the New Testament, as is true of many important themes. The subject is prominent throughout the New Testament, but always it is introduced as something already familiar to the reader. Origin and possible antecedents are not discussed, but the meaning emerges with considerable clarity.

Etymology.—The New Testament word for baptize, *baptizein,* is a strengthened form of the earlier *baptein,* the intensive or iterative suffix being added to the stem of the verb. The verb *baptein* means "to dip." The root is *baph–; and by the* simple fluctuation of the aspirates *phi* (ph) and *theta* (th), it is connected with *bath–,* the root meaning "depth," as in *bathos,* "deep," and *bathus,* "depth." [1]

In the Septuagint *baptein* occurs sixteen times, usually translating *tābhal,* to dip or immerse. In the New Testament *baptein* is used only in its proper sense, to dip (Luke 16:24; John 13:26; Rev. 19:13). Except in Luke 11:38 and some manuscripts of Mark 7:4, *baptizein* is used only in the cultic or technical sense, to immerse. It may refer to a physical immersion of the body in water or to an "immersion" of a person into Christ or into his death.

There is no room for uncertainty about the mode of baptism in the New Testament; it was an immersion of the body in water.

[1] Curtius, *op. cit.,* II, 75.

New Testament descriptions and theological deductions as well as the survival of ancient baptistries in old cathedrals, as in Italy, agree with the etymology of the word.

Antecedents.—That there were historical antecedents to the baptism of John is assumed by many and probably by the majority of interpreters. No theological problem is necessarily created by this assumption; there are no *a priori* reasons for ruling out the possibility of antecedents. To the contrary, the New Testament itself insists upon continuity as well as discontinuity with the Old. In the Sermon on the Mount, Jesus emphasized his work as fulfilment of the law and the prophets (Matt. 5:17). The epistle to the Hebrews begins with the affirmation that he who spoke in Jesus Christ is the very God who spoke in the prophets. Christianity was not isolated from the past, but bound to it. It was old and new.

Christianity was cradled in Judaism, and the New Testament stresses this fact as important. If there were Jewish antecedents to the baptism of John, this parallels the case for much else in the New Testament. It would not follow that something from the past was taken over unchanged. The old and the new, continuity and discontinuity, provide the pattern which most plausibly may be expected.

It will be the thesis of this chapter that John the Baptist adapted Jewish proselyte baptism, giving it new meaning. Christian baptism, in turn, was an adaptation of John's baptism, with new and significant meaning growing out of the baptism of Jesus and his teaching on the subject.

Jewish Proselyte Baptism

The antecedent to the baptism of John most plausibly may be sought in some once-for-all induction rite connected with the transition from one state of life to another.[2] There were many Jewish lustrations for ritual cleansing (cf. Isa. 1:16; Ezek. 36:25; Zech. 13:1; Psalm 51:7), but these repetitious lustra-

[2] Cf. W. F. Flemington, *The New Testament Doctrine of Baptism* (London: SPCK, 1948), p. 4.

tions are unlikely antecedents to John's baptism, although they may have contributed to the background of ideas. The most likely antecedent may be found in Jewish proselyte baptism.

Date of proselyte baptism.—Uncertainty surrounds the date and origin of proselyte baptism. The various Jewish lustrations in water probably formed the background to proselyte baptism; but the latter was not just another lustration, as Gilmore has well concluded:

It was an initiation ceremony, performed only once; it differed from other lustrations in that whereas they were performed in private, baptism took place before witnesses, being accompanied by a catechism and a solemn exhortation; furthermore, lustrations were self-administered, and baptism was administered by others.[3]

Probably proselyte baptism was a fusion of the idea of Levitical cleansing with the Jewish catechetical (teaching) practices, thus becoming a once-for-all, unrepeatable rite of initiation having a meaning far above mere ceremonial ritual.[4]

Proselyte baptism may itself have been an adaptation from older ceremonial rites; but whatever its origin, it came to have a significant role in Judaism. Baptism was one of three initiatory rites required of Gentiles coming into Judaism, circumcision and sacrifice being the other two. With the destruction of the Temple in A.D. 70 the sacrifice necessarily was modified. George Foot Moore concludes that actually the offering of a sacrifice (a burnt offering for which doves and pigeons sufficed) was not a condition for becoming a proselyte but only a condition for participation in a sacrificial meal (cf. *Kᵉrithôth* 8*b*).[5]

The Talmud describes the induction of the proselyte into Israel as consisting of circumcision followed, as soon as he was

---

[3] A. Gilmore (ed.), *Christian Baptism* (Philadelphia: The Judson Press, 1959), p. 66, citing H. H. Rowley, "Jewish Proselyte Baptism," in *Hebrew Union College Annual*, XV (1940), 313–34, and Torrance, "Proselyte Baptism," *New Testament Studies*, I (1954), 150 ff.

[4] Cf. R. E. O. White, *The Biblical Doctrine of Initiation* (Grand Rapids: Wm. B. Eerdmans Publishing Co., 1960), p. 58.

[5] *Op. cit.*, p. 332.

healed, by an ablution, saying: "When he comes up after his ablution he is deemed to be an Israelite in all respects" (*Yᵉbā-môth* 47b).⁶ Since many of the proselytes were women, circumcision did not become the chief initiatory rite. Consequently, baptism became the major rite of initiation of Gentiles into Judaism.⁷

Proselyte baptism was in all probability pre-Christian, although this cannot be demonstrated conclusively. The rite is not mentioned in the Old Testament, the Jewish Apocrypha, Josephus, or Philo. It is described in the Talmud, written after A.D. 70, but claiming to preserve material much earlier. It was undeniably a Jewish practice by the second century of the Christian era, and it is almost incredible that in the bitter period following A.D. 70 either Christianity or Judaism would have borrowed an induction rite from the other. That the rite, with significant adaptations, could come into Christianity from Judaism through John the Baptist poses no real problem. No conclusive or even strong evidence or argument has been offered against a pre-Christian date for Jewish baptism.

The earliest evidences for Jewish proselyte baptism are found in Epictetus and the Sibylline Oracles. Writing in Rome about A.D. 94, Epictetus (*Dissertations* 2, 9, 20) said that one is in name and in reality a Jew when he has been baptized and made his choice.⁸ Book four of the Sibylline Oracles seemingly is Jewish and was written just after the eruption of Vesuvius (A.D. 79), this catastrophe being regarded as punishment for the Roman destruction of Jerusalem (A.D. 70).⁹ In iv, 165 ff. is a possible allusion to proselyte baptism in a passage addressed to Gentiles: "In ever-flowing rivers bathe the whole body [*lousasthe holon demas*]; hands stretching heavenward, ask forgiveness for former deeds; and with praises expiate bitter impiety; God will

⁶ Unless otherwise indicated, references to the Talmud are to the *Babylonian Talmud,* translated into English under the editorship of I. Epstein (London: Soncino Press, 1935).

⁷ White, *op. cit.,* p. 63.

⁸ Flemington, *op. cit.,* p. 5.

⁹ Cf. White, *op. cit.,* p. 320, citing Moffatt.

give repentance; He will not destroy." [10] The passage connects bathing the whole body in running water with confession of sins, praise, forgiveness, repentance, and preservation. It does not employ the term baptism, but this may be alluded to. Thus this evidence is strong but not conclusive.

Rabbinic evidence from the second century, apparently preserving older tradition, points to pre-Christian proselyte baptism, the earliest reference being to a dispute between the house of Shammai and the house of Hillel (70 B.C.–A.D. 10) over t*bilāh, the ritual bath (P*sāchîm 92a; 'Eduyôth, chap. v, Mishnah 2).[11] Shammai held that the bath might follow immediately upon circumcision; Hillel contended that seven days must intervene. The reading of Mishnah 2 in 'Eduyôth, chapter v is as follows:

If one became a proselyte on the eve of Passover, Beth Shammai says: he may immerse himself and eat his Passover sacrifice in the evening. But Beth Hillel says: whoso separates himself from uncircumcision is as one who separates himself from the grace [i.e., like one having corpse defilement and requiring seven days for purification in accordance with Num. 19:19].

Although not conclusive, this seems to reflect pre-Christian proselyte baptism. Debates by Rabbi Eleazar and Rabbi Joshua over the relative merits of circumcision and t*bilāh (probably baptism) occurred around A.D. 90 (Y*bāmôth 46a). Earlier evidence appears in P*sāchîm viii, 8, where Rabbi Eleazar is cited for the conversion, circumcision, and t*bilāh of Roman soldiers who shared the Passover the same day, hence before the destruction of the Temple in A.D. 70.[12]

Meaning of proselyte baptism.—As practiced by the Jews, proselyte baptism seems to have been an initiatory rite for Gentile converts, administered once for all, possibly self-administered, witnessed by others, a total immersion in water, serving

[10] Translated from Greek cited by Flemington, *op. cit.*, p. 5, n. 2.
[11] Cf. Strack and Billerbeck, *op. cit.*, I, 102 f.
[12] Cf. White, *op. cit.*, p. 320.

as a sign of cleansing and a break with the old life through the acceptance of the new, attended by examination and instruction, marking one's incorporation into Israel.[13]

That proselyte baptism marked one's entrance into Israel as a "new person" having undergone moral change is clear from Jewish sources. Maimonides (1135–1204) summed up the requirements in saying, "And so in all ages when a Gentile is willing to enter the Covenant, and gather himself under the wings of the Shekinah of God, and take upon him the yoke of the Law, he must be circumcised and be baptized and bring a sacrifice (*Isure Biah*, 13–14)." [14]

That proselyte baptism was not concerned with mere ritual purification but with moral change is clear from the description of procedure and emphasis. One desiring to become a proselyte was asked why he wanted this and was warned as to the suffering which he would likely incur. If he acknowledged this, disclaiming any worthiness even thus to suffer, he was received. While standing in the water some of the lighter and some of the heavier commandments were read to him. After baptism the proselyte was "regarded in all respects as an Israelite" (*Y'bhāmôth* 47*a*).

Maimonides said, "The Gentile that is made a proselyte and the slave that is made free, behold he is like a child new born" (*Isure Biah*, 14. Cf. also *Y'bhāmôth* 48*a*, 62*a*, 22*a*, 97*b*.). That the proselyte was like a child newly born was taken so seriously that the question was raised about the identity of his first born, whether the child born while the father was a heathen or the one born after he became a proselyte (*Y'bhāmôth* 62*a*; *B'khōrôth* 47*a*.).

Performance of rite.—The rite of baptism was performed in the presence of two (later three) witnesses, usually the instructors of the proselyte.[15] Although challenged by some, most Jewish and Christian scholars understand proselyte baptism to have

---

[13] Cf. Gilmore, *op. cit.*, pp. 68–71; White, *op. cit.*, pp. 58–72.
[14] Quoted from Torrance, "Proselyte Baptism," p. 150.
[15] White, *op. cit.*, p. 62.

been a total immersion of the body in water.[16] The Talmud preserves the requirement that *t'bilāh* be performed in not less than forty seahs (at least one hundred gallons) of water (cf. *Mikwa'ôth* v. 6) and that there be complete bodily contact with the water.

In this connection, attention was given to types of headgear which could invalidate *t'bilāh*, surely implying that the head also was immersed (cf. *Y'bhāmôth* 47b; *Mikwa'ôth* v, 6; viii 5; ix, 1–4). Mishnah 1 of *Mikwa'ôth* ix reads: "The following interpose [between the body and the water] in the case of a person: threads of wool and threads of flax and the ribbons on the heads of girls."

Scholars are divided on the question as to whether the rite was self-administered or not. White is probably correct in saying of the proselyte, "He may have immersed himself: he did not, and could not possibly, baptise himself." [17] That is, whether or not the witnesses touched the candidate, at least they were in charge and administered the rite. It was semiprivate, but it was not to be administered at night, on the Sabbath, or feast days (*Y'bhāmôth* 46b).

Children of proselytes.—Torrance makes a point of emphasis concerning the baptism of infant children of proselytes as well as of children found or bought, holding that the "oldest evidence for the proselytism of children under three years is to be found in the Mishnah itself." [18] It is questionable that Torrance correctly interpreted the passage. At best, what he concludes is derived not from the Mishnah but the Gemara on the Mishnah. The Mishnah refers to a woman proselyte who was *converted* when "less than three years and one day old," not to one *baptized* under three years of age. The Mishnah reads: "A woman proselyte, a woman captive, and a woman slave, who have been redeemed, converted, or freed [when they were] less than three

[16] Gilmore, *op. cit.*, p. 69, cites W. O. E. Oesterley, G. H. Box, H. H. Rowley, and Israel Abrahams as among those claiming that Jewish baptism was always a total immersion.

[17] *Op. cit.*, p. 63.

[18] *Op. cit.*, p. 151.

years and one day old—their *kethubah* is two hundred [*zuz*], and there is with regard to them the claim of [non-] virginity." [19]

The Gemara upon this Mishnah quotes Rabbi Huna as saying, "A minor proselyte is immersed by direction of the court." The Gemara takes issue with Rabbi Huna, holding that the reference is to "the case of a proselyte whose sons and daughters were converted with him, so that they are satisfied with what their father does." Hence this Mishnah makes no explicit reference to immersion, and the Gemara holds the reference to be to children who consent to their father's action.

The attempt to justify the infant baptism of children born to Christian parents by analogy to proselyte baptism breaks down upon investigation. The Talmud makes it clear that the child born after his mother's baptism was not required to be baptized: "If a pregnant Gentile woman was converted, there is no need for her son to perform ritual immersion" (*Y'bhāmôth* 78a). Even if proselytes to Judaism had baptized their children, it would not necessarily follow that early Christians baptized their infants, for Christian baptism does not parallel proselyte baptism at every point. But the important fact here is that infant baptism of children born to Christian parents does not parallel —indeed, it *contradicts*—the pattern of proselyte baptism. White correctly states the point: "Any analogy drawn from proselyte baptism to Christian baptism therefore could only prove that whatever other children might receive Christian baptism the children of Christian parents are prohibited from doing so." [20]

The freedom of each person to enter Judaism by personal decision was safeguarded for servants and children. The servant was not baptized against his will (Maimonides: *Aradim* viii), and minor children who were "converted" with their father could later renounce this without suffering the penalty of apostasy: "When they have become of age they can protest against their conversion" (*K'thubôth* 11a).

[19] *K'thubôth* 11a.
[20] *Op. cit.*, p. 65.

Summary.—Proselyte baptism most likely was pre-Christian. It was an initiatory rite for Gentiles desiring to be admitted into Israel, converts who were examined as to intention by two or three men. The proselyte was immersed in not less than forty seahs of water (at least one hundred gallons), whether by self or an agent being uncertain. The initiation marked a break with the old life, the acceptance of a new life, and induction into the people of God. It was a sign of cleansing, presupposing confession and forgiveness. The proselyte was considered to be like a child newly born.

The Baptism of John

The similarities between John's baptism and proselyte baptism are unmistakable. John's baptism, like Jewish proselyte baptism, was by total immersion; it took place in flowing water (but it is not clear that this was exclusively so; cf. John 3:23); it was an initiatory rite marking induction into a new community; it was a once-for-all rite; and it presupposed a break with the old life and commitment to the new.

The differences between John's baptism and proselyte baptism are significant. Proselyte baptism was semiprivate; John's was public. Proselyte baptism was possibly self-administered; John served as the agent, the descriptive terms being conclusive. In *ho baptistēs,* the Baptist (Matt. 3:1; 11:12; 14:2; Mark 6:25; 8:28; Luke 7:20,33), the agency suffix leaves no doubt at this point. An alternate description is with the participle, *ho baptizōn,* the one baptizing (Mark 6:14,24), and points to the same fact. The "Baptist" or "Baptizer" was a descriptive addition to distinguish John from others of the same name. The role of John was possibly new and unique in that he baptized other people.[21]

The major innovation of John's baptism, however, was in the calling of Jews to repentance baptism. Proselyte baptism was for Gentiles; John baptized Jews. To John the Jews were alien to true Israel or the people of Messiah (Matt. 3:9 f.). Proselyte

[21] Oepke in Kittel and Friedrich, *op. cit.,* I, 544.

baptism marked a Gentile's entry into Israel; John's repentance baptism marked a Jew's incorporation into the community awaiting the kingdom of God. John's baptism was basically eschatological; it looked toward the coming of Messiah to establish the kingdom of God (Matt. 3:12).

John's baptism presupposed moral change, the conversion of one yielding himself to the kingship of God. The Greek *metanoiein* literally means to change the mind, but in biblical usage it may have the fuller meaning of the Hebrew *shûbh,* to turn about. The turning concerns the whole person, not just the mind. Proselyte baptism was not merely ceremonial. It, too, called for commitment to the light and heavy commandments of God; but John's baptism went even further. It announced the coming kingdom of God before which even Jews must yield in a faith-repentance. There is no evidence that those baptized were in any sense organized, but they did form a "proleptic" community or nucleus of a messianic community.[22]

John's baptism is described as a "baptism of repentance unto the remission of sins" (Mark 1:4). He refused baptism to many because they had not shown evidences of repentance (Matt. 3:8; Luke 3:8). This fact is conclusive evidence that the forgiveness of sins was bound up with repentance and not with water baptism. Had John seen saving power in the baptism itself, he would have been criminally neglectful in withholding it from the "offspring of vipers" who needed it most. He called for confession of sins (Mark 1:5) and social righteousness (Luke 3:10–14) as evidence of a radical change in one's way of life. John was not preaching reform; he was proclaiming the coming of the Lord (*Kurios*), who would "baptize with the Holy Spirit and fire" (Matt. 3:11; Luke 3:16).

Holy Spirit and fire.—The two baptisms, that of John in water and that of Jesus in the Holy Spirit (Mark 1:8; John 1:33; Acts 1:5,8; 11:16) or the Holy Spirit and fire (Matt. 3:11; Luke 3:16) are difficult, whatever the interpretation. Probably it is best to read the latter passage: "He will baptize you in the

---

[22] White, *op. cit.,* p. 77.

Holy Spirit, *even* in fire." The Greek allows this translation, and it is less difficult than the familiar one. Thus read, the Holy Spirit himself is the "fire baptism" which Jesus brings.

T. W. Manson offers a plausible solution in suggesting that John's initial reference was to a "baptism in fire" which came to be understood as the "baptism in the Holy Spirit." [23] This interpretation he bases on Acts 19:1-6, which speaks of disciples of John at Ephesus who said, "We did not even hear if the Holy Spirit is." Manson understands them to mean that they had heard nothing about the Holy Spirit, not that they had not heard that the Holy Spirit was *given*. He suggests that the statements about "baptism in the Holy Spirit and fire" reflect the coming of the Holy Spirit at Pentecost, symbolized by tongues of fire.

According to this view, then, the original statement in "Q," an early source behind Matthew and Luke, read: "He will baptize you in fire." The "fire" came to be understood as the Holy Spirit on the day of Pentecost, and this affected the readings in the Gospels and Acts. In Mark 1:8; Acts 1:5,8; 11:16; and John 1:33 the interpretation was made by reading "Holy Spirit" instead of "fire." In Matthew 3:11 and Luke 3:16, both terms were retained, "the Holy Spirit, even fire." Thus the baptism which Jesus was to bring was that of "fire," seen later to be the Holy Spirit.

Manson's interpretation could be somewhat strengthened, it seems, by looking to Jesus himself as *before* Pentecost having spoken of the baptism of the Spirit where John had spoken of the baptism of fire. Whatever the solution, it seems best to understand "baptism and [or, even] fire" as one baptism, that of the Holy Spirit. By "fire," John stressed the judgment which could be escaped only by repentance in view of the kingdom of God. Convicting the world of "sin, righteousness, and judgment" (John 16:8 f.) belongs to the work of the Holy Spirit. This interpretation is consistent with the use of fire as a symbol of judgment in other passages.

[23] *The Sayings of Jesus* (London: SCM Press, 1949), pp. 40 f.

The Baptism of Jesus

Overshadowing all else for the understanding of Christian baptism is Jesus himself: his own baptism in the Jordan River, his teaching, his death and resurrection. Although there is clearly a sense in which John's baptism was antecedent to Christian baptism, as John's in turn had its apparent antecedent in Jewish proselyte baptism, the supreme antecedent to Christian baptism is Jesus Christ. His water baptism at the beginning and his death baptism at the close of his ministry provide the true basis for the practice and meaning of Christian baptism.[24]

That Jesus was baptized of John is stated explicitly (Mark 1:9–12; Matt. 3:13–17; Luke 3:21–23). The datum is beyond dispute, being strongly attested by the fact that early Christians found it necessary to explain it. Two questions required answer: (1) why was Jesus baptized by John, and (2) why did Jesus submit to repentance baptism? Matthew is careful to point out that Jesus took the initiative in going to John and that John recognized his own subordination to Jesus (3:13–15). John recognized the case of Jesus as exceptional, asking no repentance of him.

For Jesus, his baptism was in some sense "to fulfil all righteousness" (Matt. 3:15). It was neither a magical sacrament nor a mere symbol. He said, "Thus it becometh *us* to fulfil all righteousness." It is not clear whether "us" referred to himself and John or to himself and those with whom he took his stand in accepting the baptism of John. Jesus was content to risk misunderstanding as he identified himself with the sinners whom he came to save (cf. Mark 2:17). He would create his people out of just such sinners. He would fulfil all righteousness in just such faith-obedience to the will of God. T. W. Manson seems to reach the heart of the matter in saying:

Jesus recognizes in John's effort to create a new Israel the purpose of God; and willingly enters into it. The baptism of John is from heaven (Mk. 11:29 f.). That is sufficient for Jesus. The question is not

[24] Cf. Flemington, *op. cit.,* p. 33.

whether Jesus has or has not sins to confess, but whether He is to obey the call of God which comes through the last and greatest of the prophets.[25]

The counterpart to Jesus' act of faith-obedience to the call of God was the divine presence and authentication. "He saw the heavens being split and the Spirit coming down as a dove upon him," and he heard a voice out of heaven saying, "Thou art my beloved Son, in thee I am well pleased" (Mark 1:10 f.). Regardless of the extent to which these were visible or audible to others, the primary fact is the coming of the Spirit upon Jesus and the voice out of heaven. These not only authenticated Jesus but pointed to his task. That which Jesus heard was from Isaiah 42 (less certainly from Psalm 2 also, as claimed by many). His task as Suffering Servant, endowed with the Spirit, was set before him: "Behold, my servant, whom I uphold; my chosen, in whom my soul delighteth: I have put my Spirit upon him; he will bring forth justice to the Gentiles" (Isa. 42:1). It is thus as servant that he "fulfils all righteousness."

White correctly sees a major turning point in the meaning of baptism in the descent of the Spirit at the baptism of Jesus. "Renunciation of the past is taken up into the reception of grace and power for the future. . . . The rite which had expressed mainly what man does to fulfil God's will becomes now also a rite expressing something God does to make man's obedience effective." [26] The baptism of Jesus, then, points ahead, proleptically, not only to his death in which we are to participate (see below), but also to Pentecost or the coming of the Spirit.[27]

What was at the least latent in Jesus' baptism became explicit and emphatic in his commitment and teaching. He brought together the ideas of baptism and death, saying: "A baptism I have with which to be baptized, and how I am in anguish until it be completed" (Luke 12:50). His water baptism was behind him; his death baptism, foreshadowed in his water baptism,

[25] *The Sayings of Jesus*, pp. 149 f.
[26] Gilmore, *op. cit.*, p. 91.
[27] Cf. White, *op. cit.*, p. 109.

loomed large ahead. This baptism was not only his; it was to be the necessary death through which he must bring his own in bringing them into life.

Christ expressed the demand of this in the searching question: "Are ye able to drink the cup which I drink, or to be baptized with the baptism with which I am baptized?" (Mark 10:38). Thus he spoke of a baptism which is not water baptism, a fact all-important for understanding the New Testament doctrine of baptism, especially in Pauline passages. These words of Jesus also enable us to look back at his water baptism and see it as proclaiming Calvary as well as Pentecost. The death-resurrection and the coming of the Spirit we may know only in Christ Jesus, when we are "baptized with the baptism" with which he is baptized.

Christian Baptism

It is valid to distinguish between Christian baptism—the baptism of Christians—and the baptism of Jesus. Jesus' baptism had meaning for him that ours does not have for us. He was sinless and had no sin to confess; he required no repentance. Also quite distinct, he committed himself to a task that was unique. A Christian's baptism, on the other hand, has meaning that the baptism of Jesus did not have for him. It is a sign for repentance, cleansing, death, and resurrection. Yet even here, caution must be observed, for the *identification* of Jesus with his own people is to be taken as seriously as is the *distinction* of Jesus from his people. In a real sense he did assume our sin; in a real sense he did become "incarnate in us," dying our death; and in a real sense we do participate with him in his death-resurrection and in receiving the Holy Spirit. His baptism was faith-obedience to the call of God; it did point ahead to the cross and to Pentecost.

Our baptism does affirm our death and resurrection with Christ and our being cleansed in him. There is a sense in which we cannot "follow him in baptism," for he is Christ the Lord and we are sinners saved by his grace. His baptism necessarily

Has a connotation differing from ours. And yet we do follow
him in baptism as by faith we are "baptized into Christ," "baptized into his body," "baptized into his death." In a real sense,
in our baptism we enter into his role of Suffering Servant, for
the living Lord continues his ministry in us, the body of Christ
(see chaps. 7 and 10).

No defense is required for distinguishing between the baptism
of John and Christian baptism. Between the two is continuity,
yet discontinuity. Baptism for John's disciples could not possibly
have had the fulness of meaning which baptism came to have
for those who witnessed the death of Jesus, then saw him alive,
and soon thereafter witnessed the coming of the Spirit at Pentecost. T. C. Smith cuts to the heart of the matter in saying:
"John's rite looked forward to an event in history that was to
come. He called for repentance and baptism in anticipation of
the new era. Christian baptism was a proclamation that the new
era had arrived." [28]

Baptism in Acts.—In the book of Acts several basic ideas are
closely related, although the sequence is not clear in every detail.
These related ideas are preaching (*kērugma*), teaching, conviction, repentance, trust, baptism, the coming of the Holy Spirit,
laying on of hands, and sometimes speaking with tongues (glos-
solalia). There is no one complete pattern as to inclusion or sequence. There are some fixed priorities. In the narratives, baptism in water *never precedes* preaching, conviction, repentance,
or trust. The coming of the Spirit, laying on of hands, and the
gift of tongues are mentioned sometimes before and sometimes after water baptism. Attention has already been given to
the distinction noted in Acts between John's baptism in water
and the baptism of the Holy Spirit which Jesus brought.

The following summary will indicate the problem of inclusion
and sequence in passages concerned with baptism. On the day
of Pentecost (2:14–42) the narrative sequence was preaching,
conviction, repentance, baptism, and the gift of the Holy Spirit.
In Samaria (8:12–17) the sequence was preaching, faith, bap-

[28] McCall, *op. cit.*, p. 64.

tism, laying on of hands, and the gift of the Spirit. For the Ethiopian eunuch (8:26–39) the sequence was the reading of the Scriptures, preaching, and baptism (preceded by confession of faith according to some manuscripts).

In the narratives of Paul's conversion (9:12–18; 22:6–16; 26:12–18) the sequence was conviction, trust, laying on of hands, gift of the Holy Spirit and sight, and baptism. In the conversion of Cornelius (10:44–48; 11:15–18) the sequence was preaching, the gift of the Holy Spirit, tongues, and baptism. For the Philippian jailer (16:27–34) the sequence was conviction, faith, and baptism. For the disciples of John at Ephesus (19:1–7) the sequence after John's baptism was: instruction in the meaning of John's baptism as a repentance baptism presupposing faith in Jesus, baptism, laying on of hands, the gift of the Spirit, tongues and prophecy.

It is clear from Acts, then, that baptism was closely associated with "the word" as preached and believed. Flemington suggests that it was an embodiment of the gospel. That is, baptism itself is preaching.[29] It was closely related to repentance, forgiveness, and entry into the community of Christ. It was clearly connected with the Holy Spirit, sometimes preceding and sometimes following (as with Saul and Cornelius). Surely the fact of conversion implies the presence of the Holy Spirit; there is no repentance or faith without his presence.

Possibly it was in some instances only after baptism that the fuller presence of the Spirit was felt. Just as the Holy Spirit came at Pentecost yet was present before Pentecost (as the Old Testament and the Gospels show); so the Holy Spirit came in the baptism of some, yet was already present convicting the world "of sin and of righteousness and of judgment" (John 16:8). Faith and confession were always presupposed. Acts 8:37 is not supported by the best manuscripts, but it may be a development from an oft asked question: "Do you believe with all your heart?" [30]

[29] *Op. cit.,* p. 49.
[30] *Ibid.,* p. 48.

Baptism and cleansing.—Along with its other meanings, Jewish proselyte baptism was a sign of cleansing. It was not itself
the cleansing. Christian baptism, too, included cleansing in what
it symbolized. Water baptism does not "wash away sins," but
it is a sign of the cleansing which God alone can effect in
bringing one to repentance and faith. Acts 2:38 is sometimes
cited in support of the idea of baptismal regeneration, but the
call there to repentance precludes any idea that water baptism itself can cleanse of sin.

Observing the middle voice of the verbs, Acts 22:16 may best
be translated, "Arise, get yourself baptized and get your sins
washed away, calling upon his name." Out of context, this
verse possibly could teach that baptism cleanses of sin. But the
great stress upon repentance and faith, as well as the absence of
any reference to baptism in various passages concerned with
salvation (cf. Acts 3:19; 10:43; 16:31), leaves no room for
the idea that water baptism cleanses one from sin.

Outside of the book of Acts may be found several passages
in which the idea of cleansing is related in some sense to that of
baptism. This is not surprising in view of the fact that salvation
does include a cleansing from the defilement of sin. One such
passage is Ephesians 5:26, where Christ is presented as loving
the church and giving himself up for it "in order that he might
sanctify it, having cleansed it with the washing of water in a
[the?] word." Whatever else may be said, the sanctifying and
cleansing are the work of Christ; they are based upon his giving
up of himself (*heauton paredōken*). The "washing of water"
probably is an allusion in some sense to baptism, although this
is not explicit. The cleansing is not attributed to the water itself or to man's act; Christ alone sanctifies and cleanses.

Having spoken so lightly of circumcision that is "in flesh,
handmade" (*en sarki cheiropoiētou*), hence superficial and artificial (2:11), the writer surely did not suggest three chapters
later that water baptism (also "in flesh, handmade") can actually cleanse. Water baptism has the same value and limitations
as had circumcision. It is capable of outwardly expressing what

really happens inwardly in experience,[31] or it becomes an empty rite, trusted for the accomplishment of what it cannot do. Christ does cleanse the church as he "baptizes" it into his own death. He leads men to "give themselves up" to him, and this is outwardly expressed in water baptism. The meaning of the elusive "in a [or, the] word" (en rhēmati) is uncertain. It may allude to the early Christian practice of exacting a confession of faith from the one baptized,[32] or it may refer to the Word of God with its power to cleanse.[33]

In Titus 3:5 is a possible allusion to baptism in the phrase "through the washing of regeneration and the renewal of the Holy Spirit." If there is a reference to baptism, it is not explicit. What is explicit is that salvation is strictly God's work and not man's work. This passage refutes any doctrine of salvation through man's work. There is cleansing in salvation, but God does the cleansing. No New Testament passage more forcefully stresses God's kindness, love for humanity, character as Saviour, mercy, initiative in regeneration and renewal, free grace in making righteous, and making men heirs of eternal life. The larger passage reads:

But when the kindness and love for humanity of our Saviour God was manifested, not out of works in righteousness which we did, but according to his own mercy he saved us through the washing of regeneration and renewal of the Holy Spirit; whom he poured out upon us richly through Jesus Christ our Saviour, that being justified by his grace, we might be made heirs according to the hope of eternal life (Titus 3:4–7).

That there is a "washing" in regeneration (or in regeneration and renewal) is explicit, but this is traced directly to God as his

---

[31] Cf. Dodd, The Meaning of Paul for Today (London: George Allen & Unwin, Ltd., 1930), p. 119.

[32] Flemington, op. cit., p. 65, suggests that it was some word spoken at one's baptism, possibly the formula "in the name of Jesus" but probably the confession of faith, "Jesus is Lord." Beasley-Murray favors the idea of confession of the name (Gilmore, op. cit., p. 143). White sees a reference to the kērugma (op. cit., p. 202).

[33] Cf. Schneider, Die Taufe im Neuen Testament, p. 62.

work through the Holy Spirit in Jesus Christ (cf. 1 Corinthians 6:11). Water baptism does carry a message of cleansing but it does not effect the cleansing.

Baptism in the letters of Paul.—Paul's doctrine of baptism, as was true of his theology in general, was bound up with the saving events (*Heilstatsachen*) of Jesus, his death and resurrection as the Christian's "baptism." [34] Jesus himself had brought together the ideas of death and baptism (cf. Luke 12:50; Mark 10:38). Paul's statements about baptism range from his protest that Christ sent him not to baptize but to evangelize (1 Cor. 1:17) to the bold statement that we are "baptized into Christ" (Rom. 6:3; Gal. 3:27), "baptized into his body" (1 Cor. 12:13), "baptized into his death" (Rom. 6:3). One must not so isolate any one statement as to conclude that Paul took a light view of baptism or that he viewed it as a magical sacrament (*ex opere operato*). Paul's position is clear enough, but it requires careful study.

To the Corinthians, Paul expressed thanks that he had baptized only a few of their number. He wrote of this in a tone which indicates that to him it was unimportant to recall how many and concluded: "Christ sent me not to baptize but to evangelize" (1 Cor. 1:17). This was no disparagement of baptism. Paul simply insisted that the human agency in baptism was unimportant. His fear was that one baptized by Paul might falsely hold that he was baptized "in the name of Paul." Baptism for Paul had its meaning not in terms of one's relation to the human agent but in terms of one's relation to Christ (Rom. 6:3; Gal. 3:27), to his body (1 Cor. 12:13), to his death (Rom. 6:3). To understand Paul's thought one must see his distinction between water baptism and death baptism.

A crucial passage in Paul's doctrine of baptism is Romans 6:3–11. It must be observed that this passage was written to protest the libertine tendency to justify sinful conduct on the plea that salvation is by grace rather than works. On another front, Paul found it necessary to resist the Judaistic claim that

[34] *Ibid.*, p. 43.

only law, not grace, would yield a moral life. Paul argued that only through grace is the higher life possible. He cited baptism as pointing to the Christian's death and resurrection shared with Christ. His key statement, verse 3, appears as a question: "Or, know ye not that all we who were baptized into Christ Jesus, into his death we were baptized?" Although water baptism is clearly in the picture, the immediate reference is not to baptism into water but baptism into Christ.

A parallel may be seen in 1 Corinthians 10:2: "And they all were baptized into Moses." Paul did not say that the Israelites were baptized into the Red Sea, but *into Moses*.[35] At the Red Sea, the Israelites were forced into a radical decision. They could turn back to the Egyptians and slavery, or they could commit their destinies to the leadership of Moses. Paul saw their plunging of their destinies into the hands of Moses as their baptism into Moses. The crossing of the Red Sea was outwardly expressive of this; it was the outward form of an inner commitment.

In the same manner, Paul saw water baptism as the outward form of an inner commitment to Christ in which one is brought into union with Christ. Paul wrote boldly, "We were baptized into Christ Jesus." The immersion into water is the outward form of the immersion into Christ. Schneider quotes an apt statement of Leenhardt to the effect that it is not immersion that constitutes this "baptism"; it is union with Christ.[36] Immersion into Christ was as real to Paul as was immersion in water.

For Paul, baptism into Christ was also baptism into his death (Rom. 6:3). He saw Christ's death as becoming a present saving reality (*als gegenwärtige Heilswirklichkeit*) for the one who by faith was brought into vital union with him.[37] This is vividly described (vv. 4, 5, 6, 8) by several words compounded with the preposition *sun*, meaning "with." We are buried together (*sunetaphēmen*); we have become a single plant with Christ (*sum-*

---

[35] *Ibid.*, p. 44.
[36] *Ibid.*, p. 45.
[37] *Ibid.*

phutoi); [38] the old man is crucified together with (*sunestaurō-thē*); if we died with Christ (*sun Christō*), we shall also live together with him (*suzēsomen*).

Paul apparently did not see the believer as meeting Christ at Golgotha, but rather Christ as meeting the believer here and now.[39] This would accord with the recognition elsewhere in the New Testament of the eternal aspect of Christ's death. Without detracting from the once-for-all death at Golgotha, the New Testament also sees Jesus as "the Lamb slain from the foundation of the world" (Rev. 13:8) and even still as "a Lamb standing, as though it had been slain" (Rev. 5:6). Jesus now confronts us as the "slain Lamb," as well as the living Lord. Apparently, Paul thus saw the death of Jesus, extending into the present, as the one in which the Christian shares. Hence he used the phrase "in the likeness of his death" (Rom. 6:5). Schneider states it succinctly: we can be planted together "only with a reality which is *now* and which is *here* for us [*einer Wirklichkeit, die jetzt da ist und die für uns da ist*]." [40]

It is not that one dies *of* himself and surely not *for* himself. But to Paul, anyone confronted by the transforming presence of Jesus is enabled to die *with* Christ and to be raised with him (cf. Gal. 2:19 f.; Col. 1:21 f.; 2:20; 3:9; Eph. 2:15 f.; 2 Cor. 5:14 f.; Rom. 6:1–6; 7:4). The death which the believer now dies with Jesus is like the death at Golgotha, a death to self, a yielding up of one's life to another. For Paul, this baptism into the death of Christ is outwardly expressed in water baptism, but it is never confused with water baptism.

Of course, Paul's last word for the Christian was not death. One who has died with Christ will also live with him: "If we died with Christ, we believe that also we shall live together [*suzē-*

---

[38] Cf. Cullmann, *Baptism in the New Testament,* trans. J. K. S. Reid (London: SCM Press, 1950), p. 14.

[39] This understanding of the text is contrary to Cullmann's defense of infant baptism in which he holds that all men have in principle received baptism long ago, namely "on Golgotha, at Good Friday and Easter." Arguing that we shared thus passively (!) in Golgotha, he sees no problem in an infant's sharing passively in water baptism (*ibid.,* p. 23).

[40] *Op. cit.,* p. 46.

men] with him" (Rom. 6:8).[41] The future may be future only to the condition in the sentence, meaning that this life follows the death under discussion, but probably Paul contemplated a resurrection both immediate and future. The believer experiences both death and life like that of Jesus. Both of these realities are pictured in baptism.

Galatians 3:27 equates being baptized into Christ with putting on Christ: "Whatsoever ones of you who were baptized into Christ did put on Christ." Here two analogies are used interchangeably; being immersed in Christ and putting on Christ as a robe. Paul was not confusing union with Christ and water baptism. Verse 26 is decisive, for it makes faith basic. "All ye are sons of God *through faith in Christ Jesus.*" Paul here saw Christians as not only baptized into Christ but as together forming a new solidarity. They are a new Israel as Abraham's seed, a new humanity in which there is neither Jew nor Greek, slave nor free, male nor female. Not only is being baptized into Christ equated with putting on Christ as a robe; it is equated with being "in Christ" (Gal. 3:28).

Paul's recurrent "in Christ" concept not only appears as being baptized into Christ; it appears as being baptized into "one body," apparently the "body of Christ." The picture in Galatians 3:27 of being baptized *into Christ* becomes in 1 Corinthians 12:13: "We all *into one body* were baptized." The context makes it clear that he was speaking of the church as the body of Christ in which Jews and Greeks, slaves and free men, and all are individually members of the one body. To be baptized into Christ is, for Paul, to be baptized into the church as the body of Christ—the *ekklēsia* as the people of God. This *ekklēsia* is brought into being through divine calling and hence indestructible through all eternity. That Paul was not thinking of a local organization is clear from the immediate context and from his elaborate and vigorous presentation in various epistles of the church as the body of Christ. The "body" of verse 13 obviously is the "body" of verse 12: "All the members of the body being

[41] A few manuscripts have the subjunctive, "Let us live."

many are one body; *thus also is Christ.*" The statement has the
inescapable implication: "Thus also is Christ *one body.*"

The incorporation into Christ is also incorporation into his
people, the larger "incarnation." Paul was baptized in Damascus, not in Corinth, and yet he considered himself as having
been baptized into the very body, the one body, into which the
Corinthian Christians were baptized: "All we into one body
were baptized" (v. 13). That water baptism has its meaning in
connection with one's incorporation into the people of God (i.e.,
the *ekklēsia* as the body of Christ) and not in connection with a
local organization is in principle recognized by all people who
hold that water baptism is a once-for-all event. Otherwise, one
would be baptized each time he became affiliated with a new
congregation. It must be remembered that in this Corinthian
passage, as in Romans 6:1–11 and elsewhere, Paul did not confuse water baptism with the death-resurrection baptism by
which one is "baptized into Christ."

Ephesians 4:4–6 states a basic theme already abundantly
clear in Pauline writing. The great theme of Ephesians is the
purpose of God to unite all people in Christ, creating out of
Jew and Gentile one new man (2:16). This accomplishment is
described as the church, the body of Christ (1:22 f.; 2:16;
4:13; 5:23, 29–32; and also Col. 1:18,24; 3:15). Seven major
factors of this unity are given in 4:5, including "one Lord, one
faith, one baptism." There is but one commitment to the one
Lord, one death-life shared with the one Lord. In this passage
baptism probably means death (as in Luke 12:50; Mark
10:38 f.).

In Colossians 2:11–12, Paul introduced a new analogy as he
wrote of baptism as Christian "circumcision." The identification
is explicit:

In whom [Christ] also ye were circumcised with *a circumcision not
made with hands* [*acheiropoiētō*] *in the putting off of the body of
flesh, in the circumcision of Christ,* having been buried with him in
baptism, in which [whom?] also ye were raised through faith in the
working of God, the one having raised him from the dead.

For the Jew circumcision alone was the induction rite. For the proselyte to Judaism induction included circumcision and baptism. For the Jew who became a Christian, baptism marked induction into the messianic people, even as his eighth-day circumcision had marked induction into Judaism. For the Christian, baptism alone became the induction rite. This does not carry the further implication that baptism, like circumcision, was administered to infants; this is ruled out on other grounds. Neither is this to say that baptism took the place of circumcision, becoming in the new age what circumcision was in the old.[42] In Jewish Christianity both were practiced.

On the other side, it should be observed that James, not without reason, feared that Paul's preaching would result in the dropping of circumcision by Christian Jews (Acts 21:21). Paul stood strongly against it for Gentile converts at least: "Behold, I Paul say to you, that if ye receive circumcision, Christ will profit you nothing" (Gal. 5:2). Possibly Paul discouraged it for children of Christian Jews also. The case of Timothy is not forgotten; it is said that Paul circumcised him (Acts 16:3). Possibly Paul consented to this only to acknowledge that as a Jew, Timothy should have been circumcised in keeping with Jewish custom. When Timothy was born none in his family was Christian. The Jewish rite was neglected because of his Greek father. Should Timothy attempt to work among Jews, that neglect could easily prejudice the case against him as one who, even before his conversion to Christianity, was indifferent to the traditions of his people.

Where this question of pre-Christian loyalty to Judaism was not involved, Paul may have taught Christian Jews not to circumcise their children. At least that report had reached Jerusalem (Acts 21:21); and Paul protested to the Galatians that he did not teach circumcision (5:11).

Paul, in Colossians 2:11–13, probably thought of both water baptism and death baptism (*Todestaufe*). The putting off of "the body of flesh" would be the death of the "old man" through

[42] Cf. McCall, *op. cit.*, p. 74, for a clear statement of this point.

the denial of the life attempted in independence of God. In calling this "baptism" a "circumcision not made with hands," he contrasts it not only with flesh circumcision, but also with water baptism. He was thinking of a baptism beyond water baptism, for water baptism is as definitely made with hands (*cheiropoiētos*) as is flesh circumcision.

The Christian is a new creation (2 Cor. 5:17; Gal. 6:15) and is incorporated into a new Israel or new humanity. Just as flesh circumcision was expressive of a Jewish lad's incorporation into Israel, so water baptism is the outward expression of that inward death baptism by which the believer becomes one with Christ and his church, the body of Christ. This passage is no basis for the defense of infant baptism, but it is a great text declaring that the Christian is a new man, inducted into a new people by a "baptism" or "circumcision" which is death and resurrection in Christ.

Another Pauline passage, 1 Corinthians 7:14–16, must be considered, not as offering additional light on Paul's understanding of baptism, but because of its exegetical difficulty. Paul was giving practical advice to the Christian whose spouse was not a Christian. He seems to say that such a marriage is holy and the children are holy—that the Christian does not thereby live in sin by continuing the relation. Some argue from this that the child of a Christian parent is thus by natural birth a Christian and entitled to baptism as an infant.

What is often overlooked is that Paul said of the unbelieving (*apistos*) spouse what he said of the child born to this union. The unbelieving spouse has been sanctified (*hēgiastai*) and the children are holy (*hagia*). The terms are basically the same, one a verb and one an adjective. If the child is thus saved, so is the *unbelieving spouse!* Personal salvation is not the point. Paul is simply saying that the marriage is valid. The passage offers no light for the understanding of salvation or baptism.

Very difficult is the enigmatic statement of 1 Corinthians 15:29, "Else what shall they do, those being baptized for the dead? If the dead are not at all raised, why are they being baptized for them?" The most literal interpretation of this verse is that Paul taught both "baptismal regeneration" and "proxy baptism." In other words, through one person's water baptism another person, already dead, might be saved. The Judaizers at their worst were never so crude as that. Surely Paul was not outdoing the Judaizers. Following the sound hermeneutical principle set forth by W. Vischer that the Bible is to be studied *ganzheitlich* (seen in its wholeness),[43] this passage cannot be made to refute the very position on salvation for which Paul jeopardized his whole life.

Although there are several possible interpretations, probably Paul by the "dead" means the "old man" who is put to death that the "new man" might be raised in his place. Paul's subject is resurrection, not baptism. He alludes to baptism only to point out how foolish it would be to imperil oneself before a hostile world by a baptism portraying a resurrection *if* there were no resurrection at all. The passage does support the "burial-resurrection" reference in baptism.

First Peter.—The one New Testament passage which explicitly says that baptism saves (1 Peter 3:21) so interprets the statement as to refute any doctrine of "baptismal regeneration." The reference occurs in a passage chiefly concerned with encouraging Christians then undergoing persecution by pointing out that their Lord had triumphed over all his enemies, his triumph being on a cosmic scale. Through his death and resurrection Christ conquered, even to the point of making a proclamation (judgment?) to the "spirits in prison," presumably fallen angels, who were disobedient during the time of Noah.[44] The reference to Noah led to the statement that "eight souls were saved through water" and to the further claim: "which also as an antitype now saves you, baptism." The eight in the time of Noah were saved *through* the very water which threatened to destroy them.

[43] Cf. Davies and Daube, *op. cit.*, pp. 23 f.
[44] Cf. Bo Reicke, *The Disobedient Spirits and Christian Baptism* (Copenhagen: Ejnar Munksgaard Forlay, 1946) for the definitive work on this entire passage.

Possibly to the writer baptism represented the death which both destroys and saves: one must be crucified with Christ in order to live. But lest the analogy be pressed too far, the writer hastened to rule out the idea that the water itself could save, attributing the salvation rather to "the pledge of a good conscience unto God through the resurrection of Jesus Christ" (3:21).

S. I. Buse may be followed in understanding 1 Peter 3:21 to refer to "God's pledge that a man may stand before Him without qualms of conscience." [45] The Greek *eperōtēma*, variously translated as "answer," "question," "interrogation," probably is best understood as "pledge." Christians are given the *pledge* that because of the resurrection of Jesus Christ, triumphant over death and over all enemies, they may stand before God with a good conscience. The Christian is one who has died and been raised in a "baptism" with Christ, the "baptism" with which he was "baptized" (cf. Luke 12:50; Mark 10:38). The writer could say, "baptism saves you"; but it is not water baptism that has saving value. It is Christ's "baptism" of death and resurrection which saves. This is the "pledge of a good conscience" which God is able to afford the believer. The death into which the Christian is "baptized" (Rom. 6:3) is Christ's triumphant death, and it becomes triumphant in the believer.

The Johannine writings.—The most important and most debated Johannine passage concerned with baptism (John 3:5) has been discussed in chapter 4 (see pp. 56 ff.). Of course, the word "baptism" does not occur in the passage, and many are persuaded that there is no allusion to it. The position taken in this book is that "begotten of water and the Spirit" simply acknowledges and builds upon the truth in John's statement: "I baptize you in water; but he shall baptize you in the Holy Spirit" (Mark 1:8; Matt. 3:11; Luke 3:16; John 1:33). It does not teach that water baptism is essential to salvation; rather it recognizes the limitations of John's baptism, as John himself indicated. The main point is that the new life is from God, his creative work for those "begotten from above." John 3:5 and its context trace salvation back to God, not to water baptism.

John 13, with the narrative of the washing of the disciples' feet, is commonly discussed with reference to baptism. This is highly precarious. There obviously is in the Greek of John 13:10 a play on words with far-reaching implications: "The one having been bathed [*leloumenos*] has not need except to wash [*nipsasthai*] his feet, but he is wholly cleansed; and ye are cleansed, but not all of you." Those having been "bathed" have been "cleansed," and all but Judas have been cleansed.

Jesus certainly did not mean that only Judas has not had water baptism. There was a basic, once-for-all cleansing which all but Judas had had. This may be outwardly expressed in water baptism, but it is not to be confused with water baptism. Judas would not have been cleansed by that means. The initial cleansing in conversion is eternally valid, yet it provides for and demands daily "washing of the feet"—discipline within the Christian community. God alone can "bathe" with the initial cleansing; disciples must "wash one another's feet." If the passage alludes to baptism, it is to that "baptism" which God alone can effect and which water baptism can only outwardly express.

A possible anti-Docetic thrust may be seen in 1 John 5:5–8, where Jesus as the Son of God is declared to be "the one coming through water and blood" (v. 6) and the one receiving the threefold witness of the Spirit, the water, and the blood (v. 8). Some of the Docetists sought to modify the doctrine of Incarnation by holding that the Spirit came upon Jesus at his baptism but left him before his death. Against this, John may have been claiming that the Spirit was present at his baptism and in his death, hence "the water and the blood."

A similar antidocetic teaching may appear in John 19:34, where "water and blood" are said to have flowed from the pierced side of Jesus. Taking "water" here to refer to Jesus' baptism, however, seems to strain exegesis somewhat. Certainly it is asking much of the readers to see—at least without the help of commentaries and books on theology!—an allusion to baptism and the Lord's Supper in the words "water and blood." One may allow the possibility of antidocetic teaching in John 19:34 and 1 John 5:5–8, but it is highly precarious to build a doctrine of baptism on these passages.

The Lord's command.—Matthew 28:18–20 embodies "the Great Commission" of our Lord, and it places baptism in proper relationship to discipleship and teaching. The passage has long been contested, many holding that the saying goes back only to the church and not to Jesus. Arguments against the text are weighty but not decisive. At least the passage is original to Matthew and is as well attested as other words and deeds attributed to Jesus.[46] This passage is important both for the authority which it gives to baptism and for linking baptism with making and teaching disciples. Apart from these verses, Christian baptism yet has the authority of Christ because of his own baptism and because of his forging together the ideas of death and baptism. Matthew 28:18–20, however, makes the authority explicit and in the form of a command.

In the Commission, the command centers in the verb *mathē-teusate,* "make disciples," an imperative form. Assuming that men would travel, Jesus said: "As you go, *disciple* all nations," bringing them under the discipline of Christ the Lord, calling them to obedient trust. Two participles follow, just as one precedes the imperative: "Going, disciple all nations, baptizing . . . teaching." Instruction in the observance of Christ's commands is placed alongside baptism in this command. The teaching is to continue throughout the life of the disciple, but it apparently is *to begin* simultaneously with baptism.[47]

The formula "in the name" must be understood in terms of ancient usage. In a fuller sense than we usually recognize today, the name then stood for the person. Calling the name of a person upon another carried the idea of becoming that one's property. This may be the implication of James 2:7, where Christians are admonished not to grovel before the rich as though

[46] Cf. Gilmore, *op. cit.,* p. 113.
[47] Cf. McCall, *op. cit.,* p. 65.

they belonged to them, thus blaspheming "the good name" called upon them. Smith suggests that being baptized in the name of Christ carried the idea of becoming his property.[48] In Matthew 28:19 the disciple is to be baptized "into the name of the Father, and of the Son, and of the Holy Spirit." This means that one thus comes under the authority or sovereignty of the triune God; and here, too, name stands for person.

Summary and Conclusions

The conclusions reached in this chapter may be summarized as follows:

1. New Testament baptism was always by immersion.
2. It was administered by an agent.
3. The importance of the agent was not stressed.
4. Jewish proselyte baptism, with significant differences, apparently was antecedent to John's baptism.
5. The death and resurrection of Jesus provided the supreme antecedent to Christian baptism, foreshadowed in his own baptism and made focal in his teaching.
6. Jesus himself distinguished between water baptism and death baptism, a shared death (and resurrection) by which one was "baptized into Christ."
7. Witnessing, repentance, and faith brought to confession preceded baptism.
8. Baptism signified one's incorporation into the Christian community, the *ekklēsia*, the body of Christ.
9. Baptism was viewed as Christian "circumcision," but with no suggestion of infant baptism.
10. Baptism was likened to a new robe, the putting off of the old man and the putting on of the new.
11. Water baptism was not saving. Many passages which are concerned with salvation make no mention of baptism. Persons showing no evidences of repentance were refused baptism.
12. Baptism in the New Testament is never called a symbol or a sacrament, and neither term is adequate. Water is a symbol, and burial in water is symbolic. But a symbol is a symbol of something. In a meaningful Christian baptism there is that present which goes far beyond symbolism, including: faith, obedience, confession, com-

[48] *Ibid.,* p. 68.

mitment, gratitude, acknowledgment of Christ and of the body of Christ.

In concluding, it may be suggested, with awareness of the limitations of the analogy, that water baptism is to the union with Christ what a wedding is to a marriage. Each presupposes a previous commitment and each *is* a commitment. A wedding ring is a symbol, but a wedding is more than a symbol. In a wedding the mutual commitments already made in private are brought to outward expression in community. A wedding alone is not a marriage. Even so, water baptism without a previous personal commitment to Jesus Christ is but an empty gesture. As the outward expression for an inner death baptism—death and resurrection shared with Christ—it is existentially as far above symbol as a wedding is to two persons who have become one flesh in marriage. Since some cultures do not have what we know as a wedding, a marriage may be a marriage without a wedding. But a wedding adds immeasurably to the beauty and sacredness of a marriage. Even so, union with Christ can be real apart from water baptism, but baptism adds to the beauty and sacredness of that union. It is normal and right.

The Lord's 9 Supper

THE SHARED MEAL has always been expressive of, and an encouragement to, the ties which bind people into a fellowship of love, trust, and mutual acceptance. Jesus gave only two ordinances to his church, and one is that of a shared meal. Remembrance of him, acknowledgment of his presence, confident hope in his return, fellowship (*koinōnia*) with him and his people, self-examination, gratitude, thanksgiving, and worship ideally characterize the observance of the Supper. The bread and the cup are employed as symbols, and of themselves they can be symbols only. But symbols are symbols of something. The Supper has Christian meaning when it attests to, outwardly expresses, and inwardly cultivates what it means to be the body of Christ—a fellowship of redeemed persons. This fellowship is sealed by the Holy Spirit in a new covenant through the blood of him who died for us, whose promised return is assured, and whose living presence is the most solid fact of Christian experience.

The Supper is observed under various names: Lord's Supper, Eucharist, Communion, and Mass.[1] To some it is a sacrament in the highest sense; to others it is a symbol and nothing more.

---

[1] "Mass" is in no sense a New Testament word, being a contraction of the Latin *"Missa est,"* a dismissal formula equivalent to "it is over," and used to dismiss first the catechumens then, after the Supper, the communicants. Cf. C. Anderson Scott, *Romanism and the Gospel* (Philadelphia: The Westminster Press, 1946), pp. 95 f.

Some observe it as the central interest of every service of worship; others rarely or never observe it.

The New Testament contains only a few explicit and undeniable references to the Lord's Supper, but these are highly significant. The New Testament gives importance to the Lord's Supper, and it is important to recover this meaning. Have we been so busy telling the people what the Supper is not that we have failed to tell them what it is? Has there been such concern to exclude from the Supper that few really care to be included? There can be little doubt that the earliest Christians made far more of the Lord's Supper than do many present-day churches. There are evidences that the Lord's Supper was the basis for almost every gathering of the earliest Christians, the whole service being built around the Lord's Supper observed as a full meal (cf. Acts 2:42,46; 20:7,11; 1 Cor. 11:20; Rev. 3:20).[2]

Terminology

The Lord's Supper.—The designation "Lord's Supper" occurs in the New Testament only in 1 Corinthians 11:20, and even there it is disputed as to meaning. Probably the verse is best translated, "Your coming together in one place is not to eat the Lord's Supper." The suggestion that Paul meant that the purpose of their coming together was not to eat a royal or lordly (*kuriakon*) banquet is interesting and correctly reflects exactly what they were making of the Supper, but that is not his likely meaning here. Probably Paul meant that although they called it the "Lord's Supper" it was not that in fact, for they violated its essential meaning. The adjective occurs in Revelation 1:10, where it designates the Lord's Day, not the royal or lordly day. In Corinthians it is best to translate it as the Lord's Supper.

The breaking of bread.—The expression "to break bread" was employed by the earliest Christians in describing the Supper. This expression was used for the daily meal, the breaking of the

---

[2] Cf. Cullmann, *Early Christian Worship*, trans. A. Stewart Todd and J. B. Torrance (London: SCM Press, 1953), pp. 14, 20, 29, 31, *et passim*.

bread being the signal that the meal was to begin.[3] The clearest employment of the term is found in 1 Corinthians 10:16, "The bread which we break."

Reference to the Lord's Supper as the breaking of bread is probably to be seen in Acts 2:42: "They were continuing in the teaching of the apostles, and in the fellowship [*koinōnia*], the breaking of bread, and in the prayers." Grammar favors the reference of "the *koinōnia*" (fellowship or communion) and "the breaking of bread" as being to the same thing. This *koinōnia* or "breaking of bread" was undoubtedly a full meal, the Lord's Supper being so observed by the earliest Christians. Probably Acts 20:7 also refers to the Lord's Supper observed as a full meal: "On the first day of the week as we came together to break bread."

Late manuscripts have given rise to the erroneous teaching that the Lord's Supper portrays the *broken* body of Jesus. The correct reading in 1 Corinthians 11:24, attested by third- and fourth-century manuscripts, simply reads: "This is my body for you." Late manuscripts unfortunately added either "given" or "broken" for you.

The Fourth Gospel insists that not a bone of his body was broken (19:31–37); and the spurious reading in the late manuscripts obscures Paul's emphasis in 1 Corinthians upon the oneness of the body proclaimed in the Supper (1 Cor. 10:16 f.). The Supper proclaims the body of Christ, not the *broken* body. The *breaking* of bread points to a joint participation in one loaf, not to the fragmentizing of the loaf. This agrees with Cullmann's conclusion: "The formula 'to break bread' usually meant 'to take a meal.' "[4] The idea is not that one loaf is broken into many pieces but that many people eat of one loaf. This proclaims the basic fact that all Christians participate in the one Christ.

Eucharist.—Those who term the Lord's Supper a *Eucharist*

---

[3] Arndt and Gingrich, *op. cit.,* p. 434.
[4] Cullmann and F. J. Leenhardt, *Essays on the Lord's Supper,* trans. J. G. Davies (Richmond: John Knox Press, 1958), p. 10.

employ New Testament terminology, whatever they may mean by it. As used in the New Testament, the term refers to a *thanksgiving*. The noun form is not used, but the observance of the Supper is described in the New Testament as including the giving of thanks. Used interchangeably are the participles for "giving thanks" (*eucharistēsas*) and "blessing" (*eulogēsas*). Mark describes Jesus as blessing (*eulogēsas*) the bread and "giving thanks" (*eucharistēsas*) for the cup.

Paul reversed the terms, speaking of the "cup of blessing which we bless" (1 Cor. 10:16) and describing Jesus as "giving thanks" for the bread (1 Cor. 11:24). Luke describes Jesus as "giving thanks" (*eucharistēsas*) for the bread and the cup. Obviously the terms were interchanged with no point at stake. Giving thanks or "the blessing" was a Jewish practice at all meals, each meal having a religious significance. The Lord's Supper is a "Eucharist" in the New Testament sense of the term, a thanksgiving to God for *the Bread of life,* even as at ordinary meals it was a thanksgiving for bread.

Communion.—The Lord's Supper is termed a communion by many Christians. There is New Testament ground for this, and the term, if employed in its New Testament meaning, preserves much of the meaning of the Supper. The King James Version so translates 1 Corinthians 10:16, "The cup of blessing which we bless, is it not the communion of the blood of Christ? The bread which we break, is it not the communion of the body of Christ?" The Greek word for "communion" is *koinōnia*. As seen in chapter 7, this term designates a joint participation in that which is common to two or more persons. There is gain in simply transliterating the term as *koinōnia*.

Paul's concern in the paragraph which includes 1 Corinthians 10:16 is to warn against a Christian's participation in an idol feast. In these, pagans sought communion with "gods" which to Paul were demons. Paul protested that the Christian's communion is with Christ and not with demons. The Lord's Supper as a communion of the blood and body of Christ (v. 16) excludes for the Christian any participation in a "communion of demons" (v. 20). In giving this warning Paul indicated that the Lord's Supper is a *koinōnia* with Christ, a fellowship of Christians in Christ and with Christ. Paul did not mean that Christ is in the bread or cup, but he did mean that in any true observance of the Supper one is in communion with Christ. The loaf and the cup are symbols, but Christ is not a symbol, and he is not just symbolically present. He is actually present with and in his people.

In 1 Corinthians 10:17 Paul declared that "the many of us are one loaf, one body, for all of us partake of the one loaf." Thus the *koinōnia* with Christ is also a *koinōnia* with one another. This meaning of the Lord's Supper is yet more forcefully argued in 1 Corinthians 11:21–34, where Paul insisted that the common meal is the Lord's Supper only if observed in unity. The main point of the paragraph is that the Christians must await one another, eat together, and in so doing see themselves as the body of Christ (v. 29). The word *koinōnia* is not used in this paragraph, but the idea is there. The Supper is a communion with one another and with Christ. It is the communion of the body of Christ (1 Cor. 10:16).

Further evidence that the Lord's Supper was described as a "communion" or *koinōnia* may be seen in Acts 2:42. As already observed, grammar in the Greek sentence favors the equation of "the *koinōnia*" with "the breaking of the loaf [bread]." This important New Testament term, employed in various connections, seemingly was one of several terms employed to represent the rich meaning of the Lord's Supper. *Koinōnia* would stress the participation of Christians with one another in the Lord Jesus Christ, their being members one of another as members of the body of Christ.

It must be concluded that no one term was dominant for describing the Lord's Supper, not even the term "the Lord's Supper." This significant meal was variously described in terms of its manner and meaning. Each term is valuable, for each throws its particular light on something that is too rich to be expressed by a single phrase.

The Lord's Supper and the Passover

The Jewish Passover is in some sense antecedent to, and instructive for the study of, the Lord's Supper. This is not to overlook the problem of the nature of the "Last Supper" observed by Jesus with his disciples on the night of his betrayal. Whether the Last Supper was the paschal meal or not, Jesus' death was thought of in terms of the paschal lamb.

The problem of the identity of the Last Supper is posed by the seeming conflict between the Synoptics on the one hand and John and Paul on the other. The Synoptic Gospels clearly identify the Last Supper as the Passover (cf. Mark 14:12,14, 16; Matt. 26:17–19; Luke 22:7–15). The Fourth Gospel appears to date the death of Jesus before the night of the Passover meal (John 13:1; 18:28; 19:14). Those sent to Pilate by Caiaphas, for example, did not enter the palace lest they be thus defiled and not be able to eat the Passover (18:28). Likewise, Paul seems to fix the death of Jesus at the time the paschal lamb was slaughtered, hence before the Passover meal was eaten, in writing, "Christ our passover was slain" (1 Cor. 5:7).

The problem of identifying the Last Supper, or of determining the date of the Last Supper, is real; also, the dogmatism which sees only conflict within the New Testament is unwarranted. The issue is not closed. The dogmatism which rules out a constructive solution is as untenable as the dogmatism which rules out the problem. For all the apparent conflict, there is a defensible solution which resolves the seeming conflict. As has been forcefully demonstrated by competent scholarship, the Last Supper has all the marks of the paschal meal whether described by the Synoptics or the Fourth Gospel.[5] Furthermore, the passages in Paul and in the Fourth Gospel are not conclusive against the identification of the Last Supper as the Passover.

That Paul thought of Jesus as the Passover Lamb is clear from 1 Corinthians 5:7, "For Christ our passover [*to pascha*]

[5] Cf. Joachim Jeremias. *The Eucharistic Words of Jesus*, trans. Arnold Ehrhardt (Oxford: Blackwell, 1955), pp. 1–60.

was slain." This would be more natural had the crucifixion of Jesus coincided with the slaughter of the paschal lamb on the thirteenth day of the month Nisan. The analogy is possible even if the death occurred only at the Passover season, on the day following the Passover meal. The verse is an important one to the problem, but it is not decisive.

Closer examination of John 13:1; 18:28; and 19:14, along with Synoptic passages, leaves open the possibility of actual harmonization.[6] The clue is to be found in the manner of referring to the Feast of Passover and of Unleavened Bread. Strictly speaking, there were two distinct feasts, one following immediately upon the other: the Feast of Passover, observed the night following the slaughter of the paschal lamb, and the seven-day feast of Unleavened Bread. The two feasts could be distinguished or they could be referred to as one eight-day feast, designated by *either* or *both* names. "Passover" could refer to the one-day feast in the proper sense, or to the eight-day feast combining Passover and Unleavened Bread.

The tendency to blend the two feasts may be seen in the Gospel of Mark. In 14:1 both terms appear: "The [Feast of] Passover and Unleavened Bread was after two days." [7] In verse 12 the Feast of Passover is placed within that of Unleavened Bread: "On the first day of Unleavened Bread, *when the Passover was slain,* his disciples said to him, 'Where do you wish that we go and make ready that you may eat the Passover?' " It is possible that in John 18:28 the term "Passover" is used for the eight-day feast, and not in the strict sense of the paschal meal.

The reference in John 19:14 poses no insoluable problem: "It was the preparation of the Passover [*paraskeuē tou pascha*]." The genitive in the Greek, without a preposition, does not justify the translation "preparation *for* the Passover." The term "preparation" may simply mean the day before the sabbath or "Friday" in our terminology. In present-day Greek the word

---

[6] Cf. A. T. Robertson, *A Harmony of the Gospels* (New York: Harper & Brothers, 1922), pp. 279–287.

[7] A few manuscripts omit "and unleavened bread."

for Friday is this very word *Paraskeuē*, "Preparation." Hence John 19:14 may say only that it was "Friday" of Passover Week when Jesus was crucified. This would then not rule out his having eaten the Passover meal at its regular time. John 19:31 shows that "preparation" refers only to the day before the sabbath. This is explicit in Mark 15:42, "And evening already having come, since it was preparation, which is [the day] before the sabbath." Equally clear is Luke 23:54, "And the day was preparation, and the sabbath drew on." Hence John 19:14 declares only that it was "Friday" of Passover, not that it was the day when the paschal lamb was slain.

If it may be assumed that Jesus ate the Passover with his disciples and that during that meal he instituted the Lord's Supper, there is rich background for the understanding of the Lord's Supper as will be seen in the sections to follow, these being concerned with the meaning of the Supper.

Theory of Two Early Types

Hans Lietzmann [8] has advanced the thesis that two distinct supper observances arose among early Christians, one designated by him the Jerusalem type and the other the Pauline type. The former was the table fellowship (*koinōnia*) described in the early chapters of Acts, and the latter a memorial to the death of Jesus as developed by Paul and somewhat based upon the Last Supper observed by Jesus with his disciples before his death. The Jerusalem type Lietzmann sees to have grown out of the table fellowship of the disciples with Jesus when they formed with him a Jewish *chaburāh*. The Pauline type, according to Lietzmann, arose about A.D. 50 and was based upon an old tradition found also in Mark and bound up with the Last Supper.

Lietzmann found a point of departure in what he considers the two oldest types of liturgy, the third-century Roman liturgy of Hippolytus and the fourth-century Egyptian liturgy of Sera-

---

[8] *Mass and Lord's Supper*, trans. Dorothea H. G. Reeve (Leiden: E. J. Brill, 1953), pp. 204–208, *et passim*.

pion. The former is traced back to a revelation given to Paul and the latter to the table fellowship of the disciples, begun with Jesus before his death and revived when they learned that he was alive again. According to Lietzmann, the Jerusalem type was a joyous meal realizing the spiritual presence of Jesus and looking forward to his return at the *parousia*. The Pauline type looked back to the death of Jesus, stressing its meaning for salvation.

Lietzmann's argument is strong and must be respected. On the other hand, it has not won the acceptance of many able scholars. To begin with, Lietzmann holds, without evidence, that the Jews or Jesus formed *chaburôth* as regular associations. *Chaburôth* were, in fact, concerned with the observance of the Torah and special religious duties and functions.[9] Again, he attributes the memorial aspect of the Lord's Supper back to a special revelation given to Paul, assuming that the apostle created the type of observance which shifted the emphasis from that of a fellowship meal to that of a memorial to the death of Jesus. This is unduly skeptical of Paul's own insistence that he handed on unaltered the tradition which went back to the Lord.[10]

The silence in Acts 2:42 concerning a cup in connection with the breaking of bread is scant evidence for Lietzmann's concept of a primitive type of "Eucharist" unconnected with the Passover and unconcerned with the death of Jesus. Since Acts is a direct sequel to Luke, the author could very well have expected his readers to understand from the Gospel that the cup and the bread went together. Furthermore, Paul was as much concerned with the *parousia* as were those described in Acts as joyfully breaking bread together, having stressed this very fact in saying: "For as often as you eat this bread, and drink this cup, you proclaim the Lord's death *until he comes*" (1 Cor. 11:26). No case is established for two distinct types in the New Testament, differing in origin and in content.

[9] Cf. Jeremias, *op. cit.*, pp. 25 f.
[10] Cf. Higgins, *The Lord's Supper in the New Testament* (London: SCM Press, 1952), pp. 26, 35, 57–60.

Remembrance of Decisive Deliverance

When Jesus instituted the Supper he said, "This do in remembrance of me" (1 Cor. 11:24). The Supper is more than a memorial, but it is that. It is a remembrance of the decisive event in which Christ effected at Golgotha a new "exodus" for mankind. The Passover celebrated for the Jews the mighty act of God in which he had delivered the Israelites from Egyptian bondage. The Lord's Supper looks back to the new "exodus" or the triumph over sin and death accomplished at Golgotha. At the transfiguration, Moses and Elijah were represented as speaking with Jesus concerning "his *exodus* which he was about to accomplish in Jerusalem" (Luke 9:31).

According to the Mishnah (*P'sāchîm*, x, 5*b*), each Israelite as he partook of the Passover meal was obligated to think of himself as being delivered out of Egypt. Jewish Christians, so trained, would have little difficulty in seeing themselves as delivered through the death of Jesus. Just as the Exodus from Egypt was "relived" by Israelites, so the new "exodus" in Christ was relived by his followers. The Lord's Supper was in this sense a "Eucharist," a thanksgiving to God for deliverance.

The mood of the Supper observance was properly that of joy, just as in the Passover. It was the joy of a crisis passed, of a victory accomplished. There was no funeral atmosphere, as in some present-day observances. Cullmann [11] has aptly suggested that joyous observance of the Supper may also be traceable to the fact that several of the postresurrection appearances of Jesus to his disciples occurred in connection with meals (cf. Luke 24:30 f.; 24:41–43; John 21:1–10; Acts 10:41).

The Fellowship of the Body of Christ

When Jesus said, "This is my body," he no doubt had the double reference to his own body to be given at Golgotha and to his larger "body," the church. He did not mean that the literal

[11] *Early Christian Worship*, p. 15, and also Cullmann and Leenhardt, *op. cit.*, p. 8.

bread would become his body. Burrows correctly says, "Nowhere in the New Testament is there anything approaching the idea of transubstantiation or the repeated sacrifice of the mass." [12] The loaf which he held in his hands would symbolize the body of his incarnation, given for man. It would come also to symbolize the church, the body of Christ, his larger "incarnation." Paul said as much in 1 Corinthians 10:16, "the bread which we break, is it not the *koinōnia* [communion, fellowship, participation] of the body of Christ?" Continuing, he drove home the implication of this for the Corinthians: "For one loaf, one body the many of us are; for we all partake of the one loaf" (v. 17). The bread or loaf (*artos*) stands for his body, or for himself.

Paul's one purpose in introducing the Lord's Supper into the discussion of 1 Corinthians had to do with its meaning as *koinōnia,* affirming and expressing the oneness of the people of Christ. It was their disunity, even as they pretended to observe the Lord's Supper (11:20–34), along with their consorting with pagans in their idolatrous feasts (10:18–22), which prompted Paul to explain the meaning of the Lord's Supper. Their fellowship with pagan Corinthians was too close, and their fellowship with other Christians too strained. The one loaf of which they jointly partook at the Supper was designed outwardly to express the fact that they were one people, one body, even the body of Christ. They had in common one life, that of Christ, in which together they participated: "The cup of blessing which we bless, is it not the *koinōnia* of the blood of Christ?" (1 Cor. 10:16).

It is not enough to declare negatively what the bread and the cup are not, although that must be done. It is important to declare positively what they do portray. It is not enough to declare that Christ is not in the literal bread and wine. It is important to declare where he is. Christ is present when his people come together at any time, and certainly he is present when they come

---

[12] Millar Burrows, *An Outline of Biblical Theology* (Philadelphia: The Westminster Press, 1946), p. 271.

together in the observance of the Supper. Christ is present and not as a ghost. He is present in his people, the church, the body of Christ.

When it is suggested that the bread which Jesus called his body refers to the church as well as to his crucified body, the reference is not to church in an institutional sense. The reference is to his people, wherever they may be gathered together in his name. This fact has been recognized by many Christians, including Baptists in America.

Throughout the nineteenth century it was customary for Baptist general bodies to observe the Lord's Supper when they came together. Among those to so observe it, according to W. W. Barnes, were the Boston Association in Massachusetts in the 1820's, the Charleston Association in South Carolina in the 1820's and 1830's, the Concord Association in Tennessee in 1844 with J. R. Graves as moderator, the West Fork Association in Texas in 1853, the North Carolina State Convention in 1842, the Alabama State Convention in the 1840's, and the Texas State Convention 1848–1886 and earlier.

The same practice may be found in the records of the Mississippi Baptist Association, as when it convened at Bethel Church, Bayou Sara, Mississippi Territory, September 26–29, 1807, concluding its second day of worship with the observance of the Lord's Supper. Some years later the same association in its annual meeting recommended "a union of ministers' meeting, to be held on the fifth Sundays in the following year at different places, and that the ordinance of the Lord's Supper should be observed at these meetings." [13]

Another correct insight of earlier generations into the New Testament meaning of the Lord's Supper was reflected in their attention to unity of fellowship as a condition necessary to the observance of the Supper. In earlier days, so this writer understands, it was customary in many churches to raise the question

---

[13] T. C. Schilling (ed.), *Abstract History of the Mississippi Baptist Association for One Hundred Years, 1806–1906* (New Orleans: J. G. Hauser, 1908), pp. 19, 37.

of fellowship before the Supper was observed. Where fellowship was found to be broken, the Supper was not observed until it had been restored.

Paul's insistence that each man put himself to the test before observing the Supper is not to be restricted merely to one consideration. But significantly, the one explicit charge made in the context concerned disunity (cf. 1 Cor. 11:27–34). The warning against not "discerning the body" (v. 29) presumably refers to the failure to see the church as the body of Christ. This failure to see themselves as the body of Christ was reflected in their consorting with pagans in ways untrue to their union with Christ (1 Cor. 10:18–22) and in their not even waiting for one another at the Lord's Supper (1 Cor. 11:20–21,33). They were practicing an unholy communion with the world and were failing to cultivate a real *koinōnia* with the saints.

The Lord's Supper is not a "communion" in the sense that the elements themselves embody Christ, or in the sense that the eating and drinking can communicate Christ to men. But it is in the explicit teaching of the New Testament a "communion" or *koinōnia*, the fellowship of Christians *with one another* and *in* Christ. The elements (bread and wine) are mere symbols, but the *koinōnia* is no symbol; the *koinōnia* is participation in "the blood"—the life given—and "the body"—the people of Christ. The Supper affirms that the one who is to be remembered as triumphant at Golgotha is also *present* in his people.

Faith in a Coming Consummation

The Lord's Supper not only looks back to a decisive event and to the present in its realization of Christ's presence in his body; it looks forward to his coming in the fulness of his kingdom (Mark 14:25; Matt. 26:29; 1 Cor. 11:26). The observance of the Supper is the proclamation of the Lord's death until he comes (1 Cor. 11:26). Niebuhr correctly calls the Supper "a great memory and a great hope." [14]

[14] Reinhold Niebuhr, *Faith and History* (New York: Charles Scribner's Sons, 1949), p. 241.

In its eschatological hope the Lord's Supper is found to have another point of contact with the Jewish Passover. The Jews in celebrating the Passover not only looked back to their deliverance from Egypt but to a new deliverance by Messiah whom they expected. This eschatological hope, rekindled at the Passover celebration, probably goes far to account for the reaction of the people to Jesus when he fed the five thousand (cf. John 6:14 ff.). These were pilgrims on their way to celebrate the Passover at Jerusalem who sought to take Jesus there and make him king. Eschatological hopes were especially high at this season. Likewise in the observance of the Lord's Supper, the eschatological hopes of the participants were high. The one who had come and who in a real sense was present would yet come! Significant is the Aramaic survival in 1 Corinthians 16:22, *Marana tha*, "Lord, come!"

This prayer "Lord, come!" or the affirmation of faith "Our Lord comes!" expressed the confidence of the earliest Christians that his reign would come to its consummation in the personal return of Christ. To them history was not cyclic, forever doomed to retrace its course; it was not fatalistic, doomed to end in nothing; it was not evolutionary, improving under its own power. History was *eschatological;* it was being brought forward to its goal or consummation by the very one from whom it received its beginning. It was under the sovereignty of God— ultimately to be brought fully under that sovereignty.

The eschatological hope expressed in the Lord's Supper was properly related to the death-resurrection commemorated by the same Supper; for they thus proclaimed the death of the Lord until he should come (1 Cor. 11:26). The center-point of history for the Christian, as Cullmann [15] has ably said, was found in the past, at Golgotha and the empty tomb. The future was sure because the past was sure. Christian faith looked back in order to look ahead. Eschatological hope was as strong as was their faith in the death of Jesus—death that led to resurrection.

[15] *Christ and Time*, trans. Floyd V. Filson (Philadelphia: The Westminster Press, 1950), pp. 121 ff.

The New Covenant

In each of the four basic accounts of the Lord's Supper, stress is given to the covenant (Mark 14:24; Matt. 26:28) or the new covenant (Luke 22:20; 1 Cor. 11:25) set forth in his blood. The Greek *diathēkē* may be translated "covenant" only if it be free of any idea of a contract. The terms "will," "testament," or "decree" come close to expressing the idea. In the Septuagint *diathēkē* translates *b'rîth,* the word for covenant; but in the covenants of God, he alone determined the conditions.[16] The idea is never that of an agreement negotiated between God and man. God has not invited man to meet him at a "summit conference" to work out some mutually acceptable agreements. God remains sovereign in his "covenants"; he alone determines the conditions, and he alone guarantees their validity.

When Jesus is quoted as saying "This cup is the new covenant in my blood" (1 Cor. 11:25), his reference is to God's own provision for man's proper relationship to himself and to life. God has decreed that it is by the way of the cross that man is to live. By the way of the cross man is reconciled to God. The "blood"—the life given—is the true and living way. The blood of Jesus, his life given, is the pledge or assurance of the kingdom of God (Mark 14:25; Matt. 26:29). Among other things, the cup of the Lord's Supper outwardly attests to God's new covenant, made secure in the triumphant death of Jesus Christ.

In closing, it may be observed that the Lord's Supper, as is true of baptism, employs symbols, but a true observance of the Supper or baptism involves far more than symbolism. Water, bread, and the cup are symbols. In a meaningful observance of baptism and the Lord's Supper, however, there are realities far beyond symbolism—faith, hope, love, obedience, *koinōnia,* self-examination, testimony, confession, gratitude, thanksgiving, adoration, and worship.

[16] Arndt and Gingrich, *op. cit.,* p. 182.

The
Ministry
10 of the Church

AN AMBIGUITY in the title to this chapter allows for two distinct yet related ideas. The church itself is a minister, and there are ministries and ministers within the church, as the working body of Christ. The second idea implies varied ministries within the body—apostles, bishops or elders, deacons, and others.

The Church as Minister

T. W. Manson greatly clarified the New Testament doctrine of the ministry in a small volume, *The Church's Ministry*. Building upon the New Testament teaching that Christ is alive and embodied in his church, Manson correctly said, "There is only one 'essential ministry' in the Church, the perpetual ministry of the risen and ever-present Lord himself." [1] That is, Jesus the Christ—who ministered in Judea, Samaria, and Galilee—continues his ministry through his church, his body. It is he who preaches in all true preaching; it is he who teaches, heals, comforts, judges, directs. All other ministries within the church are derived from and dependent upon that of the living Lord Jesus.

[1] Philadelphia: The Westminster Press, p. 107, *et passim*. See also Eduard Schweizer, *Lordship and Discipleship* (Naperville, Ill.: Alec R. Allenson, Inc., 1960), and especially the same author's *Church Order in the New Testament*, trans. Frank Clarke (Naperville, Ill.: Alec R. Allenson, Inc., 1961) for a thorough study of the ministry of the church.

In this view, there is provision for varied ministries, but there is no provision for a nonministering church nor for non-ministering members. The idea of "drones" or nonworking Christians is foreign to the New Testament idea of the church. To be in the body of Christ is to be a part of his working body. Were Christians to take this seriously, it would transform the life of the church. Christians who sit back, waiting to be ministered to, would see that this contradicts their calling to be the ministering body of Christ. What Jesus said of himself in the days of his flesh, "The Son of man came not to be ministered to but to minister" (Mark 10:45), holds true for him as embodied in the church.

It is valid and proper for the church to minister to its own members, just as the physical body nourishes and heals its own members; but this ministry to itself is not to substitute for, nor reduce, its ministry to the larger community. Unfortunately, most of the energies of the church are exhausted in "pump priming," "nursery tending," and other ministries to those who themselves are called to minister. A "Christian" who demands that he be waited on has missed the meaning of the Christian calling.

The continuing ministry of Christ in his church means more than simply that each Christian is to work; it means that the only true Christian ministry is that of the living Lord continued in his people. God, the Father of glory, "gave him as head over all things to the church, which is his body" (Eph. 1:17,22). Only as he is present in his people are they the church. Only as he ministers in and through them is the ministry a Christian ministry. This essential point is easily obscured as, for example, in the King James Version's mistranslation of Romans 10:14, "How then shall they call on him *in* whom they have not believed? and how shall they believe *in* him *of whom* they have not heard? and how shall they hear without a preacher?"

The American Standard Version correctly translates the Greek, "How shall they believe in him *whom* they have not heard?" One does not trust by hearing *of* Christ. To trust Christ, one must hear Christ. This is what Paul was saying. Also, one may hear Christ in preaching, and it is true preaching only when Christ preaches in the preaching. That is not to equate one who preaches with Christ nor to say that all preaching is Christ's preaching. It is to say that in true preaching Christ himself may be heard directly.

In the same way every true Christian ministry is the continuing ministry of the living Lord. His continuing ministry is the only ultimate ministry; ours is derived from, and dependent upon, his. Paul could build so heavily upon this truth as boldly to say, "Now I rejoice in the sufferings in behalf of you, and I fill up in my flesh what is lacking [2] in the sufferings of Christ in behalf of his body, which is the church" (Col. 1:24). Paul was thus saying that in his own sufferings *as a Christian,* Christ himself continued his sufferings. This thoroughly accords with all that Jesus said with reference to his relationship to his people. Jesus clearly taught that we encounter him in the persons to whom we minister or whom we neglect (cf. Matt. 25:35–46). The living Christ suffers, he preaches, and he ministers in the people in whom he is embodied.

Jesus left no doubt as to the fact or the nature of his ministry. As was seen in chapter 3 under "Christology," Jesus interpreted his whole ministry in the light of the role of Suffering Servant. His declaration that he came to minister, not to be ministered unto (Mark 10:45), was supported by his whole life and teaching. The messengers from John the Baptist, asking if he were indeed the coming one, were directed to find their answer in what they heard and saw: "The blind receive their sight, the lame walk, the lepers are cleansed, the deaf hear, the dead are raised, and the poor have the gospel preached to them" (Matt. 11:5).

Likewise, Jesus emphatically charged his followers with the same ministry. Our Lord rejected the world's standards and made the servant role the mark of greatness (cf. Mark

[2] Cf. Arndt and Gingrich, *op. cit.,* p. 72.

10:42 ff.). The greatest title which one may receive is not "Master" or "Father" or "Teacher"; it is "Servant" (cf. Matt. 23:6–11). The twelve were sent out with the commission to preach that the kingdom of heaven had drawn nigh, to heal the sick, to raise the dead, to cleanse the lepers, to cast out demons, and to give freely even as they had received freely (cf. Matt. 10:7 f.).

In a real sense each Christian is a minister. Sometimes it is said that all Christians are laymen. This is true, but it more properly could be said that each Christian is "layman" and "minister." Each is a minister in the sense that each is called to a life of service. Each is a layman in that there is no "priestly" group distinguished from the people. "Laity" is a term derived from Greek, meaning "people." All Christians are *the people* of the church. All are "clergy" in the sense that upon them the "lot" (*klēros*) has fallen. All are "priests" (cf. 1 Peter 2:9) in that each has direct access to God for himself and each has a "priestly" service to render in behalf of his brethren. Thus all Christians stand on common ground, and all participate in the continuing ministry of the living Lord as his body, the church. There are different ministries among Christians, but all are ministers.

What has been said to this point in no way overlooks the fact that some are divinely called to special ministries within the church. God called Moses, Samuel, Amos, Isaiah, John the Baptist, James, Peter, Paul, and countless others long ago; and he calls Christians today into special ministries within the church. The point is to see that these special callings fall within the basic calling, that to Christ. All Christians are called (*klētos*) persons —called to faith, discipleship, and service. The New Testament never indicates that one is called to be a farmer, merchant, or physician. One is called to be a Christian servant, whether in the work of farmer, merchant, or physician. However, the New Testament, as well as the Old, makes much of calling into particular ministries within the church. Some are given to the church as special ministers (apostles, prophets, evangelists,

pastors, and teachers). These work in the church for its up-
building that it, in turn, might minister (Eph. 4:11 f.).

Ministries Within the Church

Paul wrote of "varieties of ministries" in the oldest account we
have of the various functions within the church (1 Cor. 12:5).[3]
There are ample evidences of many and varied ministries within
the New Testament church, but no clear picture emerges of
the origin and meaning of these ministries or of their relationship to one another. To speak dogmatically of the "organization" or structure of the earliest church or of the nature of its
various ministries is altogether unwarranted.

Probably at the outset there was chiefly the intense sense of the
presence of the living Lord, or of the Holy Spirit. The Spirit held
the early Christians together as one fellowship (*koinōnia*) and
continued his work in them. There were various functional
gifts, or grace gifts (*charismata*) of God such as wisdom,
knowledge, faith, healing, miracle power, prophecy, discerning
of the spirits, tongues, and interpretation of tongues (1 Cor.
12:8–10). All these were gifts of the same Spirit, the same
Lord, the same God (1 Cor. 12:4–6,11). The list of gifts here
or elsewhere is not exhaustive but representative.

Surely no gift was the exclusive property of any one Christian. Faith, for example, was the gift of God's Spirit to all Christians, not to certain ones alone (1 Cor. 12:9). Probably
Paul meant only that some were especially endowed with
certain gifts of grace, while others had their own special endow-
ments. No two lists of gifts (*charismata*) are identical, indicating a fluid rather than a fixed teaching and practice in this connection. Nine gifts of the Spirit are listed in 1 Corinthians
12:8–10, eight such gifts in 1 Corinthians 12:28–30, seven in
Romans 12:6–8, and five in Ephesians 4:11, with the longer lists
lacking some of the gifts included in some of the shorter ones.[4]

[3] Cf. H. Richard Niebuhr and Daniel D. Williams (eds.), *The Ministry in
Historical Perspectives* (New York: Harper & Brothers, 1956), p. 1.
[4] Cf. Dale Moody, "The Ministry of the New Testament," *Review and
Expositor*, LVI (January, 1959), pp. 36 f.

What is clear in all the passages concerned with charismatic gifts is that God is the giver and that the gifts are concerned with the "building up of the body of Christ" (Eph. 4:12). These *charismata* are the grace gifts of the Triune God: the various gifts (*charismata*) are from the same Spirit (1 Cor. 12:4); God placed in the church the apostles, prophets, teachers, powers, gifts of healing, helps, rulers, and kinds of tongues (1 Cor. 12:28); the risen Christ himself gave the apostles, the prophets, the evangelists, the pastors, and teachers (Eph. 4:11).

As emphatic as the declaration of the divine *source* of these gifts is the statement of their *purpose*. They are "for the equipping of the saints unto the work of the ministry [*diakonia*], unto the building up of the body of Christ" (Eph. 4:12). Persons endowed for special ministry—apostles, prophets, evangelists, pastors, and teachers—were to equip all of the saints for the *ministry!* The whole church is thus the minister; it is the working body of Christ in which he continues his ministry.

Knox is no doubt correct in rejecting the idea that there was in the New Testament a distinction drawn between the charismatic (Spirit-given) ministry and the "institutional" ministry.[5] He correctly describes the ministry as in every part charismatic— of the Spirit. Also, it is always "institutional" in the sense that it was concerned with the proper growth and functioning of the church.[6]

On the other hand, there are in the New Testament certain ministries which in some sense were of official recognition.[7] The twelve were appointed (*epoiēsen*) by Jesus (Mark 3:14) and the seven were appointed (*katastēsomen*) to be in charge of distributing material substance to the saints (Acts 6:3). The very fact that some were known as the twelve indicates that they were recognized as having a fixed status or responsibility.

---

[5] Niebuhr and Williams, *op. cit.*, p. 10. Cf. also Heber F. Peacock, "Ordination in the New Testament," *Review and Expositor*, LV (July, 1958), p. 263, who cites to the same effect Eduard Schweizer, *Das Leben des Herrn in der Gemeinde und ihren Diensten* (Zurich: Zwingli Verlag, 1946), pp. 107 ff.

[6] Niebuhr and Williams, *op. cit.*, p. 1.

[7] Cf. Moody, *op. cit.*, pp. 34, 38–42.

The seven are not again mentioned as a group, but they were recognized as having a fixed responsibility, at least for a time.

Titus was left in Crete with instructions to appoint (*katastēsēs*) elders in each city (Titus 1:5). In Acts 14:23 Paul and Barnabas are said to have appointed (*cheirotonēsantes*) elders in each church. These elders seem to have had some "official" function, though not necessarily a permanent one in the church. Paul and Barnabas seem to have had a recognized role in appointing these elders. Probably it may best be said that in the New Testament *all ministries are charismatic—gifts of the Holy Spirit—but that additionally some were recognized as having some official status.* There was no noncharismatic ministry, but every ministry did not receive formal recognition and a somewhat fixed function within the church.

Jesus did not "organize" a church; he created a people—his church. To individual members within the church he gave certain ministries, which were themselves grace gifts (*charismata*). As the life and work of this growing community became more complex, it became increasingly necessary that various responsibilities fall in a special way to certain individual members of the group. God gave these special ministries; the church recognized them.

Ordination

Some form of ordination seems to have been practiced by Christians in New Testament times. This involved the laying on of hands, although not all laying on of hands was concerned with ordination.[8] The laying on of hands, or ordination in any sense, did not confer new rights or authority upon the one ordained; rather, it was a recognition of the presence already of some charismatic gift or ministry, an intercessory prayer for the continuation of the gift of the Holy Spirit, and the acceptance on the part of the church and the person ordained of new responsibility.[9]

---

[8] Cf. Peacock, *op. cit.,* p. 263.

[9] *Ibid.,* p. 274.

The background to the New Testament practice of the laying on of hands is probably to be found in the Old Testament, as in Genesis 48:14–16, where Jacob blessed Joseph's sons, looking to God as the one who alone could actually bestow the blessing. Laying on of hands came to be a form of intercession to God, as well as a recognition of what he had already purposed or done. This kind of laying on of hands is to be distinguished from another type in which one was thought to pour something of his own personality into another. Ordination in the New Testament —if the term may be used—did not confer authority on some one. Instead, it acknowledged three things—what God had already done, acceptance of responsibility, and prayer for God's continuing grace gifts (*charismata*).

The New Testament does not tell us whose hands were placed upon the persons thus set apart. It is altogether possible, or even probable, that the whole congregation participated in the laying on of hands.[10] In 1 Timothy 4:14 it is said that the presbytery laid hands upon Timothy, no reference being made to the congregation. However, 2 Timothy 1:6, taken alone, would exclude even the presbytery when hands were placed upon Timothy: "Because of this I bring you to remembrance to stir up the gift [*charisma*] of God, which is in you through the laying on of my hands."

Unless there is a contradiction between 1 Timothy 4:14 and 2 Timothy 1:6, one is driven to conclude that the reference to "my hands" in 2 Timothy 1:6 does not exclude "the hands of the presbytery" of 1 Timothy 4:14. If this be true, then it follows that the reference in 1 Timothy 4:14 to "the hands of the presbytery" does not necessarily exclude the larger congregation. Dogmatism is not in order at this point. There seems to have been no formally prescribed rule or procedure, these being developed gradually in the early church.

Whatever may be said for the references in the letters to Timothy, at least in Acts there is strong evidence that on occasion the whole congregation did participate in the laying on of

[10] Cf. Stagg, *op. cit.*, pp. 91, 136.

hands. The context of Acts 6:6 and the grammar of the verse
strongly suggest that the "they" who laid hands upon the seven
refers to the whole congregation. To argue a change of antecedent is to resort to "eisegesis" influenced by later Christian
practice in which ordination was the work of presbyteries. Acts
13:3 tells that hands were laid on Barnabas and Saul. Apparently the whole congregation did this, not alone the five (or
three) men mentioned in verse 1. Barnabas and Saul were two
of the five. By an alternate interpretation three of the five
would have laid hands on two, but this probably was not the
case.

The Apostles

If primacy was accorded anyone among the earliest followers
of Jesus, it was to a small group of men known as apostles. Paul,
who numbered himself among them, was explicit in saying,
"God appointed in the church first apostles" (1 Cor. 12:28). In
part this primacy would follow from the relationship of these
men to Jesus, both before his death and after his resurrection,
and from the fact of their direct appointment by Jesus.[11] Chiefly,
however, their primacy was bound up with their basic function
as witnesses to the event of God's mighty act of self-revelation
and human redemption at the center of which was the Lord
Jesus Christ.

The term "apostle" is from a Greek word meaning "sent."
The missionary role of the apostle was important; but that was
not his distinctive, for others too were sent. Paul referred to himself as a "called apostle" (1 Cor. 1:1; Rom. 1:1), literally "a
called sent one." Calling was all-important in apostleship, for
an apostle was made one by God and not by man, "not from
men nor through man, but through Jesus Christ and God the
Father, the one raising him out of the dead ones" (Gal. 1:1).
Yet calling itself was not unique to apostleship, for every
Christian is a called person (cf. "called saints" in 1 Cor. 1:2).
"Called" in Greek here is an adjective, not a part of the verb. The

[11] Niebuhr and Williams, op. cit., p. 4.

call to discipleship—the call to follow Christ—is basic; the call to apostleship was a special calling, limited to a select number.

The major significance of the apostles is to be seen in terms of their basic function, that of witnessing to Jesus Christ, with special reference to his resurrection. This was made clear in the selection of one to take the place of Judas: "It is needful for one of the men accompanying us in all the time in which the Lord Jesus went in and out among us, beginning from John's baptism until the day in which he was taken up from us, to become witness with us of his resurrection" (Acts 1:21 f.).

In the New Testament, salvation is bound up with something actually having been accomplished within history, an event in which God, incarnate in Jesus Christ, not only *acted* but *came*. The apostles were witnesses to what God had actually done in self-revelation and in redemption. The apostles were appointed by the Lord and acknowledged by the earliest followers of Jesus, who prayed: "Thou, Lord, knower of the hearts of all, show whom thou didst choose out of these two, one to take the place of this ministry and apostleship" (Acts 1:24 f.).

The earliest of the Gospels makes clear the fact that the apostles, called the twelve, were called first of all to be with Jesus, then to herald the message of which he was the center: "And he appointed [*epoiēsen*] twelve in order that they be with him, and in order that he might send them forth [*apostellē*] to preach, and to have power to cast out demons" (Mark 3:14 f.). Apostleship was thus a calling and an appointment by the Lord Jesus, and the primary work of the apostles was being witnesses to him.

The New Testament itself is basically the apostolic witness—the interpretative witness to the life, the words, and the works of Jesus. This witness was built around that of the apostles. When Christians in the early centuries struggled to form a New Testament canon, they were in general agreement that the books recognized must be apostolic, either from an apostle or one who stood in such relation to an apostle that the apostolic witness was preserved. However well they may have succeeded, at least they recognized that there was a significant difference between the apostolic witness and all subsequent witness.[12]

The term "apostle" appears seventy-nine times in the New Testament, but it is not the only and probably not the earliest designation for those often called apostles. Luke with thirty-four usages and Paul with twenty-five employed the term most frequently among the New Testament writers.[13] Mark designated these men "disciples" forty-three times and "the twelve" eleven times; Matthew designated them "disciples" sixty-nine times, "the twelve" nine times, and "the twelve apostles" once, according to most manuscripts; John never designated them "apostles." [14]

Ashcraft is perhaps correct in saying that "it seems almost certain that the term *apostolos* was catapulted into prominence" in the controversy with the Judaizers, since twenty-two of Paul's twenty-five usages occur in the four great epistles most directly related to this controversy.[15] In the earliest days there were but twelve apostles of Christ. This is clear from the first chapter of Acts, where the story is given of the replacement of Judas. The twelve apparently were considered unique, for there is no evidence that James, the brother of John, was replaced when slain by Herod (Acts 12:1 f.).

The apostles of Christ, not to be confused with apostles of churches (2 Cor. 8:23; Phil. 2:25), were a special and restricted class,[16] but they came to include others than the twelve. Paul, Barnabas, James, Andronicus, Junias, and Epaphroditus seem also to have been considered apostles of Christ. Possibly these, including Paul, are to be distinguished from the twelve, they not having followed Jesus from the time of John's baptism (Acts 1:22) as was true of the twelve. Paul, at least, insisted

---

[12] Cf. Cullmann, *Die Tradition als exegetisches, historisches, und theologisches Problem*, trans. Pierre Schonenberger (Zürich: Zwingli Verlag, 1954), pp. 31–38, and Stagg, *op. cit.*, pp. 46–48.

[13] Morris Ashcraft, "Paul's Understanding of Apostleship," *Review and Expositor*, LV (October, 1958), p. 403.

[14] *Ibid.*, pp. 405 f.

[15] *Ibid.*, pp. 405, 411.

[16] Niebuhr and Williams, *op. cit.*, p. 5.

upon the fact that he had seen the risen Lord, basing his claim to apostleship upon that experience (1 Cor. 9:1) along with his direct appointment by Jesus Christ (Gal. 1:1).

Prophets and Teachers

Next after the apostles, whose primacy in some sense is undeniable in the New Testament, are to be seen the prophets and teachers. Paul is explicit as to this order in 1 Corinthians 12:28, "God placed in the church, first apostles, second prophets, third teachers." Caution against making too much of this order must arise out of verses 8 through 10 of the same chapter, where prophecy is listed only after various other ministries:

To one through the Spirit is given the word of wisdom, to another the word of knowledge according to the same Spirit, to another faith by the same Spirit, to another gifts of healing by the same Spirit, to another workings of power, to another prophecy, to another distinguishing between spirits, to another kinds of tongues, to another interpretation of tongues.

It is further to be questioned whether "prophets" and "teachers" are designations for two distinct classes of persons, or whether they imply only a distinction in function, both of which may relate to the same person.[17]

Paul declared that prophecy was concerned with "edification, exhortation [or, comfort], and consolation" (1 Cor. 14:3), as well as with conviction of sin (vv. 24 f.). This seems to describe inspired preaching, and it is distinguished from "speaking in tongues."[18] The latter was an unintelligible vocalization, an ecstatic utterance possibly meaningful to the participant, but confusing to those who heard. Prophecy was preaching concerned with witness to Jesus as the Christ (1 John 4:1–3) and with the edification of the church. The prophet was a preacher who interpreted what God had done in Christ, indicating the implications and applications of that action for the lives of men.

[17] *Ibid.*, p. 13.
[18] Cf. Richardson, *Theological Word Book,* p. 147.

Teachers, listed as third in 1 Corinthians 12:28, were concerned with the more detailed instruction in the Christian tradition as well as in the meaning of this in daily life situations. Immediately, however, one is to be cautioned against too sharp a distinction between the work of prophet and teacher, as well as between preaching and teaching, between the *kērugma* and *didachē*.[19] The prophet teaches and the teacher prophesies. In 1 Corinthians 14:6 is suggested a multiple function traceable to one person, "How shall I benefit you unless I bring you some revelation or knowledge or prophecy or teaching?" At Antioch there were "prophets and teachers," five being named (Acts 13:1). Of the five named, Barnabas and Saul were also apostles. Thus one person could be apostle, prophet, and teacher. This is further evidence that in the New Testament the emphasis falls on function and not on office.

Further caution against finding in the New Testament a rigid system of "offices" results from the observation of Ephesians 4:11, where the risen Christ is said to have given to the church "the apostles, the prophets, the evangelists, and the pastors and teachers." Apostles and prophets are listed as first and second as in 1 Corinthians 12:28, but the evangelists rather than teachers are listed as third. Teachers are listed with pastors in a way to suggest two aspects of one work.

Bishops and/or Elders

The terms bishop (*episkopos*) and elder (*presbuteros*), although different in origin, interchange in the New Testament. *Episkopos* is Greek in origin, and it has no exact equivalent in English.[20] The literal meaning is "overseer." The office of "bishop" as known since the time of Ignatius does not correspond to anything found in the New Testament. The term *presbuteros* means "elder," and it is Jewish in background. Originally it described one in terms of his age, and later it

---

[19] Cf. Niebuhr and Williams, *op. cit.*, pp. 14 f.
[20] Cf. Burton Scott Easton, *The Pastoral Epistles* (New York: Charles Scribner's Sons, 1947), p. 227.

described a function with no necessary reference to age.

The interchange between "overseer" or "bishop" and "elder" is inescapable in Acts 20:17,28. Paul sent for "the elders [*presbuterous*] of the church" at Ephesus (v. 17), and admonished them thus: "Take heed to yourselves and to all the flock, in which the Holy Spirit placed you as overseers [*episkopous*], to shepherd [to be pastor of] the *ekklēsia* of God" (v. 28). The same men are thus elders (presbyters), overseers (bishops), and shepherds (pastors). One general function, the care of the church, has been entrusted to a group of men designated by several terms. The same interchange between "elder" and "overseer" occurs in Titus 1:5,7. In 1 Peter 2:25 "Shepherd" and "Overseer" are used together as titles for Christ. Thus "overseer" or "bishop" interchanges with "elder" in Titus 1:5,7; it interchanges with "shepherd" or "pastor" in 1 Peter 2:25; and the three terms, "elder," "bishop," and "pastor" are brought together to describe the same people in Acts 20:17,28.

Knox suggests that the earliest Jewish Christian communities closely followed the Jewish pattern whereby each community was governed by elders (cf. James 5:14; Rev. 4:4; Acts 20:17). He also intimates that the term *episkopos,* "bishop" or "overseer," was employed sometimes to make intelligible to Gentiles the meaning of *presbuteros*. Knox further states that "elder" was a rather inclusive term, employed for elders who supervised and for elders who served, the seven of Acts 6:3–6 being an enlargement of the body of elders. The elders who presided came to be designated "bishops," while the elders who served came to be known as "deacons." [21]

Initially, any elder might serve in either capacity—as a "presiding" elder or a "serving" elder. The seven, if indeed elders, seemed so to function. At least it was true of Stephen and Philip that although set apart to "serve tables," they are best known for preaching and evangelizing. Gradually there may

---

[21] Niebuhr and Williams, *op. cit.,* pp. 21 f. See also K. E. Kirk, *The Apostolic Ministry* (London: Hodder & Stoughton, Ltd., 1947), pp. 138 ff.

have come a clearer division of work, the terms "bishop" or "overseer" being employed to describe the one and "deacon" being employed to describe the other.

Should this be a correct understanding of "elder" as the inclusive term, it would explain why those appointed in the newly-formed churches were called "elders" (cf. Acts 14:23); and why in Acts 20:17 those are called "elders" who actually function as "bishops" and "pastors" (Acts 20:28). It would also account for the fact that the varied functions of visiting, praying, and anointing the sick are by James attributed to the "elders" (James 5:14 f.). In this usage "elder" described all the functions later attributed to "bishops" and "deacons."

Deacons

The origin of deacons is not made clear in the New Testament. It is traditional to trace their origin to the appointment of the seven in Acts 6. However, as has been observed many times, the seven are not called deacons. Of the seven, moreover, only Stephen and Philip are known beyond their names, and they are known for preaching and evangelizing. As indicated above, there is the possibility that the seven were elders, appointed initially to oversee the distribution of material substance among the Jerusalem Christians. This part of the elder's function may gradually have come to be assigned to men called deacons. Hence in some of the later New Testament writings reference is made to "bishops" or "elder-bishops" and "deacons" (cf. Phil. 1:1; 1 Tim. 3:1 f.,8; Titus 1:5,7).

The term deacon (*diakonos*) means servant, and it is used with its cognates to describe menial service to man or the higher service to God.[22] The idea of *diakonia,* now associated chiefly with the diaconate or deacons, is the very term which Jesus so dignified as being the true measure of greatness: "Whoever would be great among you must be your deacon [*diakonos*], and whoever would be first among you must be slave [*doulos*] of all" (Mark 10:43 f.). Jesus, in the same context

[22] Easton, *op. cit.,* p. 181.

(v. 45), described his own work as a "deaconing" or ministering (*diakonein*).[23] Paul described the various functions within
the church as "varieties of ministries," literally, "varieties of
deaconing" (1 Cor. 12:5). The work of an apostle is itself
called a *diakonia* in Acts 1:17.

In 1 Timothy 3:1–13 the moral and spiritual standards required of deacons are the same as those of bishops. The one
significant difference is in the requirement that the bishop have
an aptitude for teaching (v. 2), this not being mentioned with
reference to deacons. By the time of the pastoral epistles, it
seems that two basic functions, originally expected of all elders,
were now the special assignments of "overseers" and "deacons."
Evidence is too scant to determine whether or not the reference
in verse 11 is to deaconesses or to the wives of deacons. The
standards *demanded* of bishops and deacons are high, but they
are no higher than those *expected* of all Christians.

Church Government

Dogmatic claims for the presence in the New Testament of
one clearly defined form of church government are not war-
ranted. Some evidence may be found in the New Testament for
various subsequent developments. To find the roots of a particular system in the New Testament is not necessarily to find the
system itself there.

At the outset, the church consisted of Jesus alone and his people. He selected twelve men to serve in a special capacity as
witnesses to himself, and seemingly to these twelve and a limited
number of others, also called apostles, he gave special authority,
as the appointing of elders (cf. Acts 14:23 and Titus 1:5, where
Titus is instructed on the authority of the apostle Paul to appoint elders). Multiple functions were assigned to the elders,
a group serving each church. Gradually, as the apostles dropped
out and as the demands upon the elders grew, a natural divi-

[23] Cf. J. K. S. Reid, *The Biblical Doctrine of the Ministry* (Edinburgh: Oliver
& Boyd, 1955), pp. 1 f., who discusses the strange development in Christendom
whereby the term which Jesus applied to himself has been reduced to lesser
esteem.

sion of work resulted in the distinct, yet related, functions of bishops and deacons. The church, essentially a fellowship of persons under the sovereignty of Christ, has continued to develop organizational structure as this is found expedient for the implementation of its life and ministry.

Reicke, with sympathetic insight, finds reflected in the first chapter of Acts a mixture of governmental patterns: Peter presiding somewhat like a "bishop" or in "episcopal" fashion, the apostles functioning like a collegium or a presbytery, the whole community of believers functioning in a "democratic" or in a "congregational" capacity, yet with all in truth governed by the Lord as sovereign in a theocratic sense.[24]

Whatever "offices" or functions may appear in the New Testament, the human authority rested with the congregation. Paul, Peter, James, and John, all apostles, *appealed* to the people for the responses desired. Letters were addressed to *churches*. No official had power to coerce the people. Yet more important, the ultimate authority rested always with the Lord himself. In the strictest sense the principle of government is not episcopalian, presbyterian, congregational, democratic, or autonomous, but rather that of the sovereignty of the living and present Lord Jesus Christ. We are the church when he is present in us, and present in us as Lord. Principles of democratic or congregational government and of local church autonomy accord with early church practice, but the church must ultimately be governed by her Lord. William A. Mueller has said, "The early church was under a theonomous directive and was not autonomous in itself."

The Worship of God

By its worship the church is distinguished from all societies or clubs which function for fellowship or for the betterment of mankind. The church has in common with these clubs and societies its concern with fellowship and with service. But the church

[24] Bo Reicke, *Glaube und Leben der Urgemeinde* (Zürich: Zwingli-Verlag, 1957), pp. 25 f. See also Grant, *op. cit.*, pp. 273 f.

is more than a fellowship or service club. It is that particular fellowship (*koinōnia*) of persons created by the Holy Spirit and made one under the sovereign rule of God through his Anointed, Christ Jesus. Thus, if it be the church, worship is not only proper but indispensable. Without the worship of God it is not the church, only another secular club.

The importance of worship to the earliest Christians is reflected throughout the New Testament. This was in part their heritage from Judaism. It may best be understood in terms of the impact made upon them by the presence of the risen Lord. Thomas was not alone in acclaiming him "My Lord and my God!" The early chapters of Luke reflect the adoration and praise of the worshiping church (cf. 1:46–56, 67–80; 2:13–14, 28–32). Paul's theological discussions are often abruptly interrupted as he breaks out into spontaneous worship (cf. Rom. 11:33–36; Gal. 1:5; Eph. 1:6,12,14; 3:20 f.; Phil. 4:20).

The book of Revelation is saturated with awe, praise, thanksgiving, and worship. The Aramaic *Marana tha,* "Come, Lord!" survives in the Greek New Testament, witnessing to the "vertical dimension" in the early services. The Christians were not just meeting with one another; they were gathered together in the Lord's presence. Possibly the major threat to much of Christendom today is that of practical atheism, services without a true sense of God's presence and thus without worship.

Stauffer has well observed that the Bible knows man not primarily as *homo sapiens* (knower) or *homo faber* (worker) but as *homo orans* (worshiper), created by and for God, and that "theology is doxology or it is nothing at all." [25] H. Richard Niebuhr has remarked that revelation is not acknowledged by a third-person proposition which says, "There is a God"; it is acknowledged in direct confession of the heart which says, "Thou art my God." [26] An ancient Greek quotation describes the theologian as "the one saying God, from God, in the pres-

[25] *Op. cit.,* pp. 60, 88.
[26] *The Meaning of Revelation* (New York: The Macmillan Co., 1946), pp. 153 f.

ence of God, and unto His glory." [27] God is known to faith not as
an inference from logic but as a presence continually invading
our lives.[28] Thomas fell at the feet of the risen Lord and said,
"My Lord and my God!" (John 20:28). Adoration, awe, worship, praise, and thanksgiving belong to the essential life of the
church. Likewise, the cultivation of worship among her people
belongs to the primary ministry of the church.

Worship in the New Testament, as Bo Reicke shows, is to be
seen from "two points of view: (1) what God gives to man, and
(2) how man is to receive the gifts of God." There is in the New
Testament no idea of worship as the offering of something to
God as in Jewish Temple worship.[29] Paul at Athens was emphatic
in saying, "God is not worshiped with men's hands, as though
he needed anything" (Acts 17:25). The only sacrifice required
of man is that he yield himself to God in his whole bodily existence (Rom. 12:1), the Christian life itself being an "offering." [30]

Even in worship, however, God is always the active agent behind man's attitudes and actions.[31] In prayer, it is the Holy Spirit
who "intreats with groanings unutterable" (Rom. 8:26). Man's
part is that of response or answer to God, the response of awe,
adoration, gratitude, thanksgiving, and praise made to God's
presence and his gifts. In worship, man stands before God to
receive and to acknowledge what already he has received.

Evangelism and Missions

Evangelism is the telling of the good news of what God has
done for us in Jesus Christ. Man's first privilege and obligation is
to *receive*. Having received, his continuing privilege and obligation is to *tell*. The actual work of saving is Christ's alone; man
may simply accept it in faith and then witness to it in gratitude.

---

[27] Cited by Karl Barth, *The Doctrine of the Word of God* (*Church Dogmatics*, Vol. I [Edinburgh: T. & T. Clark, 1936], trans. C. T. Thomson), p. 1.
[28] Baillie, *Our Knowledge of God*, p. 174.
[29] Higgins, *New Testament Essays*, pp. 197–98.
[30] Cf. Otto Michel, *Der Brief an die Römer* (Göttingen: Vandenhoeck &
Ruprecht, 1955), p. 260.
[31] Higgins, *New Testament Essays*, p. 207.

"Soul-winning" is a term which may easily obscure the role of God in salvation and misrepresent man's role. We do not save souls or win them; we witness to the One who alone is able to save. The extent to which "soul-winning" has overshadowed evangelism may be seen in the dependence placed upon techniques designed to make soul-winning easy. There is nothing inherently wrong with the term soul-winning (cf. Prov. 11:30); the problem is with those of us who forget that we cannot save anyone. A saved person is one who has been begotten from above, not one overcome by our techniques.

A second danger in the substitution of "soul-winning" for evangelism is in the impoverishment of the term "soul." In the New Testament "souls" are persons (cf. Luke 12:19 f.; Acts 2:41,43; Rom. 13:1; Rev. 6:9). Salvation is not concerned with some mere extraction or separable part of a person. "Soul" in this sense is a Greek idea, not a biblical one. A soul is a self. Salvation is concerned with the whole thinking, feeling, volitional, moral, spiritual, bodily self. It is concerned with man in all his relationships to God, to other persons, and to things.

The Christian is under orders to evangelize, to make disciples of all nations. Witnessing to what God has done for us is to be the natural and normal function of the Christian. The Commission expressed in Matthew 28:19 f. is not "Go," but rather it is "Disciple all nations as ye go." Jesus assumed that we would be "on the go" and we are. Our proper function is to bear our witness to him as we go.

This, of course, does not overlook the great importance of deliberate missionary efforts, which have an abundance of New Testament precedents. Jesus sent out various disciples upon missionary journeys (cf. Luke 10:1–24), and he appointed twelve men to devote their lives to witnessing (Mark 3:13–19; Luke 6:12–16). The risen Lord declared that his disciples, empowered by the Holy Spirit, should be his "witnesses in Jerusalem, and in all Judea and Samaria, and unto the end of the earth" (Acts 1:8). The carefully planned missions of Philip, Peter, Barnabas, and Paul were carried out under the direction of the Holy Spirit. Thus in the New Testament, witnessing in evangelism and missions is seen to have been both spontaneous and normal, as well as studied and deliberate.

Preaching the Gospel

A further word needs to be said about the "gospel" which is ours to declare. It is not enough merely to observe that gospel (*euangelion*) means "good news." It is the good news that God has come in his power to establish his kingdom, bringing evil under his judgment, overcoming forces hostile to himself, and offering deliverance to all who will receive it. The gospel is judgment and promise. The Bible knows no "gospel" without judgment; the gospel requirement of judgment can be compared to therapy that requires surgery.

The Greek *euangelion* first designated a reward for the bearer of good news. Next it came to stand for the good news itself. But New Testament usage cannot be determined from secular usage in the Greek world. The New Testament usage came from the Hebrew Bible through the Septuagint. The Hebrew *b'sōrāh* is rendered by the Greek *euangelion*, designating the good news that God has come to establish his rule and to deliver his people.

Background for New Testament usage may be studied in Isaiah 40:9; 41:27; 52:7; 61:1 and their contexts. The herald is to declare the gospel that "The Lord God comes with might and his arm rules for him" (Isa. 40:9 f.). The preacher of the gospel is to declare to Zion, "Your God Reigns" (Isa. 52:7) and that he has "bared his holy arm" (52:10). Of course, the gospel magnifies the promise of God to heal the brokenhearted, to liberate the captives, to comfort all who mourn (Isa. 61:1 f.), and to gently care for his flock (Isa. 40:11).[32]

The gospel in the New as well as in the Old Testament always combines judgment and deliverance. The gospel is never mere denunciation. Neither is it ever promise without judgment

---

[32] See Kittel and Friedrich, *op. cit.*, II, 705–735, and Sherman E. Johnson, *The Gospel According to St. Mark* (New York: Harper & Brothers, 1960), pp. 31 f.

and demand. The bad news of man's sin is not the good news of Jesus Christ. But the good news of Jesus Christ is never proclaimed except against the background of man's sin and hostility which must be overcome by God's kingdom. Mark's Gospel is introduced as "The beginning of the gospel of Jesus Christ," and immediately there is given the command that crooked paths are to be made straight. The naturalistic or humanistic philosophy that man needs only to "be" himself or "express" himself gets no support from the Bible.

John the Baptist presented the Coming One as one who should "thoroughly cleanse his threshing floor," separating the wheat from the chaff (Luke 3:17). Significant is the sentence which follows: "With many other exhortations, therefore, he *preached the gospel* unto the people" (v. 18). Jesus so preached the gospel in the Nazareth synagogue, spelling out its implications and applications, that his fellow townsmen tried to push him off a cliff for thus preaching the "good news" (Luke 4:16–30). In Romans, Paul set forth the gospel which he preached (1:16), beginning it with the judgment of God under which all men are found false (1:18 to 3:20). In Thessalonica he preached the gospel *in much agony* (1 Thess. 2:2). In Revelation, the angel "having an eternal *gospel* to proclaim" to all people on earth began thus: "Fear God, and give him glory; for the hour of his *judgment* is come" (14:6 f.).

It belongs to the ministry of the church to preach the gospel. This gospel is to be understood as it is set forth in the New Testament against the background of such passages as Isaiah 40:9; 41:27; 52:7; and 61:1. The gospel is the good news that God has come in the person of his anointed, the Christ, to establish his kingdom rule, judging and overcoming all hostility and providing deliverance to all who will receive it. If the church is to be able to claim with Paul that it has not counted its life dear to itself and that it is clean from the blood of all, *having held back no part of the gospel* (Acts 20:20, 24, 26,27), then must it properly relate judgment and promise in its proclamation of the gospel.

Teaching

No sharp distinction between preaching and teaching is to be found in the New Testament. From the earliest days *kērugma* (what was preached) and *didachē* (what was taught) together made up *euangelion* (the gospel). H. G. Wood [33] probably is correct in rejecting the generally accepted theory that the *kērugma* (what Jesus did) and the *didachē* (what Jesus taught) were for a time separately transmitted, only later to be combined into the gospel (*euangelion*). The earliest preaching (*kērugma*) included teaching (*didachē*). The tradition (*paradosis*) known to Luke was concerned with what Jesus both did and taught (Luke 1:1–4; Acts 1:1). Jesus went about "teaching in the synagogues" and "preaching the gospel of the kingdom" (Matt. 4:23; 9:35; 11:1). Paul referred to the tradition (*paradosis*) as having been taught by word and epistle (2 Thess. 2:15).

Although no sharp distinction is to be made between *kērugma* and *didachē*, preaching and teaching, some difference in emphasis is to be observed. The early Christians continued daily in teaching and evangelizing (Acts 5:42). Paul and Barnabas, with many others, were teaching and preaching the word of the Lord in Antioch (Acts 15:35). In Ephesians the teaching ministry is closely tied to that of the pastor (Eph. 4:11). The very term "disciple" suggests the New Testament emphasis upon the teaching of those who are evangelized. There must be an element of teaching in all preaching, and there must be careful and continual preaching to those initially evangelized.

It should be observed that in the Great Commission the command to teach is really "teaching them to observe" the commandments of Christ (Matt. 28:20). The reference here is not to the teaching of facts but the teaching of obedience to Christ. The Scriptures are profitable for *teaching*, but this is spelled out as including reproof, correction, and discipline in righteousness,

---

[33] Higgins, *op. cit.*, pp. 306–14; Wood credits others with significant contributions at this point.

equipping the man of God for every good work (2 Tim. 3:16 f.). Doctrine (teaching) is instruction for life! Doctrine is not to be an end in itself. Teaching is an important ministry of the church; basically it is to be instruction for life, "teaching them to guard whatsoever things" Christ has commanded (Matt. 28:20). The ultimate test of doctrine is the life produced.

Discipline

Discipline is the continuing work of discipleship. Disciple (noun and verb) and discipline (noun and verb) both come from the same Latin word, *discere*, meaning "to learn." They are closely related to the word *docere*, "to teach." To "disciple all nations" includes "teaching them to observe all the things" which Jesus has commanded (Matt. 28:19 f.). The Greek text employs two distinct words for making disciples (*mathēteusate*) and teaching (*didaschontes*), but they represent one continuing work. Becoming a disciple of Christ occurs in a specific conversion experience. Being taught to guard his commandments is a lifelong discipline. Latin has happily given us two words, based upon one root, bringing these two significant ministries into closest possible relationship. It is the function of the church to "*disciple* all nations" and to *discipline* its own membership.

To discipline is to provide treatment suited to a disciple or learner (Webster). It is to educate. Such is the meaning of the word derived from Latin. This accords with the intention of the Greek New Testament as it describes the duty of Christians to care for one another. Discipline is not mere punishment, although painful corrective measures may be inescapable to the discipline exercised in love.

God himself, precisely because he is love, chastens his own: "Whom the Lord loves he chastens, and he scourges every son whom he receives" (Heb. 12:6). The risen Lord said to the Laodiceans, "Whatsoever ones I love, I rebuke and chasten" (Rev. 3:19). The word for rebuke (*elegchō*) means to expose with a view to correction. The word for chasten (*paideuō*) describes the discipline given a child (*pais*) in training or "bringing him up." The intention of discipline as it relates to the person is positive and redemptive, not negative and destructive. Of course, it is the intention of discipline to destroy the evil which destroys the person.

In Matthew 18:15–35 specific instructions are given for church discipline. The individual Christian and the church as a whole bear inescapable responsibility in the matter of *giving* and *receiving* discipline. When one brother sins against another, the wronged person is to take the initiative in correction and reconciliation. Of course, the responsibility also rests upon the offender to go to the one whom he has wronged (Matt. 5:23 f.), but the very fact that he has done wrong reduces his capacity for bringing about a proper relationship.

Jesus warned the wrongdoer against trying to appear before God *without* his brother, for one cannot divorce his relationship to God from that to his brother. One must be willing to come *with* his brother to the altar, else he cannot come at all *to* the altar. Such is the teaching in Matthew 5:23 f., concerned with the imperative for the wrongdoer. In Matthew 18:15–35 attention is given to to the responsibilities of the wronged to the wrongdoer.

The intention of church discipline, as set forth in Matthew 18:15–35, is redemptive. It is to gain the brother, not to get rid of him. The offended bears the first responsibility in seeking reconciliation. This calls for a "remembering together" of the wrong on the part of the wronged and the wrongdoer. They must see it together, condemn it together, then forget it together.[34] Should the offender reject the overtures of the offended, a committee is to arbitrate. One function of the committee is the establishing of the facts, as far as that is possible.

Should the offender not heed the committee, discipline becomes the inescapable responsibility of the church. Should the offender refuse to hear the church, the church can only recog-

[34] See Knox, *Chapters in a Life of Paul*, p. 147, for an excellent discussion at this point.

nize the painful fact that he is not one of them. Strictly speaking, the church does not *exclude* him; it simply recognizes that he is not one of them. *Belonging to*—in the sense of being owned by—the church is to be taken literally. A Christian *belongs* to Christ, and he *belongs* to the church. The church does have authority over its member. To deny this is to confess that one does not belong. The church, assuming the guidance of the Holy Spirit, has the necessary function of "binding" and "loosing" (v. 18), of declaring that one is, or is not, in its fellowship.

In John 13:1–17 is found another basic lesson in church discipline. When Jesus washed the feet of the disciples, he gave a lesson in humility; but the lesson goes beyond that. He taught something which was not immediately obvious to Peter: "That which I am doing, you do not know just now, but you will know after these things" (v. 7). There was nothing new to this group about the simple act of washing feet. Jesus, however, was teaching a basic lesson about "foot washing" in a nonliteral sense.

In verse 10 is an important play on words: "The one having been bathed [*leloumenos*] has no need except to have his feet washed [*nipsasthai*], for he is wholly a cleansed person [*katharos*]." Jesus thus distinguished between an initial cleansing, likened to a bath, and further cleansing, likened to having one's feet washed. When next he said that they all were cleansed persons except the betrayer (vv. 10–11), he was referring to their spiritual condition. He was not implying that Judas had come to the supper without a physical bath. The eleven had been "bathed" in a spiritual sense, but they needed further cleansing. Judas needed more than to have his "feet washed"; he needed the initial cleansing which belongs to conversion.

Several lessons emerge from the thirteenth chapter of John. "Foot washing" without the "bath" is meaningless. Those "having been bathed" need never again be "bathed," yet they need to have their "feet washed." Further, it is the responsibility of the Christian to offer this ministry of "foot washing" to his brother, who, in turn, must accept this ministry from his brethren. When Jesus said, "Ye ought to wash one another's feet" (v. 14), he taught humility, but with special reference to the ministry of discipline—the responsibility within the church to help one another in our sin problems. Humility is never tested more severely than in a true ministry of love expressed in "washing one another's feet."

Of course, the ministry of the church to its own membership goes far beyond correction in matters of error and evil. It includes all that is implied in the "care of souls." Comfort, counseling, guidance, encouragement, visiting the sick, sharing with the needy, and all else which gives meaning to life must belong to the larger ministry of the church. One of the strangest of all remarks, often altogether incomprehensible, is that of the "minister" who says, "I feel that I have completed my ministry in this community." Presumably, he means that he has achieved all the statistical gains to be hoped for. His ministry in its broadest and deepest sense may just have begun.

The Christian
11 Life

THERE IS something arbitrary about calling this chapter "The Christian Life," for that caption could as well be placed over other chapters. The thought here, however, is to give attention to the Christian in various relationships: with God in prayer, with people in matters of stewardship, with his family, and with the state. The considerations in this chapter are sometimes called "practical" matters. In the New Testament no sharp distinction is made between the theological and the practical. The theology of the New Testament is not speculative in interest; it is always concerned with the "practical"—life as it is to be lived. Doctrine is always instruction for life. Of course, attention is sometimes weighted in the direction of interpretation and sometimes in the direction of application. The two are wedded, however, and are not to be divorced.

Prayer

The disciples of Jesus once petitioned him, saying: "Lord, teach us to pray, just as John taught his disciples" (Luke 11:1). Jesus in response gave specific instructions about prayer, indicating its proper spirit, nature, purpose, and content. By implication he may have indicated that although one may be taught that he *ought* to pray and although he may be taught *how* to pray, he cannot be taught *to* pray. Prayer is quite natural and spontaneous. It is almost universal. Instruction does not of itself induce prayer, although it may encourage prayer. Instruction is most helpful in giving such guidance that prayer becomes more meaningful.

Futility in prayer.—Jesus gave three basic warnings with reference to prayer. He taught that prayer is empty and futile if it is an attempt to impress God (Matt. 6:7 f.), or to impress other people (Matt. 6:5), or to impress one's self (Luke 18:11–14). Faith is not to be in prayer itself, but in God. If faith is in prayer then it is in the one praying. The faith that leads to valid praying is that which is in God, not in ourselves. It is faith in God's wisdom and love as well as in his power. This faith seeks the will of God, not the bending of his will to that of the one praying. "Thy will be done" must be deeply embedded in every true prayer.

Prayer is not to be an attempt to impress other people, to be seen or heard of men (Matt. 6:5). If one prays to be seen of men, he will be seen and that will be his total reward. The command to pray within one's private room (v. 6), however, is not a prohibition to all public prayer. Jesus himself prayed in public. It is direction for one whose temptation is to impress other people. The closed door will not alone solve his problem, for within his private room he yet may seek to impress God or himself.

Prayer's purpose is not to impress God, as is attempted by the pagans (Matt. 6:7). It is not to inform God, for he already knows our needs (Matt. 6:8). Its purpose is not to win God's favor, for already we are the objects of his good will (Matt. 6:26; Luke 2:14; Rom. 5:8; 8:31). It has been aptly said, "Prayer is not overcoming God's reluctance; it is laying hold of God's willingness." [1] Prayer is not magic, and it is well that it is not. We have neither the wisdom nor the integrity to make an Aladdin's lamp safe in our hands.

Prayer is futile when one tries to impress himself. Jesus described the sham and futility in the Pharisee who "prayed to

[1] Georgia Harkness, *Prayer and the Common Life* (New York: Abingdon Press, 1948), p. 28.

himself" (Luke 18:11). Although verbally addressed to God, the prayer was actually to himself (*pros heauton*). Of course as he admired himself, he did ask God to join in the adoration. He went home worsened, not helped by this mockery at prayer.

New Testament terminology.—The English word "prayer" may account for the mistaken idea that prayer is primarily asking. The English word does mean just that. "Prayer" is from the Latin *prex* meaning request or entreaty. It is like the Sanskrit *prach*, the Anglo-Saxon *frignan*, and German *fragen*, all meaning "to ask." It must be recognized that asking is at the heart of prayer, but prayer is far more than asking. Prayer in the New Testament is adoration, communion, worship, thanksgiving, confession, and commitment, as well as petition and intercession. The rich New Testament meaning of prayer must be found in its many Greek terms, not in the limited English word "prayer."

The New Testament term most general in meaning and most widely used is *proseuchē*. This term describes prayer in general, always that which is addressed to God. It stresses no particular aspect of prayer.

That petition is a valid aspect of prayer is reflected in the employment of various terms, including *deēsis*, *aitēma*, and *hiketēria*. The term *deēsis* is employed for petition for particular benefits, addressed almost always to God but sometimes to man. These petitions are not restricted to things but may be for salvation (Rom. 10:1), for health and forgiveness (James 5:16), or for anything which one would beg of another. *Aitēma* appears only twice in the New Testament as a petition addressed to God (Phil. 4:6; 1 John 5:15). It simply designates what is asked for. *Hiketēria* formerly described a symbol of supplication. In the only New Testament occurrence (Heb. 5:7), it designates the supplication itself.[2]

The wide range of what may be included in petition is indicated by the Model Prayer itself, where Jesus teaches us to pray for the coming of God's kingdom and for daily bread. Thielicke

[2] R. C. Trench, *Synonyms of the New Testament* (Grand Rapids: Wm. B. Eerdmans Publishing Co., n.d.), p. 180.

observes that we are taught to pray for the greatest and least matters, for the spiritual and material, the inner and the outer matters. Prayer is to be total, omitting no area or concern of life. Happily we do not have a stepfather but the Father of our Lord Jesus Christ, concerned with daily bread and with warm clothing for the winter.[3]

The noun *enteuxis* appears only twice in the New Testament, apparently with the meaning of intercession in 1 Timothy 2:1 and of thanksgiving in 1 Timothy 4:5.[4] The verb *entugchanō* describes a falling in with another person or a going to meet another for the purpose of conversation, consultation, or supplication.[5] The idea expressed is that of intercession (Rom. 8:27, 34; 11:2; Heb. 7:25). When prayer is described as *enteuxis*, probably what is stressed is boldness of approach to God.[6] Actual prayers of intercession in the New Testament outnumber the occurrences of this descriptive term.

Eucharistia, with its cognates, expresses thankfulness or thanksgiving. It is grouped with *deēsis* (petition), *proseuchē* (prayer in general), and *enteuxis* (entreaty) in 1 Timothy 2:1. It stresses gratitude to God for his benefactions and is thus distinguished from petition for further blessings. At the Last Supper Jesus "gave thanks" (*eucharistēsas*) as he took the cup and gave it to the disciples (Mark 14:23). This has for many given the name "Eucharist" to the Lord's Supper, a name that stresses the thankfulness which belongs to the true observance of the Supper.

A little-used but important word in the New Testament for prayer is *euchē*. In Acts 18:18 it clearly describes a vow. Probably its meaning in James 5:15 is to be so understood: "And the *euchē* [prayer as pledge or vow] of faith shall save the sick." The word here may be translated "prayer," but the emphatic

[3] Helmut Thielicke, *Das Gebet das die Welt umspannt* (Stuttgart: Quell-Verlag, 1953), pp. 80 ff.

[4] Arndt and Gingrich, *op. cit.*, p. 268.

[5] J. H. Thayer, *A Greek-English Lexicon of the New Testament* (New York: American Book Co., 1889), p. 219.

[6] Trench, *op. cit.*, p. 178.

idea probably is that of a pledge or vow to God. Prayer for health is to include a pledge to God as to what is to be done with life and health. Prayer described as *euchē* is asking but it also is pledging. One may pray for the sick, but he is to "anoint with oil" (James 5:14) and pledge himself in faith to God. "Anointing with oil" presumably refers to the household medicinal remedies of the day.[7] One must gratefully utilize the resources which God already has given, otherwise it is ingratitude and impudence to pray for more.

Nature and content.—The wide selection of terms employed in the New Testament suggests what the contexts bear out, that prayer is inclusive of many things as to its content and purpose. Worship, adoration, praise, communion, thanksgiving, confession, petition, intercession, and comitment all belong to prayer as present and as described in the New Testament.

The Model Prayer (Matt. 6:9 ff.; Luke 11:2 ff.) begins with the adoration of God: "Our Father . . . Hallowed be thy name!" In Revelation are many prayers or prayer hymns addressed to God, as Father and Son. The four living creatures and the twenty-four elders give glory, honor, and thanks in worship and say, "Worthy art thou, our Lord and our God, to receive the glory and the honor and the power, for thou didst create all things and because of thy will they were and were created" (4:11). There is no true prayer without worship, for one cannot consciously come into God's presence without a sense of awe.

Thanksgiving belongs essentially to prayer. The Philippians were admonished thus: "In everything, in prayer and petition, with thanksgiving, let your requests be made known to God" (4:6). Gratitude, remembering God's blessings, and thanksgiving characterize biblical faith and are reflected in true prayer (cf. Col. 1:3,12; 2:7; 3:15 ff.; 4:2).

Prayer may be confession, personal and specific, without being exhibitionism. Public display is not to be confused with confession of sins, yet when one's sin is public his confession

[7] Arndt and Gingrich, *op. cit.*, p. 34.

may well be public. To pray God to forgive us our sins with no painful awareness of specific sins, our own and those of our group, is to make mockery of confession. To ask forgiveness without prayer for deliverance from future sin is to confuse forgiveness with indulgence. Jesus taught us to pray, "Forgive us our sins . . . and do not lead us into temptation" (Luke 11:4).

Petition is valid to prayer and is prominent in the prayers of the New Testament. Petition need not be selfish. It can be redeemed. It can be purged and redirected.[8] One may ask for health, strength, material substance, guidance, courage, or the sense of God's presence. One may *ask anything;* he must *demand nothing.* The Christian life is to be one open to God: asking, seeking, knocking (Luke 11:9 f.). One is not promised that he will receive what he asks, find what he seeks, or see opened the door on which he knocks. But one may be assured that he will *receive,* that he will *find,* and that he will *see opened* some door. Faith asks, but faith does not demand. When one demands, his confidence is in his own wisdom and integrity. Faith in God includes faith in his wisdom and love.

The promise is made to the Christian that with assurance he may ask anything in Jesus' name (John 14:13 f.). This is true, but it is important to observe the context and meaning of the promise. To ask in Jesus' *name* is to ask in terms of his character and purpose. That excludes all selfish requests. Moreover, the promise was coupled with that of the Christian's continuing the work of Christ (v. 12). The Christian may ask *anything* which enables him to fulfil his own Christian calling, that which enables him to do the works which Christ does (v. 12). It does not follow that one will get an oil well or a fur coat for the asking. Asking is to be conditioned upon our abiding in Christ and his word's abiding in us (15:7).

God's best gift is himself. Prayer grants us no license to ask God to give us things apart from himself. Gift and giver go together. Thielicke points out the half truth in the familiar warning that "in prayer one should grasp the hand of God and

8 Harkness, *op. cit.,* p. 61.

not the coin in His hand." There should be no "either-or." The coin is to be accepted from God's hand, but it is evil to want to accept the coin apart from the hand.[9]

Prayer is commitment to God. Jesus prayed for the removal of a cup, yet he drank it (Matt. 26:39). Paul asked three times for the removal of a thorn in the flesh, yet he accepted it (2 Cor. 12:7 ff.). Prayer reaches one of its major goals when from the heart one can pray, "Not my will but thine be done." This is not a mere psychological victory which one wins for himself; it is no mere pep talk which one gives himself. It is being brought under the sovereignty of God as one encounters him and converses with him in prayer.

No doubt the most difficult aspect of prayer to understand is intercession. Yet Jesus prayed for others, the early Christians prayed for others, and we are commanded to pray for one another (cf. Matt. 5:44; 1 Thess. 5:25; 2 Thess. 1:11; 3:1; Heb. 13:18; James 5:14,16). Harkness is correct in saying that to doubt the validity of intercessory prayer is to doubt that God has anything to do with it.[10] To some extent intercession is understandable, for in praying for another one may be brought into better relationship with God and with the other—thus becoming a more suitable instrument through which God may work. In intercessory prayer one prays not only for the other; he prays for himself, for his own right attitude and relationship.

There remains a dimension of intercessory prayer yet unexplained: how can one person's praying affect another person? Should this remain not only unexplained but unexplainable, that does not necessarily make it invalid. In faith and experience all does not yield to rational analysis. However, some explanation may be possible.

Buttrick offers the "parable" of the clearing up of a lung infection by the injection of serum in the arm.[11] An objector may reply that this is no parallel, for the arm and the lung be-

[9] *Op. cit.*, p. 86.

[10] Harkness, *op. cit.*, p. 76.

[11] George A. Buttrick, *Prayer* (New York: Abingdon-Cokesbury, 1942), pp. 108 f.

long to the same body. This is precisely the point Buttrick would make. Christians belong to the same body, the body of Christ; and there are mysteries belonging to "the hidden channels of our common life" known only to God. To some extent this would apply to the human race as a whole. All persons, because they are persons, stand in a relationship with one another and with God, a relationship as full of mystery as it is of reality.

Intercessory prayer is not magic. It is not coercive upon God nor upon one's neighbor for whom one prays. But persons are so bound up with one another and with God that there is meaning for this relationship when one person prays for another. DeWolf asks "Shall we suppose that what is best for all in a situation where no one prays is always best when someone does pray?" [12]

Conclusion.—Praying is not something achieved just by the study of prayer. Some who have had no formal study of prayer can pray effectively. The scholar may fail to pray. One prays naturally and spontaneously when conditioned for it. Awareness of one's needs or of needs already met, and awareness of God from whom comes all that one has is the basic conditioning for prayer. Study may help one pray more worthily or more meaningfully, but the study of prayer will not of itself enable one to pray.

The parable of the friend at midnight (Luke 11:5–8) is a strong encouragement to pray, but it also is a reminder that praying is what one does naturally and spontaneously when properly conditioned for it. The friend who had unexpected guests at midnight needed only the awareness of his need and the presence of a neighbor to know what to do. He went to his neighbor in his need, not to the library for a book on what to do when surprised at midnight by unexpected guests.

Prayer occurs somewhat as a by-product, more so as a result of meditation upon our needs and blessings than as the outcome of a deliberate and studied effort to pray. Even though that be

[12] L. Harold DeWolf, *A Theology of the Living Church* (New York: Harper & Brothers, 1953), p. 361.

true, there is still reason to study the subject of prayer. It is
only partially true that "Everybody talks about the weather, but
nobody does anything about it." Man has not changed the patterns of cold and warm fronts or of high and low pressure systems, but he has developed heating and cooling systems. He
also has had some success in forecasting weather changes.
Some gain has thus resulted from talking about the weather. So
with prayer, talking about it may be a mere substitute for praying, but it can lead to more meaningful prayer.

Stewardship

Stewardship in the New Testament is always person-centered.
Attention is never fixed upon money and things as such. Collection of money is never made an end in itself. New Testament
interest is in God, the Christian, and his fellow man. This study
will give special attention to the teachings of Jesus, of James, and
of Paul on the subject of men and the material.

Jesus' teaching concerning men and money.—Jesus seemed
to have two basic concerns with reference to a man and the material—that a man be free from the tyranny of things and that he
be actively concerned for the needs of his brother. He taught that
our attitude toward our brothers reflects our true attitude toward, and relationship to, God. He taught that the only way we
can give to him as our Lord is to give to his people. The measure
of giving is always personal, never quantitative.

Jesus repeatedly warned against the tyranny of the material.
Freedom from this tyranny, he taught, may be found only in
submission to the sovereignty of God. Only by seeking first the
kingdom of God, his sovereign rule, may one escape the tyranny
of things (Matt. 6:33). One must choose between God and
mammon (v. 24), which is hoarded wealth. One cannot belong
(*douleuein*) to God and to mammon.

That one may be destroyed by the tyranny of things Jesus
taught by parable as well as in the Sermon on the Mount. In the
parable of the rich farmer (Luke 12:16–21) Jesus described
the folly of the man who was owned by what he thought he

owned. This farmer dreamed of greater crops and barns and eventual retirement only to be confronted suddenly with his folly. The text may best be translated, "Fool, in this night they are demanding from you your soul" (v. 20). The Greek *apaitousin* expresses the demand for the return of something—a loan or stolen property.[13] The thought may be that the man who thought that he owned himself must give himself back to God. Or the thought may be that the crops and barns which the farmer thought he owned are now claiming him. He owned nothing; he simply had fallen under the tyranny of what he mistakenly thought he owned.

A major burden in the Sermon on the Mount is to free men from slavery to things. Jesus warned against living for the "treasures" which perish (Matt. 6:19–21). He warned that to have an "evil eye" is to live in darkness (vv. 22 f.). "Evil eye" was an idiomatic expression for envy or stinginess (cf. Deut. 15:9; Prov. 23:6; Matt. 20:15; Mark 7:22). The "single eye" is the generous one, giving a life full of light (cf. Prov. 22:9; James 1:5; 2 Cor. 8:2; 9:11; Rom. 12:8). Jesus warned against distraction over what one is to eat or wear (Matt. 6:25–34).

The main verb in Matthew 6:25 is *merimnate,* and it is best translated: "Be not distracted." Jesus did not say "take no thought," "fret not," nor even "be not anxious." He warned against "going to pieces" over things. There is a proper attention which one may give to the material needs of himself and others. Jesus warned against being under the tyranny of things and of worrying to distraction over them.

The alternative to this is trust in God. Distraction over things is unnecessary, as can be seen from God's care of the birds about us (v. 26). It is futile, for one cannot thus increase his stature or extend his life (v. 27). It is evil, characteristic of pagans but not of those who trust God (v. 32). Jesus climaxed his instruction at this point by commanding that we "seek first the kingdom and his righteousness" with the assurance that all these things will then fall into proper place (v. 33). The

[13] Arndt and Gingrich, *op. cit.,* p. 79.

kingdom or sovereignty of God is the only alternative to the tyranny of things.

Jesus' desire to free the rich young ruler (Luke 18:18) from the tyranny of things probably accounts for the surprising answer given him when he inquired about eternal life. Jesus commanded him to sell his possessions and distribute to the poor (v. 22). Since the Lord did not make money the issue with each inquirer, apparently the key to this man's trouble was in the tyranny of his money. Jesus contended that it is easier for a camel to go through the eye of a needle than for a rich man to enter the kingdom of God (v. 25). Either would be a miracle. To enter the kingdom of God is to come under his sovereignty. One enslaved to money is not in the kingdom of God.

Embedded in the parable of the unrighteous steward is the strange command, "Make to yourselves friends out of the mammon of unrighteousness, in order that when it fails they may receive you into the everlasting tents" (Luke 16:9). Gollwitzer may be correct in understanding this to mean that money, which usually divides, may be made to bring people together in fellowship.[14] Viewed as one's possession, it can only cause estrangement. To say that it is mine is to say that it is not yours and that it is not God's. Seen as a sacred trust from God and exercised as a stewardship, it becomes the occasion for acknowledging God as the giver and man as one's neighbor or brother.

Money as such is neither good nor evil. It is the *love* of money which is the root of all evil (1 Tim. 6:10). In the story of the rich man and Lazarus (Luke 16:19–31) there are two rich men. One is in torment, and one, Abraham, is in heaven. Wealth exercised in stewardship could have become the rich man's opportunity. Considered as a possession, it became his crime. His attitude toward Lazarus reflected his true attitude toward God. Again, money divided persons where it could have united them.

For Jesus the measure of giving was not quantitative or statistical. It was qualitative and personal. A widow who gave two

14 Helmut Gollwitzer, *Die Freude Gottes* (Berlin: Buckhardthaus Verlag, 1952), p. 181.

small copper coins gave more than did the rich, for she gave her very living while they gave only out of an excess (Luke 21:1–4). *The only gift possible to one is himself.* As Paul L. Stagg has put it, "fragmentary giving—money but not self, a fixed part of one's money but not the responsible use of all— [cannot take] the place of wholeness in giving." [15] The idea that a tenth given at church meets the obligations of stewardship is a shameful distortion of New Testament teaching. The idea that a tithe is a debt paid and that one makes an offering from the remaining nine-tenths falsely assumes that one possesses the nine-tenths.

Stewardship, if true, must acknowledge that to be in the kingdom of God—to be under his sovereign rule—is to be under the absolute and ultimate claims of God. One can never discharge his debt. When we have done all that is commanded us, we can only say, "We are unprofitable bondservants; we have done what it was our duty to do" (Luke 17:10). For the Christian, even duty is grateful response to the grace of God. "The bondage of law takes the place of the freedom of the Spirit" whenever "mathematical calculation overshadows the spontaneity of love in giving without measure." [16]

Mary anointed Jesus for his burial; she did it directly. We can give to Jesus only by giving to his own people. This is his teaching. He clearly taught that our true relationship to him is reflected in our relationship to others. At the judgment, so he taught, the King will say either "Come here, ye blessed of my Father" (Matt. 25:34) or "Depart from me" (v. 41). Which verdict one is to hear, Jesus related directly to what one did with reference to the hungry, the thirsty, the stranger, the naked, the sick, and those in prison (vv. 35–46). "In that ye did it not to one of the least of these my brethren, ye did it not to me" (v. 45). Jesus so identified himself with his own that the solidarity cannot be broken. Jesus never offered himself apart from his people. We can give to him *only* in giving to his own.

[15] McCall, *op. cit.,* p. 148.
[16] *Ibid.*

The teaching of James.—The Epistle of James has much in common with the Sermon on the Mount and with the teachings of Jesus in general. Its basic plea is for a faith that is validated in works or fruits. It does not put works over against faith but holds them to be inseparable. Genuine faith will yield its appropriate fruits. The epistle stresses nothing as an evidence of faith more than it does one's relationship to other persons in respect to things material.

James taught that worship that is pure and undefiled is characterized by charity and chastity (1:27). His word *thrēskeia* designated the worship of God or religion as it is actively expressed.[17] Cultic practice or religious expression that is cleansed (*kathara*) of God is characterized by the care of widows and orphans and by a personal life that is clean. James did not intend to give an exhaustive description of religion. He did intend to set forth some of its basic and indispensable markings.

James strongly condemned the placement of monetary value upon those present in a worship service. He scorned the special attention given the rich and branded as sin anything which belittled the poor (2:1–13). Partiality he labeled as sin, "If ye have respect of persons [partiality], ye commit sin, being convicted by the law as transgressors" (v. 9). The church must not have categories of first- and second-class persons within it. This discrimination is evil. To rate according to money is to make distinctions on the basis of the irrelevant.

James insisted that genuine faith is validated by the works it produces. It is significant that much of his development of this theme was in terms of material substance given to those in need. He scorned the hypocritical "sympathy" that is content to give mere advice. He scorned the piosity which is content to advise the hungry to get food and the poorly clad to get themselves warmed (2:15 f.). James was in agreement with the demand of John the Baptist: "He that hath two coats, let him impart to him that hath none; and he that hath food, let him do likewise." This is stewardship in the New Testament.

[17] See Arndt and Gingrich, *op. cit.*, p. 364.

The Lord of sabaoth is mentioned twice only in the New Testament. Paul mentioned his mercy in saving a remnant (Rom. 9:29). James referred to him as the one into whose ears reach the cries of those workmen whose wages are held back from them (5:4). "Sabaoth" does not mean sabbath. *Sabaōth* is a Greek transliteration of the Hebrew plural for "army." The Lord of sabaoth is the Lord of armies (hosts). Those who defraud the poor by failing to give them a living wage may thus trample upon the poor, but they have yet to answer to the Lord of armies! The New Testament does not relegate the problem of economic justice to the state; the New Testament represents this as a moral issue which does concern the Christian faith.

Paul's doctrine of giving and receiving.—Paul praised the Philippians for having had fellowship with him "in the matter of giving and receiving" (4:15). Christian giving and Christian receiving are traced to the same grace of God. Paul recognized the importance to fellowship (*koinōnia*) of both giving and receiving. He spent several years promoting an offering, in which he sought to lead some to give and some to receive and thus bring them into a more meaningful fellowship with one another (Rom. 15:30–33; 2 Cor. 8–9).

Paul quoted Jesus as saying, "It is more blessed to give than it is to receive" (Acts 20:35). This accords with all that Jesus taught. Paul himself, however, made much of the relationship between giving and receiving. They cannot be separated. Because it is better to give than to receive, it is proper to receive. One cannot give unless someone will receive. One of the best of gifts is to give another the opportunity to give. The grace of God so operates within Christians as to enable them "to have fellowship in giving and receiving."

Paul's most sustained appeal for stewardship is found in 2 Corinthians 8–9. For some time he had been asking the churches of Achaia, Macedonia, and Asia to contribute a sum of money for the relief of the poor at Jerusalem. His concern was twofold—to give material substance to those in need and to bring about a happier relationship between Jewish and Gentile Christians. He thus sought to cultivate a fellowship (*koinōnia*) of giving and receiving.

It is significant that in 2 Corinthians 8–9 there is a total absence of legalism, regimentation, and appeal to the profit motive. Giving is not placed on a bargaining basis. Paul recognized giving to be a duty, but he emphasized it as a matter of grace. This is the recurring theme throughout the two chapters. Stewardship he saw to be rooted in the very grace from which comes our salvation. He appealed to gratitude for blessings already received, not to the desire for something more. In Greek the word *charis* is usually translated grace, but it sometimes means "thanks." In these chapters, Paul used the word for both grace and thanks. The word "joy" is from the same root, spelled *chara*. Grace, gratitude, and joy are the words most prominent in Paul's appeal for giving.

Paul described the giving on the part of the Macedonians as the grace of God at work among them (2 Cor. 8:1). The dynamic behind their generous and joyful giving was divine grace, not money-raising gimmicks (see also vv. 6–7). Their joy (*chara*) in giving was traceable to the grace (*charis*) of God. Their giving was out of deep poverty (v. 2). They gave liberally, beyond their means (v. 3). They gave voluntarily, even begging for the privilege (*charin,* grace) and the fellowship (*koinōnia*) of this ministry to the saints (v. 4). The cultivation of this *koinōnia* among Christians, especially in bringing Jewish and Gentile believers into a closer fellowship, was the main objective for Paul. This was not fragmentary giving, separating gift from giver, for first they gave themselves to the Lord and to their brethren (v. 5). Such is the true spirit of stewardship in the New Testament.

With the example of the Macedonians before them, Paul appealed to the Corinthians to give as an expression of their love (*agapē*). Grace is the love of God in operation. Christian giving is the outward validation of the love of God in the Christian (v. 8). The example of Christ is the primary one, for his grace was shown by his becoming poor that we might be rich (v. 9).

Paul appealed to no arbitrary rule or legalism in urging the Corinthians to give. One was to give as he was able (vv. 11 ff.). Giving should aim at equalizing material resources, so that none would have an excess and none a lack (vv. 13–15). Giving was to be liberal and free, not grudgingly or of necessity (9:6 f.). Although there is a spontaneity in Christian giving, it is also to be according to deliberate purpose (v. 7).

Paul was concerned for the grace in giving which would help both those giving and those receiving. It was to be a ministry or service unto the saints (8:4; 9:1). It was to relieve a present need (9:12). It was to stimulate them to pray and long for one another (v. 14). It was to be a worship experience, a thanksgiving to God (vv. 11 f.). It was to be a fellowship (*koinōnia*) with the saints (v. 13). Paul followed Jesus in a person-centered emphasis in stewardship. Jesus stressed faith in God, freedom from the tyranny of things by coming under the sovereignty of God, and active care for those in need. Paul was concerned that "giving and receiving" be a fellowship of persons in the love and grace of God.

To this point, tithing has not been discussed in detail. The New Testament does not once introduce tithing into the grace of giving. Tithes are mentioned only three times in the New Testament: (1) in censoring the Pharisees for neglect of justice, mercy, and faith while giving meticulous care to the tithing of even garden produce (Matt. 23:23; Luke 11:42); (2) in the exposure of the proud Pharisee who "prayed to himself," boasting that he fasted twice each week and tithed all his possessions (Luke 18:12); and (3) in arguing for the superiority of Melchizedek, and hence of Christ, to Levi (Heb. 7:6–9).

It is clear that Jesus approved tithing as a part of the Temple system, just as in principle and practice he supported the general practices of the Temple and the synagogues. But there is no indication that he imposed any part of the Temple cultus on his followers. Tithes were chiefly produce, formerly eaten at the sanctuary by the one tithing and later eaten by the priests. Tithing as set forth in the Old Testament could be carried out only in a religious system built around a system of animal sacrifice. Many Christians find the tithe to be a fair and workable plan for giving. So long as it is not made to be a coercive or legalistic system, it may prove to be a happy plan. However, one may not validly claim that tithing is taught in the New Testament. It is recognized as proper for Jewish observance (Matt. 23:23; Luke 11:42), but it is not imposed upon Christians. In fact, it is now impossible for Jews or Christians to tithe in the Old Testament sense. Tithing today only faintly resembles the ancient ritual practice belonging to the sacrifical system of the Jews. Paul Stagg has summed it up:

While much may be said for adopting the tithe voluntarily as a standard for one's giving without rigidly imposing it upon others as a Christian requirement, it is clear in adopting such a practice that one is not carrying on the Old Testament practice. At most one is doing something only remotely analogous to the tithing practice of the Old Testament, which was a tax to support the Temple and the priestly system, a social and religious system which no longer exists. Tithes were obligatory in Judaism as a tax until the destruction of the Temple in A.D. 70, but they are not thus binding upon Christians.[18]

This is not to discredit tithing, but it is to clarify its relationship to the New Testament. It is to deny that the New Testament supports the coerciveness, legalism, profit motive, and the bargaining which so often characterize the tithing appeals today. As a voluntary system, tithing offers much; but it must be redeemed by grace if it is to be Christian. To plead that "it works" is only to adopt the pragmatic tests of the world. Much "works" that is not Christian. Tithing, if it is to be congenial to New Testament theology, must be rooted in the grace and love of God.

The Sabbath and the Lord's Day

Special days and seasons are given no special recognition in the New Testament. It is not hostile to the idea of special days

[18] McCall, *op. cit.*, p. 151.

and seasons, yet it refuses to allow them to become an end in themselves.

It was the custom of Jesus to attend the synagogue service on the sabbath day (Luke 4:16). He went up to Jerusalem for certain of the Jewish feasts (John 2:13; 5:1; 7:10; 10:22; Mark 14:12). He did not disapprove Jewish observance of special days and feasts. On the other hand, he constantly was in conflict with the Pharisees over the proper meaning of the sabbath (Mark 2:23–28; 3:1–6; John 5:1–47). He healed the sick and permitted his disciples to pluck grain and rub off the husks on the sabbath. In defense of his position he made two basic claims. First, "the sabbath was made for man, and not man for the sabbath." Second, "the Son of man is Lord even of the sabbath" (Mark 2:27–28).

Paul, along with other Jewish Christians, attended synagogue services on the sabbath day and gave no disapproval of the day in principle (Acts 13:27,42,44; 15:21; 18:4). However, he did censure any disposition of Christians to make much of special days and seasons. In protest of a legalistic trend in the Galatian churches, he wrote, "Ye observe days, and months, and seasons, and years. I am afraid of you, lest in vain I have bestowed labor upon you" (4:10–11). Paul counted that work lost which led to their making days and seasons ends in themselves. He warned the Colossians against this very peril: "Let no one judge you in the matter of eating and drinking, or in the matter of a feast or new moon or a sabbath, which things are but shadows of the things coming" (2:16 f.).

The sabbath.—The New Testament gives no evidence that early Christians were taught to observe the sabbath day. The earliest Christians were Jews. They worshiped in the synogogues and at the Temple with other Jews. Their sabbath observance is to be understood against this background. With the inclusion of Gentiles in the church there came an ultimate separation between synagogue and church. Gentile Christians did not observe the Jewish sabbath.

Hebrews indicates the meaning "sabbath" is to have for Christians. Life in Christ is the promised "rest" or "sabbath" (4:1–11). The whole Christian life is a "sabbath" for the Christian. The seventh day was'but a "shadow," the fulfilment or reality for which is Christ. To the author of Hebrews, Christ is our sabbath—just as to Paul, Christ is our passover (1 Cor. 5:7). The seventh day is the Jewish sabbath; Christ is the Christian sabbath.

The Lord's Day.—Little mention is made in the New Testament of the first day of the week as the Lord's Day, yet the special significance given it by Christians seems to go back to the apostolic days. Apparently, without specific command for it, the followers of Christ made much of this day because of the resurrection. There is no explicit record of the setting apart of this day. Presumably this was a free and spontaneous act of primitive Christians.

Jesus arose from the dead on the first day of the week (Mark 16:2; Luke 24:1; John 20:1), and it was natural that his followers met together when reports of his appearances began to circulate (Luke 24:33 ff.; John 20:19 ff.). It would have been incredible had they not done so, such was their excitement and amazement. Subsequent meetings on the first day of the week can be understood only as a deliberate memorializing of the resurrection. That Jesus *chose* to appear on Sunday night one week after his resurrection may be significant (John 20:26). By this act, he may have encouraged the setting apart of the first day of the week for the assembling of his followers.

There are outside the Gospels a few traces of Christian observance of the first day of the week. When Paul was promoting a collection for the poor of the saints at Jerusalem, he wrote, "Upon the first day of the week let each of you put something aside, storing it up, as he may prosper" (1 Cor. 16:2). This seems to imply a Christian assembly on the first day of the week. At the time of Paul's last recorded trip to Jerusalem (about A.D. 55), he met en route with the saints at Troas on the first day of the week. Luke writes, "Upon the first day of the week, when we were gathered together to break bread, Paul discoursed with them, intending to depart on the next day" (Acts 20:7). After an all-night service, he resumed his journey toward Jerusalem.

The lone reference to "the Lord's Day" is in the book of Revelation. John wrote, "I was in the Spirit on the Lord's day" (1:10). Presumably this was the first day of the week, but it is not so designated. Revelation was written probably about A.D. 95. By that time "the first day of the week" may have come to be known to Christians as "the Lord's Day." Sunday (the day anciently dedicated to the sun or its worship) is a term of pagan origin and appears nowhere in the Bible.

The Lord's Day is not the sabbath. The two days are distinct as to origin and character. The sabbath was a day of rest from work. The Lord's Day has its true meaning in its positive emphasis, memorializing the resurrection of Christ. The day can have Christian meaning to those alone who know the risen Christ. The day is best observed by assembly, worship, and witnessing to the risen Christ. To force the day upon unbelievers is comparable to forcing baptism upon them. The hope for giving the day its Christian meaning is in Christ's becoming so real in his presence to us today that we will be moved by the same impulse which brought together an excited band of early believers, thrilled to proclaim, "It is the Lord! He is risen!"

Marriage, Family, and Divorce

In the New Testament marriage is thought of as normal and proper. It is to be "held in honor among all" (Heb. 13:4). Weddings are described as times of joy, and the union between Christ and the church is likened to marriage (Eph. 5:21–33; Rev. 19:7 ff.). Marriage is considered in its ideal according to the purpose of God; it is also considered in its actual occurrence, sometimes involving failure. Hence, the New Testament speaks also on the subject of divorce.

Marriage.—In Mark 10:6–9, in statements attributed to Jesus, two important passages from Genesis (1:27; 2:7–25) are brought together. This passage in Mark sets forth the basic position of Jesus with reference to marriage. It is the completion of man, for "male and female he created them." It is a union so real that "the two become one flesh."

Genesis 1:27 describes man as created in the image of God, and as created male and female. It is the second affirmation which is important for the study of marriage. The relationship of husband and wife is necessary to the completion of man. Sex is not evil, as in gnostic teaching. Sex is the creation of God, and it is essential for the multiplication of the race (v. 28). Its first importance lies in the fact that God made mankind "male and female." Jesus quotes this part of Genesis 1:27.

Genesis 2:7–25 gives a second account of the creation of man, giving the basis for the view that "the husband is the head of the wife" (Eph. 5:23). This passage in Genesis also teaches that the two in marriage become one flesh (v. 24). Ephesians stresses the headship of the husband in the home. Jesus gave no stress to this, but he did quote from the passage in Genesis containing this teaching. As Jesus blended Genesis 1:27 and 2:24, it was to stress the oneness of husband and wife and the indissoluable nature of that union (Mark 10:6–9).

Husband and wife.—Paul was very insistent that "the husband is the head of the wife" (1 Cor. 11:2–16; Col. 3:18; Eph. 5:23). Peter likewise taught that the wife is to subject herself to her husband (1 Peter 3:1). This accords with one emphasis of Genesis 2:7–25, that God created man first and that woman was created for man. In some real sense the husband is recognized throughout the New Testament to be the head of the wife. This, however, must not be taken out of context, nor may attendant teachings be overlooked.

In another most important sense, there is no priority of one over·the other. As *persons* husband and wife are of equal value. In truth, they are one. It is only to the extent that certain responsibilities fall to the husband that he is "the head of the wife." Protection and support of the wife normally belong to the responsibilities of the husband. It is inescapable that the role of one be subordinated to the role of the other. The Bible teaches what is generally recognized, that normally it is proper for the role of the wife to be subjected to that of the husband. She takes his name, and normally she adjusts to his place of work and standard of living. She is his helper (Gen. 2:18). But as persons, the two become one. They are of equal importance and are due equal love and honor.

It should be observed that the husband is never authorized to subject his wife to himself, and she is never in the New Testament told to obey her husband. In Colossians 3:18, the wives are the ones addressed, not the husbands; and they are admonished to *subject themselves* to their husbands. The wife is instructed to make her role subordinate to that of her husband and thus become his helper. But the husbands are commanded to love their wives and not embitter them (Col. 3:19). Again, husbands are told to love their wives as Christ loved the church (Eph. 5:25). They are not to be brutish, crude, and rude; but they are to be understanding and considerate of their wives as being persons with feelings and rights. The wife is a *person* to be loved and respected, not a *thing* to be used.

Parents and children.—According to Genesis, the first word which God spoke to man was a command, "Be fruitful and multiply" (1:28). Little more is said in the Bible to this effect, and little more was required. The desire for children was so great among the people of Israel that they needed little such encouragement. It was a sorrow or actual shame among them to be without children. There should be meaning to marriage apart from the bearing of children, yet children are normal and proper to marriage. Marriage without the *desire* for children is foreign to any biblical view of marriage.

Children are commanded to obey their parents in everything, that being pleasing to the Lord (Col. 3:20). In Ephesians the command is blunt, "Children, obey your parents in the Lord, for this is right!" (6:1). Manuscript evidence is equally divided over the inclusion of "in the Lord." Appeal is made to the Ten Commandments in underscoring the importance of obedience to parents. The modern idea of a home as a "pure democracy" is foreign to the Bible. Authority rests with the parent over the child. As persons they are of equal value, due the same measure of love and honor. But the role of child is not to be confused with that/ of parent.

The parent has basic responsibilities for the child which require corresponding authority. Whenever responsibility is assumed there must be a corresponding authority, such authority as is necessary to the discharge of the responsibility. The driver of an automobile may not be a better driver than his passengers; but as long as he has the responsibility of driver, he has to have the authority of the steering wheel. Parents are not more important than children, but they have inescapable responsibility requiring certain authority.

Stern warning is given to fathers not to abuse their authority over their children. Children are *persons,* not things. Colossians is especially emphatic: "Fathers, do not irritate [or, embitter] your children, lest they be made to lose heart" (3:21). Ephesians likewise has a strong warning coupled with positive instruction: "Fathers, do not provoke [make angry] your children, but nurture them in the discipline and admonition of the Lord" (6:4). The husband is rightful "head of the wife," and parents have necessary authority over the children, but that home is happiest where mutual trust and love are so strong that these "roles" do not require assertion.

Divorce.—At one point there is no room for uncertainty as to the New Testament teaching concerning marriage. It is that God's intention is that marriage be a union between a man and a woman *not to be broken by any human being.* God is the one who has ordained marriage, and man must not destroy it (Mark 10:9). It is clear from Mark 10:2–12 that "Jesus regarded marriage as an indissoluble union and that he placed husband and wife in a relationship of equality." [19] Marriage is to be a union for life, to be dissolved by death alone (Rom. 7:3). Any departure represents failure, the missing of God's will. God's commandment is clear and uncompromising, "That which God has joined together, let no person put asunder" (Mark 10:9).

[19] Taylor, *The Gospel According to St. Mark,* p. 421.

Divorce always represents failure. It always represents a deviation from God's will. That does not mean that God has no place or no will for a divorced person. Theft is a sin and is always condemned of God, yet God does not close the door to the one who has stolen. There is grace and redemption where there is contrition and repentance. Where marriage ends in divorce, there is failure; and there are wounds and scars which are never fully healed. Where a marriage had been broken, there is no "right" or "ideal" way left. From this point it is a matter of salvaging as much as is possible. There remain grace and redemption for those of a contrite heart. Following the wreckage, a new life can be made; but it falls short of the life God intended at the outset.

There is no clear authorization in the New Testament for remarriage after divorce.[20] Many see it as a valid deduction from the gospel of grace that there is always a new life open to the one of a contrite heart. This does not make divorce right. It is failure. It also represents wrong on the part of at least one spouse.

Paul claimed to have the commandment of the Lord (Jesus) on the subject of divorce as he wrote, "To the married I charge, not I but the Lord, that the wife not leave her husband—but if she be separated, let her remain unmarried or be reconciled to her husband—and [I charge] the husband not to leave the wife" (1 Cor. 7:10 f.). There is no authority here for remarriage. Should one go contrary to this charge, it does not necessarily follow that he is banished from God's presence. Judgment and grace alike operate here as elsewhere. The judgment of God upon divorce is nowhere retracted or relieved; the grace of God is never limited.

Matthew 5:32 is concerned with divorce, but its chief concern is to condemn the criminal act of the man who divorces an innocent wife: "Everyone divorcing his wife, except for the cause of fornication, makes her to be adulterous, and the one marrying the divorced woman is made adulterous." The "except

[20] See Kenneth E. Kirk, *Marriage and Divorce* (London: Hodder & Stoughton, Ltd., 1948), pp. 49 f. *et passim.*

clause" makes sense here if the passage is concerned with the
offending husband. To put away a guilty wife would not be "to
make her adulterous," for she already would be that.

Jesus was rebuking the husband who victimizes an innocent
wife and thinks that he makes it right with her by giving her a
divorce. Actually, he thus treats her as though she were an
adultress. She is thrust out just as he would thrust out an
adultress. She is stigmatized; and her husband, should she
marry, is stigmatized. The Greek text does not say that she
commits adultery but that she is made adulterous. The passive
voice appears in *moicheuthēnai*. She is made a victim. The right
of an innocent wife is to be loved and honored, not divorced
like an adultress.

Jesus refused to be trapped by the Pharisees into choosing between the strict and liberal positions on divorce as then held in
Judaism. They asked him, "Is it lawful for a man to divorce his
wife for any cause?" (Matt. 19:3). He answered by reaffirming
the will of God as set forth in Genesis (1:27, 2:24), that God
created them male and female—for marriage. In marriage husband and wife are made one flesh, and what God has united
man must not separate (Matt. 19:4–6). When they said that
Moses had commanded (*eneteilato*) divorce, Jesus corrected
them at two points: (1) it was not a command, it was a *con-
cession*—Moses permitted (*epitrepsen*) divorce, and (2) this
was in violation of God's purpose.

Jesus then declared remarriage after divorce to be adultery
(Matt. 19:9). Manuscripts disagree as to the presence of the
phrase "except for fornication." Possibly he excepted the "innocent" party in his pronouncement that remarriage after divorce is adultery. Luke 16:18 is without modification: "Everyone divorcing his wife and marrying another commits adultery,
and the divorced woman who marries commits adultery."

To summarize, it has been the will of God from the beginning
that marriage be a union indissoluble except by death. Any
divorce is failure and represents sin on the part of at least one
spouse. The New Testament nowhere authorizes a second mar-

riage while one's first spouse is alive, unless such provision is made in the "except clause" of Matthew 5:32; Jesus did not legislate concerning divorce. For one who is divorced and remarried the laws of judgment and grace are valid, just as in reference to any other sin. Judgment must not be lightened by condoning, and grace must not be limited.

The Christian and the State

Caesar and God.—The familiar reply of Jesus to messengers of the Pharisees and Herodians asking about the lawfulness of paying tax to Caesar discloses much of his position on the subject (Mark 12:13–17). They probably represented a view that it was a betrayal of their nation to pay tax to the Roman Caesar, and their strategy was to force him into the dilemma of offending either Roman or Zealot interests. Jesus did not evade the issue, nor did he take a neutral position. By calling for a coin, he demonstrated that they were already in business with Caesar. They were using his coin, and this but suggested many benefits which already they were accepting from Rome. Payment of tax would rightly follow the acceptance of services.

The heart of Jesus' answer was in the words, "Give back to Caesar the things that are Caesar's and the things of God to God" (v. 17). This is a clear recognition of the claims of the state upon the individual. Jesus was not, however, saying that the state has claims independent of God. He did not teach that there is a realm over which Caesar has absolute and ultimate authority. Caesar is not God. Caesar's authority is limited; he is answerable to God. God alone is sovereign over all. Jesus told Pilate, the Roman governor, "You would have no authority against me were it not given you from above" (John 19:11). It is proper to pay taxes to the state and to give a proper allegiance to the state, but ultimate allegiance is to be given to God alone.

The state as ordained of God.—Paul recognized the state to be ordained of God, and he admonished the Roman Christians to subject themselves to "the powers that be" (13:1). Cullmann has argued that Paul is thinking primarily of angelic powers behind the state, but he recognizes a reference to both angel powers and the state.[21] Barrett, however, seems to have the better of the argument in seeing Paul's reference to be to the state, appointed by God to restrain the "demonic powers" (see 2 Thess. 2:6 f.) which war against man.[22] Stauffer calls these the "powers of chaos."[23] So long as the state exercises this function it is the appointed servant of God and is to be respected.

The state ceases to be the instrument of God when it becomes idolatrous—when it becomes an end in itself. Cullmann has well described the proper limits of the state under God.[24] When it becomes totalitarian, demanding the absolute and ultimate allegiance of man, then it has "deified" itself and is idolatrous. This is what the state had done when the Revelation was written, hence it was the beast (Rev. 13). When the state remains within its proper bounds, it is to be supported by the taxes and prayers of the people. When it becomes idolatrous, its claims are to be rejected even at the price of martyrdom. "We must obey God rather than men" (Acts 4:19; 5:29). We are to "fear God and honor the king" (1 Peter 2:17).

Church and state.—The principle *intended* by those advocating "separation of church and state" is a proper one, but the statement of it is quite unsatisfactory. Separation of church and state, taken strictly, is contrary to the teaching of the New Testament and contrary to what apparently is intended by those using the term. Actual "separation of church and state" can only end in one's destroying the other.

Proper relationship, not separation, of church and state is what is to be sought, each free to become its true self. Neither is to encroach upon the proper limits of the other, yet each has its own responsibility to the other. Were separation complete,

---

[21] Cullmann, *The State in the New Testament*, (New York: Charles Scribner's Sons, 1956), p. 98, and *Christ and Time*, trans. Floyd V. Filson (Philadelphia: The Westminister Press, 1950), pp. 191–210.

[22] C. K. Barrett, *The Epistle to the Romans* (New York: Harper & Brothers, 1958), pp. 244–49.

[23] *Op. cit.*, p. 197.

[24] *The State in the New Testament*, pp. 86–92.

the church could not even pray for the state, to say nothing of judging it. Were separation complete, the state could offer no protection to the church, not even protection for freedom of worship. Proper relationship, not separation, is that which is to be sought. Each under God, each answerable to God, giving him alone absolute and ultimate allegiance, is what is to be desired.

Eschatology:
the Goal
12   of History

WHATEVER may be said about the *meaning* of
the *eschaton*, the *fact* of eschatology in the New Testament is
beyond dispute. The entire New Testament is eschatological in
that it sees history as being moved under God toward a goal. On
the negative side this goal is to be understood as judgment; on
the positive side it is redemption. The extent to which this goal
or *eschaton* has been realized or remains unrealized is subject to
debate, but that the entire New Testament assumes an *eschaton*
is conclusive. Only Philemon and 3 John, twenty-five and fifteen verses respectively, are without references "to hopes and
expectations concerning the future and the 'last things.' " [1] To
make eschatology the *last* chapter in a book, as is done here, is
itself somewhat misleading, for eschatology belongs to the whole
study of New Testament theology. It is not just an addendum.[2]

The eschatological view of history which characterizes the
New Testament contrasts with various nonbiblical views. There
was a cyclic view in which history was seen as repeating itself,
periodically retracing its steps. This cyclic view, providing for
the recurrence of events and even the reincarnation of individual
persons, is not that of the New Testament. The evolutionary view

[1] H. A. Guy, *The New Testament Doctrine of the Last Things* (New York:
Oxford University Press, 1948), p. 173.
[2] Cf. W. D. Davies, *Paul and Rabbinic Judaism* (London: SPCK, 1948), p.
285, who agrees with A. Schweitzer, *Paul and His Interpreters* trans. W.
Montgomery (London: A. and C. Black, 1912), p. 53, in this conclusion.

in which history is seen as progressing under its own power is likewise foreign to the New Testament. In the eschatological view God is seen to be at the beginning of history, above it yet within it, and moving history toward its goal.

Eschatology is an understanding of history as seen from its end or goal. It is not something simply tacked on at the end of theology. Its concern is "not for providing a map for the future, but for supplying a criterion for the present." [3] Eschatology is about last things (*eschaton* means last) and about the end (*telos*), but its concern is thus with the eternal consequences of the present. The fact that history is moving toward its goal—when judgment and deliverance will be brought to consummation—makes clear the importance of decision now.

Present and Future Reality

Realized eschatology.—The term "realized eschatology," stressing the present reality of the kingdom of God, is chiefly associated with the name of C. H. Dodd.[4] The idea was actually set forward by earlier writers. E. von Dobschütz in *The Eschatology of the Gospels*, 1910, wrote of a "transmuted eschatology already at hand during the lifetime of Jesus" (p. 150), and William Manson in *Christ's View of the Kingdom of God*, 1918, wrote of "the Kingdom as already being fulfilled" (p. 83).[5]

Dodd, however, is chiefly responsible for the present emphasis and for much of the understanding of the *eschaton* as already realized. He argues convincingly that in Jesus Christ "the *eschaton* has entered history; the hidden rule of God has been revealed; the age to come has come." This realization or inauguration of the *eschaton* within history is indicated in several ways: [6]

(1) Fulfillment—Jesus preached the gospel of God, saying, "The time is fulfilled, and the kingdom of God is at hand" (Mark 1:15).

---

[3] Robinson, *Jesus and His Coming*, p. 94.
[4] Cf. *The Parables of the Kingdom, The Apostolic Preaching*, and *The Interpretation of the Fourth Gospel, passim.*
[5] Cf. Guy, *op. cit.*, pp. 71 f.
[6] *Apostolic Preaching*, pp. 85 f.

Paul wrote that "when the fulness of time came, God sent forth his Son" (Gal. 4:4).

(2) The supernatural—the miracles of the New Testament are eschatological. They anticipate what ultimately will be the complete overcoming of possession by demons, sickness, and death by the kingdom of God.[7]

(3) Overthrow of the powers of evil—Jesus thus explained the significance of exorcisms: "If by the Spirit of God I am casting out demons, indeed the kingdom of God has arrived" (Matt. 12:28).

(4) Judgment—the gospel (b'sōrāh or euangelion) of God is the good news that he has come in judgment and to deliver his people. The coming of Christ was judgment as well as deliverance (John 3:19). Hence the gospel calls for repentance as well as faith (Mark 1:15).

(5) Eternal life—the life of the age to come has come in Jesus Christ (John 3:16; 6:54, 58). It is life under the kingdom of God.

Eschatology is thus concerned with the view that history has a goal in which judgment and redemption are brought to ultimate expression. Realized eschatology is the view that when Jesus came into the world, this very judgment and this redemption came. What will ultimately be complete is already present in Jesus. When the Word became flesh, God came into history with his ultimate gift and demand. Jesus cited his works, in particular the casting out of demons, as evidence that the kingdom of God had come and was overcoming the kingdom of Satan. He said, "If by the Spirit of God I am casting out demons, then the kingdom of God has come upon you" (Matt. 12:28).

Unrealized eschatology.—To say that the kingdom of God has come is not to deny that it is yet to come in its consummation. To see the *eschaton* as realized is to see it as inaugurated but not exhausted in history. Paradoxically, the *eschaton* has come and is yet to come.

Dodd is thought by many of his critics, at least in his earlier writings, to have excluded any future idea from eschatology. Possibly this is unfair to Dodd, for in 1936 he wrote:

[7] Cf. Alan Richardson, *The Miracle-Stories of the Gospels* (London: SCM Press, Ltd., 1941), pp. 38–58, and Grant, *op. cit.*, pp. 155 ff.

While, however, the New Testament affirms with full seriousness that the great divine event has happened, there remains a residue of eschatology which is not exhausted in the "realized eschatology" of the gospel, namely, the element of sheer finality. While history still goes on, a view of the world, which, like the prophetic and Christian view, insists that history is a unity, must necessarily represent it as having an end as well as a beginning, however impossible it may be for philosophy to admit the idea of finite time. Thus the idea of a second coming of Christ appears along with the emphatic assertion that his coming in history satisfies all the conditions of the eschatological event, *except* that of absolute finality.[8]

Here Dodd seems to understand history to have an "end" bound up with the "second coming" of Christ. Whatever be true of Dodd, this appears to be the teaching of the New Testament.

Jesus spoke about the coming of catastrophic events, as described in Mark 13 and its parallels (Matt. 24:1–36; Luke 21:5–36). Apparently, one of his major purposes was to give assurance that life is to go on beyond those events. "The end [*telos*] is not yet" (Mark 13:7). His death and the destruction of Jerusalem would both make heavy demands on his disciples' faith. Each would seem like the end—but not so. The end in its ultimate sense was to be connected with his death-resurrection. Jesus anticipated a time when he would be taken away from his disciples (Mark 2:20), and yet they would not be orphaned, for in a real sense he would be with them (John 14:18).

The last days.—New Testament writers saw themselves as living in the last days. On the day of Pentecost, Peter interpreted the coming of the Holy Spirit as the fulfilment of the promise in Joel that God would pour out his Spirit "in the last days" (Acts 2:17). In Hebrews, God's speaking in his Son is described as being "at the last of these days" (1:2). John explicitly said, "It is the last hour" (1 John 2:18). Conditions described as belonging to the last days (2 Tim. 3:1; Jude 18) are meant to characterize the writer's days. The perilous and wicked times described were those of the writers and the readers. The "last times" had begun when the Word became flesh.

[8] *Apostolic Preaching,* p. 93.

The future reference, as well as a present one, is found in John's reference to "the last day," the singular for "day" being employed (John 11:24). Jesus declared himself to be the resurrection and the life (v. 25). In John 6:39–40 eternal life is considered a present reality, but reference is made in a future sense to a resurrection "in the last day." There is a future element in the reference to a judgment to come "in the last day" (12:48). Thus judgment is not only a present reality (3:19); it also belongs to the last day, considered as future (12:48).

The paradox which runs through so much of the New Testament is found in the phrases "the last days" and "the last day." The judgment is present and future. Likewise, the resurrection is present and future. Both judgment and the risen life come now in Christ; both will come in fulness in Christ. What is to come in fulness is already present in him. The last days came with him; the last day awaits us at his coming.

The Parousia

Terminology.—"*Parousia*" is a New Testament term whose precise meaning is somewhat elusive. Etymologically, it means "being alongside." Sometimes it signifies no more than the simple idea of presence (*parousia*) as distinguished from absence (*apousia*) as in Philippians 2:12 and possibly in 1 Corinthians 16:17. It describes in 2 Corinthians 7:6 the arrival (or presence) of Titus and in Philippians 1:26 the arrival (or presence) of Paul.[9] As a technical term it developed in two directions. It could designate the coming of a divine person or the visit of a royal person.[10] In the New Testament it is used prevailingly to designate the coming of the risen Christ to his people at the conclusion of an interval of undetermined length following his resurrection (cf. Matt. 24:3,27,37,39; 1 Cor. 15:23; 1 Thess. 2:19; 3:13; 4:15; 5:23; 2 Thess. 2:1,8; James 5:7 f.; 2 Peter 1:16; 3:4, 12; 1 John 2:28).

"Second coming" is not a New Testament term; the nearest

---

[9] Kittel and Friedrich, *op. cit.,* V, 857.
[10] Arndt and Gingrich, *op. cit.,* p. 635.

approach to it is in the statement in Hebrews that "He shall appear a second time, apart from sin, to those awaiting him, unto salvation" (9:28). The earliest use of the term "second coming" seems to be by Justin Martyr, about the middle of the second century.[11]

Not only is "second coming" not a New Testament term, but it obscures the close relationship between the "coming" of Jesus in his death-resurrection and that "at the end of the world." The New Testament term *parousia*, meaning both *presence* and *coming,* brings together the two all-important facts that he has already come and that he is yet to come. This paradox runs through the New Testament and is essential to its message. Christ is present with his people, yet his coming is to be awaited. At no time is he an absentee Christ, yet a future coming is awaited. The future coming is not an isolated event; it is the completion of a *parousia* begun with his death and resurrection. The triumph of the death-resurrection event is what assures the triumph of the future coming.

Already but not yet.—The *parousia* is present and future. Christ is present and he is to come. Paradoxically, Jesus could say, "while I was with you" (Luke 24:44) and "lo, I am with you always" (Matt. 28:20). In Acts 2:29–36 Jesus is already enthroned through his resurrection, already made Lord and Christ, and he is already present and active in his church through the Holy Spirit. In Acts 3:19–21 he is the Christ "whom the heaven must receive until the times of restoration of all things," the one to be sent from the presence of the Lord.

Paul clearly looked forward to the coming of Christ in a future sense (1 Thess. 2:19; 3:13; 4:15; 5:23; 2 Thess. 2:1,8; 1 Cor. 15:23; Phil. 3:20), yet he based his whole Christian faith and life upon the claim that Christ appeared to him (1 Cor. 15:8). In the Thessalonian letters, precisely where the future coming is so emphatic, Paul thought of Christ not as absent in heaven but as present, directing his ways and theirs. The *presence* and the future coming of Jesus are brought together in one

[11] See Robinson, *Jesus and His Coming,* pp. 156 f. for early occurrences.

prayer that "Our Lord Jesus direct our way to you . . . the Lord make you to abound in love . . . to the end that he may establish your hearts unblameable in holiness . . . at the *parousia* of our Lord Jesus with all his saints" (1 Thess. 3:11–13). In Philippians, Christ is already exalted through suffering and he already reigns (2:5–11) and to die is to be with him now (1:21 f.), yet from heaven "we wait for a Saviour, the Lord Jesus Christ" (3:20). In Ephesians, Jesus has *descended* to the church with his gifts to it in the very act of ascending on high (4:8–10).

The Gospel of John is emphatic about a future coming (14:3,18 f.,28; 16:16,22) and it speaks clearly of the resurrection and final judgment "in the last day" (5:28 f.; 6:39 f., 44,54; 11:24; 12:48); yet throughout this Fourth Gospel, eternal life, judgment, and resurrection are present realities (3:18 f.; 4:23; 5:25; 6:54; 11:23 ff.; 12:28,31; 13:31 f.; 14:17; 17:26). In Hebrews God's "rest" is both present and future; men enter it, and must strive to enter it.[12] Christians are "at the end of these days" (1:2; 9:26), yet they see "the day drawing near" (10:25).

In a real sense Christ's death and resurrection constituted his *going* to the Father in triumph: "From now on [*ap arti*] you will see the Son of man sitting on the right hand of power, and *coming* upon the clouds of heaven" (Matt. 26:64). Based on Psalm 110:1 and Daniel 7:13, this describes the *going* to the Father of the Son of man, vindicated and brought to triumph through suffering and death.[13] Christ thus enters upon his triumphant reign through death and resurrection (Acts 2:29–36). He reigns from the resurrection onwards (*ap arti*) rather than waiting to start his reign at a future "second coming."[14]

Paradoxically, this "coming on the clouds" *to* the Father was also his coming to his disciples. The *ascent* to the Father was also

---

[12] Cf. Davies and Daube, *op. cit.*, p. 371.
[13] See T. W. Manson, "The Son of Man in Daniel, Enoch, and the Gospels," p. 174; and Robinson, *Jesus and His Coming*, pp. 44 f.
[14] Robinson, *Jesus and His Coming*, pp. 50 f.

his *descent*, through the Holy Spirit, to his people. "The one having descended is himself the one having ascended above all the heavens, that he might fulfil all things" (Eph. 4:10). Jesus spoke of something not distant but immediate in saying, "I will not leave you orphans; I come unto you . . . I go away and I come unto you" (John 14:18,28). His *going* to the Father was his *coming* to his disciples as the risen Christ in the Holy Spirit.

The *continuity* between the *parousia* as present and the *parousia* as future is obscured by the English "hereafter" in Matthew 26:64. The King James Version reads, "Hereafter shall ye see the Son of man sitting on the right hand of power, and coming in the clouds of heaven." This refers to one event, not two. "Hereafter" translates *ap arti,* which means "from now on" or "henceforth." The parallel in Luke has *apo tou nun,* "from now on" (22:69). The English "hereafter" is misleading if it suggests a point in the indefinite future; it is correct if it is understood to mean *here* after—from here on.[15]

It is important to see that the coming at "the end of the world" is connected with the "coming in the clouds" through the triumph of the death-resurrection event. The one who is to come is already present. The victory which is to be completed in the *parousia* has already been won in his death and resurrection. He entered "from here on" (*ap arti* or *apo tou nun*) into his glory when he arose from the dead (Matt. 26:64; Luke 22:69; Acts 2:29–36).

A real coming.—The *parousia* refers to a real *coming* of Christ to his people, not simply a *going* to the Father. It is probably correct to see in Mark 14:62 a reflection of Psalm 110:1 and Daniel 7:13, and to understand "coming with the clouds" (Mark 14:62) or "coming in clouds" (13:26) to refer to the Son of man's triumphant ascent to the Father. But in the New Testament this is made to refer to a future coming of Christ to earth, not just an ascent to the Father through the resurrection.[16]

[15] *Ibid.,* p. 159.
[16] According to Beasley-Murray, *Jesus and the Future,* p. 259, and *A Commentary on Mark Thirteen,* pp. 90 f., the view which would reject the traditional

John A. T. Robinson holds that the dividing of the eschatological event of the coming of Christ into two comings is to be traced to the church, not to Jesus. This division he traces to the church's hesitation to believe that the messianic event already had taken place fully, asking, "Art thou really and fully, 'he that should come' or are we to look even for 'this same Jesus' again?" [17] Robinson holds that in the oldest view Jesus was seen to have been exalted in glory and to have completed his ascent to the Father by his reunion with the disciples in the Father, this mutual indwelling being the essence of the parousia.[18] He thus equates the parousia with the body of Christ, recognizing but one coming: "begun at Christmas, perfected on the Cross, and continuing until we all are included in it." [19]

Robinson's argument throughout is careful and logical and to many scholars quite convincing. The argument is necessarily highly subjective, and its conclusion that Jesus did not anticipate a "second coming" beyond that which occurred in his death-resurrection is extremely precarious. It is not contested that the New Testament writers expected Jesus to return on clouds from heaven. It is less certain what precisely Jesus meant by the Son of man's coming on clouds.

It is clear that Jesus did visualize an *end* to history, a final judgment (Matt. 5:21–30; 7:22; 10:15; 11:21–24; 12:36, 41 f.; Luke 10:12–15; 11:31 f.), a general resurrection (Mark 12:25–27; Luke 14:14), and a final separation between the saved and the lost (Matt. 8:11 f.; 13:24–30,36–43,47–50; 25:31–46).[20] He also expected that there would be a time on

---

interpretation of Mark 13:26 and 14:62 on the ground that Daniel 7:13 describes not the Son of man's descent to earth but his ascent to the Father in heaven, was introduced in 1864 by Timothy Colani, *Jesus Christ et les croyances messianiques de son temps*, p. 20, and was followed by Holsten, Appel, Wellhausen (who said that he received the idea from Smend), Lagrange, Glasson, and Duncan. Recently it has been strongly defended by Robinson in *Jesus and His Coming*, 1957.

[17] *Jesus and His Coming*, p. 152.
[18] *Ibid.*, pp. 132, 178, *et passim*.
[19] *Ibid.*, pp. 184, 185.
[20] *Ibid.*, p. 37.

earth when his disciples would have to go about their work without his visible presence. This would be a time for fasting, the bridegroom having been taken away (Mark 2:20), and also a time of joyous remembrance, celebrated often through the "bread" and the "cup" (Luke 22:17–20; 1 Cor. 11:24 f.).[21]

Robinson's best contribution is exactly where he himself puts the emphasis, arguing that the important thing is not that "the coming on the clouds" is an ascent rather than a descent, but that the triumphant entry of Jesus into his glory was *from the resurrection onwards* and not only at some *second* coming.[22] This properly ascribes to the death-resurrection event the primary place in his triumph. The New Testament writers who clearly expected a "second coming," or a *parousia* at the end of history, based that assurance upon the victory already won at Golgotha and in the resurrection.

Imminence and delay.—The fact that the *parousia* as a visible return of Jesus to earth did not take place within the first generation posed serious problems for the early Christians. At Thessalonica, some of the saints could think of nothing else than an imminent return of the Lord, some in excitement and disorder and some in fear or disappointment (1 Thess. 4:13 to 5:11; 2 Thess. 2:1–2; 3:6–13). Second Peter deals with "mockers" who ask, "Where is the promise of his parousia?" (3:4). The extended "delay" is difficult to explain in the light of the expectation of an imminent *parousia* attributed to Jesus in the New Testament.

Jesus did urge his disciples to expect an imminent *parousia,* saying, "This generation shall not pass away until all these things be accomplished" (Mark 13:30; Matt. 24:34). "Generation" is to be taken in its normal sense of contemporaries to Jesus. But it is to be observed with Beasley-Murray that "a saying which implies the incidence of the end in a short time nevertheless leaves room for the correction of all statements that

---

[21] Cf. Kümmel, *op. cit.,* pp. 64–83, for a careful argument that Jesus expected some interval between his resurrection and *parousia.*

[22] *Jesus and His Coming,* pp. 50 f.

declare it will come shortly." [23] Jesus himself is quoted as saying, "But of that day or that hour knoweth no one, not even the angels in heaven, nor even the Son, but only the Father" [24] (Mark 13:32; Matt. 24:36).

It is not likely that the church would thus have placed a limit on the knowledge of Jesus; the statement is best understood as going back to Jesus himself. He predicted the fact of the *parousia*, but he denied knowing the time of its realization. He also warned his followers against trying to know what is known to the Father alone. Jesus did leave room for the realization of the *parousia* in an immediate sense, "Lo, I am with you always" (Matt. 28:20), and in a future sense following an absence implied by his saying, "while I was with you" (Luke 24:44). He who came and who is to come is in a real sense present now. [25]

The end.—The word *telos*, normally translated "end," is not as simple as it might appear. It may designate a termination or cessation, a close or conclusion, an end or goal, or it may have some adverbial force. [26] Its eschatological use in Mark 13:7 (and parallels in Matt. 24:6; Luke 21:9) and 1 Corinthians 15:24 concerns us here.

Jesus referred to "the end" in a warning to the disciples not to be misled by false prophets or false messiahs and not to mistake "wars and rumors of wars" for signs of the end. Presumably the wars would be those brought on by Jewish Zealots, who thought that they could thus bring about the kingdom of God. Jesus said that these things would come, "but the end is not yet" (Mark 13:7). Paul spoke of the resurrection of the people of Christ at his *parousia*, adding "after that [*eita*] the end" (1 Cor. 15:24).

[23] *Jesus and the Future*, p. 189.

[24] Manuscript evidence against the inclusion of "not even the Son" is insufficient to discredit it in Matthew 24:26, and its originality to Mark 13:32 is not contested.

[25] Kittel and Friedrich, *op. cit.*, V, 868, sums it up in saying, "The meaning of the Parousia in the New Testament is that the tension between unfulfillment and fulfillment, here and yonder, hope and having, being hidden and revealed, faith and sight is overcome and that therefore the decisive has already taken place in Christ."

[26] Arndt and Gingrich, *op. cit.*, p. 819.

Kennedy finds *telos* to mean far more than "termination," holding that it expresses the idea of goal. He sees it to refer to "the final consummation, the perfect realization of the Divine aim," made possible by the abolishing of every rival rule, or authority, or power.[27] The end (*telos*) is distinguished from the *parousia*,[28] although the word "after" (*eita*) need not imply an interval of any duration.[29]

Davies is probably correct in rejecting the interpretation given by J. Weiss and H. Lietzmann, according to which *to telos* means not "the end" but "the rest of the dead." The two examples cited for this meaning of *telos* are not convincing. Davies is also to be followed in rejecting the view of F. C. Burkitt and Karl Barth, who see in *to telos* an adverbial usage, "finally." [30] For Paul the resurrection of Jesus was the "beginning of the end" in which the powers of the age to come were already present, and for him the *parousia* would usher in the consummation (*telos*) in terms of the resurrection of the dead and the final judgment.[31]

The "end" or goal thus designates the complete overcoming of all hostility to God, putting all the enemies under his feet, the last enemy being death (1 Cor. 15:25 f.). Jesus warned that the "end" or goal would not be brought on by such "messianic" wars as represented the hope of many (Mark 13:7). Paul wrote that the "end" or goal is reached when death as the last enemy is overcome in the resurrection of those who are of Christ (1 Cor. 15:22–26).

The millennium.—"Millennium" is a term of Latin origin, employed to designate the thousand-year reign mentioned in

---

[27] H. A. A. Kennedy, *St. Paul's Conceptions of the Last Things* (London: Hodder & Stoughton, Ltd., 1904), pp. 319 ff.

[28] Stauffer, *op. cit.*, p. 219.

[29] Kennedy, *op. cit.*, p. 323, cites John 13:4 f.; 19:26 f.; and 1 Corinthians 15:5–7, for examples of the use of *eita* where only momentary or brief periods are implied.

[30] *Op. cit.*, pp. 293 f.

[31] Cf. *ibid.*, pp. 295–298, for careful treatment of the view that the *parousia*, according to Paul, will be followed immediately, or at least shortly, by a general resurrection and judgment, the final consummation or end (*telos*) thus ensuing as the perfected kingdom of God.

Revelation 20:4–6. The New Testament has no other reference to this reign of a thousand years. This reign is attributed to the Christian martyrs who were slain because of their witness to Christ and their refusal to "worship the beast, or his image" (v. 4). Of them it is said, "they lived and reigned with Christ a thousand years" (v. 4).

Although this is often termed the millennial reign of the martyrs with Christ, the concern seems to be with the martyrs, with their vindication and triumph in Christ. This accords with the concern throughout Revelation to challenge persecuted Christians to be true to Christ with the assurance that even in martyrdom they were triumphant.

It is not likely that the author of Revelation intended that the thousand years be taken literally.[32] The author has given hints and clues throughout the book to the effect that something other than the literal meaning is to be sought (e.g., 1:1,20; 13:18; 17:9). Elsewhere in Revelation there is no indication that numbers are to be taken in a literal sense. They seem to have qualitative rather than quantitative significance. A thousand is probably a round number symbolizing completion. This in Revelation is a highly dramatic way of assuring the Christian martyrs that they with Christ will reign completely. This contrasts with the complete overthrow of Satan, who is to be bound for the same period of a thousand years (20:2,7).

To understand the "millennium" not as a literal period of a thousand years but as a dramatic portrayal of the triumph through the life-giving of Christ and his people accords with the nature of apocalyptic and the message of the entire New Testament. Apocalyptic is a dramatic-poetic type of literature with its own way of conveying its message. To take it seriously

---

[32] Concensus of scholars by no means amounts to proof, but at this point critical scholarship is virtually agreed. The position that the language of the whole book of Revelation is to be taken as symbolic and not literal was assumed by so balanced a scholar as Conner, *The Faith of the New Testament*, p. 493. See also E. A. McDowell, *The Meaning and Message of the Book of Revelation* (Nashville: Broadman Press, 1951), and Ray Summers, *Worthy Is the Lamb* (Nashville: Broadman Press, 1951), for a full treatment of the book of Revelation.

and honestly one must not take literally apocalyptic imagery that was never meant to be taken literally.

According to the Gospels Jesus rejected physical force as a means to victory, and Revelation does not contradict this. Jesus chose to overcome the power of evil by giving life, not by taking it. He did so through the cross, not a sword. Revelation honors this principle in what it says of those who were victorious over "the great dragon . . . the old serpent, he that is called the Devil and Satan, the deceiver of the whole world" (12:9). Revelation says, "They overcame him because of the blood of the Lamb, and because of the word of their testimony; and they loved not their life unto death" (v. 11).

Victory over Satan will not come through a literal battle fought against "Gog and Magog" (20:8). The victory is in the death-resurrection of Jesus, his own and ours as we are brought into its reality with him. The "martyrs" who reign with Christ are those who have been "beheaded for the testimony of Jesus and for the word of God" (v. 4). Christ already reigns! Revelation supports what is taught throughout the New Testament.

Christ has already "overcome to open the book [of destiny] and its seven seals" (5:5). The Lamb is already with "him that sits upon the throne" (v. 13). Already "the kingdom [rule] of the world is become that of our Lord and his Christ, and he shall reign for ever and ever" (11:15). The saints already have been loosed from their sins by his blood and already made a kingdom—made to reign with Christ (1:5 f.). Already it can be said of the saints that Christ "made them unto our God a kingdom and priests, and they reign upon the earth" (5:10).

Christians were suffering persecution, probably under the Emperor Domitian, when the Revelation was written. All were under orders to offer sacrifice to Caesar as God. No true Christian could do this. Revelation's answer to any tendency to worship a man is clear: "See that you do it not" (22:9). The positive command is, "Worship God" (22:9). The emperor had placed all under orders to worship himself. But Christians were already under orders to worship no mere man, but to worship God. In this situation all Christians were potential martyrs. The purpose of Revelation—in what it says of the thousand years and otherwise—is not to give in advance a description of events which Jesus himself said belonged to the knowledge of the Father alone. The purpose is to assure threatened saints that to give their lives to and for Christ is to be made to reign with him who is "King of kings and Lord of lords" (19:16).

The Resurrection

Two conflicting concepts.—It is important at the outset to distinguish between the ideas of "immortality of the soul" and "resurrection of the body." [33] Both are ancient and widely-held views. "Immortality of the soul" is often called the "Greek view," but this is misleading. The Greeks have held many views, this one among them. Not all Greeks believed in "immortality of the soul," and many non-Greeks did and do so believe. According to this view the "soul" exists before its habitation in a body, and it survives after being freed from the body when the body dies. In some systems the "soul" is considered to be the essential self, the body being the "prison" or "tomb" from which the "soul" is freed by death. Thus death is considered to be the friend of the "soul."

All of this is foreign to the theology of the New Testament. Its doctrine of man, seen in his wholeness, calls for that of resurrection, not "immortality of soul." Man *is* a soul; he does not just *have* one. Body and soul both describe the total man, each from its own perspective (see chap. 2 on the doctrine of man).

The belief in bodily resurrection is ancient and widely held. The antiquities of Egypt, with their elaborate tombs and burial arrangements, are eloquent in their witness to this ancient belief. The simple faith of the early American Indian in a "happy hunting ground" is another expression of this belief.

[33] See Cullmann, *Immortality of the Soul or Resurrection of the Dead,* for a brief but cogent treatment of this theme.

In the Old Testament this expectation comes only to gradual expression and is never prominent. In the New Testament it is basic. As has been said many times, there would have been no church or New Testament except for the faith that Jesus was raised from the dead. Paul went so far as to say that the *kērugma* (what we have to preach) and our faith are empty and we are deluded if there is no resurrection (1 Cor. 15:13–19). He did not exaggerate the importance of belief in the resurrection to the New Testament.

To speak of resurrection as "bodily" is a redundancy, for resurrection implies body as an essential aspect of the total self. Man is a bodily self in creation, at birth, and always. To speak of "resurrection" simply as survival is to confuse it with "immortality." It is indefensible to explain the resurrection of Jesus as simply the growing conviction of the disciples that Christ was yet with them. All Christians have a sense of his presence, but this is not what is described in the Gospels. It also is not what Paul meant when he wrote:

I delivered to you the first [or, as the main thing] that which also I received, that Christ died for our sins according to the scriptures; and that he was buried; and that he has been raised on the third day according to the scriptures; and that he was made visible [*ōphthē*] to Cephas; after that to the twelve; then he was made visible to above five hundred brethren at once, out of whom the majority remain until now, but certain ones fell asleep; then he was made visible to James; afterwards to all the apostles; and last of all, as to one untimely born, he was made visible to me also (1 Cor. 15:3–8).

This does not describe a mere awareness of his presence. Paul was speaking of visible appearances which may be named and numbered. Had he meant only a sense of his presence, he could not have written "and last of all to me also." This does not *prove* the actuality of the resurrection of Jesus, but it is nonsense to confuse the faith of the New Testament with anything short of resurrection in its fullest sense.

The nature of the risen body.—The nearest approach to a description of the resurrected body is in 1 Corinthians 15:35–

54. This passage deals explicitly with the question concerning the "kind of body" the risen ones will have (v. 35). It employs the analogy of seed and harvest, indicating that there is both continuity and discontinuity in each case (vv. 37–38). The seed that is sown has to die. The seed or grain produced has a new body, yet it is the same continuing life. The body that dies and the one raised are the same, yet not the same.

Paul argued that the body is sown a natural body, but it is raised a spiritual body (1 Cor. 15:44). By "sown" he may refer to one's birth into the world, not his physical death.[34] By "spiritual body," he does not mean ghostlike. A spiritual body did not mean for Paul an immaterial one. "The 'spirit' had a physical nuance for Paul such as it often had for his Rabbinic contemporaries." [35] His meaning is indicated in saying, "It is sown in a state of being perishable [phthora], it is raised in an imperishable state; it is sown in humiliation [atimia], it is raised in glory; it is sown in weakness, it is raised in power" (vv. 42 f.).[36] We now have a body like that of "the first man Adam," but we shall have one like that of "the last Adam"— Christ Jesus (vv. 45–49).

Those who are alive at Christ's parousia will be "changed," and the dead will be raised when the "last trumpet" sounds (vv. 51 f.). Paul's chief concern here was to say that the "spiritual body" will be deathless (vv. 53–57).

Descriptions of the risen body of Jesus are most difficult to bring together in a harmonious whole. He was not recognized by Mary until he called her name (John 20:15 f.), in part because she did not expect to see him. The two disciples on the way to Emmaus did not recognize him until he was disclosed to them in the breaking of bread (Luke 24:30 f.). He appeared to the ten in a room where the doors were closed (John 20:19); yet he could show them his hands and feet, and he ate a piece of broiled fish (Luke 24:39,43). A week later he offered to show

---

[34] Guy, op. cit., p. 115.
[35] Davies, op. cit., p. 308.
[36] Cf. Arndt and Gingrich, op. cit., p. 865, for the meaning of phthora.

Thomas the nail prints in his hands and the wound in his side (John 20:26–28).

Apparently Luke and John meant to insist that it was a body of flesh in which Jesus arose, thus having conquered death. Possibly it was at some subsequent point that his body was "changed." Probably it is best simply to conclude that there was continuity and discontinuity between "the body sown" and "the body raised"; it was the same body, yet a changed body. It may best be thought of as a spiritual body which could manifest itself in spatial limits and yet overcome or transcend the limits of space.[87] Regardless of its precise nature, Jesus' resurrection body clearly was real.

An intermediate state?—The New Testament is not clear as to the state of those who have died. It never speaks of an "intermediate state," and it is not clear that it makes room for one.[88] It never speaks of a "disembodied state," and this idea seems foreign to the New Testament. There are isolated verses which may imply a disembodied state, but this is by no means certain. Never does a biblical writer envision a person as disembodied. Moses and Elijah at the transfiguration are represented in bodily state, making the suggestion of tents possible (Luke 9:33). The rich man in Hades is represented as wanting water for his *tongue,* so his was at least not complete disembodiment (Luke 16:24)!

However else these stories may be interpreted, they at least demonstrate that those in the life beyond are not thought of as disembodied. Paul expressed horror at the very thought of "being found unclothed"—not having a body (2 Cor. 5:1–8). The New Testament may best be understood as providing for no "intermediate state," the "spiritual body" being an immediate replacement of the "natural body." Whatever unanswered ques-

---

[87] Emil Brunner, *Eternal Hope* trans. Harold Knight (London: Lutterworth Press, 1954), p. 149.
[88] Davies, *op. cit.,* p. 318, holds that there is "no room in Paul's theology for an intermediate state of the dead." He cites for this view G. B. Stevens, *The Pauline Theology* (rev. ed.; New York: Charles Scribner's Sons, 1903), pp. 358 f. This holds for many New Testament writers.

tions may be left to us, these seem to be the lines along which New Testament thought proceeds.

There are passages in the New Testament which seem to indicate that when the Christian dies he is immediately with the Lord (Mark 9:4; 12:26 f.; Luke 16:19–31; 23:43; 2 Cor. 5:1–10; Phil. 1:23). There are also many passages which seem clearly to relegate the resurrection and the *parousia* to the future as has been demonstrated earlier in this chapter under the heading "already but not yet." These two apparently different views appear in a single writing, such as Philippians: to die is to be with Christ (1:23), yet the "day" of Christ is ahead (1:6, 10). The Saviour, the Lord Jesus Christ, is awaited out of heaven (3:20).

Two Corinthian views?—It is not easy to harmonize 1 Corinthians 15:20–28, 49–54, which seems to assume that the new body will be given at the *parousia*, with 2 Corinthians 5:1–10, which seems to teach that the new body is given immediately at one's death. Some would suggest a change in Paul's own position in the brief time between the two letters. But something of the same problem appears in Philippians, written some years later, so it seems necessary to study the passages together.

Probably the differences between the two Corinthian passages are those of emphasis, traceable to varying problems behind them. In 1 Corinthians 15 Paul was concerned with the *fact* of the resurrection and with the *nature* of the resurrected body. He had to fight on two fronts: against a spiritualizing of "resurrection" into mere immortality and against a crude doctrine of "fleshy" resurrection.[39] Paul insisted upon the actual resurrection of Jesus, witnessed by himself and others (vv. 3–8). He also explained that the risen body was a changed one, not a mere restoration of the old body, as expected by many Jews of his day.

In 2 Corinthians 5:1–10, Paul was more concerned with the *time* at which one receives the new body. His recent experiences in Asia where he "despaired even of life" and felt within him-

[39] Davies, *op. cit.*, p. 308, citing Johannes Weiss.

self "the sentence of death" (2 Cor. 1:8 f.) may have caused him to think more definitely about death and the time when one receives his heavenly body. The thought of a "naked soul" was abhorrent to Paul as a Jew and as a Christian (5:3). He saw the "building from God" as the replacement for the "earthly house" (v. 1), and apparently this would occur at once, so that one not be found "naked"—disembodied.

Paul's concern to have this new body immediately at death seems to be reflected in his groaning not to be "unclothed" but to be "clothed upon," "that the mortal may be swallowed up by life" (v. 4). His further statement about being "absent from the body" to be "at home with the Lord" (v. 8) probably means only the loss of the present visible body as occurs in death.

Cosmic redemption.—The counterpart to the resurrection of the body is the redemption of the "creation." The redemption which begins with the liberation and renewal of the inner man is continued in the redemption of the body (Rom. 8:23). But just as the body as an essential component of man is to be redeemed, so is the created world. Paul thus saw a cosmic redemption as bound up with that of man:

For the eager expectation of the creation awaits the revelation of the sons of God. For to vanity was the creation subjected, not voluntarily, but because of the one subjecting it, in hope; wherefore the creation [*ktisis*] shall be liberated from the bondage of corruption unto the freedom of the glory of the children of God. For we know that all the creation groans together and is in travail until now; and not only so, but we ourselves having the firstfruit of the Spirit, groan within ourselves, awaiting the adoption, the redemption of our body (Rom. 8:19–23).

In its fulness, then, redemption provides for an inner renewal ultimately completed by a renewed body in a renewed creation. Paul seems here to teach that the cosmos will not be destroyed but rather renewed.

Second Peter describes "the day of the Lord," (3:10) or "the day of God" (v. 12) as a time when the heavens and the elements (*stoicheia*) are to be dissolved by fire and the earth is to be found out [eurethēsetai]; but the assurance is also given of "new heavens and a new earth" (vv. 10–13). In apocalyptic imagery this may reflect, as in Romans 8, the expectation that the creation or cosmos itself is to be redeemed. It would accord with the expectation of a new heaven and a new earth in Revelation 21. Manson observes that "New Heavens and a New Earth signify not the final destruction or displacement of the cosmos, but its *renovation* (*palingenesia, kainē ktisis, apokatastasis*) by the power of God." [40]

However difficult it may be to imagine a cosmic redemption, the difficulties are already present in relation to the redemption of the body. If the body can be redeemed in a resurrection, the cosmos itself may be brought to a comparable redemption. It is well to consider with Berdyaev that "Materiality and corporeality are not one and the same thing." What is thought of as "the other world" is also a bodily world "in the sense that there exists an eternal form, eternal countenances, and the eternal impression upon them." [41] The strength of this view is that it sees the whole man redeemed and placed within a cosmos suited to his larger life.

Time and Eternity

A proper understanding of the meaning of time and eternity may help resolve what appears to be a discrepancy between the view that at death one goes immediately in a bodily state to be with the Lord, and the view that one is raised to be with the Lord only at a future *parousia*.[42] There are passages in the New Testament which seem to teach that Christians who have died already have their risen bodies, and there are passages which seem to teach that these bodies are to be awaited.

[40] William Manson, "Eschatology in the New Testament," *Scottish Journal of Theology Occasional Papers* (Edinburgh: Oliver & Boyd, Ltd., 1952), p. 15.

[41] *The Beginning and the End* trans. R. M. French (New York: Harper & Brothers, 1952), p. 242.

[42] Recent studies on the meaning of time and eternity include those of Berdyaev, *The Beginning and the End;* Cullmann, *Christ and Time;* John Marsh, *The Fulness of Time* (London: James Nisbet & Co., Ltd., 1952); Brunner, *Eternal Hope;* and Bultmann, *The Presence of Eternity.*

Is there any contradiction here? Probably not. What appears to be a time interval to us who are bound by time may be no interval at all to God or to those who through death have entered into eternity with him. The resurrection which is future to those within time may be present reality to those who have died and who are now with the Lord in a bodily state. The nature of time and eternity and their relationship to one another are to be studied with a view to the problem above and the far-reaching implications for the meaning of history.

The difficult question of the nature and meaning of time is not a study as such in the New Testament. However, a near approach to one aspect of the question may be found in 2 Peter 3:8, "But do not forget this one thing, beloved, that one day with the Lord is as a thousand years and a thousand years as one day." Time is a proper study for physics and philosophy as well as for theology. Few men, and this writer is not one of them, have the competence to discuss time as such. But however difficult, the subject cannot be avoided here. It does seem, at least, that the New Testament poses no barrier to the view that time is not a factor in eternity. In this view eternity is qualitatively different from time, although related to it; and God transcends time.

Time is to be distinguished from eternity, though related to it. Marsh observes, "We cannot say that eternity precedes or succeeds time, or that it is contemporaneous with it, or contained in it." Time and eternity are related, for "the historical order is that within which the eternal has revealed itself and in which it may be entered." [43] It was when "the fulness of time" came that "God sent forth his Son, born of a woman" (Gal. 4:4). When "the Word became flesh and tabernacled among us" (John 1:14), the eternal was present in time. The coming of Christ meant that "the time [kairos] has been fulfilled and the kingdom of God has drawn near" (Mark 1:15).

This season or kairos was that of a demand for decision, a commitment of faith to be made within historical time and affecting eternity. This kairos is the moment of decision in which "the

[43] Op. cit., pp. 144 f.

yield of the past is gathered in and the meaning of the future is chosen." [44] One may enter eternal life here and now (John 6:54, 68; 10:28; 17:3). Thus time and eternity, though qualitatively different, are related. The Eternal has become present in history, and decisions made within time are significant for eternity. The Word has become flesh (John 1:14); and Jesus, the one born of woman (Gal. 4:4) is now standing at the right hand of God (Acts 7:55 f.). In a once-for-all event, eternity made its entry into time. "He who is above and beyond all time—Christ, the same yesterday, today, and forever—has entered into time." [45]

Many attempts have been made to describe time in terms of some graph, but none is adequate. It is commonplace today to reject the "Greek view" of cyclic time in favor of the linear view. The problem of time, however, is not to be solved simply by choosing between the cyclic and linear views. The linear view, time seen as a line moving on with each event unique and unrepeatable, comes nearest the New Testament view, but it is inadequate. The New Testament sees two ages (*aiōnes*) as overlapping. The Christian lives in these two orders at once—the historical-chronological, and the eternal, which transcends time but is related to it. A further and all-important factor in the New Testament conception of time is that the end (*eschaton*) is seen to have already entered into history and become a part of it.[46]

The cyclical view, commonly called the Greek view,[47] represents history as repeating itself, events recurring in cycles similar to those of seasons and crops in nature. According to this view,

---

[44] Adapted from Bultmann, *The Presence of Eternity*, p. 141.
[45] Brunner, *Eternal Hope*, p. 47.
[46] This is the view ably developed by Marsh, *op. cit.*
[47] According to Bultmann, *The Presence of Eternity*, p. 24, this view grew out of Oriental astronomy and was developed in Greek philosophy chiefly by the Stoics, who "evolved the doctrine of universal conflagration (*ekpurōsis*) which leads the world back to Zeus, out of whom it radiates again as a new world." He quotes Chrysippus as saying that Socrates, Plato, and every man will exist again, doing and suffering the same things, and that this restoration will be repeated without limit or end.

Plato and his disciples will reappear in history as the cycles recur. Thus understood, history is going nowhere and has no ultimate significance. The "spiral" view sees progress in the cycles of history, repetition with differences, but no goal and no ultimate significance. The linear view sees time and history as moving on a line which does not provide for lingering, reversibility, or repetition of a particular event, each being unique or unrepeatable.

As stated above, the New Testament understanding of time and history is nearer the linear view than the cyclical or spiral, but it is not identical with it. The great difference is that in the New Testament view the end of the linear process has already appeared in the middle of the line; the *eschaton* (the end) has already entered history in the person of Jesus Christ.[48] It was when "the fullness [*plērōma*] of time" came that God sent his Son (Gal. 4:4). Christ is the goal of history. Time and history are not endless, and they will not just end like a clock run down. Were either true, time would be linear but without meaning. The whole Bible, however, is *eschatological* in that it assumes that time and history are being moved to an end which is a goal (*eschaton*).

This *eschaton* has already entered history in the person of Christ who is "the first and the last [*eschaton*], and the living one" (Rev. 1:17–18). Thus the "end" of the line has entered into the line and become a part of it. History will not move on endlessly, nor will it end without meaning. It is being caught up into the eternal and is thus given its significance. Christ is the one through and unto whom all things were created (Col. 1:16), and in Christ all things are summed up (Eph. 1:10). Christ, who is the beginning and the end, has appeared in the center as Jesus of Nazareth. In him history is brought to its fulfilment (*plērōma*), to its end or goal (*eschaton*). Eternity does not simply take up where time leaves off, nor is eternity just endless time. In Christ—the first and the last, the living one—the eternal has entered history to redeem it.

[48] Marsh, *op. cit.*, p. 169.

Berdyaev finds time to be of three sorts: cosmic, historical, and existential.[49] For him, cosmic time is that of calendars and clocks, calculated mathematically on the basis of movement around the sun and symbolized by the circle.[50] He describes historical time as likewise calculated by mathematics in terms of decades, centuries, and millennia and symbolized by a line. This sort of time, to him, stretches out into the future and is unrepeatable. The third type, existential time, he holds not to be subject to mathematical measurement. He sees it to be characterized by intensity of experience and symbolized by a point—movement in depth. This third sort of time Berdyaev finds to be "akin to eternity, having no distinction between the future and the past, between the end and the beginning."[51]

These distinctions and descriptions are serviceable so long as it is recognized that time in each sense is *related* to eternity, that existential time is *akin* to eternity, but that no time is to be confused with eternity. The New Testament does not distinguish between cosmic and historical time, but it does distinguish between chronological time (*chronos*) and a season of opportunity, fulfilment, or decision (*kairos*).

Chronological or historical time is for us a "one-way street." One in it may not move backward as well as forward, as is possible in space. Historical time allows no lingering or turning back as "not yet" gives way to "no longer."[52] In this sense it is linear, being neither cyclic nor reversible. It moves on, but it moves on toward an end. It has both beginning and end. God himself is not imprisoned within time. "In the beginning God" (Gen. 1:1; cf. John 1:1) does not mean "in the beginning time." Time is real to God, but God is above it as its creator.

The Christian is within time, yet in Christ he already is transcending it. The fathers of old in Israel "drank of the spiritual Rock that followed them, and the Rock was Christ" (1 Cor.

---

[49] *The Beginning and the End,* p. 206.
[50] Some mathematicians would say that time is egg-shaped, due to the factor of velocity in its dimensions.
[51] *The Beginning and the End,* p. 207.
[52] Brunner, *Eternal Hope,* pp. 43, 53.

10:4). Hence those who according to chronological time lived B.C., actually transcended this linear time and lived A.D.—in Christ.[53] If time can to this extent be overcome, the way is open to see a further transcendence of it by those in Christ, certainly for the Christians who have died.

Althouth eternity and time are related, there is a qualitative difference between them.[54] Both are real to God and to man. Eternity is not endless time, as Marsh[55] and Brunner[56] have ably argued against Cullmann.[57] There is more than a quantitative difference between God's way of existence and that which we know within the limits of time.

God is above time, his "present" not being one which "crumbles away" as the "not yet" becomes the "no longer."[58] Time belongs to creation, but God is the creator. God is the Lord of time, "for whom the distinctions of time, time-distances, have no significance."[59] For him there is no past or future. Hence the psalmist could say, "from everlasting to everlasting, thou *art* God" (90:2). For this reason Christ could say, "Before Abraham was, I *am*" (John 8:58) and "I am the first and the last and the living one" (Rev. 1:17–18). As the Lord of history, God "can survey time in its entire extension."[60]

If eternity thus transcends time and is not merely an endless succession of time, it is possible to harmonize what appears to be two parallel New Testament doctrines. At death the Christian is at once with the Lord in bodily state, and we await the resurrection at his *parousia*. Both can be true at once, if those with the Lord have transcended time with him. That is to say, the Christian's death and the *parousia* may be divided by an interval of time to us, but it does not follow that this interval is a factor to God or to those who have died to be with the Lord.

[53] Marsh, *op. cit.*, pp. 156 f.
[54] Brunner, *Eternal Hope*, p. 53.
[55] *Op. cit.*, pp. 174–181.
[56] *Eternal Hope*, p. 53.
[57] *Christ and Time*, pp. 62, 65, *et passim*.
[58] Brunner, *Eternal Hope*, pp. 43, 50, 52, *et passim*.
[59] *Ibid.*, p. 54.
[60] Marsh, *op. cit.*, pp. 180 f.

What to us is future is eternally present as seen "from the other side." Brunner states it thus:

The date of death differs for each man, for the day of death belongs to this world. Our day of resurrection is the same for all and yet is not separated from the day of death by intervals of centuries—for these time-intervals are here, not there in the presence of God, where "a thousand years are as a day." [61]

If this understanding of time and eternity is correct, then it is only to us who are yet within time (Berdyaev's historical time) that the *parousia* and the resurrection are future. This understanding of time and eternity allows for both New Testament teachings. We await the coming of Christ, yet to die is to be with Christ in bodily state.

Since it belongs to the essence of salvation to be in new relationship with the people of Christ as his body, it must be seen that the resurrection in its fulness awaits the completion of the body of Christ. The church as his body is "the fulness of him" (Eph. 1:23), and it is thus the fulness of the individual Christian. Something of each Christian is to be found in each other Christian. Thus one cannot be "fully risen" until all are joined together with the Lord at the end of history. No Christian can be complete without his brethren in Christ. One is brought to the fulness of his redemption when the body of Christ is brought to its fulness.

This means that even though one at death is brought immediately into the presence of Christ and brought there in a bodily state, his resurrection in its fullest sense awaits the *parousia* at the end of history. One's "embodiment" is completed only in Christ who is himself embodied in the church and in it brought to his own fulness (Eph. 1:23).

Judgment and Eternal Destiny

Judgment.—That judgment before God is inescapable to each man is the unmistakable teaching of the New Testa-

[61] *Eternal Hope,* p. 152.

ment. Each one of us must stand before the judgment seat of God and give account of himself to God (Rom. 14:10–12). This judgment is based upon our relationship to Christ as reflected in the good or bad practiced through the body (2 Cor. 5:10). The New Testament provides for no escape through annihilation nor through the loss of individual identity within the family, nation, or church. Each must enter into eternal life alone, passing through "the strait gate—which admits only one"; and "each must alone and unaccompanied appear before the Judge." [62]

Paradox is found in the New Testament doctrine of judgment, as in much else. Judgment is present and future. That it is present is emphatic in John: "This is the judgment, that light is come into the world and men loved darkness rather than the light, for their works were evil" (3:19). Assurance is given to the one who believes (trusts) that he has life eternal and that "he comes not into judgment but has passed out of death into life" (5:24). In John 12:31 judgment is present: "Now is the judgment of this world; now is the prince of this world cast out." Later in this same chapter it is future: "The word that I spoke, the same shall judge him in the last day" (12:48).

Judgment has a future aspect as well as a present one. Men of Nineveh and "the queen of the south" will stand up in the judgment and condemn more-privileged generations (Matt. 12:41 f.). A future judgment apparently is meant in 2 Corinthians 5:10, which says that all of us "must be brought into openness before the judgment seat of Christ, in order that each may receive back the things which he practiced through the body, whether good or bad." A final judgment involving all nations is described in Matthew 25:31–46. Likewise, a final judgment before the "great white throne" is described in Revelation 20:11–15. But the judgment which awaits us at the "end of the world" is the outward disclosure of the judgment accomplished in the presence of Christ now.

Furthermore, the full meaning of any act now, good or

[62] *Ibid.,* pp. 168–69.

evil, may be seen only when its full course has been run. An act today is the beginning of a "chain reaction" which continues in an ever-widening path until the end of the world. Some sins are immediately apparent as to their character, but some are seen in their true character only as later their ugly fruits are harvested. Something of this is taught in 1 Timothy 5:24, "The sins of some men are open, running before them unto judgment, but they also follow after some."

The full effect of a lie, of the incitement of another to lust, greed, jealousy, prejudice, ill will, or malice is to be seen only at the final judgment. Hence final judgment is possible only at the end of time, when the full course has been run by deeds done here. Likewise, the full measure of good deeds is to be seen only at the final judgment. Of those who die in the Lord it is written, "Blessed are the dead who die in the Lord . . . that they may rest from their labors, for their works follow after them" (Rev. 14:13).

The most important fact about judgment is that we are judged in relation to Christ. In turn, this is a judgment in relation to his people. Our true relationship to him is reflected in our relationship to his people. To serve them is to serve him and to neglect them is to neglect him (Matt. 25:31–46). Never does the New Testament allow one to divorce his relationship to Christ from that to other people. To persecute them is to persecute him (Acts 9:1–2,4–5; 22:4,7–8; 26:10–11,14–15). To sin against the brethren is to sin against Christ (1 Cor. 8:12). Though we are not saved by our works, we are judged by them; for they reflect our true relationship to Christ and his grace. Judgment is merciful toward them that accept judgment, and judgment is merciful toward them who are merciful (Matt. 5:7).

Separation.—A final separation between the people of God and those who are unwilling to be his people seems to be the inexpressibly sad yet positive teaching of the New Testament. It is unthinkable that any but one of a distorted mind could take pleasure in this. It is understandable that one should recoil from the teaching, as one recoils from the thought of the dreadful scourge of cancer. But to refuse to acknowledge the fact of cancer is not to remove it. That there is a fundamental difference between the people of God and those who refuse to be, and that there is a final separation between them are terrifying facts to be acknowledged. Salvation is never coercive. Becoming a child of God is an opportunity offered but never a relationship imposed.

The activity of God as set forth throughout the Bible leads always to judgment (*krisis*) and separation between persons. Even the coming of Jesus into the world was announced as "set for the falling and rising up of many" (Luke 2:34).[63] Jesus came to save, but the light which he brings remains judgment alone for those who refuse to see (John 3:19; 9:39). The chasm between the rich man and Lazarus cannot be crossed in the realm beyond this one (Luke 16:26). The door remains shut to those who ignore the conditions for entry into the marriage feast of the bridegroom (Matt. 25:10 f.). The separation is final between "the sheep" and "the goats" at the judgment when the Son of man comes in his glory (Matt. 25:31–46). Many, to their own surprise and amazement, will be "cast forth without" when people from east, west, north, and south are gathered together with "Abraham and Isaac and Jacob, and all the prophets, in the kingdom of God" (Luke 13:28 f.).

Escape from the teaching of a final separation cannot be achieved validly by a doctrine of universalism or annihilation. That one should find a doctrine of universal salvation attractive is altogether commendable. The long-suffering of God is evidence that he does not purpose that any perish but "that all should find room [*chōrēsai*] for repentance" (2 Peter 3:9). But the longing that all be saved does not dispose of the painful fact that many are lost.

Those who seek to defend the doctrine of universal salvation are not without supporting texts, depending of course upon how they are interpreted. If 1 Corinthians 15:22 means that automatically all were lost in Adam, then it follows inescapably that *all* shall be made alive in Christ. Of course, Paul is saying

[63] Cf. Stauffer, *op. cit.*, p. 220.

neither of these things. He is saying that one is saved in Christ in the manner (*hōsper . . . houtōs*) that he is lost in Adam,—by commitment to the one or the other. Paul is not teaching that being lost or saved is arbitrary.

Some interpreters find universal salvation in Romans 11:32, "For God shut up all together unto disobedience that he might have mercy upon all." Those who find universalism in this verse are no more literalistic than are others who find in Romans 11:26 the promise that all Israelites shall be saved. Each verse must be studied in context. Paul was not teaching that every person will be saved (v. 32) any more than he was teaching that every national Israelite will be saved (v. 26). In each case he was indicating that God's will is exercised in the direction of salvation for all men. The very agony expressed throughout the Roman letter precludes any doctrine of universal salvation for mankind or even for Jews. Incredible as it may seem, "disobedient and gainsaying people" can and do reject the outstretched hands of God (Rom. 10:21).

As to the doctrine of annihilation, it is without support in the Bible. The idea of total extinction is found nowhere in Old or New Testament.[64] The minimum belief was never less than that of some shadowy existence in Sheol. This, of course, reached a full and clear doctrine of resurrection to "life" or to a "living death." The New Testament warns that a person may be destroyed, or self-destroyed, but this does not mean annihilation. A watch is destroyed as a watch when it is smashed, but it does not thus vanish. It remains in its ruined state a sad contrast to what it was designed to be. Jesus taught that "whoever wishes to save his life shall destroy [*apolesei*] it" (Mark 8:35); but he did not mean that one would thus vanish.

The New Testament offers no escape from the doctrine of final separation through either universalism or annihilation. Instead, it warns against the dreadful fate of "eternal death." It tells of God's concern to save all, and it locates responsibility of each believer to be witness to God's power to save.

[64] Richardson, *Theological Word Book*, p. 106.

Will the saved in heaven have awareness of the lost in hell? This question has been asked countless times. The New Testament offers little help at this point, but it certainly does not teach that those in heaven will not have such awareness. The assurance so often given that certain memories will be blanked out is without New Testament support. One may ask, why is it that Christians are so eager to forget the lost? Does it relate to our criminal neglect of them in this life? Why do we always want pleasure without pain? If Luke 16:19–31 may guide us here, it may be observed that Abraham was aware that the rich man was in torment.

The "joy in heaven over one sinner who repents" (Luke 15:7,10) assumes that there was something lacking in joy before he repented. Why should Christians in heaven not share with Christ in his sorrow over the lost? John Marsh probably is correct in saying, "The supreme folly of worldliness is that it seeks pleasure without pain; the glory of heaven is that it knows a joy that is not destroyed, but enriched, by tragedy." [65]

Hades.—The Greek word *hadēs* according to its etymology means "the unseen." In the Old Testament it is the usual translation for the Hebrew *sh"ôl*, the place of the dead. In the New Testament it seems only to refer to the place of the dead, without distinguishing between the "wicked" and the "righteous." In Luke 16:23 it may be that the rich man only, and not Abraham and Lazarus, is thought of as being in Hades. However, in Matthew 16:18 "the gates of Hades" is best understood as simply a reference to death. In Revelation (1:18; 6:8; 20:13–14), Hades is closely associated with death and may mean simply the place of the dead.

The most decisive usage is probably in Acts 2:27,31, where it is declared in effect that Hades could not hold the crucified Christ Jesus. Some would take this as a text to support the doctrine that Jesus "descended into hell," but it is most precarious to do so. Never does the New Testament say that Jesus descended into hell. The obscure reference in 1 Peter 3:19 is to his making

[65] *Op. cit.*, p. 152.

proclamation (or preaching) to "the spirits in prison." It is an open question as to whether the reference is to human beings or to fallen angels (cf. Jude 6; 2 Peter 2:4). In 2 Peter 2:4 the reference is to angels who were cast down into *Tartarus,* not into hell (*gehenna*). The terms "hell" and "paradise" are employed to distinguish the abodes of the "wicked" and "righteous" respectively, but Hades seems not to make this distinction. It was Hades (death) which could not hold Jesus (Acts 2:27,31).

Hell.—The term "hell" is the proper translation for the Greek *gehenna.* In turn, *gehenna* translates the Hebrew for "valley of Hinnom." Originally this designated the valley just southeast of Jerusalem, where children were sacrificed to Moloch (2 Chron. 28:3; 33:6). It seems that later this valley served as a garbage dump, where the fires burned continually.

Gehenna came to symbolize destruction, condemnation, and punishment.[66] In the New Testament the term appears only in Mark (9:43,45,47), Matthew (5:22,29 ff.; 10:28; 13:42, 50; 23:15,33), Luke (12:5), and James (3:6), and is characterized as unquenchable fire, eternal fire, and a furnace of fire. Possibly it gathers up all the elements of censure, reproach, shame, and anguish bound up with its various usages through many centuries. It is sufficient to see that in the New Testament it represents the indescribably tragic and irretrievable state of those who choose not to know God (Rom. 1:28). "Know" here means, of course, recognizing God for what he truly is and responding appropriately.

Heaven.—The term "heaven," and its plural form, is used many times in the New Testament to describe the sky above the earth. It is also used to describe the abode of God and of the righteous. In this sense it contrasts with *gehenna* and it corresponds to paradise (Luke 23:43; 2 Cor. 12:4; Rev. 2:7). The term "paradise" was originally a Persian word for a garden or park. In the New Testament it always describes the abode of the saved.

The New Testament is very reticent about precise descriptions

66 Richardson, *A Theological Word Book,* p. 107.

of heaven, as it is about hell. It is enough to know that heaven is where God is (Matt. 6:9). To be in heaven is to be with him. It should be sufficient to Christian faith to leave to God: "Which things eye has not seen nor ear heard, and which have not come up upon the heart of man, whatsoever things God makes ready for those loving him" (1 Cor. 2:9). Christian faith may well take seriously the admonition of John: "Beloved, now are we the children of God, and not yet does it appear what we shall be. For we know that if he be manifested we shall be like him, for we shall see him just as he is" (1 John 3:2).

Bibliography

ARNDT, W. F., and GINGRICH, F. W. *A Greek-English Lexicon of the New Testament and Other Early Christian Literature.* Translated and edited from W. BAUER'S *Griechisch-Deutsches Wörterbuch zu den Schriften des Neuen Testaments und der übrigen urchristlichen Literatur,* fourth edition, 1952. Chicago: University of Chicago Press, 1957.

ASHCRAFT, MORRIS. "Paul's Understanding of Apostleship," *Review and Expositor,* LV (October, 1958), 400–12.

BAILLIE, JOHN. *The Idea of Revelation in Recent Thought.* New York: Columbia University Press, 1956.

———. *Our Knowledge of God.* New York: Charles Scribner's Sons, 1939.

BARRETT, C. K. *The Epistle to the Romans.* New York: Harper & Brothers, 1958.

———. "The Lamb of God," *New Testament Studies,* I. New York: Cambridge University Press (February, 1955), 210.

BARTH, KARL. *The Doctrine of the Word of God.* (*Church Dogmatics,* Vol. I.) Translated by E. G. THOMSON. Edinburgh: T. & T. Clark, 1936.

———. *The Epistle to the Romans.* Translated by EDWYN C. HOSKYNS. London–New York: Oxford University Press, 1933.

BARTH, MARCUS. *The Broken Wall.* Philadelphia: Judson Press, 1959.

BEASLEY-MURRAY, GEORGE R. *A Commentary on Mark Thirteen.* New York: St. Martin's Press, 1957.

———. *Jesus and the Future: The Eschatological Discourse, Mark 13 with Special Reference to the Little Apocalypse Theory.* London: The Macmillan Co., 1954.

BERDYAEV, NICHOLAS. *The Beginning and the End.* Translated by R. M. FRENCH. New York: Harper & Brothers, 1952.

BERDYAEV, NICHOLAS. *The End of Our Time.* Translated by DONALD ATTWATER. London: Sheed & Ward, 1933.

BERNARD, J. H. *St. John.* ("International Critical Commentary," Vol. II.) Edinburgh: T. & T. Clark, 1928.

BLACK, MATTHEW. *An Aramaic Approach to the Gospels and Acts.* Oxford: The Clarendon Press, 1954.

————. "Servant of the Lord and Son of Man," *Scottish Journal of Theology,* VI. Edinburgh: Oliver & Boyd. (March, 1953), 1, 10.

————. "The 'Son of Man' in the Teaching of Jesus," *The Expository Times,* LX (November, 1948), 2, 32.

BONHOEFFER, DIETRICH. *The Cost of Discipleship.* Translated by R. H. FULLER. New York: The Macmillan Co., 1949.

BOWMAN, JOHN WICK. *The Intention of Jesus.* Philadelphia: The Westminster Press, 1943.

BRIGHT, JOHN. *The Kingdom of God.* Nashville: Abingdon-Cokesbury Press, 1953.

BROADUS, JOHN A. *Commentary on the Gospel of Matthew.* ("An American Commentary on the New Testament," ed. ALAN HOVEY, Vol. I.) Philadelphia: The American Baptist Publication Society, 1886.

BROWN, F., DRIVER, S. R., and BRIGGS, C. A. (eds.). *A Hebrew and English Lexicon of the Old Testament.* Oxford: The Clarendon Press, reprinted 1952.

BRUNNER, EMIL. *Eternal Hope.* Translated by HAROLD KNIGHT. London: Lutterworth Press, 1954.

————. *The Misunderstanding of the Church.* Translated by HAROLD KNIGHT. Philadelphia: The Westminster Press, 1953.

————. *Der Römerbrief.* Stuttgart: Oncken-Verlag, 1948.

BULTMANN, RUDOLF KARL. *Das Evangelium des Johannes.* Göttingen: Vandenhoeck & Ruprecht, 1953.

————. *Jesus Christ and Mythology.* New York: Charles Scribner's Sons, 1958.

————. *The Presence of Eternity.* New York: Harper & Brothers, 1957.

————. *Theology of the New Testament.* Translated by KENDRICK GROBEL. Vol. I. New York: Charles Scribner's Sons, 1951.

BURROWS, MILLAR. *An Outline of Biblical Theology.* Philadelphia: The Westminster Press, 1946.

BUTTRICK, GEORGE A. *Prayer.* New York: Abingdon-Cokesbury Press, 1942.

CALVIN, JOHN. *Institutes of the Christian Religion.* Translated by JOHN ALLEN. Vol. I. Grand Rapids: Wm. B. Eerdmans Publishing Co., 1949.

CARVER, W. O. *The Self-Interpretation of Jesus.* Nashville: Broadman Press, reprinted 1961.

CHARLES, R. H. *The Revelation of St. John.* New York: Charles Scribner's Sons, 1920.

COATES, J. R. (trans. and ed.). *Bible Key Words.* Vols. I and II. New York: Harper & Brothers, 1951, 1958. Cf. entry below under "Kittel."

CONNER, W. T. *The Cross in the New Testament.* Nashville: Broadman Press, 1954.

——. *The Faith of the New Testament.* Nashville: Broadman Press, 1940.

CROSS, F. L. (ed.). *Studies in the Fourth Gospel.* London: A. R. Mowbray & Co., Ltd., 1957.

CULLMANN, OSCAR. *Baptism in the New Testament.* Translated by J. K. S. REID. London: SCM Press, 1950.

——. *Christ and Time.* Translated by FLOYD V. FILSON. Philadelphia: The Westminster Press, 1950.

——. *The Christology of the New Testament.* Translated by SHIRLEY C. GUTHRIE and CHARLES A. M. HALL. Philadelphia: The Westminster Press, 1959.

——. *Early Christian Worship.* Translated by A. STEWART TODD and J. B. TORRANCE. London: SCM Press, 1953.

——. *Immortality of the Soul or Resurrection of the Dead.* New York: The Macmillan Co., 1958.

——. *Königsherrschaft Christi und Kirche im Neuen Testament.* Zollikon-Zürich: Evangelischer Verlag, 1950.

——. *Peter: Disciple, Apostle, Martyr.* Translated by FLOYD V. FILSON. Philadelphia: The Westminster Press, 1953.

——. *The State in the New Testament.* New York: Charles Scribner's Sons, 1956.

——. *Die Tradition als exegetisches, historisches, und theologisches Problem.* Translated by PIERRE SCHONENBERGER. Zürich: Zwingli-Verlag, 1954.

——, and LEENHARDT, F. J. *Essays on the Lord's Supper.* Translated by J. G. DAVIES. Richmond: John Knox Press, 1958.

CURTIUS, GEORGE. *Principles of Greek Etymology.* Translated by AUGUSTUS S. WILKINS and EDWIN B. ENGLAND. 2 vols. London: John Murray, 1875.

DALMAN, GUSTAF H. *Jesus-Jeshua.* Translated by PAUL P. LEVERTOFF. London: SPCK, 1929.

——. *The Words of Jesus.* Translated by D. M. KAY. Edinburgh: T. & T. Clark, 1902.

DANA, H. E., and GLAZE, R. E., JR. *Interpreting the New Testament.* Nashville: Broadman Press, 1961.

DAVIES, W. D. *Paul and Rabbinic Judaism*. London: SPCK, 1948.
————, and DAUBE, D. (eds.). *The Background of the New Testament and Its Eschatology*. New York: Cambridge University Press, 1956.

DEWOLF, L. HAROLD. *A Theology of the Living Church*. New York: Harper & Brothers, 1953.

DIBELIUS, MARTIN. *Gospel Criticism and Christology*. London: I. Nicholson & Watson, 1935.

DODD, C. H. *According to the Scriptures*. New York: Charles Scribner's Sons, 1953.

————. *The Apostolic Preaching and Its Developments*. New York: Willett, Clark & Co., 1937.

————. *The Interpretation of the Fourth Gospel*. New York: Cambridge University Press, 1953.

————. *The Johannine Epistles*. New York: Harper & Brothers, 1946.

————. *The Meaning of Paul for Today*. London: George Allen & Unwin, Ltd., 1930.

————. *The Parables of the Kingdom*. London: James Nisbet & Co., 1946.

DUNCAN, GEORGE S. *Jesus, Son of Man*. New York: The Macmillan Co., 1949.

EASTON, BURTON SCOTT. *The Pastoral Epistles*. New York: Charles Scribner's Sons, 1947.

EPSTEIN, I. (ed.). *Babylonian Talmud*. London: Soncino Press, 1935.

FILSON, FLOYD V. *Jesus Christ the Risen Lord*. New York: Abingdon Press, 1956.

FLEMINGTON, W. F. *The New Testament Doctrine of Baptism*. London: SPCK, 1948.

FLEW, R. N. *Jesus and His Church*. London: The Epworth Press, 1938.

FOAKES-JACKSON, F. J., and LAKE, KIRSOPP (eds.). *The Beginnings of Christianity*. Vol. I. London: Macmillan & Co., Ltd., 1920.

FOULQUIE, PAUL. *Existentialism*. Translated by KATHLEEN RAINE. London: Dennis Dobson, 1950.

GILMORE, A. (ed.). *Christian Baptism*. Philadelphia: The Judson Press, 1959.

GOLLWITZER, HELMUT. *Die Freude Gottes*. Berlin: Buckhardthaus Verlag, 1952.

GOODSPEED, EDGAR J. *How Came the Bible?* New York: Abingdon Press, 1940.

————. "Some Greek Notes," *Journal of Biblical Literature* (Philadelphia), June, 1954.

GRANT, FREDERICK C. *An Introduction to New Testament Thought.* New York: Abingdon Press, 1950.

GRENE, MARJORIE. *Dreadful Freedom: A Critique of Existentialism.* Chicago: University of Chicago Press, 1948.

GUY, H. A. *The New Testament Doctrine of the Last Things.* New York: Oxford University Press, 1948.

HARKNESS, GEORGIA. *Prayer and the Common Life.* New York: Abingdon Press, 1948.

HIGGINS, A. J. B. *The Lord's Supper in the New Testament.* London: SCM Press, 1952.

———. (ed.). *New Testament Essays.* Manchester: Manchester University Press, 1959.

HODGSON, LEONARD. *The Doctrine of Atonement.* London: James Nisbet & Co., 1951.

HORT, F. J. A. *The Christian Ecclesia.* London: Macmillan & Co., Ltd., 1897.

HUNTER, A. M. *Introducing New Testament Theology.* Philadelphia: The Westminster Press, 1957.

JEREMIAS, JOACHIM. *The Eucharistic Words of Jesus.* Translated by ARNOLD EHRHARDT. Oxford: Blackwell, 1955.

JOHNSON, SHERMAN E. *The Gospel According to St. Mark.* New York: Harper & Brothers, 1960.

KENNEDY, H. A. A. *St. Paul's Conceptions of the Last Things.* London: Hodder & Stoughton, Ltd., 1904.

KIRK, KENNETH E. *Marriage and Divorce.* London: Hodder & Stoughton, Ltd., 1948.

———. (ed.). *The Apostolic Ministry.* London: Hodder & Stoughton, Ltd., 1947.

KITTEL, GERHARD, and FRIEDRICH, GERHARD (eds.). *Theologisches Wörterbuch zum Neuen Testament.* Stuttgart: W. Kohlhammer, 1933—. Sections in English translation published as *Bible Key Words;* cf. entry above under "Coates."

KNOX, JOHN. *Chapters in a Life of Paul.* New York: Abingdon-Cokesbury, 1950.

———. *Christ the Lord.* New York: Willett, Clark & Co., 1945.

———. *The Death of Christ.* New York: Abingdon Press, 1958.

———. *On the Meaning of Christ.* New York: Charles Scribner's Sons, 1947.

KÜMMEL, W. G. *Promise and Fulfilment: The Eschatological Message of Jesus.* Translated by DOROTHEA M. BARTON. Naperville, Ill.: Alec R. Allenson, Inc., 1957.

KUNKEL, FRITZ. *Creation Continues.* New York: Charles Scribner's Sons, 1947.

LANGTON, EDWARD. *Essentials of Demonology*. London: Epworth Press, 1949.

LEIVESTAD, RAGNAR. *Christ the Conqueror*. New York: The Macmillan Co., 1954.

LIETZMANN, HANS. *Mass and Lord's Supper*. Translated by DOROTHEA H. G. REEVE. Leiden: E. J. Brill, 1953.

McCALL, DUKE K. (ed.). *What Is the Church?* Nashville: Broadman Press, 1958.

McDOWELL, E. A., JR. *The Meaning and Message of Revelation*. Nashville: Broadman Press, 1951.

————. *Jesus and His Cross*. Nashville: Broadman Press, 1944.

MACKINTOSH, H. R. *The Christian Experience of Forgiveness*. New York: Harper & Brothers, 1927.

————. *The Doctrine of the Person of Jesus Christ*. New York: Charles Scribner's Sons, 1912.

MACLAREN, ALEXANDER. *Expositions of Holy Scripture*. Grand Rapids: Wm. B. Eerdmans Publishing Co., 1932.

MACMURRAY, JOHN. *Conditions of Freedom*. London: Faber & Faber, 1950.

MANSON, T. W. *The Church's Ministry*. Philadelphia: The Westminster Press, 1948.

————. *The Sayings of Jesus*. London: SCM Press, 1949.

————. *The Servant-Messiah*. New York: Cambridge University Press, 1953.

————. "The Son of Man in Daniel, Enoch, and the Gospels," *Bulletin of the John Rylands Library*, XXXII (1950), 171–93.

————. *The Teaching of Jesus*. New York: Cambridge University Press, 1935.

MANSON, WILLIAM. "Eschatology in the New Testament," *Scottish Journal of Theology Occasional Papers*. Edinburgh: Oliver & Boyd, 1952.

————. *The Epistle to the Hebrews*. London: Hodder & Stoughton, Ltd., 1951.

————. *Jesus the Messiah*. Philadelphia: The Westminster Press, 1946.

MARSH, JOHN. *The Fulness of Time*. London: James Nisbet & Co., Ltd., 1952.

MICHEL, OTTO. *Der Brief an die Römer*. Göttingen: Vandenhoeck & Ruprecht, 1955.

MOFFATT, JAMES. *Grace in the New Testament*. New York: Ray Long & Richard R. Smith, Inc., 1932.

MOODY, DALE. "The Ministry of the New Testament," *Review and Expositor* (Kentucky), LVI (January, 1959), 36 f.

MOORE, GEORGE F. *Judaism in the First Centuries of the Christian Era, the Age of the Tannaim.* 3 vols. Cambridge: Harvard University Press, 1927–1930.

MOWINCKEL, SIGMUND. *He That Cometh.* Translated by G. W. ANDERSON. New York: Abingdon Press, 1956.

NIEBUHR, H. RICHARD. *The Meaning of Revelation.* New York: The Macmillan Co., 1946.

———, and WILLIAMS, DANIEL D. (eds.). *The Ministry in Historical Perspectives.* New York: Harper & Brothers, 1956.

NIEBUHR, REINHOLD. *Faith and History.* New York: Charles Scribner's Sons, 1949.

———. *The Nature and Destiny of Man.* New York: Charles Scribner's Sons, 1949.

OESTERLEY, W. O. E., and BOX, G. H. *The Religion and Worship of the Synagogue.* New York: Charles Scribner's Sons, 1907.

OTTO, RUDOLF. *The Kingdom of God and the Son of Man.* Translated by FLOYD V. FILSON and BERTRAM LEE-WOOLF. London: Lutterworth Press, 1951.

PEACOCK, H. F. "Ordination in the New Testament," *Review and Expositor* (Kentucky), LV (July, 1958), 262–74.

PLATO. *The Dialogues of Plato.* Translated by B. JOWETT. 5 vols. Oxford: The Clarendon Press, 1953.

RAWLINSON, A. E. J. *The New Testament Doctrine of the Christ.* New York: Longmans, Green & Co., 1949.

———. *The Gospel According to St. Mark.* London: Methuen & Co., Ltd., 1925.

REICKE, BO. *Glaube und Leben der Urgemeinde.* Zürich: Zwingli-Verlag, 1957.

———. *The Disobedient Spirits and Christian Baptism.* Copenhagen: Ejnar Munksgaard Forlay, 1946.

REID, J. K. S. *The Biblical Doctrine of the Ministry.* Edinburgh: Oliver & Boyd, 1955.

RICHARDSON, ALAN. *An Introduction to the Theology of the New Testament.* New York: Harper & Brothers, 1959.

———. (ed.). *A Theological Word Book of the Bible.* New York: The Macmillan Co., 1950.

———. *The Miracle-Stories of the Gospels.* London: SCM Press, 1941.

ROBERTSON, A. T. *A Harmony of the Gospels.* Nashville: Broadman Press, 1950.

ROBINSON, JOHN A. T. *The Body: A Study in Pauline Theology.* Chicago: Henry Regnery Co., 1952.

ROBINSON, JOHN A. T. *Jesus and His Coming.* New York: Abingdon Press, 1957.

SCHILLING, T. C. (ed.). *Abstract History of the Mississippi Baptist Association for One Hundred Years, 1806–1906.* New Orleans: J. G. Hauser, 1908.

SCHNEIDER, JOHANNES, *Die Taufe im Neuen Testament.* Stuttgart: W. Kohlhammer, 1952.

SCHWEITZER, A. *Paul and His Interpreters.* Translated by W. MONT-GOMERY. London: A. & C. Black, 1912.

SCHWEIZER, EDUARD. *Lordship and Discipleship.* Naperville, Ill.: Alec R. Allenson, Inc., 1960.

———. *Church Order in the New Testament.* Translated by FRANK CLARKE. Naperville, Ill.: Alec R. Allenson, Inc., 1961.

SCOTT, C. ANDERSON. *Romanism and the Gospel.* Philadelphia: The Westminster Press, 1946.

SOUTER, ALEXANDER. *The Text and Canon of the New Testament.* New York: Charles Scribner's Sons, 1913.

STAGG, FRANK. *The Book of Acts.* Nashville: Broadman Press, 1955.

STAUFFER, ETHELBERT. *New Testament Theology.* Translated by JOHN MARSH. London: SCM Press, 1955.

STRACK, H. L., and BILLERBECK, PAUL. *Kommentar zum Neuen Testament aus Talmud und Midrasch.* München: Beck, 1922–1956.

SUMMERS, RAY. *Worthy Is the Lamb.* Nashville: Broadman Press, 1951.

TAYLOR, VINCENT. *Forgiveness and Reconciliation.* London: The Macmillan Co., 1941.

———. *The Names of Jesus.* New York: St. Martin's Press, 1953.

———. *The Gospel According to St. Mark.* London: The Macmillan Co., 1952.

THAYER, J. H. *A Greek-English Lexicon of the New Testament.* New York: American Book Co., 1889.

THIELICKE, HELMUT. *Das Gebet das die Welt umspannt.* Stuttgart: Quell-Verlag, 1953.

THORNTON, L. S. *The Common Life in the Body of Christ.* London: The Dacre Press, 1950.

TILLICH, PAUL. *The Courage to Be.* London: James Nisbet & Co., Ltd., 1952.

TORRANCE, T. F. *The Doctrine of Grace in the Apostolic Fathers.* Edinburgh: Oliver & Boyd, Ltd., 1948.

———. "Proselyte Baptism," *New Testament Studies.* New York: Cambridge University Press, 1954.

TRENCH, R. C. *Synonyms of the New Testament.* Grand Rapids: Wm. B. Eerdmans Publishing Co., n.d.

WHITE, R. E. O. *The Biblical Doctrine of Initiation*. Grand Rapids: Wm. B. Eerdmans Publishing Co., 1960.

WOLF, WILLIAM J. *No Cross, No Crown*. New York: Doubleday & Co., Inc., 1957.

Scripture Index

Subject Index